Woodrow Wilson
LIFE AND LETTERS

WOODROW WILSON
FROM A PAINTING BY F. GRAHAM COOTES, PHOTOGRAPHED
BY RUSSELL SHELK, WASHINGTON, D. C.

Woodrow Wilson

LIFE AND LETTERS

Facing War

1915—1917

BY

RAY STANNARD BAKER

Illustrated

VOLUME SIX

Garden City, New York
DOUBLEDAY, DORAN & COMPANY, INC.
1937

PRINTED AT THE *Country Life Press*, GARDEN CITY, N. Y., U. S. A.

PREFACE

THIS volume of the biography of Woodrow Wilson, like its predecessors, is founded primarily upon the enormous collection of letters and documents, both public and private, a large part of it hitherto unpublished, which Mrs. Wilson made available to the author soon after the President's death in 1924, and upon which he has been at work for thirteen years. He has added largely in understanding and illumination of the events here chronicled by conversation and correspondence with members of Mr. Wilson's cabinet, members of Congress, and others, who were most closely associated with him, and with many intimate friends and relatives.

The task has grown steadily more difficult. Each year has added its quota to the list of biographies, autobiographies and memoirs dealing with the stupendous events of the period in which Woodrow Wilson was President, and pointing, as though drawn by some magnetic force, toward the man who more than any other represented the constructive opinion, and influenced the mighty affairs, of his time.

All this new material has had to be examined and related to the President's own documents, especially in dealing with the highly controversial period, here under consideration, in which the United States decided finally to go into the war. During the years devoted to this exacting labour, the author, aware that irate partisans nursing unpublished memoirs, or undiscovered admirers treasuring priceless letters, might still be waiting in ambush to spring out upon him, has often recalled the comment of Woodrow

Wilson, himself then a student of history, in one of his early essays:

"It is a wonder that historians who take their business seriously can sleep at night."

It would, indeed, have been a task impossible of achievement if it had not been for the loyal, unfailing, generous assistance of many friends. Wholly inadequate, but heartfelt, acknowledgments of the author's appreciation have been made in the body of this volume.

The author wishes to express, especially, his indebtedness to Dr. Harley A. Notter, formerly of Leland Stanford Junior University, now of the Research Section of the Department of State, whose scholarly assistance in the analysis of the documentary material has been invaluable in the preparation of this work. Dr. Notter is a devoted student of the writings and addresses of Woodrow Wilson; his book, *The Origins of the Foreign Policy of Woodrow Wilson*, being in process of publication by the Johns Hopkins press. The coöperation of Dr. Notter has not only contributed to the scope of this volume, but it has added an enthusiasm of common endeavour which has lightened the task.

The author acknowledges, in no less degree, the continued and increasingly valuable assistance of Katharine E. Brand, who has been connected with these studies from the beginning. Her knowledge of every source of material used, and her thoroughness, as a research historian, in checking every authority, have added immeasurably to the value of the work.

RAY STANNARD BAKER.

Amherst, Massachusetts
July, 1937

CONTENTS

VOLUME VI

LIST OF ILLUSTRATIONS

LIST OF FACSIMILES

Woodrow Wilson
LIFE AND LETTERS

Woodrow Wilson
LIFE AND LETTERS

CHAPTER I

WILSON AND NATIONAL PREPAREDNESS

"Democracy is the most difficult form of government, because it is the form under which you have to persuade the largest number of persons to do anything in particular."

Address at Washington, September 28, 1915.

"We regard war merely as a means of asserting the rights of a people against aggression. . . . We will not maintain a standing army except for uses which are as necessary in times of peace as in times of war . . ."

Address to Congress, December 7, 1915.

"What is America expected to do? She is expected to do nothing less than keep law alive while the rest of the world burns."

Address at Des Moines, February 1, 1916.

I. PERIOD OF ANXIETY AND AGITATION

AS THE World War deepened, two powerful and sincere bodies of opinion developed in America as to the best methods of meeting the problems presented by our neutrality, how we should guard our manifold interests, avoid being drawn into the conflict itself, and yet be of use in the ultimate settlements.

The first of these groups advocated a steady and vigorous pressure for peace as the surest way out; the second demanded military preparation. Both groups soon ripened into bitter antagonism, and both had to be recognized and wisely dealt with by the President.

Both were early in the field. If Bryan was the typical leader of the pacifists, Theodore Roosevelt, raging at Oyster Bay, was the outstanding spokesman of those who demanded immediate and extensive additions to the American army and navy. This last movement was confined largely to the East, and based upon industrial and financial interests rather than upon agricultural. What it lacked in numbers it made up in economic power.

In the beginning Wilson regarded both of these movements as unnecessary and extreme: they tended to "rock the boat," which he was endeavouring to hold steady; but he was far more opposed to the preparationists than to the pacifists. It was the part of statesmanship to keep them both in leash and so direct his course that the nation might preserve a united front.

Garrison, Wilson's Secretary of War, had been agitating for a reorganization of the army since he took office. He regarded the authorized strength of 100,000 men—with only 90,000 recruited and 35,000 immobilized in coast defenses and army posts—as utterly inadequate.[1] But this was commonly the excited attitude of new Secretaries of War and nobody, least of all Congress, paid much attention. With the outbreak of the war in Europe, however, the military and naval situation of the United States became an outstanding issue. General Leonard Wood, who had been Chief of Staff, began to agitate with characteristic blunt vigour for "a sound, national military policy."[2] Our situation as to preparedness was "thoroughly unsatisfactory."[3] In October Representative A. P. Gardner of Massachusetts, chairman of the House Committee on Military Affairs, declared for the creation of a National Security Commission to report upon defense conditions

---

[1]Lindley M. Garrison, in a statement to the press, March 12, 1913.
[2]Hermann Hagedorn, *Leonard Wood*, Vol. II, pp. 131, 133.
[3]Memorandum written by Wood in early November.

in the United States.[1] Senator G. E. Chamberlain was also active, and on December 1st the National Security League, made up of an ardent group of advocates of preparedness, came into being. Extensive agitation began in the Eastern press;[2] many thoughtful men believed that if we took a strong position in our notes to European nations—insisting, for example, upon strict accountability—we should, if challenged, be in a position to back up our demands.

"No man should draw a pistol who dares not shoot. The government that shakes its fist first and its finger afterward falls into contempt. Our diplomacy has lost its authority and influence because we have been brave in words and irresolute in action."[3]

The President's earlier attitude toward this agitation was one of avoidance and opposition. He would not comment on Gardner's demand,[4] and when Colonel House, who had been conferring with General Wood, insisted that "it was time to do a great constructive work for the army and one which would make the country too powerful for any nation to think of attacking us," the President remarked that he "did not believe there was any necessity for immediate action; he was afraid it would shock the country. He made the statement that, no matter how the great war ended, there would be complete exhaustion; and, even if Germany won, she would not be in a condition seriously to menace our country for many years to come."[5]

---

[1] New York *Times*, October 16, 1914.

[2] "There is no tendency among the American people toward militarism, but there is a just demand that we shall be prepared for emergencies, and there is ample testimony that our army and navy and our coast defenses need immediate improvement." *Ibid.*, December 7, 1914.

[3] Elihu Root, February 15, 1916.

[4] New York *Times*, October 20, 1914.

[5] Colonel House's diary entry, November 4, 1914. *The Intimate Papers of Colonel House*, Vol. I, p. 298.

In this position he had the strong support of Bryan, who was "in violent opposition to any kind of increase"[1] of the army. Wilson himself hated war—he had as a youth seen the results of it in the post-bellum South—and he knew as an historian that for a century national policy had vigorously opposed a great military establishment.

It was the general expectation that the President would treat the subject of preparedness in his annual message at the opening of Congress on December 8, 1914: and the expectation was not disappointed. The "uproarious ovation which continued for several minutes"[2] gave evidence of his popularity at that time.

"We never have had, and while we retain our present principles and ideals we never shall have, a large standing army."

We should be ready to defend ourselves but should not "turn America into a military camp" nor "ask our young men to spend the best years of their lives making soldiers of themselves."

He declared that we were "at peace with all the world," we did not dread any other nation, we were not "jealous of rivalry in the fields of commerce." ". . . we threaten none, covet the possessions of none, desire the overthrow of none."

It was right enough that citizens who were willing to volunteer should be "made familiar with the use of modern arms, the rudiments of drill and maneuver, and the maintenance and sanitation of camps," and that "the National Guard of the States should be developed and strengthened," but to do more than this "carries with it a reversal of the whole history and character of our polity."

---

[1] Diary entry of November 8, 1914. *The Intimate Papers of Colonel House*, Vol. I, p. 300.

[2] New York *Times*, December 9, 1914.

He stood almost where Jefferson had stood more than a century earlier.

"A powerful navy" he recognized as our legitimate means of defense: but here changes must await the studies of experts and the lessons of modern war.[1]

The reception of the address was unexpectedly enthusiastic. ". . . even some of the Republicans joined in the applause." When the President said, "we shall not alter our attitude because some amongst us are nervous and excited," the Democrats broke into loud laughter. Representative Gardner sat through this thrust "silent and solemn-faced."[2] There was little doubt where the majority in Congress stood.[3]

In general the comment in the country was favourable. The President had not yielded to "mob hysteria,"[4] nor heeded the "shrill screams of the jingoes."[5] An analysis of some sixty letters and documents commenting on the address, remaining among the President's papers, shows that forty either condemn the Gardner resolution or felicitate the President on his message; ten take issue with the President, and five petitions bearing one hundred

---

[1]*The Public Papers of Woodrow Wilson*, Vol. III, pp. 215–228 for entire address.

[2]New York *Times*, December 9, 1914.

[3]The Committee on Rules of the House on that day refused even to give Congressman Gardner a hearing on his resolution. *Ibid.*, December 9, 1914.

[4]Hamilton Holt, editor of the *Independent*, to Wilson, December 9, 1914.

[5]L. W. Nieman of the Milwaukee *Journal*, to Wilson, December 11, 1914. The President's addresses seemed always to awaken admiration for their oratorical finish. An editorial in the Boston *Herald* of December 9th remarked:

"It sometimes seems as if the days of oratory had passed . . . But here is Woodrow Wilson, practical-minded enough to become President of the United States, who writes with the charm of the old rhetoricians, and demonstrates anew the power of the literary quality. If you have any doubt of this, read the closing passages of his message, particularly those which deal with the ancient ideals of the republic, and the hopes that may be cherished as to its place in the future of the nations. . . . If anyone doubts that this literary quality means added power to its possessor, let such a doubter consult the concern which had planned to unload munitions of war on Uncle Sam, as a result of the present furore. Whether anyone agrees with the President's affirmative theory or not, one must respect the broad basis of historical scholarship on which it rests and the sustained idealism with which it is set forth."

and fifty signatures express a fervid opposition to war and warlike preparations.[1]

The President himself was well pleased with the reception:

"Well, the broadside has been fired off and I hope sincerely that it will have the desired effect in quieting those who are seriously in danger of making trouble for the country."[2]

Nevertheless the agitation was not stilled. Some of the extremists were beside themselves with indignation. Theodore Roosevelt declared that Wilson and Bryan were the "very worst men we have ever had in their positions . . . they are worse than Jefferson and Madison. I really believe that I would rather have Murphy, Penrose or Barnes as the standard-bearer of this nation in the face of international wrong-doing."[3] But there was also steady pressure from leaders like Mr. Taft who, while deploring "hysteria," demanded that both army and navy be increased.[4] And General Wood and other strong believers in increased armaments continued to agitate, much to the President's irritation. He wrote to Garrison on December 21st:

---

[1] The canny old "laird of Skibo," Andrew Carnegie, wrote to the President on January 29, 1915, endorsing his position on armies and armaments.

"After this war is over . . ." he said, "no nation we have to fear will be in condition, or be in the mood, to begin war, for some years, thus giving us plenty of time to consider what is needed to give us Naval Power, up to date."

[2] Wilson to Colonel E. M. House, December 9, 1914.

[3] Theodore Roosevelt to Henry Cabot Lodge, December 8, 1914. *Selections from the Correspondence of Theodore Roosevelt and Henry Cabot Lodge*, Vol. II, p. 450.

[4] In an address at Somerville, Massachusetts, December 9, 1914. New York *Times*, December 10, 1914.

The New York *Times* quoted Mr. Bryan as saying that "if this country needed a million men . . . the call would go out at sunrise and the sun would go down on a million men in arms." It commented as follows:

"More foolish words than these of the Secretary of State were never spoken by mortal man in reply to a serious argument. . . .

"There has been no talk about raising an army of a million men. There have been no sane prognostications of impending war. All that hundreds of thousands of reasonable citizens are asking is ably and clearly expressed in Secretary Garrison's annual report." December 11, 1914.

". . . I do think that General Wood is pursuing a questionable course hardly consistent with the right spirit of the service and much too individualistic."

Of the speeches of Representative Hobson he wrote: "I am sincerely sorry that any man holding a responsible position should try to stir up such feelings and thoughts, but I am heartily glad to know how little serious effect that particular speech of Mr. Hobson had."[1]

At least two of the members of the cabinet, Houston[2] and Garrison, were ardent preparationists—Garrison to the point, by February 1, 1915, of threatening to resign.

Meanwhile the situation in Europe was becoming steadily more alarming. Early in February came the news of the German war zone declaration: enemy ships were to be ruthlessly sunk: neutrals were warned against travelling on them. Wilson responded, as we have seen, that Germany would be held to "strict accountability" for damages that affected the United States; nevertheless several ships were torpedoed, involving the loss of American lives: and in May came the appalling shock of the *Lusitania*. During the same period a large section of American opinion was also becoming more and more irritated by the high-handed methods of the British blockade, and there were not wanting prophecies that if we did not fight the Germans we should be compelled to fight the British.

All of these things immensely stimulated the agitation for preparedness in America. Garrison was writing articles and making addresses.[3] General Wood, wholly without official authority, was canvassing the larger universities of

---

[1] Wilson to Frederic C. Howe, December 21, 1914.

[2] See David F. Houston, *Eight Years With Wilson's Cabinet*, Vol. I, p. 127.

[3] He wrote an article on national defense for the *Century Magazine* of March, 1915, and on April 10th he addressed a Democratic Club at the Hotel Astor in New York, stressing the need of a larger standing army, trained reserves for the regulars and similar reserves for the militia.

the North in the interest of universal military training.

In spite of the President's strong feeling in the matter, something plainly had to be done. On February 8th, four days after the German war zone decree, the President seems for the first time to have turned the full powers of his mind to a consideration of concrete plans. He discussed with Garrison proposals for increasing the "militia," and considered suggestions for the adoption of a military system based upon Swiss experience. "It is a matter," he wrote to H. L. Higginson, "to which I have been giving a great deal of thought."[1]

On March 3rd he signed the Naval Appropriation bill carrying $45,053,801 for the increase of the navy. On May 5th, two days before the sinking of the *Lusitania*, he was writing quite frankly:

". . . I am very glad that you feel the confidence you do in my willingness to consider very fully any plan which looks towards increasing the efficiency of the Army or improving the army system in any way . . ."[2]

He was willing to "consider very fully any plan," even though, a few days later, he was telling a great audience in Philadelphia that there was "such a thing as a man being too proud to fight."

But it was not until July that in his judgment the accumulating evidence had become so convincing as to warrant positive action. He was then preparing and dispatching his third and last *Lusitania* note. Who could tell what a new day might bring forth?

There is no doubt that the President moved with profound hesitation and a tormenting sense not only of the futility of war but of the hazards of victory: nevertheless on July 21st he took his first great step, writing to Garrison and Daniels to draw up programmes for the develop-

---

[1]March 1, 1915.
[2]To John Brisben Walker.

ment and equipment of the two arms of the service. To Garrison he wrote:

"I have been giving scarcely less thought than you yourself have to the question of adequate preparation for national defense, and I am anxious, as you know, to incorporate in my next message to Congress a programme regarding the development and equipment of the Army and a proper training of our citizens to arms which, while in every way consistent with our traditions and our national policy, will be of such a character as to commend itself to every patriotic and practical mind."

The two Secretaries were to confer with their professional associates, draw their plans, and then the President would discuss the proposals with them. In each letter he was careful to say:

"Whether we can reasonably propose the whole of it to the Congress immediately or not we can determine when we have studied it. The important thing now is to know and know fully what we need. Congress will certainly welcome such advice and follow it to the limit of its opportunity."

Having thus taken the entire subject in hand, the President followed it up with characteristic vigour and thoroughness. He knew far better than many of the hot-headed advocates of a great army and navy the real attitude of the people and of the fight that he must face in a Congress which reacted so sensitively to that opinion. He knew well that it would require able and persistent leadership to secure united action. He began immediately to bring together his following on Capitol Hill, writing on August 2nd to the outstanding leaders of the military and naval affairs committees of both Houses. The letter to Congressman Hay is representative:

"I am sure you have had as much in mind as I have the whole matter of what it is wise and necessary to do in the matter of national defense. I have been taking steps to get full recommendations from the War and Navy Departments and I am hoping that after I get back to Washington[1] it may be convenient for you to come up and have a talk with me as to the best way in which the whole thing can be handled, so that we shall all have a single judgment in the matter and a single programme of action. I shall value your advice in the matter very much indeed."[2]

On August 12th Secretary Garrison submitted a general outline of the military policy desired by the War Department, and suggested that it be made public at once, in order to arouse popular interest and discussion. But this was not at all the President's conception of the method of handling a matter so delicate; it would tend to decentralize and weaken leadership by setting up controversies, possibly between the President himself and his Secretary of War, certainly between the War Department and the excited pacifist organizations, supported by no inconsiderable part of the membership of the Congress. The government must move as a unit, Congress must be kept firmly behind the administration, and there must be a clear understanding as to what the programme was to be, and how much it would cost in dollars and cents. The President wrote Garrison at once:

"My judgment does not coincide with yours as to the publicity test. There is this danger in that, that a subsequent modification of the suggested policy might be given

---

[1] He was then at Cornish, New Hampshire, on his vacation.

[2] He considered the proposals as non-partisan and endeavoured to enlist the support also of Republicans, some of whom had been his unrelenting critics. He wrote to James R. Mann, Republican leader of the House:

"I hope that you are planning to be in Washington at least a little while before the opening of the session of Congress. I would greatly value a conference with you on one or two of the more important matters which are to come before the Congress, matters which are or should be entirely non-partisan in the treatment given them and in which I would very much value your advice and coöperation; such, for example, as the question of national defense." (November 18, 1915.)

the color of a difference of opinion between yourself and myself, which I am sure you would not wish any more than I would. If we should differ, I may have the good luck to convince you,—I have always found you very open-minded,—and I think that a matter of as much consequence as this should, of course, be a matter of common counsel. My judgment is, therefore, that it is best to keep the matter for the present for private consideration.

"The desires of the nation, I think, are quite clear in this matter and our duty equally clear, but I think the detail of the policy the country is generously willing to leave to us. It must, necessarily, be a matter of official information and expert opinion."[1]

Two days later, after reading the report "with very studious attention," he wrote again:

"I am sorry to say that it does not contain what I hoped it would. In view of what you wrote me in your letter, it is evident that you were thinking chiefly while preparing it of making the test of public opinion to which you referred. The paper is, therefore, lacking in the detail which is necessary before I can really form a personal judgment about it.

"I want to say that the general idea contained in it interests me very much and seems to me a feasible one, but the method by which the thing could be done, I mean by which the training of the citizen soldiery could be carried out, and also the cost, it is of the first importance that I should know.

"I learn from Mr. Breckinridge that the War College is now at work on the figures of cost. I hope that it will be possible for you to get them to finish these reckonings at as early a date as possible, and I am going to ask that you will be good enough to have drawn out for me a succinct plan in definite items summing up this paper that I have

---

[1] August 16, 1915.

and sufficiently developing the method of administration
to enable me to form a practical as well as a general
judgment."

Here were hard-headed, practical demands, asking for
just such facts and figures as the President well knew he
would need to use upon skeptical congressmen who were
asked to appropriate money, and upon a still more doubtful popular mind, if a public appeal should become necessary. Wilson knew that competent leadership required
thorough, even scholarly, preparation. This was one of
the reasons why he seemed often so slow to move: it was
also one of the reasons why, when he did move, his leadership was commonly so effective.[1]

It was thus a question of method, rather than a difference of judgment as to ultimates, that caused the rift
between the President and his impatient, individualistic,
tactless, but wholly sincere and really able Secretary of
War—a rift that was now to widen rapidly. The President
was prepared to go farther in mollifying the extreme
preparationists than was his Secretary in admitting any
element of reason in the demands of the pacifistic groups.
It must have been with something of a wry face that
Wilson wrote to General Wood regarding the training
camp at Plattsburg—but he wrote!

"I have followed as well as I could at a distance what
has been done at Plattsburg and have followed it with the
greatest interest. I think all concerned ought to be congratulated upon the success of the experiment."[2]

---

[1]The only other statesman of the period, in the writer's judgment, who approached
Wilson in appetite for thoroughness, in determination to go to the bottom of every
subject he really attacked, was Senator Robert M. La Follette of Wisconsin. Both
Wilson and La Follette succeeded largely because they knew more than their opponents: their own confidence in themselves being the bulwark of the confidence which
they aroused in the public mind. Both were great orators, but neither ever rested upon
oratory alone. It was not emotion they sought to arouse; although both did arouse
emotion; it was men's reason they struggled to convince.

[2]August 16, 1915.

What he especially wished to avoid was an excited and emotional appeal such as Roosevelt made a few days later at Plattsburg wherein he made a vitriolic attack on "college sissies" and, talking with reporters after leaving the camp, by inference attacked the President in a contemptuous reference to "elocution as a substitute for action."

Some of Wilson's ardent friends feared that the Plattsburg movement was being turned into political and personal channels, and again urged that the President himself speak at Plattsburg; but he was not to be turned by political alarums from the method he considered most soundly effective.

"I realize," he wrote Dudley Field Malone, "to the full the force of what you say about the desirability of my coming to the military camp at Plattsburg, but I am sure that I could convince you if I had a chance at you in conversation that it would not be the timely or all-wise thing to do. What I want to say about preparedness I must say to the Congress and I don't think that any partisan use that can be made of the camp at Plattsburg will really do anybody any harm except those who try to turn it to such purposes."[1]

It was a wise judgment; for when it began to appear— the news inevitably leaked—that the President was even beginning to consider a programme of preparation, a tremendous pother arose among the pacifistic groups. It was not confined to cranks and fanatics; it included many men and women of high attainments, leaders in nearly all walks of life. The protests revealed that the country was not at all united on the preparedness issue.[2]

---

[1] August 19, 1915.

[2] Reports from reliable sources found among the President's papers indicate that Iowa, Maryland, Missouri, Nebraska, Oklahoma, Oregon, Minnesota, Wisconsin, and parts of Pennsylvania were either indifferent or violently opposed to the issue. Texas

In this turmoil of excitement and agitation we find the President steadily and patiently trying to mollify and moderate both extremes, arguing that Americans were no swashbucklers, and urging coöperation in preparation, "not for war, but for defense."[1]

"I do not think there need be any fear that the country will go too far in the policy to be adopted. I think its thought is, on the whole, very self-restrained and judicial and that it will wish to see a course pursued that lies between the extremes in every particular."[2]

To an even more violent extremist in the other direction, who wrote that he had seen Bryan "address 3,000 traitors" and that "every man in that organization should be in jail," and who proposed to "stir the nation up" with books and moving pictures, the President wrote:

"I must frankly say to you that I am sorry after reading the synopsis of your new enterprise, because I think the thing a great mistake. There is no need to stir the nation up in favor of national defense. It is already soberly and earnestly aware of its possible perils and of its duty, and I should deeply regret seeing any sort of excitement stirred in so grave a matter."[3]

---

was split on the question. Organizations sprang up whose sole purpose was opposition to preparedness. Three hundred and fifty thousand members of the United Brethren Church were said to be against it; twelve thousand farmers in Wisconsin were of the same opinion. One hundred and three Women's Single Tax Clubs opposed it, and when on October 4, 1915, at Houston, Texas, Bryan delivered an anti-preparedness address, he was cheered by eight thousand Texans. These groups generally believed that preparedness was a step inevitably leading to war.

Secretary Lansing gives this convincing testimony:

"The majority of my callers during the summer and autumn of 1915, and for many months after that time, senators, representatives, and men high in financial and business circles, frankly said that they were against war, or else stated that, though they favored it, the bulk of the people with whom they came in contact were opposed to it." *War Memoirs of Robert Lansing*, p. 24.

[1]Address to the Civilian Advisory Board of the Navy, October 6, 1915. *The Public Papers of Woodrow Wilson*, Vol. III, p. 373.

[2]To Oswald Garrison Villard, an ardent pacifist, September 7, 1915.

[3]To Thomas Dixon, author of *The Birth of a Nation*, and other propagandist works, September 7, 1915.

In October, when a committee of the Conference on National Defense, a body representing several preparedness and military societies, sought an interview to present a petition for extensive measures, the President was reluctant to grant it.

". . . the promoters of this League," he wrote to Tumulty, "are by no means friends of ours, but I suppose I ought to receive their petition."

In some cases the attacks from both sides, though avoiding direct criticism of the President, became intensely personal, endeavouring to undermine the policies he advocated by making charges against, or ridiculing, various members of the administration. It is the familiar, inevitable and utterly despicable method of opponents who in their violence and excitement cannot or will not meet reason with reason. Every strong administration has known such attacks. In the earlier part of the Wilson administration Bryan was the favourite butt; they shifted later to Daniels and Baker, since both were supposed to have pacifistic leanings. Few things irritated Wilson more than these methods. We have a record of how the President met a slighting reference to Daniels, who was supposed to have forbidden the singing of "Tipperary" in the navy. It was at a luncheon at the White House:

"I have never seen the President angry before. I never want to see him angry again. His fist came down on the table:

"'Daniels did not give the order that "Tipperary" should not be sung in the navy. He is surrounded by a network of conspiracy and of lies. His enemies are determined to ruin him. I can't be sure who they are yet, but when I do get them—God help them.'"[1]

Months later we find him expressing in a letter the deep-

---

[1] January 5, 1915. Narrative by Mrs. Crawford H. Toy, who was a guest at luncheon.

est resentment at "the partisan, puerile, and most grossly unjust attacks on Secretary Daniels."[1]

Late October found the work of drawing up tentative military and naval plans about completed. Secretary Daniels announced a five-year building programme for the navy involving what was then considered the enormous expenditure of $502,482,214.[2] With Garrison's military plan, submitted a little later, the President was not wholly satisfied, urging that more attention be given to the existing National Guard—a difference of emphasis that was afterwards to become more pronounced.

Having these definite reports in hand, he was ready to go to the people—in preparation for the opening of Congress in December. As the occasion for an address he had chosen a dinner of the Manhattan Club of New York, scheduled for November 4th. So important did he consider the initial statement of his proposals that, contrary to his usual method, he worked out his address beforehand and sent a copy to Mr. Garrison. The blunt, undiplomatic Secretary of War, standing behind every item of his proposals, was frank in his criticisms of two statements— that the continental army "was not to be organized," and that the National Guard could be used as a training corps. Wilson commented on Garrison's letter in a memorandum which Mr. Tumulty undoubtedly showed to the Secretary:

"It is too late to change the speech. The two statements to which the Secretary refers are not likely to be mis-

---

[1]Wilson to John R. Dunlap, September 15, 1915.

No President was ever more loyal or determined in his defense of his close associates than Wilson—as again and again in the case of Bryan and Baker as well as Daniels. In several instances we also find him stoutly defending his secretary, Mr. Tumulty, absurdly charged with being an agent of the Pope.

"The attitude of some people about this," he wrote to Tumulty on August 6, 1915, "irritates me more than I can say. It is not only preposterous, but outrageous and of course you know it never makes the slightest impression on me."

[2]New York *Times*, October 20, 1915.

understood. The men referred to will of course *not* be organized as a standing force, and, while everybody knows that we do not and cannot *command* the national guard we can, and I think we should, call upon them for voluntary services of any kind. The plan suggested by the Secretary is susceptible, fortunately, of adaptation."[1]

Wilson knew well the difficulties of convincing the people as to any comprehensive programme whatever—especially if it contained the least semblance of a "standing army"—and he was well aware how impossible it was to carry out to its last detail any bureaucratic programme whatsoever: that "adaptation," otherwise compromise, was of the essence of a favourable solution.

It was a tremendous gathering the President found in New York, the great hall of the Biltmore Hotel crowded to the last place.

"Wave after wave of applause greeted President Wilson after Mr. Britt had said, in presenting him to the company, that history would accord him a place by the side of Washington and Lincoln, and 'that this country is not now plunged into that inferno of bloodshed that is devastating Europe is attributable to the cool head, great mind, and patriotic heart of Woodrow Wilson.'"[2]

The President began by setting forth, as frequently in the past, what he considered to be definitely established American principles: that we had put aside all aggressive purposes, that we would "never again take another foot of territory by conquest." "For ourselves we wish nothing but the full liberty of self-development . . ." But the world was "ablaze with terrible war"; how far were we "prepared to maintain ourselves against any interference with our national action or development"?

Turning to concrete proposals, he called "for the train-

---

[1] November 1, 1915.
[2] Henry Watterson, *A History of the Manhattan Club*, p. 113.

ing within the next three years of a force of 400,000 citizen soldiers . . . who . . . would not be organized as a standing force but would be expected merely to undergo intensive training for a very brief period of each year."[1] The National Guard, which we were not to "supersede" or "subordinate," "would be used as part of the instrumentality by which training would be given the citizens who enlisted under the new conditions." The navy was to be, as it had always been, "the first and chief line of defense"; we should "hasten our pace" in its further development.[2]

It was as far as possible from being an extreme or excited presentation of the new proposals. While there was no doubt as to the cordiality of the reception to the President himself, the proposals elicited no great enthusiasm.[3]

The address seems to have satisfied neither extreme of opinion. To Theodore Roosevelt it was a "shadow program."[4] Wilson's "half preparedness" was as dangerous as the schemes of Bryan and Henry Ford.[5]

A little later a member of the Naval Advisory Board, Henry A. Wise Wood, an ardent advocate of preparation, sent a sharp letter of resignation to Secretary Daniels:

"I have done this in order that I shall be free to attack the thoroughly inadequate, and therefore dangerously

---

[1]It was the phrase, "would not be organized as a standing force," that had especially aroused Garrison's criticism.

[2]*The Public Papers of Woodrow Wilson*, Vol. III, pp. 384–392.

[3]William Allen White, who was present, commented that the applause was perfunctory "but not much more."

[4]Public statement published in the New York *Times*, November 12, 1915.

[5]Interview with Theodore Roosevelt, published in the Chicago *Daily News*, quoted in the New York *Times*, November 19, 1915. Roosevelt's diatribes, however, caused Wilson no anxiety. They defeated themselves by their violence. The *Times* said in an editorial on December 7th:

"Scanning the gall and vinegar of his adjectives, hearing that curious staccato of impetuous speech, the indulgent critic can only take refuge in the theory of the Everlasting Juvenile, the boy who has never grown up, as Dr. Eliot said of him. As Mrs. Berry in 'The Ordeal of Richard Feverel' remarked delightedly of Dick's baby: 'Ain't he got passion? Ain't he a splendid roarer?'"

weak, naval and military policy of the President, as expressed in Secretary Garrison's and your own recommendations, and to urge publicly that the recommendations of the General Board of the navy and General Staff of the army, as contained in their original reports, be substituted therefor."[1]

The pacifists were equally excited: Bryan issued a formal statement attacking the President's proposals. Still worse, there was a positive and unfavourable reaction from members of Congress, even of his own party, upon whom the President knew he must depend if he was to secure any new armament at all. Congressman Kitchin, for example, one of the powerful Democratic leaders of the House, thought the programme was "stupendous" and would "shock the civilized world."[2]

To make matters still more difficult, Secretary Garrison had given out the text of his plan for publication apparently without consulting the President, thus enabling opponents to pounce upon the more definite and drastic items which it contained.

Wilson met all the attacks generously, kept his temper, and seems to have retained the respect of most of his critics.[3] He was trying, as he had said in his Manhattan Club address, to "purge" his heart "of all personal and selfish motives"; and he recognized that in a democracy sharp public opposition and discussion were the price of unity of action. As he wrote to an old friend:

"I can't help being disturbed that Mr. Bryan should

---

[1]December 22, 1915. New York *Times*, December 23, 1915.

[2]*Ibid.*, November 19, 1915.

[3]To Rabbi Wise of New York, one of the sincere critics, he wrote:
"I have your letter of November twelfth and I need not say that it distresses me very deeply. I always mistrust my own judgment when I find myself disagreeing with you, but in this case I fear the disagreement is inevitable. I want you to know, nevertheless, that it does not affect in the least my estimate of you or my personal feeling. It is painful to go different ways but we can thoroughly respect one another in doing so." (November 18, 1915.)

see things as he does. My own feeling towards him remains of the most cordial sort, but evidently everything must be worked out by contest, and I dare say it is best so. Only in that way are things threshed to the bottom."[1]

The President was now ready for the struggle with Congress. He knew the opposition he would have to meet, and he gave unusual care and thought to the preparation of his annual message.[2] We find him shutting himself away in his study, refusing appeals to consider this or that subject in his recommendations, sharpening the entire document as far as possible to a single impressive point—the need of preparation.[3]

One is impressed, at this time, by the sheer weight of the President's responsibilities. Well had he observed in previous years, knowing as an historian the burdens placed

---

[1] Wilson to Frank P. Glass, November 10, 1915.

[2] His papers give remarkable evidence of the thoroughness with which he attacked the entire problem. He demanded not only complete facts and figures from the War and Navy Departments, but he fortified himself to the last degree with knowledge of the condition of the Treasury. He wrote on his own typewriter to Secretary McAdoo on November 22nd:

"Will you not be kind enough to have the enclosed information furnished me, very succinctly, in the form I have here indicated? This is for use in my message."

The memorandum enclosed was as follows:

"FINANCES:

"Deficit at the end of the present fiscal year if the taxes enacted by the last Congress lapse and the sugar duty ceases.

"Position of the Treasury at the end of the present fiscal year if these taxes and that duty are continued.

"Additional appropriations estimated for for the next fiscal year if the new programmes of the army and navy are approved and adopted.

"Resulting deficit (a) assuming the continuance of the present taxes and duties. (b) assuming the loss of their discontinuance.

"The several sources and objects of revenue and taxation mentioned in the Secretary's report with the estimated amount each would yield.

"The amount of 'Panama' bonds which the Treasury is authorized to issue, as of this date."

[3] In explaining to a delegation of woman suffragists, on November 6th, why he could not discuss their desired reforms, he remarked:

". . . I have a habit—perhaps the habit of the teacher—of confining my utterances to one subject at a time, for fear that two subjects might compete with one another for prominence. I have felt obliged in the present posture of affairs to devote my message to one subject . . ." Inez Haynes Irwin, *The Story of the Woman's Party*, p. 115.

upon the shoulders of American Presidents, that a "wise and prudent athlete"[1] should be chosen for the place. There were those who criticized Wilson for his "isolation,"[2] usually because they themselves could not reach him, but the record gives evidence of days of crowded appointments and concentrated labour. He was not only giving his closest thought to his message to Congress, and beginning the campaign by reasoning with senators and representatives, but he was meeting an unending train of visitors, delegations, committees.

"Congressmen are rushing upon me from every quarter and it is hard to say when, if at all, I can have a moment of my own . . .

"Congress meets to-morrow; Tuesday I must address it; Wednesday I am to entertain the Democratic National Committee at lunch."[3]

It is scarcely surprising that he should have had to exercise stern self-discipline, refuse even to see old friends, or that he should have renewed his attempts to organize his time.[4]

And yet the White House records show that every day, or nearly every day, the President took long automobile rides, or on favourable days played golf. His extraordinary intensity as a worker made necessary a stern adherence to a daily programme of rest and exercise, lest his burdens break his health.

---

[1]*Constitutional Government in the United States*, p. 80.

[2]As for example O. G. Villard's article, "Isolation of the President," in the *Independent*, December 6, 1915.

[3]Wilson to Edith G. Reid, December 5, 1915.

[4]On December 1st the following schedule was issued regarding the President's engagements:

"On Mondays, Wednesdays, and Thursdays he will receive those who merely want to pay their respects, then senators and congressmen who have no engagements. Then he will spend thirty minutes in signing public documents and devote an hour and a half to special engagements.

"On Tuesdays and Fridays, after an hour devoted to persons with engagements, he will spend from 11 to 1 o'clock with his cabinet." New York *Times*, December 2, 1915.

His days were not, however, without relaxation and delightful interludes; intimate friends or relatives were often at luncheon and dinner, and in these months the President was spending many of his evenings with Mrs. Galt, whom he had become engaged to marry.[1]

Both labour and rest, activity and relaxation, were ordered aspects of a life of extraordinary personal discipline. In his early years Wilson had adopted the principle that if a man really masters his task there is no need of working overlong at it. He had learned through the years to think everything clear before speaking or acting[2]—his long daily automobile rides, during which he was usually silent, prepared him for the duties of the hour—so that he never did anything twice, rarely made false motions, or needed to excuse or explain. All his letters are short and to the point; his addresses, compared with those of most Presidents, are concentrated, organized and aimed, to a superlative degree. After a paper was finished, an address delivered, a delegation met, an argument concluded, he dismissed it completely and went forward to the next task. He never, or rarely ever, corrected or even wished to see copies of the addresses he delivered, though they were usually extemporaneous. He said what he wanted to say, exactly in the form he desired to say it, the first time.[3] He had, probably, at this period in his career, as nearly complete mastery of his mind, of his time, of his work, of his play as it is given to men to attain. It was one of the things that the ordinary loose-minded politician, who

---

[1]Their engagement had been announced on October 6th.

[2]In his boyhood, as we have seen, his father trained him rigorously never to speak until he knew exactly what he wanted to say, and then to say it in the fewest possible words.

[3]The present writer, who was with President Wilson during the entire period of the Peace Conference at Paris and was responsible for the distribution of his addresses— many of which were of momentous importance—recalls only one instance, and that of minor importance, in which he desired a change made in the text of any of them after delivery.

18 December, 1915

THE WHITE HOUSE
WASHINGTON

Dear Mr. Secretary

Here is the note with my alterations — which, as you will see, are alterations of form only.

Thank you for its prompt preparation. Please do not hesitate to communicate with me at the Hot Springs, West Virginia.

In haste,

Cordially and Sincerely Yours,

Woodrow Wilson

Letter from Woodrow Wilson to Secretary Lansing, enclosing the draft of a note to Austria regarding the sinking by a submarine of the Italian ship, *Ancona*, with Americans aboard. This was written on the wedding day of the President and Mrs. Norman Galt.

commonly captures his thoughts and forms his decisions in conferences, could never appreciate.

On December 7th the President delivered his preparedness address before Congress. It was generously, though not enthusiastically, received. Many of the men sitting there before him in that great hall, some of his own party, did not believe that he was right and did not intend to follow him. What he asked Congress to do was to accept without curtailment the measures recommended in the reports of the Secretaries of the War and Navy Departments. "We cannot do less." He also emphasized again the need of a more efficient merchant marine—a sore point —and pleaded for a sound financial programme. "Borrowing money is short-sighted finance . . . we should pay as we go." Such stern advice, with the inevitable corollary of higher taxes, never sounds cheerful in congressional ears!

With this address the gauge was thrown down: the fight began.

II. WILSON GOES TO THE COUNTRY ON THE PROBLEM OF ARMAMENT

It was plain enough, after the preparedness address to Congress, that the President had a genuine fight on his hands. His spirits rose accordingly. Deep down in the man the Covenanter spirit, once convinced of the rightness of a cause, dearly loved the battle to win it.

". . . I always accept, perhaps by some impulse of my native blood, the invitation to a fight. . . ."

". . . I do not traduce my antagonists. . . . I wish that the best argument and the right purpose shall prevail."[1]

In all the course of the bitter struggle that was to follow, there is seldom to be found in his letters or documents a

[1]Address at New York, January 27, 1916. *The Public Papers of Woodrow Wilson*, Vol. IV, pp. 3 and 4.

single word of personal attack or of personal criticism, but everywhere, as we shall see, an effort to convert his critics with arguments and with reason. In the later years of his life, and especially after the breakdown in his health at Paris in April 1919, this was not always true; but in the great years from 1915 onward through the war he was at his best, physically and mentally.

It is beautiful, indeed, in these months, to see him flinging aside the attacks on both flanks—from extremists who were militarists and extremists who were pacifists— and marching straight forward to win the cause he had espoused, carrying the fight into Congress, and when opposition proved serious there, going to the country in a determined campaign to secure the backing of public opinion.

He had need of resourcefulness and determination. The address to Congress, so far from allaying controversy, seemed to inflame it. The militarists began at once to demand, in hearings before the committee, far more than the administration had proposed. They wanted a still larger army; they wanted compulsory military service. The navy men, not contented with the half-billion dollars that Daniels was asking, demanded a fleet equal to that of the strongest naval power.[1]

The anti-preparationists were even more vocal and far more numerous. Not long before,[2] the Ford peace ship, representing a considerable body of naïve American opinion, had sailed away to Europe to "stop the war." Anti-preparationist meetings were being held in New York and Washington, petitions, one of them "fifteen miles long," were being sent to the President.[3] There were really widespread doubt and opposition among the people

---

[1]Vote of the National Security League. New York *Times*, January 23, 1916.

[2]December 4, 1915.

[3]New York *Times*, January 28, 1916.

regarding the programme—which found immediate expression among timid congressmen and senators, acutely aware of the coming fall elections. Even the chairman of the Committee on Military Affairs of the House of Representatives, Mr. Hay, upon whom the President must depend for leadership, was frank to express his disapproval of certain vital aspects of the programme.[1]

The President knew that his chief difficulty lay with an "uninformed public opinion." He could write confidently enough that there need be no fear "that the jingoes will force or even hurry me into anything,"[2] but there were masses of people, especially in the Middle West, not at all pacifists in the sense of having thought the subject through and taken a stand upon conviction, but merely, in his judgment, unawakened to the gravity of the situation. He therefore determined, before opposition in Congress could solidify, to go to the country with the proposals to which he had committed his leadership.

The "swing-around" that followed, as far east as New York, as far west as Missouri and Kansas, was one of the most successful he ever made; and the records show that he thoroughly enjoyed the campaign. He began in his first speech, in New York, by boldly facing reality:

"We live in a world which we did not make, which we cannot alter, which we cannot think into a different condition from that which actually exists."

It was not the ambitions of America he must consider: it was the safety. To "keep a free hand to do the high things that we intend to do," we must look to the strengthening of our defensive forces.

He met, in forthright manner, the charges that he was inconsistent, that he had reversed the position so strongly taken the year before:

---

[1] New York *Times*, January 12, 1916.
[2] Wilson to Mrs. John W. Kern, January 24, 1916.

". . . I would be ashamed if I had not learned something in 14 months. The minute I stop changing my mind with the change of all the circumstances of the world, I will be a back number."[1]

Two days later he spoke at Pittsburgh, but it was not until the evening address at Cleveland that he began really to warm to his theme, kindling with the response he received. There was "no mistaking either the effectiveness of his argument or the spontaneous outbursts of applause and approval" which greeted him. His "solemnity inspired awe."[2] The nation, he said, was "daily treading amidst the most intricate dangers . . . no man in the United States knows what a single week or a single day or a single hour may bring forth."[3]

And yet, neither in this speech nor in any other during the crusade, did he lose sight of the dangers of militarism. We must be prepared: we must avoid, if humanly possible, the use of that preparation.

"You may count upon my heart and resolution to keep you out of the war, but you must be ready if it is necessary that I should maintain your honor."[4]

What he was asking for was the power to protect the nation "against things that I cannot control, the action of others. And where the action of others may bring us I cannot foretell."

---

[1]January 27, 1916. *The Public Papers of Woodrow Wilson*, Vol. IV, pp. 5, 7, 10. In an unused passage of his prepared speech, he further explained his thought: "It is our duty, therefore, just because we respect . . . the rights of others, to provide ourselves with the ready and adequate means of making it certain that others will respect our rights." (From the original.)

[2]David Lawrence, *The True Story of Woodrow Wilson*, pp. 158–159. Mr. Lawrence accompanied the presidential party, and his press reports are at first hand.

[3]*The Public Papers of Woodrow Wilson*, Vol. IV, p. 42.

[4]*Ibid.*, 44. At another time he defined what he meant by that tricky term, honour: ". . . the basis of honor is right, is peaceful intention, is just action, is the treatment of others as we would wish to be treated ourselves, is the insistence upon the rule of a free field and no favor." (At Topeka, February 2, 1916. *Ibid.*, Vol. IV, p. 88.)

Altogether Cleveland was "awestruck"—"not alone the few thousands who obtained the precious tickets for the armory and squeezed their way into the auditorium, but the hundreds of thousands more who read the alarming headlines and excerpts from the speech in black type the next day."[1]

The addresses in Wisconsin, Illinois, Iowa, Kansas, and Missouri followed much the same line and awakened much the same enthusiasm. The speech at Kansas City on February 2nd was probably the most effective.

"The crowd was enormous, taxing powers of description. Fancy an immense auditorium jammed to the roof with tiers of cheering humanity, many thousands of little American flags waving to and fro, almost coloring the air itself, and you have an idea of the demonstration which President Wilson received as he walked down the steps of a banked stage to the platform from which he spoke. There was no mistaking the enthusiasm of the people. They had waited—nearly 18,000 of them—in the tightly packed Convention Hall for two hours, while a crowd, almost as large, stood disappointedly outside, hoping the police lines would break and give them but a moment's glimpse of the President. . . .

"Many times the President was interrupted by applause, and often, too, by the remark of someone here and there in the crowd who shouted, 'We're with you!' or 'You can raise 500,000 men in Missouri' . . ."[2]

---

[1]David Lawrence, *The True Story of Woodrow Wilson*, pp. 161–162.

[2]*Ibid.*, p. 169. There were many evidences that these people were not in any sense pacifists. It was as the President himself had believed, that they were uninformed: that if they could understand the full meaning of the situation they would respond in their decisions just as he himself had done. A telegram from a man in Kansas City, on January 29th, is a sample of Western opinion:

"Referring to your speech at Pittsburgh you say that if all could see the dispatches I read every hour of the day they would know how difficult it has been for me to maintain peace. Why don't you publish some of these dispatches and you will get the support of the West. We are for you if the danger is real."

His appeals gained fire and fervour as he advanced into the deeper West.

"You have either got to make the men of this Nation in sufficient number ready to defend the Nation against initial disaster, or you have got to take the risk of initial disaster. Think of the cruelty, think of the stupidity, of putting raw levies of inexperienced men into the modern field of battle! We are not asking for armies; we are asking for a trained citizenship . . .

"Have you ever let your imagination dwell upon the enormous stretch of coast from the Canal to Alaska,—from the Canal to the northern corner of Maine? There is no other navy in the world that has to cover so great an area of defense as the American Navy, and it ought, in my judgment, to be incomparably the greatest [most adequate] navy in the world."[1]

"Incomparably the greatest navy in the world," was a torchlike phrase to light up the press of the nation, awakening emotion, support, fear, opposition. It was what the extreme advocates of preparation were demanding. It had, truly, a warlike sound.

It is quite as important, in considering the entire content of his message, to emphasize what he did not say as what he did say. His campaign was no indiscriminate appeal to the passions of patriotism: it is to be noted, as an astonishing aspect of such a crusade, that there was no hatred in it. It was a call to arms with no enemy in view. What moved him was the consideration that war might

---

[1] At St. Louis, Missouri, February 3, 1916. *The Public Papers of Woodrow Wilson*, Vol. IV, pp. 112–114.

In his actual address the President said, "incomparably the greatest navy in the world." On the train after the party had left St. Louis, Walter Lippmann reports, someone called attention to the sentence as being injudicious, and Wilson replied that he was "intoxicated by the exuberance of his own verbosity!" It is interesting to note that the sentence in the official House document recording the speech reads "incomparably the most adequate navy in the world." (Lippmann to the author.)

arise out of the circumstances of a world on fire and that it was wise to be prepared for the contingency.

"... I have tried for my own part to hold off from every passion."[1]

He was still confessing his inability to assess the rights and wrongs of the war:

"No man for many a year yet can trace the real sources of this war, but this thing we know, that opinion did not bring it on and that the force of opinion, at any rate the force of American opinion, is not going to stop it."[2]

As for keeping the country out of war, he told his Milwaukee audience:

"So far I have done so, and I pledge you my word that, God helping me, I will if it is possible."[3]

His reason was not merely the interest of America, but concern for the welfare of the entire world—"... we can show our friendship for the world and our devotion to the principles of humanity better and more effectively by keeping out of this struggle than by getting into it."[4]

And he gave glimpses of his vision of a fairer world beyond the mighty conflict—a vision of a league of nations born of the travail then in being, to which he was later to devote his highest energies, and finally lay down his life:

"I pray God that if this contest have no other result, it will at least have the result of creating an international tribune and producing some sort of joint guarantee of peace on the part of the great nations of the world."[5]

On the whole, the "swing around the circle" was a tremendous success.[6]

---

[1] At Pittsburgh, January 29, 1916. *The Public Papers of Woodrow Wilson*, Vol. IV, p. 17.

[2] At Chicago, January 31, 1916. *Ibid.*, p. 61.

[3] January 31, 1916. *Ibid.*, p. 48.

[4] At St. Louis, February 3, 1916. *Ibid.*, p. 108.

[5] At Des Moines, February 1, 1916. *Ibid.*, p. 75.

[6] "The frankness, the vigor, the suasion, the patriotism of his words carried conviction. He did not, of course, create, he awakened and reinforced the sound patriotic

While it was impossible to avoid some talk of politics—with the national conventions only a few months away and the presidential election in November—the President made a determined effort to keep his appeal upon a non-partisan basis, in itself really the canniest, as well as the wisest, attitude for any leader who happens to be President.   His popular appeal was everywhere most effective. He threw off restraint and mixed with the people. "He jested with them over the rail of his car . . . was generous with his back-platform speeches . . . handled himself unusually well in the big crowds in the cities."[1]

He returned to Washington on February 4th, vastly reassured, stimulated, eager for the struggle that was to come.

"The President is cheerful, regarding his Western tour as one of triumph."[2]

He found himself at once involved in a storm of controversy. Every Congress of every President is more or less antagonistic to most cabinet secretaries who come asking for huge appropriations to carry out their cut-and-dried programmes. Congress was especially suspicious and critical of Garrison. He exhaled a kind of military impatience and authority, highly irritating to the men on the Hill. Before Wilson left for the West there had been a sharp disagreement between the Secretary and Congressman Hay, the former emphasizing the need of enlarged federal control of the new army, the latter supporting a

feeling of the Middle West, a country retaining the courage, the energy, the Americanism of its pioneers, inheriting the traditions of the rude, heroic breed of founders and early settlers." New York *Times*, February 4, 1916.

   "The President 'got' the people. They showed for him a remarkable reverence; a hero-worship that was almost affection itself; something of the demonstrative enthusiasm which the West would never have dreamed of bestowing on the cold, impassive Wilson they had heard about." David Lawrence, *The True Story of Woodrow Wilson*, p. 171.

[1]*Ibid.*, p. 173.

[2]Franklin K. Lane to his wife, February 5, 1916. *The Letters of Franklin K. Lane*, p. 201.

federalized National Guard. Garrison was peremptory and abrupt.

"The issue," he wrote the President on January 12th, "must be plainly and clearly drawn. It has nothing whatever to do with the numbers of men to be raised or with the means of raising them, as Mr. Hay would have it appear that it has. It is between two absolutely different systems, one of which is based upon the Nation undertaking upon its own responsibility the raising and management of the national troops; and the other of which leaves us in the position that we have always been in since the institution of the Government,—to rely upon the States doing this thing for the Nation,—a situation in which the Nation is relying upon a military force that it does not raise, that it does not officer, that it does not train, and that it does not control."

He felt, he wrote later, that he could show his sincerity only by declining to "admit the possibility of compromise" with respect to the fundamental principle.[1]

There was great force in the Secretary's contentions. History supported him. The wars of the nineteenth century had abundantly demonstrated that reliance upon state militia was a hopelessly ineffective way to combat an enemy. It had led to endless confusion in the War of 1812 and to a great deal more in 1861. The defeat at the first Bull Run was a rout of a motley aggregation, mostly militiamen, from the several states. Wilson himself clearly recognized the need of unified control: he had in general endorsed and advocated Garrison's plan.

But Garrison was impolitic and intolerant. His initial report, as we have seen, had been prepared as though he and not the President were speaking for the country: and he had later made it public without consulting the White House—a course that might have given just cause of

---

[1] In a letter to the President of January 14, 1916.

offense. He failed to consider the problems confronting the administration in a democracy, where statesmanship, if it is to continue virile, must rest its leadership upon reason, and convince rather than drive its following. Wilson's reply on January 17th was patient but reproving. It illuminated the entire situation, and revealed his own clear conception as to his duties and functions as a leader:

"I am very much obliged to you for your letters of January twelfth and January fourteenth. They make your views with regard to adequate measures of preparation for national defense sharply clear. I am sure that I already understood just what your views were, but I am glad to have them restated in this succinct and striking way. You believe, as I do, that the chief thing necessary is, that we should have a trained citizen reserve and that the training, organization, and control of that reserve should be under immediate federal direction.

"But apparently I have not succeeded in making my own position equally clear to you, though I feel sure that I have made it perfectly clear to Mr. Hay. It is that I am not irrevocably or dogmatically committed to any one plan of providing the nation with such a reserve, and am cordially willing to discuss alternative proposals.

"Any other position on my part would indicate an attitude towards the Committee on Military Affairs of the House of Representatives which I should in no circumstances feel at liberty to assume. . . .

"I do not share your opinion that the members of the House who are charged with the duty of dealing with military affairs are ignorant of them or of the military necessities of the nation. . . .

"My own duty towards them is perfectly plain. I must welcome a frank interchange of views and a patient and thorough comparison of all the methods proposed for obtaining the objects we all have in view. So far as my own participation in final legislative action is concerned, no one will expect me to acquiesce in any proposal that I regard as inadequate or illusory. If, as the outcome of a free interchange of views, my own judgment and that of the Committee should prove to be irreconcilably different and a bill should be presented to me which I could not accept as accomplishing the essential things sought, it would manifestly be my duty to veto it and go to the country on the merits. But there is no reason to anticipate or fear such a result, unless we should ourselves take at the outset the position that only the plans of the Department are to be considered; and that position, it seems to me, would be wholly unjustifiable. The committee and the Congress will expect me to be as frank with them as I hope they will be with me, and will of course hold me justified in fighting for my own matured opinion.

"I have had a delightfully frank conference with Mr. Hay. I have said to him that I was perfectly willing to consider any plan that would give us a national reserve under unmistakable national control, and would support any such scheme if convinced of its adequacy and wise policy. More he has not asked or desired."

On the following day he wrote a letter to Congressman Hay so frank, so winning, so adroit and yet so firm, that it laid the soundest possible foundation for the coöperation that was to result, in the end, in a triumph for his leadership. There is much of the essential Woodrow Wilson at his best in this letter:

"I feel we are under a sort of obligation to each other to keep one another posted and, therefore, I venture to write you a few lines as to a recent interchange of views on my part with the Secretary of War. I want you to know just what I said to him about my position with regard to the way in which the programme for preparation is to be handled."

After reporting what he had written to Garrison, he continued:

"Frankly, as I told you, I do not believe that such a reserve can be supplied through the National Guard because of the apparently insuperable constitutional obstacles to a direct control of training and organization by the National Government. I feel certain that the country will demand of us imperatively a genuine nationalization of the reserve forces which we are about to create. But it would, of course, be ridiculous for me to say that I would not consider methods which men thoroughly acquainted with the subject matter felt ready to propose. I wish with all my heart that the Committee could see its way to a direct and immediate acceptance of the plan for a Continental Army and I believe that it will ultimately find that it must turn in that direction."

The President had hoped thus to conciliate both sides to the controversy, but upon his return to Washington on February 4th he found that the situation had grown even more difficult. Both the Secretary and his assistant, Mr. Breckinridge, had lost ground by favouring a policy for compulsory military service which went far beyond their own previously submitted plan. Many congressmen were alarmed, especially members from the South, because it might mean enlisting large numbers of Negroes. It was no doubt the blunt and honest opinion of well-informed military men: it was the worst of politics and diplomacy.

Garrison was in a fighting mood. To his unyielding nature, it was all—and all at once—or nothing. He had inflexible convictions and did not hesitate to declare them "definitely and unmistakably." He was not only displeased with the attitude of the President and Congress on the military measures, but he was much aroused by the proposed Clarke amendment favouring the withdrawal of the United States from the Philippines:

"I consider the principle embodied in the Clarke amendment an abandonment of the duty of this nation and a breach of trust toward the Filipinos; so believing, I cannot accept it or acquiesce in its acceptance."[1]

If the President did not agree with his views he decided that he must withdraw from the cabinet. Wilson made a strong appeal for patience and fair-mindedness:

"This is a time when it seems to me patience on the part of all of us is of the essence in bringing about a consummation of the purpose we all have in mind."[2]

But Garrison's determined spirit would not delay. His letter of resignation arrived that very day, and the President wrote him immediately:

"I must confess to feeling a very great surprise at your letter of today offering your resignation as Secretary of War. There has been no definite action taken yet in either of the matters to which your letter of yesterday referred. The whole matter is under debate and all the influences

---

[1]February 9, 1916. In his attitude upon the Philippines issue, the President and his Secretary were as far apart as the Poles. Wilson much more nearly approved the views of Bryan, who was urging early independence. He also considered the problem in reference to the World War, as in his annual message, December 7, 1915:

"We must be free from every unnecessary burden or embarrassment; and there is no better way . . . than to fulfill our promises and promote the interests of those dependent on us to the utmost." *The Public Papers of Woodrow Wilson*, Vol. III, p. 418.

He had not favoured giving full independence to the Islands so soon as originally provided in the so-called Clarke amendment (which proposed to grant independence not less than two nor more than four years after the approval of the Act, the President having authority to extend the time if circumstances warranted). He thought the Filipinos were hardly ready for it; but he gave his approval, feeling that action a little too early was preferable to no action at all. It was the passage of this amendment by the Senate, on February 4th, which aroused Garrison's ire. However, when a final agreement was reached between the Senate and the House, an indefinite promise was accepted: the independence of the islands was to be recognized "as soon as a stable government can be established" therein. Wilson rejoiced at this more moderate solution; it brought about a "new and happier order of things." (Message to the Philippine Legislature, October 14, 1916.)

It was, indeed, upon this statement of policy, and this promise, that the President's record, so far as the Philippines were concerned, was to rest to the end of his administration.

[2]February 10, 1916.

that work for clarity and judgment ought to be available at this very time.

"But since you have felt obliged to take this action and since it is evident that your feeling in the matter is very great indeed, I feel that I would be only imposing a burden upon you should I urge you to retain the Secretaryship of War while I am endeavoring to find a successor. I ought to relieve you at once and do hereby accept your resignation because it is so evidently your desire that I should do so.

"I cannot take this important step, however, without expressing to you my very warm appreciation of the distinguished service you have rendered as Secretary of War, and I am sure that in expressing this appreciation I am only putting into words the judgment of our fellow citizens far and wide.

"With sincere regret at the action you have felt constrained to take . . ."[1]

While Wilson personally regretted the loss of Garrison— he could not doubt his ability or his honesty, or the sincerity of his convictions—there is little doubt that it relieved a difficult situation and made the task of leadership in Congress much easier.

". . . it has not on the whole set back the cause we are fighting for."[2]

He was prompt in filling Garrison's place: on March 5th he telegraphed Newton D. Baker of Cleveland:

"Would you accept Secretaryship of War? Earnestly hope that you can see your way to do so. It would greatly strengthen my hand."[3]

The offer was wholly unexpected—it came "like a

---

[1] The Assistant Secretary of War, Henry Breckinridge, who had been closely sympathetic with his chief, resigned at the same time.

[2] Wilson to John R. Dunlap, February 16, 1916.

[3] Palmer, *Newton D. Baker*, Vol. I, p. 10.

thunderbolt"—and Baker was doubtful as to his own qualifications. To his telegram of tentative acceptance, however, the President replied:

"My judgment and desire in the matter are clear . . . With your permission I will send in the nomination at once . . ."[1]

Three days later Baker went to Washington, to "point out all the reasons why he should not be Secretary of War." When he had finished, Wilson asked, "Are you ready to take the oath?"[2]

Baker entered upon his new service March 9th and soon became one of Wilson's most trusted advisers. His qualities of mind, and his ideals, approached more closely to those of the President, probably, than those of any other member of the cabinet.

Garrison having resigned, Wilson began to work with Congress with a new spirit of coöperation and good will. Congressman Hay wrote on February 11th that he had been instructed by the Committee on Military Affairs of the House "to convey to you the very great appreciation which the committee feels for the confidence which you have shown in its good faith and patriotism; and to assure you of its desire to work in harmony with you in perfecting a plan which would be of the greatest benefit to the country."

But the opinion of the country generally was chaotic. It was not yet clear what was happening at Washington; or where, exactly, the President now stood. A year earlier he had been opposed to military preparation: he was now vigorously demanding it. He had aroused the anxiety of the nation: and had temporarily disappeared in a fog of controversy at Washington. Both extremes were critical and dissatisfied. Bryan charged that Wilson was "joy-

---

[1] March 6, 1916. The appointment was announced the same day.
[2] Newton D. Baker to A. H. Meneely, March, 1928.

riding with the jingoes."[1] And if the resignation of Garrison pleased the pacifists, it seemed to confirm the common criticism of Wilson's inability to work with his associates. As yet there was no perceptible flow of opinion in Congress that promised decisive action either for or against the President's recommendations. At the same time conditions in Europe were growing steadily worse, with less hope of any immediate settlement.

It was one of those moments of disillusion and doubt, when new and grave circumstances demand drastic action, with no clear conviction, at least upon the part of the people, as to what that action should be. It was the "valley of hesitation," vastly distressing to the individual human spirit, still more a test of the fortitude, the faith, the vision of the leader. Well may the President have glanced up at the copy of Kipling's poem which stood framed upon his library table:

"*If you can keep your head when all about you*
Are losing theirs and blaming it on you . . ."

Henry Morgenthau writes:
"I spent the first few days after my return to the United States with my old political friends in Washington, and I was shocked at the prevailing political atmosphere. Not one of the numerous men high in the Administration with whom I talked had the slightest hope that President Wilson could be reëlected that fall."[2]

This time of disillusion and doubt, the apparent uncertainty of strong leadership, was accompanied, as usual, with bitter attacks upon the administration. It was charged that the President was shaping his course on preparation, dramatizing it with the vivid "swing-around" through the West, on political grounds; that he had in view

[1]Public statement, published in the New York *Times*, February 19, 1916.
[2]*All in a Life-Time*, pp. 234–235.

the fall elections. This he met sharply in an address at the Gridiron dinner at Washington on February 26th:

"It is not a new feeling on my part, but one which I entertain with a greater intensity than formerly, that a man who seeks the Presidency of the United States for anything that it will bring to him is an audacious fool. The responsibilities of the office ought to sober a man even before he approaches it."[1]

The President himself was extremely anxious, knowing that his leadership was meeting a supreme test.

"I never go to bed without realizing that I may be called up by news that will mean that we are at war."

And yet he must avoid "hasty action"; it was his duty not to "see red."

A visitor, reporting these remarks, carried away "a feeling of the tremendous difficulty under which he constantly lived," and yet was convinced that he had "steeled himself to see it through."

"It strengthened my confidence in him."[2]

It was indeed the lowest ebb of his leadership during the period of American neutrality. The events of the next few weeks, involving the revolt in Congress connected with the McLemore and Gore resolutions, and the so-called "Sunrise Conference," are of such importance that they must be given separate attention.

---

[1] *The Public Papers of Woodrow Wilson*, Vol. IV, p. 125.

Worse even than these charges, were the attacks of human jackals on the personal character of the President, always underhanded, always secret, which began at this time and were to continue with increasing volume until the fall election.

[2] Ida M. Tarbell's report of a dinner at the White House, where she was a guest, and of her conversation with the President afterwards. Quoted in William Allen White's *Woodrow Wilson*, p. 290.

CHAPTER II

MARRIAGE

"... we dread to see these ... days of quiet and seclusion come to an end."

Letter to Mrs. Francis B. Sayre, December 29, 1915.

A WEEK before Christmas, 1915, Woodrow Wilson and Mrs. Norman Galt were married.

It was the culmination of a romance which had begun in the early spring and in its later phases, after the announcement of the engagement in October, had awakened national interest.

Mrs. Galt, born Edith Bolling, had come of an old Virginia family which had intermarried with the Randolphs and was connected with Thomas Jefferson. Through the Rolph line she was a descendant of that most romantic figure of early Virginia, the Indian maiden, Pocahontas. Her grandfather Bolling was a physician who had a plantation in Bedford County, and her father attended the University of Virginia, studied law under Judge Brockenborough, and became himself a judge. Like most of the men of the old South, both were early swept into the Civil War, leaving to the mother and grandmother the management of the plantation with only Negro slaves about them.

Their home lay in the path of marching armies. Northern troops soon took everything of value except the family silver, which was hidden by a faithful Negro servant. The grandfather came home wounded to find the plantation house serving as a hospital for the soldiers of both armies. He died there before the war ended.

41

After Lee's surrender at Appomattox the father found himself, like so many of the soldiers of the lost cause, quite impoverished. One mule survived: and the still dependent Negro servants were near starvation. He hitched up the mule and drove into Lynchburg, but the federal officer in command was able to provide only a scant load of food, hardly enough to feed his dependents for a single week. One of the hardest things her father ever had to do, Edith Bolling relates, was to tell his Negroes that he could no longer care for them, that they were really free.

The family removed to the town of Wytheville, in Wythe County, where the grandfather had owned a small property, and here the daughter Edith, seventh in a family of eleven, was born. It was a narrow, pinched and difficult existence: no servants, no money, but with a hospitable home crowded with children and relatives. Often the Episcopal rector and his wife were guests for considerable periods of time. The Judge was commonly away from home, travelling his circuit, driving an old black horse.

In those hard years of Reconstruction, there were no public schools of any value, nor did the Bolling family believe in them. Education for gentlefolk must be conducted at home. The main reliance in all matters of education, as of religion, was the grandmother Bolling—a remarkable character, a lady of the old school.

She was a cripple and walked with a staff, but she dominated the entire household. She lived in the large front room with a high four-poster bed to which she ascended on carpeted steps. Being lame she had always to be assisted up at night, but she could get down in the morning. Here she held her court and commanded the activities of the day. Although without much formal early education, she had become a vast reader, and had taught herself Latin and French, which, having had no instruc-

MRS. WOODROW WILSON

tion, she pronounced in the most original ways. She was passionately devoted not only to books, but to birds and flowers.

One of her chief interests was the rearing of canaries; she had as many as twenty-nine birds in her room at one time. These she could not herself, of course, attend to, and she did not trust the Negroes. Her granddaughter Edith remembers the infinite tasks connected with the care and feeding of this numerous family. Nests had to be made and lined exactly so, with white flannel. In winter, fires had to be kept up night and day, and the children were often stirred sleepily from their beds to mend them.

The old lady wore a particular lace cap which had to be laundered, always, in her sight—as she sat, throned in her great bed. She had a special tub, washboard, and flatiron which upon stated days the little Edith or some other member of the family brought into her room and there, under minute instructions, performed the indispensable ritual.

She was a strict and indefatigable teacher. Edith must study Latin and French and other subjects appropriate for a lady to know. Besides the family prayers conducted every morning by Judge Bolling and a regular course of instruction by him on Sunday—for none of the children was ever allowed to attend Sunday school—she must also commit to memory long passages from the Bible and learn the catechism. It is scarcely surprising that she was prepared for Confirmation at the age of nine years.

If there were these severities of discipline, there were long evenings of intense interest, for the wonderful old grandmother took delight in reading to the children, or in having them read to her while she knitted—*Children of the Abbey* and *Lorna Doone*, or as they grew older, Thomson's *Seasons* and *Tristram Shandy*. She believed that no one ought ever to be idle for a moment: the little girl remembered hearing the click of her grandmother's knitting needles in the dark, and she could knit and read at the same time. During the later years she cut out all the garments that the children wore, and supervised the making of many of them.

In her last years she had a horror of dying in the dark, and if she felt in the least indisposed, she would call out many times in the night, so that the little girl or one of her brothers would come in to fix the fire, or see who was at the door, or take care of the birds—anything to have someone in the room.

Edith Bolling's early ambition was to become a musician, and at fourteen she went off to a boarding school at Abingdon—a poverty-stricken place with the poorest possible living quarters and the worst of food, but she practised four hours a day in a room with no heat, and came back so thin at Christmas that her family hardly recognized her. Later she had a happy year at a school in Richmond. In 1896 she married Norman Galt, a business man of Washington, who died in 1908.

It was not until the spring of 1915 that she met Woodrow Wilson. She had seen him three times before, once at a Princeton banquet in Philadelphia, once while he was Governor of New Jersey, at a review of state troops—she remembered a "thin man on a horse. He was wearing a frock coat and a high hat"—and once again, soon after the inauguration in 1913, she saw him at a play at the National Theatre in Washington.

One of her warm friends of the Washington years was Miss Alice Gordon,[1] with whom she made two trips to Europe. In October 1914 Dr. Grayson, who was the President's physician, was much concerned about the health of Miss Helen Bones who, after the death of the first Mrs. Wilson, had, with Miss Margaret Wilson,

---

[1] Afterwards the wife of Dr. (Rear-Admiral) Grayson.

assumed many of the responsibilities of the mistress of the White House. Miss Bones was a cousin of President Wilson. Dr. Grayson asked Mrs. Galt to let him introduce Miss Bones with the hope that she might find diversion in new friendships. They became fond of each other at once: both were Southern and had many interests in common. They drove and walked in Rock Creek Park, afterwards returning to Mrs. Galt's home for tea. Sometimes one of the President's daughters was included in the excursions.

It was in March 1915 that Miss Bones, arguing that she had been having tea for months at Mrs. Galt's home, insisted that she be allowed to reciprocate: she invited Mrs. Galt to the White House.

"I promise you will not see a soul; it is the hour when Cousin Woodrow plays golf."

They had had a long walk and returned to the White House muddy and blown. As they stepped out of the elevator, they met the President and Dr. Grayson face to face. The golf players had unexpectedly come in. There were introductions all around, and Miss Bones said that she had brought Mrs. Galt to have tea with her.

"I think you might ask us," said Dr. Grayson.

Instead, therefore, of having tea in Miss Bones's apartment, as they had intended, they transferred to the Oval Room. Mr. Wilson made himself extremely entertaining.

A few days later Miss Bones brought the President with her, and they went together for a ride, returning to the White House for tea. This soon came to be a common practice; and that summer Mrs. Galt spent a month at the vacation home at Cornish with the Wilson family.

Early in their acquaintance the President began sending her copies of his favourite books—Wordsworth's poems, and the works of Bagehot and Burke and Lord Bryce, and as the sincerest evidence of his confidence in her interest, he read aloud to her many of his favourite passages. It was not long before he was talking with her about the great problems he was facing, opening his whole mind, seeking her suggestions and opinion, as he continued to do as long as he lived. It soon became a relationship based upon the deepest understanding and sympathy.

All the Wilson family, and the nearest friends, from the beginning looked with the warmest approval upon the new friendship. The loneliness that followed the death of the first Mrs. Wilson had been desolating. His friends feared for him. ". . . no one can offer Cousin Woodrow any word of comfort, for there is no comfort . . ."[1]

"I can see the lonely figure of the President now, walking down the long hallway, the hair so much whitened in the few months."[2]

With the ripening friendship with Mrs. Galt, everything began to change. The intimate letters of the summer and early fall of 1915 give many evidences of a renewal of hope and of health. His friends "never saw the President looking better."[3] His daughters referred to their love and admiration for Mrs. Galt;[4] they gave their entire approval to the new relationship.

". . . we are all," wrote Stockton Axson, a brother of the first Mrs. Wilson, "thoroughly thankful that the great man doesn't have to keep on being a *lonely* great man . . ."[5]

A little later he wrote:

"Isn't she a *vivid* person? And with all that, most sweet and lovely."[6]

The President's own letters to his old friends radiate his happiness:

[1]Helen W. Bones to Agnes V. Tedcastle, November 16, 1914.
[2]Stockton Axson, *The Private Life of President Wilson.*
[3]E. T. Brown to his wife, July 20, 1915.
[4]Margaret Woodrow Wilson to her father, August 16, 1915.
[5]To Mrs. E. T. Brown, September 25, 1915.
[6]To Mrs. E. T. Brown.

"Something very delightful has happened to me which I am not yet at liberty to tell others but which I want you to know among the first. A great happiness and blessing has come to me in the midst of my loneliness. Mrs. Norman Galt, a lovely Washington woman (born in Virginia) whom I first met in April last through Helen, who had become her fast friend, has promised to marry me. When you know her you will know why it was inevitable that I should fall in love with her, for she is wholly delightful and lovable. . . . You would think that it was only love that was speaking if I were to tell you what she is like, how endowed and made distinguished in her loveliness, but you will, I am sure, find out for yourself how truly wonderful she is in gifts both of heart and of mind.

"Please for the present keep this as an absolute secret. We are not yet ready to let others know of it, though we shall, of course, make public announcement of the engagement in due time."[1]

To his long-time friend, Mrs. Hulbert, he wrote on October 4th:

"Before the public announcement is made, I want you to be one of the first to know of the good fortune that has come to me. I have not been at liberty to speak of it sooner. I am engaged to be married to Mrs. Norman Galt of this city, a woman I am sure you would admire and love as every one does who knows her, and I feel that a blessing greater than I can measure in words has come to me. . . .

"I am writing in great haste, amidst a pressure of clamorous engagements that cannot be gainsaid, but you will know in what spirit. Helen joins me in affectionate messages."

And to another of his dearest friends, Mrs. Reid of Baltimore, he wrote on October 5th:

---

[1]Wilson to Mary W. Hoyt, an old family friend, cousin to Ellen Axson Wilson, September 26, 1915.

"The last fourteen months have seemed for me, in a world upset, like fourteen years. It is not the same world in which my dear Ellen lived; and one of the very last things she said to me was that she hoped that what has happened now would happen. It seemed to me incredible then, and would, I think, have continued to seem so if I had not been brought into contact with Mrs. Galt. She seemed to come into our life here like a special gift from Heaven, and I have won a sweet companion who will soon make me forget the intolerable loneliness and isolation of the weary months since this terrible war began.

"I hope that you will sympathize and approve.

"My thoughts constantly seek you out. I wish that I could see you and have an old-fashioned talk. Things crowd upon me so every day that I hardly have time for any indulgences of that sort; but I must find it or starve."

On October 6th the formal announcement of the engagement was made, the President himself writing it out:

"The announcement was made today of the engagement of Mrs. Norman Galt of this city, and President Woodrow Wilson."

The betrothal was celebrated on the next evening by a gay family dinner at the White House:

". . . Mrs. Bolling[1] was at the President's right Cousin E at his left & I had the honor of being next to her . . . when you come to know her better you will (as all who know her) love her dearly. One of the most charming incidents occurred at dinner—Cousin E . . . had occasion to address the President and when she came to calling his name, with a slight but natural embarrassment it was 'Woodrow'—and as she afterwards confided to me, it was the *first time* she had ever called him by his first name.

"It all happened in such a simple natural way that it

---

[1]Mrs. Galt's mother.

brought down the table . . . I don't think I ever saw the President enjoy anything quite so much.

"He is perfectly happy—and looking better than he has for months."[1]

The response throughout the country was instant and impressive. So many telegrams and letters of congratulations arrived that an extra staff of operators and clerks had to be installed at the White House.[2]

But the reaction among Democratic politicians was one of alarm, almost of panic. Many of them were of the opinion that if the President remarried before November 1916 he would destroy all chances of reëlection.

The political leaders knew well enough the difficulties they were facing. In the fall of 1915 the President's prestige, as we have seen, was nearing its lowest ebb. He was confronted with tremendous and insoluble foreign problems: the country was apparently drifting toward a war that few people wanted: the President was beginning his campaign for preparedness which was to cause a break in his cabinet and a hard struggle with his own party leadership in Congress. To add to this weight of difficulty such an unexpected and startling personal adventure was, in the minds of the politicians, to outrage fate. For there were no inconsiderable number of people to whom the President's marriage, little more than sixteen months after the death of his first wife, was not short of shocking. This feeling was fomented by one of the most despicable campaigns of secret slander ever known in American politics. Political enemies who dared not attack in the

---

[1] E. T. Brown to his wife, October 8, 1915.

[2] A single folder among the President's papers contains nearly five hundred letters and messages. A cablegram from the King of Italy and a message from the President of France are included. The President himself answered scores of them. To his old friend and Princeton classmate, Hiram Woods, he wrote:

"I will have to have the old gang over here sometime to make sure that Mrs. Galt gets authentic information about my past. I hope when the time comes you will all be easy on me." (October 14, 1915.)

open used this vile means of besmirching the President's character. Lying innuendo regarding his relationships with his friend Mrs. Hulbert[1] circulated everywhere: he was charged with inattention to the first Mrs. Wilson, and even with the neglect of her grave after her death![2]

Panicky Democrats who were close to the President urged one another to expostulate with him: but no one apparently dared to do it.[3] Several friends did, however, warn him guardedly concerning the campaign of slander of which, strange as it may seem, he had known practically nothing up to that time.[4] If the intent of some of these protesters was to prevent or at least postpone the marriage to Mrs. Galt in the interest of his political future, as it apparently was, the effect upon the President was quite the reverse. Shocked and angry, he went at once to Mrs. Galt and told her the whole story.

---

[1]Who had been Mrs. Peck.

[2]An incident related by David Lawrence illustrates the character of this campaign: ". . . about a year after the death of Mrs. Wilson, on the night before Thanksgiving Day, 1915, several of the more important newspaper bureaus in Washington were called on the telephone and mysteriously given a tip to the effect that important court proceedings had been filed involving Mr. Wilson. The newspapermen could not afford to ignore the information and yet they disbelieved it. Many of them spent the better part of a week investigating the story and found it baseless. Dissatisfied with this, the rumor-mongers tried another tack and insisted that prominent lawyers knew the circumstances. Every lawyer named was visited but none knew anything about it. The fact was the story was made out of a whole cloth. . . . " David Lawrence, *The True Story of Woodrow Wilson*, p. 134.

[3]"There was much hurried whispering, and it was finally decided," Secretary Daniels told the author, "that someone must tell Wilson. They tried to wish the job on me, but I refused to have anything to do with it."

[4]One of these friends was Frank P. Glass, editor of the Birmingham *News* of Alabama, who had been at Princeton with Wilson. He relates (in a memorandum written for the author) that he had planned to refer only broadly to the slanders, but the President's interest "became intense, and he proceeded to question me closely, requiring every detail that I could give him. Seeing my reluctance and shamefacedness, he insisted that I was doing him a very great service, that he was astonished that he had been kept in such ignorance. . . . Before he got all of my story, tears came into his eyes, while his voice and demeanor showed that he was profoundly moved. He had not imagined that his enemies could be so unjust, so cruel. I reminded him of George Washington's experiences. . . .

"When I was parting from him, he took both of my hands in his, and thanked me in the warmest way for what he regarded as a service of personal friendship."

The engagement was announced to-day of Mrs.
Norman Galt and President Woodrow Wilson.

Mrs. Norman Galt is the widow of a well known
business man of Washington who died some eight
years ago. She has lived in Washington since
her marriage in 1896. She was Miss Edith Bolling
and was born in Wytheville, Virginia, where her
girlhood was spent and where her father, the Hon-
William H. Bolling, a man of remarkable character and charm, won distinction as one of the
ablest, most interesting and most individual
lawyers of a State famous for its lawyers. In
the circle of cultivated and interesting people
who have had the privilege of knowing her Mrs.
Galt has enjoyed an enviable distinction, not
only because of her unusual beauty and natural
charm, but also because of her very unusual character and gifts. She has always been sought
out as a delightful friend, and her thoughtful-
ness and quick capacity for anything she chose
to undertake have made her friendship invaluable
to those who were fortunate enough to win it.

It was Miss Margaret Wilson and her cousin
Miss Bones who drew Mrs. Galt into the White
House circle. They met her first in the early
part of the present year, and were so much attracted by her that they sought her out more and
more frequently and the friendship among them

AT THE TIME OF THE ANNOUNCEMENT OF HIS ENGAGEMENT
TO MRS. NORMAN GALT, OCTOBER 6, 1915, PRESIDENT WILSON
WROTE OUT A STATEMENT ON HIS OWN TYPEWRITER, GIVING
THE ESSENTIAL FACTS. THIS FACSIMILE IS FROM THE ORIGINAL
DOCUMENT.

quickly ripened into an affectionate intimacy.
It was through this association with his daughter and cousin that the President had the opportunity to meet Mrs. Galt, who spent a month
at Cornish this summer as Miss Wilson's guest.
~~There she was thrown, too, with Mrs. Sayre, the~~
~~President's second daughter, , who promptly be-~~
~~came as warm a friend and admirer as her sister~~
                    already
~~and cousin were.~~ It is, indeed, the most interesting circumstance connected with the engagement
just announced that the President's daughters
should have picked Mrs. Galt out for their special admiration and friendship before their father did.

"There is nothing in any letters I ever wrote," he said, "that I am ashamed to have published."

At that time there had been some talk between them of delaying the marriage until a year later: "I want to marry the man and not the President," she had told him: but he now urged an immediate marriage.

"Why wait when I need you now? Why wait a year?"

She objected that public criticism might seriously injure his leadership.

"If the people do not trust me," he said, "now is the time to find it out."[1]

Accordingly the date of the wedding was announced almost immediately[2] and took place on December 18th. The simple ceremony was at the home of Mrs. Galt,[3] with only a small party of relatives and the most intimate friends in attendance. The presiding ministers were the Reverend Herbert Scott Smith, a former student of Mr. Wilson's, then rector of St. Margaret's Episcopal church, of which Mrs. Galt was a member, and the Reverend James H. Taylor, of the First Presbyterian church, which the President attended.

The honeymoon, which lasted through the holidays, was spent at Hot Springs, Virginia. While public matters of the greatest moment constantly crowded upon the President's attention, it was a "heavenly time."

"... I shall go back to Washington feeling complete and strong for whatever may betide. I am indeed blessed beyond my (or any other man's) deserts. ... There is little to do here but walk and ride and play golf and loaf and spice it all with a little work, not to forget that there *are* duties as well as pleasures in the world. Every day we feel

---

[1] The facts here set forth are based upon conversations between Mrs. Wilson and the author.

[2] December 4, 1915.

[3] At 1308 Twentieth Street, N. W.

fresher and fitter (Edith was very tired, of course, with the last distracting rush of things, when she got here) and our dear native State is giving us most hospitable weather and refreshment."[1]

On one of the days of the honeymoon, December 28th, the President celebrated his fifty-ninth birthday.

Complications connected with the war in Europe—the crisis precipitated by the sinking of the British ship *Persia* —compelled the return to Washington[2] somewhat earlier than the President had intended. A few days later, January 7th, Mrs. Wilson made her first public appearance as the mistress of the White House, the occasion being a large reception—there were 3,328 guests—in honour of the Latin-American diplomats. From that time onward the whole atmosphere of the White House was changed. It lost its recent monastic seclusion and took on colour and life; there were flowers and music and the stir of social activity.

For Edith Bolling brought into the President's life an abundant vitality. She had gaiety, she had courage, and above all, she had humour. Her devotion to the President, whether in the great years of his labour and achievement or in the weary months of helpless suffering after he was stricken, was absolutely unsparing. To those friends who were there, and saw, and knew, such loyalty was beyond praise.

The President's papers reveal the fact that almost at once Mrs. Wilson began to coöperate with her husband in his lonely labour. In February we find notes and memoranda showing that she was helping him with the difficult tasks of coding and decoding the most confidential dispatches to and from Europe. They worked together, she with the secret code keys, spelling out the messages word

---

[1] Wilson to Lucy and Mary Smith, December 27, 1915.
[2] They arrived at the White House early on the morning of January 4th.

by word, and he at his typewriter, setting them down. Or they reversed the process, he writing out his dispatches and she translating them into the code symbols ready for transmission. They spent many hours of many nights in this painstaking employment. To the end of his life Mrs. Wilson shared in all of the President's labour: he discussed every public problem with her.[1]

It is difficult to overestimate the importance in the President's life of this new relationship. It steadied and calmed his highly wrought and sensitive nature. It filled the need, so plainly marked from his youth onward, so tragically evident after the death of Ellen Axson Wilson, of intimate companionship based upon sympathy and complete understanding. Beginning in the fall of 1915, the note of anxiety, the sense of futility, the loneliness and longing for personal sympathy, so marked a feature of his correspondence for many months, completely disappears from his letters. With his remarriage there is a cessation of inner discord, a recovered joy in life, a new power of concentrated effort. He finds his experiences, however difficult and trying, newly "interesting and inspiring," full of "electrical thrills."[2] A visitor who dined at the White House in February describes him as "gay."[3]

Mrs. Wilson accompanied the President into the West on the preparedness campaign—as she accompanied him everywhere in the years that followed. Although the two years that followed were marked by problems as difficult and burdens as great as any President, probably, has

---

[1]During the Peace Conference at Paris Mrs. Wilson followed, minutely, the course of every day's discussion. It was the duty of the present writer to call upon the President at his house in the Place des États Unis after each session of the Council of Four, listen to his summary of the secret discussions, and decide what should be made public. These conversations were usually held in Mrs. Wilson's salon, so that she could listen to the President's report. Sometimes she took part in the discussions, her questions assisting greatly in clarifying difficult subjects.

[2]Wilson to Richard Olney, February 7, 1916.

[3]Ida M. Tarbell.

ever had to bear, no period of Woodrow Wilson's life gives evidence of better health, a calmer mind, a surer command of all his powers. It is not to be doubted that this was due largely to the companionship and sympathy of Edith Bolling.

CHAPTER III

COMPLICATIONS IN LATIN AMERICA

"... the states of America have become ... more clearly conscious of the many common sympathies and interests and duties which bid them stand together."

Address to Congress, December 7, 1915.

"... we are already spiritual partners with both continents of this hemisphere and ... America means something which is bigger even than the United States ..."

Address at West Point, June 13, 1916.

"What makes Mexico suspicious of us is that she does not believe as yet that we want to serve her."

Address at Detroit, July 10, 1916.

"The two Americas can be knitted together only by process of peace, friendship, helpfulness, and good will, and the nation which must of necessity take the initiative in proving the possibility of these processes is the United States."

Article in the Ladies' Home Journal, *October, 1916.*

I. CIVIL WAR IN MEXICO

AS IF the storm in Europe were not sufficiently threatening, President Wilson was compelled to turn aside frequently during the years from 1914 to 1917 to deal with the smouldering fires of civil strife in Mexico. More than once he approached what seemed at the moment the last bearable provocation, testing his patience to the uttermost. He averted, narrowly, the open warfare that might immeasurably have increased his difficulties, not only in meeting the incalculable crisis in Europe, but in dealing with sensitive and suspicious South American powers.

Following the triumph of his policy of "watchful wait-ing," when the Indian Huerta had fled and Carranza[1] had come into power, it had seemed that the Mexican difficulty was, at length, really quieted.

While he was well aware that the situation was "still a little blind," he could not have imagined the confusion that was yet to be, or the irritation the problems were still to cause him.

Hardly were the Constitutionalists in power before quarrels between Carranza and Villa resulted in so much disorder that Secretary Garrison, ever eager to apply military remedies, urged drastic action. Wilson's reply showed that his determination to avoid war, based upon the highest ideals of American responsibility, remained unalterable:

"We shall have no right at any time to intervene in Mexico to determine the way in which the Mexicans are to settle their own affairs. I feel sufficiently assured that the property and lives of foreigners will not suffer in the process of the settlement. The rest is political and Mexi-can. Many things may happen of which we do not approve . . . but I say very solemnly that that is no affair of ours. Our responsibility will come after the settlement and in the determination of the question whether the new govern-ment is to receive the recognition of the government of the United States or not. There are in my judgment no conceivable circumstances which would make it right for us to direct by force or by threat of force the internal processes of what is . . . a revolution as profound as that which occurred in France. All the world has been shocked ever since the time of the revolution in France that Europe should have undertaken to nullify what was done there, no matter what the excesses then committed.

----

[1]He made a "triumphal entry" into the capital on the morning of August 20, 1914. *Foreign Relations*, 1914, p. 588.

"I speak very solemnly but with clear judgment in the matter, which I hope God will give me strength to act upon."[1]

Carranza, however, rendered non-intervention a difficult policy. With a comprehensive suspicion unrestrained either by tact or fear of consequences, he ordered a number of foreign diplomats out of the country. The British minister was informed that if he did not leave immediately he would be given his passport by a policeman. A great international hubbub arose, not quieted by a message from the State Department of the United States urging moderation and adherence to conventions.[2]

". . . we are dealing with a very difficult person in Carranza. . . ."[3]

One demand all the warring Mexican leaders—Carranza, Obregon, Gonzales, Villa—were vigorously agreed upon: the withdrawal of American forces from Vera Cruz. The presence of the "invading" troops offended their "dignity as patriots."[4] The risks of friction increased with every day's delay. On Mexican Independence Day (September 15th) Wilson made his crucial decision to withdraw, and Carranza was requested to take over the administration of Vera Cruz.[5] Delay ensued because Carranza was reluctant to guarantee protection to the Mexicans who had served the United States in governing Vera Cruz; and because, in spite of the promise that Amer-

---

[1]Wilson to Garrison, August 8, 1914. When Cardinal Gibbons wrote of his fears for the safety of Catholics and the future of the Catholic Church, long allied with the conservative landed and governing classes, the President replied, August 21, 1914: "Alas I am sorry to say that it is not true that 'one word from me . . . would relieve the sad condition of affairs' in Mexico with regard to the treatment of the priests, for I have spoken that word again and again. . . .

". . . we shall have to await the subsidence of the passions which have been generated by the unhappy condition of the country."

[2]August 22, 1914. *Foreign Relations*, 1914, p. 589.

[3]Wilson to Bryan, August 25, 1914.

[4]Obregon to Villa, September 9, 1914. *Foreign Relations*, 1914, p. 595. *Cf.* also p. 596.

[5]*Foreign Relations*, 1914, pp. 597–598.

icans would turn over to the new authorities the funds they had collected, he refused to give assurances that he would not impose a second levy of taxes and import duties.[1]

The President felt that this delay "would make a very bad impression not only in Mexico, but in Latin-America generally . . . My wish is to get out at the very earliest possible date."[2]

When he permitted the Navy Department to withdraw certain vessels, Garrison was highly indignant, but Wilson scouted his fears:

"It is a bit inconceivable to me that, with the trouble they have on their hands . . . Carranza or Aguilar should make any demonstration against our troops at Vera Cruz."[3]

His judgment was confirmed. Facing rebellion on every hand, Carranza finally gave sufficient assurances, and the American withdrawal from Vera Cruz was completed November 23, 1914.[4]

During the remainder of 1914 and the spring of 1915, the civil war continued indecisively. The Brazilian minister notified the State Department, February 3rd, that the "situation grows worse every day."[5] European nations were becoming thoroughly alarmed. When Carranza gave up Mexico City and moved his headquarters to Vera Cruz, the attacks upon Wilson's policy in the United States became even more violent—especially from American owners of property in Mexico, from Roman Catholics indignant over the treatment of their churches and priests, and from political opponents who were looking forward

[1]The United States authorities had promised these protections. (Bryan to Wilson, September 9, 1914, Garrison to Wilson, September 22, 1914, Lansing to Wilson, October 3, 1914.)

[2]Letter to Bryan, October 2, 1914.

[3]Wilson to Garrison, November 5, 1914, replying to a letter of the day before. General Aguilar was Governor of the state of Vera Cruz.

[4]*Foreign Relations*, 1914, pp. 620–622, 626.

[5]*Cf. ibid.*, 1915, p. 650.

eagerly to the campaign of 1916. Even when in December 1914 rifle shots in Mexico wounded citizens in Arizona and it seemed impossible to avoid sending troops across the border,[1] Wilson held with absolute firmness to his patient idealism:

"There is one thing I have got a great enthusiasm about . . . and that is human liberty. . . . I hold it as a fundamental principle, and so do you, that every people has the right to determine its own form of government; and until this recent revolution in Mexico, until the end of the Diaz reign, eighty per cent. of the people of Mexico never had a 'look in' in determining who should be their governors or what their government should be. Now, I am for the eighty per cent! It is none of my business, and it is none of your business, how long they take in determining it . . . [or] how they go about the business. The country is theirs. The Government is theirs. The liberty, if they can get it, and Godspeed them in getting it, is theirs. And so far as my influence goes while I am President nobody shall interfere with them. . . .

"Do you suppose that the American people are ever going to count a small amount of material benefit . . . to people doing business in Mexico against the liberties and the permanent happiness of the Mexican people? Have not European nations taken as long as they wanted and spilt as much blood as they pleased in settling their affairs . . . ?"[2]

Conditions grew steadily worse. With great sections of Mexico being literally devastated, the policy of letting the

---

[1] *Foreign Relations*, 1914, pp. 650–651. For the military arrangements to render American interference unnecessary, see *ibid.*, pp. 652–653.

[2] Address at Indianapolis, January 8, 1915. *The Public Papers of Woodrow Wilson*, Vol. III, pp. 247–248. Wilson wrote to Bryan, September 18, 1914, regarding a memorandum prepared by F. J. Kearful of Mexico City:

"When I read on page four . . . about the agrarian problem . . . and that in Mexico 'it is commonly considered as a dream or a joke' I closed the paper with something like disgust, at any rate with the deepest disappointment that the fundamental thing should be taken so lightly and with so little understanding."

settlement come by civil war began to be intolerable.[1] Notes were finally dispatched (March 6th) notifying Carranza and Obregon that the United States government would hold them "personally responsible" for injury to the lives and property of Americans at Mexico City. The First Chief was further informed that serious talk by other nations of "joint action . . . to protect their legations and their nationals" had again arisen.[2] This gave Carranza pause, but in his reply he argued vigorously that the charges against the Constitutionalists were only the efforts of reactionaries to bring about "complications which may cause the failure" of the Revolution. He hoped that all foreign residents would retire temporarily from Mexico.[3]

Wilson would not soften his demands:

"Nothing will stir . . . [world] sentiment more promptly or more hotly or create greater dangers for Mexico than any, even temporary disregard for the lives, the safety or the rights of the citizens of other countries, resident within her territory, or any apparent contempt for the rights and safety of those who represent religion. . . .

"To warn you concerning such matters is an act of friendship . . . To speak less plainly or with less earnestness would be to conceal from you a terrible risk which no lover of Mexico should wish to run."[4]

Wilson, however, was learning that words apparently meant nothing more in Mexico than they did in Europe. Several foreigners had been killed.[5] Raids across the American border in search of food were increasing. "I am daily

---

[1]Charles W. Eliot proposed, in a letter February 19th, "an American League to set Mexico, and perhaps Hayti and San Domingo, in order . . ." Wilson replied, February 23rd: "The suggestion you make as to a possible means of settlement in Mexico would commend itself to me more strongly if it did not seem to involve the use of force. I feel that nothing but the extreme necessity would justify that."

[2]*Foreign Relations*, 1915, pp. 659–661.

[3]March 9, 1915, *ibid.*, pp. 666–668.

[4]Reply to Carranza, March 11, 1915. *Foreign Relations*, 1915, pp. 668–669.

[5]Bryan to Silliman, March 12, 1915. *Ibid.*, p. 671.

fearful that something imprudent may be done at Browns-
ville," wrote the President to Garrison, March 31st. He
directed that the War Department coöperate with the
Red Cross "in every way possible" to relieve the distress.[1]
And he warned Americans to leave Mexico and arranged
assistance for them in doing so.[2] He had determined to
avoid the use of force if it was humanly possible.

Within the limit of moral pressure, however, one thing
more was possible: to support one of the chief leaders.
Backed by American approval, that leader could more
speedily terminate the tragedy. The question was, whom
to support.[3] Secretary Lane favoured supporting Don
Eduardo Iturbide, but Wilson was suspicious about the
concealed financial interests backing Iturbide.[4] Villa, who
was the boldest fighter, had the loyalty of many Mexicans,
but he was unable to keep order even where he was
nominally in control.

"The trouble is he is so unsteady . . . when he is under
excitement. . . ."[5]

---

[1]Wilson to Garrison, June 3, 1915.

[2]In this connection, Bryan wrote to Wilson, May 21, 1915: "I think we ought to
refuse to support those who insist on staying there. We have advised them to leave
Mexico City and they have refused to do so on the ground that they had business
there that they could not leave. This reason could hardly apply to those who are
destitute."

[3]Wilson had begun to take the measure of the leaders in this regard as early as
February 1915. He had sent Duval West, of Texas, to Mexico with the following letter
of instructions, dated February 5th: "My wish in general is this: To have you meet
and, as far as possible, assess the character and purposes of the principal men down
there of the several groups and factions, in the hope that you may be able to form a
definite idea not only as to their relative strength and their relative prospects of success,
but also as to their real purposes.

"Above all, I want to find out just what prospects of a settlement there are and what
sort of settlement it would be likely to be. If the settlement contemplated is not seriously intended for the benefit of the common people of the country, if the plans and
ambitions of the leaders center upon themselves and not upon the people they are
trying to represent, of course it will not be a permanent settlement but will simply
lead to further distress and disorder. I am very anxious to know just what the moral
situation is, therefore, and just what it behooves us to do to check what is futile and
promote what promises genuine reform and settled peace."

[4]Lane to Wilson, undated but probably May 25, 1915; Wilson to House, July 3, 1915.

[5]General Scott to Wilson, September 3, 1915; Wilson to Scott, September 7, 1915.

Lind wrote urging the recognition of Carranza,[1] but that general was the least amenable to friendly counsel of any of the leaders. However, the administration gradually began to lean toward Carranza,[2] whose recent military victories left, in fact, little doubt that the Constitutionalists would ultimately crush the opposition.

The decision to act was probably precipitated by reports that the plight of the starving non-combatant population was so desperate that the people would soon be attacking anyone in the country or near the border who had food. This might lead to incidents causing intervention.[3] Wilson announced his new step in a message sent to the various authorities in Mexico, June 2nd:

"Mexico is starving and without a government. . . .

". . . the people and Government of the United States cannot stand indifferently by and do nothing. . . ."

The American government, therefore, "must presently do what it has not hitherto done or felt at liberty to do, lend its active moral support to some man or group of men, if such may be found, who can rally the suffering people of Mexico to their support in an effort to ignore, if they cannot unite, the warring factions of the country, return to the constitution . . . and set up a government at Mexico City which the great powers of the world can recognize and deal with, a government with whom the program of the revolution will be a business and not merely a platform."[4]

Carranza thereupon issued an adroit and effective

---

[1]Lind to the Secretary of State, April 21, 1915.

[2]The First Chief detected the growing favour, and inferred that it was somehow preordained. The United States government, he declared in a proclamation May 3rd, "begins to have the conviction of the justice of our cause" and to recognize in the Constitutionalist party, led by himself, "the only party capable of carrying out . . . social and political reforms . . . and sufficiently strong to implant a truly democratic government." (Received by Wilson, May 25, 1915.)

[3]Canova to Bryan, May 24, 1915; David Lawrence to Wilson, May 27, 1915.

[4]*The Public Papers of Woodrow Wilson*, Vol. III, pp. 339–340.

manifesto to the Mexican people announcing that full guarantees to foreigners would be given by the Constitutionalist government under his leadership, that responsibility to all legitimate financial and property obligations would be assumed, that religious freedom would be held inviolate, that there would be no confiscations in the agrarian reforms enacted, and that without waiving any civil responsibilities involved, in "due time an amnesty shall be declared."[1]

This being in line with the advice Wilson had given all the leaders months before, Lansing instructed Special Agent Silliman to "intimate cautiously that it is within the possibilities ... that the United States might recognize General Carranza in view of the way in which things appear to be shaping themselves ... but that if General Carranza does not go the full length of conciliation and conference with all the principal factions ... the situation thus created may prevent ... it."[2]

Carranza proved as obdurate as ever in his determination to go his own way to a complete military victory, and Silliman wired back: "The intimation of possible recognition did not in the least affect his impassive face." Carranza argued that history showed no example of civil war "terminating by the union of the contending parties. One or the other must triumph."[3]

For the next few weeks utter confusion prevailed throughout central Mexico. Every leader sought victory in order to get the coveted recognition. Mexico City

---

[1]June 11, 1915. *Foreign Relations*, 1915, pp. 705–707. Wilson did not, however, expect an early improvement of the condition of the people. On June 16th he wrote to Miss Mabel T. Boardman, of the Red Cross: "The Mexican situation certainly seems a most distressing and difficult one and apparently we are going to have a good deal of trouble with the so-called authorities of that distracted country in trying to send assistance to those who so sorely need it."

[2]June 18, 1915. *Ibid.*, pp. 715–716.

[3]Silliman to Lansing, June 22, 1915, quoting Carranza to Silliman, June 21st. *Foreign Relations*, 1915, pp. 718–719.

changed hands time and again; each time adding to the ruin. The patient Brazilian minister finally burst out that it was "unbearable" and "dreadful." "As to food, we have nothing."[1]

Wilson was at Cornish, New Hampshire, on a vacation— "the first real one I have had since I went into politics." He wrote to Colonel House that the Mexican situation was growing "ominously worse and more threatening day by day."[2] House was privately deploring Wilson's "propensity for lagging in the Mexican situation";[3] but the President was apparently pleasing the majority of the people of the nation; Congress voted a resolution "heartily" endorsing his conduct of Mexican relations.[4]

Wilson and Lansing finally decided upon consultation with the diplomatic representatives of certain of the South and Central American powers, with a view to agreeing upon the leader to recognize.

"I hope with all my heart," wrote Wilson, "that something will come out of it."[5]

The sentiment was shared by the general public in the United States and by almost all the principal newspapers of Latin America.[6] The conferees sent a friendly plea to the military and political chiefs to meet together to agree on a provisional government[7]—an old idea, except that it was now voiced by men speaking the anxiety of the peoples of the entire Western Hemisphere.

When replies were tallied, one significant fact stood out: with a single unimportant exception, every Constitutional-

[1]Oliveira to Lansing, July 29, 1915. *Foreign Relations*, 1915, pp. 731–732. Also two telegrams, Silliman to Lansing, July 28th, 8 A. M. and 11 A. M., sent to Wilson, July 29th.

[2]July 7, 1915.

[3]*The Intimate Papers of Colonel House*, Vol. II, p. 19.

[4]Original House concurrent resolution in Wilson's files, dated June 29, 1915.

[5]To Colonel House, August 4, 1915.

[6]New York *Times*, August 5, 1915; Barrett, head of the Pan-American Union, to Wilson, August 4, 1915.

[7]*Foreign Relations*, 1915, pp. 735–736. Message dated August 11th, sent August 13th.

ist deferred to the authority of Carranza.[1] In addition it was clear that Carranza's *de facto* government controlled about three quarters of the territory of Mexico.

Wilson had preserved his sense of humour in the wearying business.

"He laughingly said that Carranza had once or twice put it over us and in a very skillful way. He thought ... we would perhaps have to recognize Carranza."[2]

When the formal notification was given by the United States, October 19, 1915,[3] Wilson had real cause for satisfaction:

"We have been put to the test in the case of Mexico, and we have stood the test. Whether we have benefitted Mexico by the course we have pursued remains to be seen. Her fortunes are in her own hands. But we have at least proved that we will not take advantage of her in her distress and undertake to impose upon her an order and government of our own choosing ... that we seek no political suzerainty or selfish control."[4]

However, the great test of non-intervention was yet to come. During the remainder of 1915, and especially the spring of 1916, President Wilson faced the most critical problems he ever had to meet in his relations with Mexico. Power did not make Carranza any more amiable, nor was there an observable increase of his military control especially along the Rio Grande. Armed Mexicans were firing daily at American troops across the border and had killed

[1] *Ibid.*, pp. 753–755. Lansing reported the results of the conference to the President, September 18, 1915.

[2] *The Intimate Papers of Colonel House*, Vol. I, pp. 223–224.

[3] *Foreign Relations*, 1915, p. 771; see also Lansing's report to the President, February 17, 1916. *Ibid.*, 1916, pp. 469–473. To support the recognized *de facto* government in its efforts to bring about order, an embargo on arms and munitions was at once laid down in such a way as to cut off supplies to rebel-ridden areas. *Ibid.*, pp. 772–773, 781–782.

[4] From his annual message to Congress, December 7, 1915. *The Public Papers of Woodrow Wilson*, Vol. III, pp. 408–409.

or wounded several men already. Carranzista soldiers joined in some of the raids on American villages near the line.[1] Worst of all, Villa had been antagonized by the recognition of Carranza and had set out to revenge himself.[2] On November 26th some of his troops began shooting at American soldiers at Nogales, and on December 21st General Pershing gave orders "to vigorously return any deliberate firing from Mexican side."[3]

In the midst of this disappointing and threatening condition, Wilson held tenaciously to his charted course. Ignoring the vicious incidents along the Rio Grande, he sent to the Senate the nomination of Henry P. Fletcher as ambassador to Mexico.[4] He had tried to find a "man of the right principles but a man thoroughly versed in Latin-American affairs and accustomed to dealing with a sensitive people in a way they wish to be dealt with."[5] Before the appointment of Fletcher was confirmed, however, many weeks were to pass, and before he was to go to his post, many months.[6]

With the opening of 1916 we find Wilson seeking a more comprehensive plan and firmer support—nothing short of a coöperative understanding among all the nations of the Western Hemisphere. On January 6th he outlined the main elements of a proposed Pan-American peace pact and declared that the friendship of American nations must be "founded on a rock."[7] The projection of this great structure of peace, however, was almost instantly jeopardized. On January 10th some of Villa's bandits held up

[1]*Foreign Relations*, 1915, pp. 809–810. Also Wilson to Lansing, September 8; Lansing to Wilson, September 10, 1915.

[2]*Ibid.*, p. 775.

[3]*Foreign Relations*, 1915, pp. 820–821.

[4]December 17, 1915.

[5]Wilson to Frederic C. Howe, November 1, 1915.

[6]Confirmation was made in February 1916; he reached Mexico City on February 18, 1917.

[7]*The Public Papers of Woodrow Wilson*, Vol. III, pp. 439–445.

a passenger train carrying seventeen American mining men, all but one of whom were deliberately killed.[1]

The news startled and angered the entire nation.[2] Resolutions authorizing intervention were hastily introduced in the Senate by Republicans.[3] Representative Frank W. Mondell, of Wyoming, delivered an emotional but dangerous attack in the House, January 20th,[4] and a week later Representative William E. Humphrey, of Washington, ridiculed Wilson's policy as "characterized by weakness, uncertainty, vacillation, and uncontrollable desire to intermeddle in Mexican affairs."[5]

The State Department meantime prodded the *de facto* government to take action against the bandits. Carranza promised, but took distinctly longer strides on paper than on the trail of Villa.[6]

Wilson was "pretty sad about the Mexican situation."[7] He was now on the defensive more than ever before; but he neither forsook his ideals nor changed his policy of untiring patience. He replied to his bitter critics[8] January 27th:

"We have slowly, very slowly indeed, begun to win the

---

[1]*Foreign Relations*, 1916, pp. 650–653. At this time the Yaqui Indians were committing depredations in the great Yaqui Valley, adding to the conviction that the *de facto* government was incompetent. *Ibid.*, pp. 660 *et seq.*

[2]Senator A. B. Fall, of New Mexico, rabid advocate of intervention, if not, indeed, of the conquest of Mexico, had already secured the passage, on January 6th, of a Senate resolution calling for information, so phrased as to condemn the administration's policy. *Cong. Rec.*, 64–1, pp. 501, 589–603.

[3]In the debate, Senator Stone warned of the danger in making the matter "the subject of partisan politics." *Ibid.*, pp. 1004, 1060–1069, 1189–1196.

[4]*Ibid.*, pp. 1318–1322.

[5]*Ibid.*, p. 1636.

[6]*Foreign Relations*, 1916, pp. 653 *et seq.*

[7]Wilson to Cleveland H. Dodge, January 17, 1916.

[8]The feeling of Catholics was caustic and personal in the extreme. A Catholic official sent the President a protest stating that "the sixteen millions" of Catholics in the United States felt "profoundly outraged" because of his support of the Carranzista faction. Tumulty was told that his attitude "shocked" the Church, and that he had almost turned out to be a "traitor" to his Church to please his "*protestant* president." (Reverend J. Gheldof to Tumulty, February 17, 1916.)

confidence of the other States of the American hemisphere.
... Have gentlemen who have rushed down to Washington
to insist that we should go into Mexico reflected upon the
politics of the world? Nobody seriously supposes, gentlemen, that the United States needs to fear an invasion of
its own territory. What America has to fear, if she has anything to fear, are indirect, round-about, flank movements
upon her regnant position in the Western Hemisphere."[1]

In March Villa was riding north determined to provoke
hostilities. On March 9th his nondescript cavalry, some
four hundred men, crossed the border without hindrance
from the *de facto* government, galloped into Columbus,
New Mexico, and killed or wounded several men of the
American garrison and a few civilians. After looting and
burning part of the town, they raced back into Mexico.
The news instantly flashed to Washington. Lansing wired
Carranza curtly that this was "the most serious situation"
in the whole period of Mexican unrest; he expected him
to use every power to "pursue, capture, and exterminate
this lawless element."[2]

Angry soldiers on the border desired to pursue Villa at
once; unless he was caught, they believed he would continue his raids into the United States and attack Americans in Mexico.[3] Wilson felt himself compelled to take
immediate action and directed that an armed force be sent
across the border "with the sole object of capturing Villa
... and with scrupulous regard to sovereignty of Mexico."[4]
He declared his intention of acting in friendly coöperation
with the constituted authorities of Mexico.

There were no illusions about the possibilities of danger

---

[1]Address in New York. *The Public Papers of Woodrow Wilson*, Vol. IV, p. 9.

[2]*Foreign Relations*, 1916, pp. 478–481.

[3]*Ibid.*, pp. 481–482.

[4]Telegram, Adjutant General McCain to General Funston, March 10th. *Foreign Relations*, 1916, p. 483. For a discussion of Wilson's power in the matter, see C. A. Berdahl, *War Powers of the Executive in the United States*, pp. 65–67.

in such an incursion. Lansing directed all consuls except those near the border to advise Americans to "leave for the border or nearest port," and they were themselves ordered to withdraw if they deemed it safest to do so.[1]

The factor most in doubt was beyond American control: Carranza. While he showed some enthusiasm for the extermination of Villa and his "horde," he at once suggested that actual pursuit by American forces should be preceded by an agreement providing "that armed forces of either country might freely cross into the territory of the other . . . if the raid effected at Columbus should unfortunately be repeated at any other point on the border."[2] The next day he declared that if the United States would not consider mutual permission to pursue bandits, and insisted upon "sending an operating army" into Mexico, "my Government shall consider this act as an invasion of national territory." This would mean war, the very end that Villa sought.[3] Since American troops were already massing along the border, Carranza appealed to the Mexican people "to be prepared for any emergency" in case "the territory of Mexico be invaded . . . and the dignity of the Republic outraged."[4]

The United States government tried to quiet such fears regarding its intentions. With Wilson's approval, Lansing on the 13th accepted the proposal for reciprocal pursuit of bandits across the boundary and gave notice that "the arrangement is now complete and in force and . . . may accordingly be exercised by either Government without further interchange of views."[5]

---

[1]*Foreign Relations*, 1916, pp. 684, 689. Carranza in a proclamation, March 12th, requested Mexican authorities to extend all guarantees to American citizens. *Ibid.*, p. 487.

[2]March 10, 1916, midnight. *Ibid.*, p. 485.

[3]March 11, 1916, delivered March 12, 1916. *Ibid.*, p. 486.

[4]March 12, 1916. *Foreign Relations*, 1916, p. 487.

[5]*Ibid.*, pp. 487–488.

The foreign secretary of the *de facto* government received this notice with marked pleasure;[1] but no evidence of coöperation from Carranza was forthcoming. The pursuit expedition, though "deliberately intended to preclude the possibility of intervention,"[2] might result in war in spite of the President's efforts. William Kent propounded the question:

". . . s'posin' Villa should become the popular hero of Mexico, and that Carranza should go into eclipse . . . Then the question would be as to what we were going to do about this new dictator. . . ."[3]

To which the perturbed President replied:

"Your game of 'S'posin' ' puts a very poignant question which has been very much in my mind. The whole problem down there looks very much less simple to me than it seems to appear to some other people, and your question has accentuated my own anxious speculations about the future turn of events down there."[4]

He discussed his doubts with Tumulty, who argued that if he did not now send an expedition it would be disastrous to the party, and to his influence, and "humiliating to the country."[5] Lane wrote, too, that he thought that "to fail in getting Villa would ruin us in the eyes of all Latin-Americans . . . like children they pile insult upon insult if they are not stopped when the first insult is given."[6]

Fully awake to the fact that "not all the pitfalls" in this "very thorny matter"[7] had been disclosed, the President decided that the expedition must be sent. American troops crossed the boundary, March 15th; Congress agreed over-

---

[1]March 13, 1916. *Ibid.*, p. 488.
[2]Public statement by President Wilson, March 13, 1916. *Ibid.*, p. 489.
[3]Representative William Kent to Wilson, March 14, 1916.
[4]March 15, 1916.
[5]Tumulty to Wilson, March 15, 1916.
[6]March 13, 1916.
[7]Wilson to Representative E. W. Pou, March 15, 1916.

whelmingly on the 17th to a resolution approving the President's purpose.[1] On March 25th he took one last precaution against being driven beyond the objective of that pursuit by requesting the American press to temper their reports of the expedition and Mexican affairs so as not to inflame opinion.[2]

Carranza expostulated sharply, declaring that "an expedition described as punitive" had entered Mexican territory without permission, and that his original proposal, which the United States had accepted, applied only to future raids, not to this one.[3]

Astonished officials of the State Department explained that the acceptance of Carranza's own terms had been considered sufficient, but that any suggestions for securing approval of the present expedition would be gladly received.[4] It seemed that patience could go no further.

Greatly perplexed, the President studied every phase of these developments, read every dispatch. Demands for intervention now swelled into a roar wherever Wilson's critics foregathered, with Senator Lodge and Theodore Roosevelt sounding the tocsin. Senator Fall visited the border, vowing that, if American troops withdrew without capturing Villa, he would "open up a bombardment in the Senate which will make the past revolutions in Mexico look like a sane Fourth of July celebration."[5]

---

[1] *Foreign Relations*, 1916, pp. 491–492.

[2] The idea was suggested by David Lawrence. (Lawrence to Wilson, March 13, 1916; Wilson to Polk, March 14, 1916.) *The Public Papers of Woodrow Wilson*, Vol. IV, pp. 132–133.

[3] March 18, 1916. *Foreign Relations*, 1916, pp. 493–494.

[4] March 19, 1916. *Ibid.*, pp. 494–495.

[5] El Paso *Times*, March 27, 1916; Fall to Senator Jacob H. Gallinger, March 27, 1916; Gallinger to the Secretary of War, March 28, 1916. Wilson wrote to Secretary Baker: "I would trust Senator Gallinger to try to tell the truth but I do not think that Senator Fall even tries. . . ." (March 31, 1916.) The President on March 31st ordered the War Department to make an investigation of Fall's charges against his policy. The report of the investigation, April 5th, found the charges "a confused jumble of rumors, some of which have slight foundation, some of which have none, and none of which appear to have been wholly justified. . . ."

Wilson exclaimed in a letter to Lane:

"What Machiavellis these men are who are trying to stir up war!"[1]

American citizens in Mexico were also among those who were deliberately fomenting intervention. The President, thoroughly indignant, typed out a list of "American Plotters and Liars in Mexico," his muster roll containing twenty-four names.

Meanwhile Lansing's efforts to negotiate an agreement covering the pursuit expedition broke down. Carranza remained of the opinion that Mexican dignity was offended and its sovereignty violated by the presence of any American troops on Mexican soil. He cut off negotiations on April 12th.[2] The next day the first clash between American troops and Mexican citizens occurred at Parral.

The situation was now acute. To reach some understanding, the United States suggested that General Scott confer on the border with General Obregon, who headed the Carranzista forces. Carranza accepted.[3] Rumours persistently sprang up in the United States that the expedition was to be withdrawn. When Senator Smith, of Arizona, protested to the President, he received the exasperated reply that the press knew "absolutely nothing about what is intended in Mexico."[4]

While the trail of Villa was soon lost, Wilson felt that the expedition must be kept in Mexico to hold the bandits inactive and to guard the border until security to life and property was assured—in short until Carranza's troops should carry out their responsibilities.[5]

---

[1]April 12, 1916. Lane himself wanted Wilson to go to the point of war, to show "strong leadership." (Lane to the author, April 13, 1916.)

[2]*Foreign Relations*, 1916, pp. 507–517.

[3]*Ibid.*, pp. 527–533. The discussions began April 30, 1916.

[4]April 25, 1916.

[5]Newton D. Baker to Wilson, April 23, 1916; Adjutant General to General Scott, April 30, 1916; *Foreign Relations*, 1916, pp. 534–535; undated telegram [May 1 ?]

A tentative agreement by the generals on May 3rd seemed to promise a solution. Secretary Baker and the President, gladly enough, prepared a statement for publication, to be issued when Carranza gave his approval:

"The agreement drawn up and approved by both governments contemplates the gradual retirement of the American force toward the border, the prosecution of the search for Villa, and the dispersal of his remaining following by the Mexican forces, and the entire withdrawal of the American expedition so soon as either Villa shall have been captured or the Mexican forces shall have secured such complete control . . . as to render us safe . . .

"The ratification . . . removes all controversy . . . and I have therefore decided officially to receive Mr. Arredondo, ambassador-designate of Mexico, and shall direct Mr. Fletcher presently to proceed to Mexico City. . . ."[1]

While Wilson was prepared, in good faith, to settle everything, Carranza would not sign the agreement because it did not set a date for the completion of withdrawal.[2] Unfortunately, just at this time, a new crisis developed, with raids on Glen Springs and Boquillas, Texas.[3] The border states were now growing impatient, and their militiamen were called out. On the 9th more troops were sent to the front.[4] A clash with the forces of the suspicious and obstinate First Chief seemed now only a matter of time.

The President referred to the situation in a conversation with the author, May 11th:[5]

War Department to General Scott. "This Government cannot withdraw troops from Mexico until it is satisfied that danger to our people on the border is removed."

[1]The statement was never used.

[2]*Foreign Relations*, 1916, pp. 535, 538–539, 547.

[3]May 5, 1916. *Ibid.*, pp. 540, 542.

[4]New York *Times*, May 10, 1916.

[5]"I was shown into the study a few minutes before he arrived and had a moment to look about. Two very large paintings, one a fine copy of Watt's 'Love and Life,' with a written poem on the bookcase at one side, also entitled 'Love and Life.' The other

"He said his Mexican policy was based upon two of the most deeply seated convictions of his life. First, his shame as an American over the first Mexican war, and his resolution that there should never be another such predatory enterprise. Second, upon his belief in the principle laid down in the Virginia Bill of Rights, that a people has the right 'to do what they damn please with their own affairs.' (He used the word 'damn.') He wanted to give the Mexicans a chance to try. He said he had asked a man named ———, formerly with the British Embassy at Mexico, who had come to see him, to name a single instance in history in which the blessings of free government had been bestowed upon a people from above, and had not come with struggle and trial from below. He wants to give the Mexicans a chance, but he is not dogmatic about the method of approach. Here, as always, he respects facts.

"'It may prove,' he said, 'that we shall have to go in finally and make peace.' He . . . said that the greatest trouble was not with Mexico, but with people here in America who wanted the oil and metals in Mexico, and were seeking intervention in order to get them. He referred to the Mexican boundary as one of the longest in the world, and declared with shut jaw that he would not be

---

painting represented the moment of the signing of the Treaty with Spain, in the McKinley administration. President McKinley is represented as standing at the end of the table, a fine figure, Hay and the Spanish ambassador as sitting and signing the treaty. Genthe's photograph of the new Mrs. Wilson had a prominent place on a near-by bookcase. A book by Earl Grey on fly fishing lay on the corner of the table. On Mr. Wilson's desk was a great litter of books and papers, the filing cabinet behind it, the stenographer's desk in the corner. It is a quiet place, at the back of the house, where, he told me, he does all of his serious work.

"He came in, stepping quickly and lightly.

"'How are you, Baker?' . . .

"I have never talked with any public man who had such complete control of his whole intellectual equipment as he. . . . The rise and fall of his intelligent interest and enthusiasm express themselves especially in his eyes. . . . He pounces upon things as they are said, and consumes them before they are well out of one's mind. And his pounce is sure, accurate, complete. He instantly adds what you give him, whether fact or opinion, to his own view of the situation, so that, to an extraordinary degree, you go along with him, and arrive at that meeting of the minds which is so rare a thing in discussion." (From notes made at the time by the author.)

forced into war with Mexico if it could possibly be avoided. He does not want one hand tied behind him at the very moment that the nation may need all of its forces to meet the European situation. He emphasized the enormous undertaking it would be to pacify Mexico: 'Five hundred thousand men at least.'"[1]

Determined to force the issue, Carranza directed his agent, Arredondo, to deliver on May 31st a protest against the entire action of the United States—a long insulting note, imputing bad faith and hidden motives on the part of the American government, and culminating in a demand that the troops be withdrawn immediately.[2] Arredondo said when delivering it that it was not an ultimatum but "merely a continuation of the diplomatic discussion"[3]—a distinction, in this case, without real difference. The State Department found the note "impertinent" and debated sending it back.[4]

A general Mexican attack was believed to be imminent.[5] The excited attitude of the Mexicans was displayed on June 18th in the port of Mazatlan; two American naval officers were arrested and a boat crew fired upon—a more serious offense than that at Tampico.[6]

The American reply to Carranza's note, June 20th, minced no words. The course pursued by the United States was defended at every point. To Carranza's warning that if necessary he would "appeal to arms" to repel the so-called invaders, the answer was courteous but peremptory:

"... the execution of this threat will lead to the gravest

---

[1]From notes made at the time by the author.

[2]*Foreign Relations*, 1916, pp. 552–563. The note was dated May 22nd.

[3]Polk to Wilson, May 31, 1916.

[4]Polk to Wilson, June 1, 1916.

[5]Funston to the Adjutant General, June 18, 1916. New York *Times*, June 19, 1916. Nearly all the militia in the state were called to patrol the border June 18th.

[6]*Foreign Relations*, 1916, pp. 578–580.

consequences. While this Government would deeply regret such a result, it cannot recede from its settled determination to maintain its national rights and to perform its full duty in preventing further invasions of the territory of the United States. . . ."[1]

The inevitable clash took place at Carrizal, June 21st. Seventeen American soldiers were reported taken prisoner, a figure later corrected to twenty-three.[2]

"The break seems to have come in Mexico; and all my patience seems to have gone for nothing," wrote Wilson the next day. "I am infinitely sad about it. I fear I should have drawn Pershing and his command northward just after it became evident that Villa had slipped through his fingers; but except for that error of judgment (if it was an error) I cannot, in looking back, see where I could have done differently, holding sacred the convictions I hold in this matter.

"Right or wrong, however, the extremest consequences seem upon us. But *INTERVENTION* (that is the rearrangement and control of Mexico's domestic affairs by the U.S.) there shall not be either now or at any other time if I can prevent it."[3]

And he wrote to Louis Wiley, the same day:

"We are apparently getting into deep waters to the south of us, but we must be the more careful in entering them to do nothing which will put any doubt upon our purpose and our ability to keep faith with Latin-America in all matters that touch independence and territorial integrity."

The immediate tasks were to dispose our troops for war, get the prisoners released, and arrive if possible at an accommodation with Carranza. Available guardsmen were

---

[1]*Foreign Relations*, 1916, pp. 581–592.
[2]*Ibid.*, pp. 592 *et seq.*
[3]To Colonel House, June 22, 1916.

dispatched, and the President was authorized by a joint resolution of Congress to draft the National Guard into the military service of the United States.[1] Formal demands for the release of the prisoners and for a statement of Carranza's intentions were made on the 25th.

Wilson conferred with Senators Stone and Lodge and Representative Flood preparatory to making a statement regarding his course. At this time he was composing a message to Congress—not, as it turned out, to be delivered. The border must be quieted, he wrote, and the *de facto* government would neither use its forces effectually nor allow the United States to do so. The *de facto* government had been recognized because it seemed able to establish order and resume constitutional processes, "and because it did not bear upon it the infamous stain of blood guiltiness and of having laid violent hands upon the constitution itself that the lawless Huerta bore. We do not know whether it represents the people of Mexico or not. We shall not know until it has been judged by the people at the polls."

If there were a "regularly constituted" and responsible government in Mexico "it would obviously be my duty to advise the Congress to exercise its constitutional power to declare war. But we are not dealing with such a government. There has been no such government in Mexico since February 1913."

The condition of the Mexican people was pitiful: war would be a "heartless and unrighteous thing." Instead he would recommend:

". . . that the Congress authorize me to use the military and naval forces of the Government in any way that may be necessary to guard our frontier effectively, if necessary to enter on Mexican soil and there require the entire sus-

---

[1] June 23, 1916. *Cong. Rec.*, 64–1, pp. 9870 *et seq.*

pension, in the states which touch our own of all military activities of every kind on the part of the Mexican people until by the establishment of a responsible and adequate authority among themselves they are prepared to resume their full obligations to us as a neighbouring and friendly state."[1]

This would not mean intervention:

". . . I feel bound in conscience, as the official representative of the American people, to act in these critical circumstances as a friend of the people of Mexico even when proposing to use force against those who profess to be their government, but do not govern. I am not willing to be ["unasked" he later added in pencil] a party to intervention in the internal affairs of Mexico. By intervention I mean an attempt to determine for the Mexican people what the form, the circumstances, and the personnel of their government shall be, or upon what terms and in what manner a settlement of their disturbed affairs shall be effected. . . .

"Very few of those who desire a settlement of Mexican affairs by the force and power of the United States desire it for the sake of Mexico. It does not lie with the American people to dictate to another people what their government shall be or what use shall be made of their resources, what laws or rulers they shall have or what persons they shall encourage or favour. . . .[2] I know what American history means and what spirit in affairs the American people have most passionately and habitually preferred. I know that they desire no one who professes to speak for them to interfere with the liberties of any people and that I am speaking their deepest principle of action when I say that

[1]This military plan was Wilson's, but the phrasing was mainly Secretary Baker's. (Baker to Wilson, June 26, 1916.)

[2]When reading the proposed message, Lansing wrote in the margin: "Haiti, S. Domingo, Nicaragua, Panama." No attempt was made by the President to meet the question of consistency thus raised.

we wish not a single foot of Mexican territory, not a single hour of political control in Mexico."

This plan to compel order in northern Mexico came to nothing for several reasons. It would have been an unwise step when we might at any time be forced into the European war. Its justification was in doubt because there was some question as to the judgment of the captain who had commanded the American force at Carrizal.[1] And there was a strong public opinion against war or anything approaching it, shown by the many letters Wilson received.

And, finally, Carranza released the prisoners.[2]

An opportunity to avoid hostilities was the very thing Wilson most wanted; in spite of the overwhelming provocations south of the border, and the bitter criticisms at home, he determined to try again for a peaceful solution, using the offices, as he had done before, of a Joint American-Mexican Commission.[3] It was a momentous decision, and it undoubtedly kept us out of a miserable conflict the repercussions of which, especially as related to the European war, we could not have foreseen.

It was well, indeed, that he acted quickly, for the forces of irritation and the demands for stern intervention were rapidly getting out of hand. Great Britain was fretting about the fate of the oil fields and the investments of her citizens,[4] and interventionists were working with a zeal that was beginning to persuade great numbers of Americans. Representative C. P. Caldwell on July 11th wrote to the President that he had on the previous day intro-

---

[1] Report of General Pershing, June 23, 1916. *Foreign Relations*, 1916, p. 594.

[2] *Foreign Relations*, 1916, p. 597. Samuel Gompers' telegram, June 28, 1916, urging release of the prisoners may have had influence with Carranza. On July 1st Wilson saw the telegrams exchanged by Gompers and Carranza. (Wilson to Secretary Wilson, July 3, 1916.)

[3] Lansing suggested such a commission. (Lansing to Wilson, July 3, 1916; see also Arredondo to Lansing, July 12, 1916. *Foreign Relations*, 1916, p. 601.) Several Latin-American countries had offered their "friendly mediation."

[4] Secretary Baker to Wilson, June 26, 1916; Palmer, *Newton D. Baker*, Vol. I, p. 23.

duced a resolution to purchase certain portions of northern Mexico, including Lower California. The President at once replied:

"I beg that you will not at this time press the resolution. It would constitute a very serious embarrassment and probably make a new complication in our Mexican affairs."[1]

Indeed, the President practically confessed that he had barely avoided committing himself to war:

"I can lose my temper in a minute . . . I think that if you were to subject my Scotch-Irish blood to the proper kind of analysis, you would find that it was fighting blood, and that it is pretty hard for a man born that way to keep quiet and do things in the way in which his intelligence tells him he ought to do them."[2]

The crisis was a profound personal test of Wilson; and it threatened for a time to be a powerful factor in his campaign for reëlection which was just then beginning. His course was being sarcastically described by political critics as "a combination of meddling and muddling without any definite cohesive plan from beginning to end."[3] The chambers of the Senate and the House of Representatives rang with volley after volley of Republican oratory.[4] But the criticism ran headlong into the impressive fact that Wilson had kept the country at peace with Mexico and had protected the border probably as well as was humanly possible during a period of revolution and civil war.

With the acceptance of the proposal for a joint commission, Wilson's struggle against intervention was at

---

[1] July 13, 1916. As early as October 1, 1915, McAdoo had suggested to Wilson that a part of Mexico's debt to the United States might be liquidated by buying Lower California, and a border strip which could be neutralized.

[2] Address at Toledo, Ohio, July 10, 1916. *The Public Papers of Woodrow Wilson*, Vol. IV, p. 246.

[3] Ellery Sedgwick, of the *Atlantic Monthly*, reporting opinion to Colonel House. Letter quoted in House to Wilson, July 15, 1916.

[4] *Cong. Rec.*, 64-1, pp. 11647–11661, 12138–12149, 12189–12190, 12319–12326, etc.

length victorious. Even though Carranza opposed a really comprehensive inquiry,[1] Wilson considered that the arrangements were "in as satisfactory a position as we can get. . . ."[2]

The President had some difficulty in finding men to serve on the commission, "men whom I can absolutely trust to be honest with themselves and with the Mexicans and with the public."[3] Secretary Lane, Dr. John R. Mott, and Judge George Gray finally accepted; an able group.[4] L. S. Rowe, an expert on Latin-American affairs, acted as secretary.

To hasten the negotiations, Wilson himself conferred with the Mexican commissioners on September 12th,[5] at New London, where he had been called by the last illness of his sister. But he did not attempt to guide the proceedings, being occupied to the limit of his time with the election, with problems of military preparedness, and with harassing European affairs.

After weeks of fruitless negotiation, the American commissioners, though convinced that the *de facto* government was both incompetent and ill-intentioned, concluded that

---

[1] *Foreign Relations*, 1916, pp. 601, 605, 606. One of the problems Wilson wished to touch was, for example, "adequate and rightly safeguarded financial assistance from this side the border" to stabilize Mexican affairs. (Wilson to R. Olney, August 13, 1916.) David Lawrence [?] in a letter of July 27th warned the President that any attempt at broad inquiry was foredoomed to fail, for Carranza would not and in fact could not permit discussion of any internal problem of Mexico without losing prestige at home, a prestige he needed desperately.

[2] Wilson to Frank L. Polk, August 10, 1916. Wilson at this period gave some thought to a possible meeting between himself and Carranza at the border. (Wilson to Amos Pinchot, August 11, 1916.)

[3] Wilson to Thomas D. Jones, August 17, 1916. Richard Olney, T. D. Jones, and Justice Brandeis were unable to accept, and objection was raised by the State Department to Dr. Charles W. Eliot on the ground of hasty temper. (Polk to the author, February 9, 1926.) To the suggestion that he name ex-President Taft, Wilson answered that Taft seemed unfitted "to handle any business that requires firmness and definiteness of view." His personal feeling toward Taft remained "altogether agreeable," nevertheless. (Wilson to Senator H. F. Hollis, a letter which Tumulty persuaded the President not to send, August 12, 1916.)

[4] See *Foreign Relations*, 1916, pp. 606–608.

[5] New York *Times*, September 13, 1916.

the choice was between bad and worse; they proposed as the only solution that full diplomatic relations be re-established and the troops withdrawn.[1] We should retire to the border, patrol it, and hold Mexico responsible for any encroachments.

Pershing and the last ten thousand American cavalry-men rode out of Mexico February 5th.[2] On March 3, 1917, Ambassador Fletcher presented his credentials. Eight days later Carranza was constitutionally elected President of Mexico, a fact still worthy to be noticed, but on the inside pages of newspapers:[3] for Mexican relations had dropped from sight as we stood on the brink of war with Germany.

It is not too much to say that if it had not been for Woodrow Wilson's determination that the American nation should act always toward Mexico upon a plane of honour, tolerance, helpfulness, patience, consonant with our power and responsibility, we should certainly have been at war: and good relations with the rising nations to the south of us which have been developing so hopefully since that time might have been long delayed.

II. STABILITY IN THE WESTERN HEMISPHERE

Seeking a Pan-American Pact

One of the great purposes upon which Woodrow Wilson had set his heart, since it was a sincere expression of his fundamental ideals, was to win the confidence of Latin America. He strove to forge permanent bonds of peace in the Western Hemisphere, to encourage constitutional government, and to better trade relationships. Early in his

---

[1]January 3, 1917, *Foreign Relations*, 1917, pp. 936–938.

[2]This was the day that, unknown to Americans at the time, orders to begin a dis-cussion of a German project of alliance with Mexico in case of American entrance into the World War were sent from Berlin to the German minister in Mexico. *Official German Documents*, Vol. II, p. 1338.

[3]*Foreign Relations*, 1917, p. 910. New York *Times*, March 12, 1917.

administration, as already pointed out, he had spoken and written hopefully of a closer union.

During 1914 Andrew Carnegie was urging Wilson to "banish war from the American continent"; a league of twenty-one republics would be "an example" to the world.[1] Wilson replied, September 29th:

"I am warmly obliged to you for lodging in my mind a suggestion which may later bear fruit."

Through Wilson's initiative practical coöperation with the countries to the south—the only solid basis for such a movement—was indeed already in process. Mediation had been accepted in the Tampico affair, and Latin-American nations were being informed from time to time as to American intentions in the Caribbean and in Mexico. In September a Pan-American Congress was being arranged[2] and plans for another conference, on business matters, were begun as early as October 1914.[3]

Conditions were ripe for a further step. In December we find the President writing out what he considered the two basic articles for a Pan-American pact: (a) that independence under republican forms of government and territorial integrity were to be mutually guaranteed, and (b) that all the governments concerned would agree to take full control of the production and sale of munitions.[4]

Conversations with the ambassadors of Argentina, Brazil, and Chile were soon under way. Suarez, of Chile, was not enthusiastic, partly because of the boundary dispute between Chile and Peru.[5] Naon of Argentina was

---

[1] September 26, 1914.

[2] Bryan to Wilson, September 4, 1914.

[3] Held in May 1915. McAdoo to Wilson, October 28, 1914, and December 24, 1914; Wilson to McAdoo, November 3, 1914. A Scientific Congress was held in December 1915 and January 1916.

[4] *The Intimate Papers of Colonel House*, Vol. I, pp. 209–210.

[5] He also resented any suggestion from the United States, especially one which could possibly be interpreted as taking a position of initiative and tutelage over

pleased. Da Gama of Brazil thought it desirable. And the Senate Committee on Foreign Relations seemed favourably disposed.[1]

Months passed with no perceptible progress, but in October 1915 the matter was again under discussion. House wrote that Lansing was "pushing the South American proposal."[2] Chile's obstruction was, however, so baffling that Wilson typed out a new draft, retaining both of the original guarantees, but adding a provision relating to the settlement of current boundary disputes by an arbitral tribunal. The core idea of the Bryan treaties of investigation and delay was added in another clause.[3]

Even with these changes, and others drafted later by Lansing,[4] the negotiations did not prosper. Suarez, of Chile, might appear to agree, as he frequently did,[5] but a definite agreement could not be reached. Wilson plainly failed to realize at the time the immense weight of suspicion and inertia that had to be overcome. He was likely, when a course seemed so utterly reasonable as this, to overestimate the capacity of men for understanding and prompt action. We find him speaking too hopefully of the outlook in his annual message in December 1915, and in his address to the Pan-American Scientific Congress, January 6, 1916.[6] He wrote to Stone and to Flood, January 12th:

"... our relations with the Central and South American

Chile. (Grey to House, March 23, 1916, transmitted to Wilson April 8, 1916. Printed in *The Intimate Papers of Colonel House*, Vol. I, pp. 229–230.)

[1]*Ibid.*, pp. 213–218.

[2]*Ibid.*, p. 225. House to Walter H. Page, October 19, 1915.

[3]This fourth clause provided for arbitration of all questions not affecting "the honour, independence, or vital interests of the nations concerned or the interests of third parties ..." Wilson's draft is not dated.

[4]In place of the earlier munitions clause there was substituted a provision forbidding the exportation of munitions destined for revolutionists.

[5]Lansing to Wilson, November 18, 1915; Lansing to House, November 18, 1915.

[6]*The Public Papers of Woodrow Wilson*, Vol. III, pp. 407, 409, 444.

countries are now upon a happier footing than ever before. . . ."

His heart was indeed set upon the achievement of the new pact, for its implications were far flung. If he was to ask the war-torn world to accept the basic elements of such an agreement in forming a League of Nations, he must omit no effort to apply it practically in the Western Hemisphere. It would make us "partners" with South and Central America, "rather than guardians." He thought it "a great step in advance."[1] In March, therefore, he authorized Polk to discuss the possibility of going ahead without Chile.[2]

For a time there seemed to be some hope of success, despite the imbroglio on the Mexican border which made for new suspicion of the United States throughout Latin America,[3] but by August Chile had become so "decidedly opposed to the treaty" that Argentina and Brazil were reluctant to proceed.[4] If progress toward a real agreement had then to be dropped, the President had laid down the new principles, had applied them practically in efforts to solve the Mexican difficulties, and had begun the negotiations for more comprehensive coöperation which in later years and calmer times were to bear rich fruit. Moreover, his experience with the problems of the Western Hemisphere was of great value in fortifying his stand for the mightier structure, a league of all nations, to which he was now devoted and which he hoped would bring about a new world order.

---

[1] Author's notes of conversation with President Wilson, May 11, 1916.

[2] Interview between Wilson and Polk, March 14, 1916; Polk to Wilson, March 17, 1916.

[3] Wilson asked Ambassador Fletcher, who was being delayed by the border troubles from taking his post in Mexico, to work with Colonel House in gaining agreement. (Wilson to Lansing, April 3, 1916.)

[4] Fletcher to House, August 9, 1916. *The Intimate Papers of Colonel House*, Vol. I, pp. 231–232.

Revolutions in Haiti and Santo Domingo

Wilson was not only defeated in his vision of capping his Latin-American policy with a comprehensive peace agreement, but his problems in the Caribbean and Central America continued to be irritating and highly complex. A full exposition of his early difficulties and the principles he endeavoured to apply has been given in a former volume of this biography.[1] He had already met and tried, not too successfully, to solve the problems of Nicaragua and Colombia; the Dominican Republic and Haiti continued to be sore spots. Conditions there appeared to be superficially similar to those in Mexico—revolution, insecurity of life and property, and a feeble development of the attitudes and customs which underlie steady self-government. Actually the island "revolutions" lacked even as sound a basis of social, economic, or political reform as that in Mexico. Strife between rivals seeking position and plunder was accompanied by peculiar external complications. The little republics, rich in resources, admirably situated strategically, were so weak politically that they were easy victims of foreign exploitation. The island containing the two republics lay between two great trade routes that linked the Panama Canal with the important ports of the United States and Europe. On the northwest the Haitian harbour, Mole St. Nicholas, faced, across the busy Windward Passage, the new American naval base in Cuba, Guantanamo Bay; and on the east the Dominican harbour in the Bay of Samana looked across Mona Passage to Porto Rico. Americans were thus deeply concerned in the stability and security of the island, and Wilson had to consider inexorable strategic and economic interests as well as his cherished hope of stabilizing the hemisphere by promoting constitutional government.

[1] Vol. IV, *President*, pp. 426–451.

Both the President and Bryan gave much thought to the increased importance that Haiti would assume with the use of the Panama Canal.[1] Concerning the natural naval base of Mole St. Nicholas, which it was understood that Germany "coveted," Bryan wrote to the President:

"I am satisfied that it will be of great value to us and even if it were not . . . it is worth while to take it out of the market so that no other nation will attempt to secure a foothold there."[2]

Wilson replied, ten days later: "I fully concur. . . ."

The main objective, however, was not, at the moment, so much to get a base as to assure stability. The method which seemed most likely to succeed was to starve the revolutions by helping to put Haiti's customs collections, and possibly her finances as well, on a firm basis.[3] A gloss of indirection was to be employed in the method (Haiti was to *request* "assistance") but the plain objective was American control.

Early in February 1914 revolution by General Oreste Zamor brought forth a new *de facto* government, which was immediately occupied with a revolution led by one Davilmar Theodore. With Wilson's consent, the State Department tried to negotiate with Zamor for financial reform, lighthouses along the coast, and an understanding that no other power should be given a foothold at Mole St. Nicholas.[4] It was useless. The fighting intensified. As a consequence the French and German diplomatic representatives informally proposed that their governments join the United States in control over the customs, a plan which was unacceptable to Bryan, and decidedly so to Wilson.[5] This suspicious foreign interest proved that a

[1]Bryan to Wilson, January 21, 1914.
[2]Bryan to Wilson, June 14, 1913.
[3]State Department memorandum, January 23, 1914, in Mr. Wilson's files.
[4]*Foreign Relations*, 1914, pp. 338–340.
[5]Bryan to Wilson, March 24, 1914; Wilson to Bryan, March 26, 1914.

determined effort to get reforms could no longer be postponed.

Bryan—an eloquent crusader against imperialism, now faced with the realities of power—suggested that the only practicable course was to make a convention along the lines negotiated with the Dominican Republic in 1907, with the addition of provisions for a financial adviser and authority to prevent interference with the customs receipts. Wilson agreed, June 25th.[1]

Negotiations came to nothing; by November, Theodore had reached the capital city, Port-au-Prince, and set up a new government. Lansing consulted Wilson, arguing that the American naval force there had best be increased at once, "not only for the purpose of protecting foreign interests, but also as evidence of the earnest intention of this Government to settle the unsatisfactory state of affairs which exists." Here were inexorable facts, and Wilson again agreed.[2]

When Bryan wrote on January 7, 1915, that the "situation in Haiti is still embarrassing and we have apparently made no progress," and that a new revolution was about to burst upon the unfortunate capital, Wilson sharpened his demands. He proposed that a commission should be sent to Haiti at once to say to the faction leaders "as firmly and definitely as is consistent with courtesy and kindness that the United States cannot consent to stand by and permit revolutionary conditions constantly to exist there. They ought, as in San Domingo, to insist upon an agreement for a popular election under our supervision and to be told that the result of that elec-

---

[1] *Cf. Foreign Relations,* 1914, pp. 347–350.

[2] Lansing to Wilson, October 28, 1914; memorandum of telephone conversation, October 29, 1914. See also *Foreign Relations,* 1914, pp. 354 *et seq.* The decision was not made from any urgent claim of naval necessity. The General Board of the Navy Department notified the State Department that there was no necessity for naval purposes to have a station at Mole St. Nicholas. (Noted in Lansing to Wilson, August 9, 1915.)

tion would be upheld by the United States to the utmost. "Is not this your judgment?"[1]

It was. The commissioners, John Franklin Fort, A. Bailly-Blanchard, and Charles Cogswell Smith,[2] met in Port-au-Prince March 5th, the day after the Haitian Congress elected another new president, Vilbrun Guillaume Sam. With histrionic dignity, Sam declined to treat with the commissioners until after his formal recognition by the United States.[3] France, Germany, and Italy soon recognized him, and to add to the complications, preparations for a new revolution became visible.[4] In these circumstances, Paul Fuller was sent by Wilson and Bryan as special commissioner, first to negotiate a treaty agreeing to the reforms thought necessary, and then to deliver a letter of recognition.[5] He also failed: democratic machinery absolutely would not work.

In June there was pillaging in Cape Haitien; French sailors were called to protect the French Consulate and the bank. On July 27th Sam took refuge in the French Legation, and the next day a mob dragged him out and dismembered him. American marines were landed at once; the British and French were assured that the American forces would protect foreign interests; and they were asked not to land marines.[6]

"The matters in Haiti have certainly come to a head . . ." wrote Wilson on August 2nd. "Fortunately, we are now in control and I am confidently hoping that it will be possible to bring some order out of the chaos."[7]

[1] Wilson to Bryan, January 13, 1915.

[2] Fort and Smith had been members of the commission sent to the Dominican Republic in 1914. See *Woodrow Wilson, Life and Letters*, Vol. IV, *President*, p. 447.

[3] Commissioners' report, March 13, 1915.

[4] *Foreign Relations*, 1915, pp. 469–470.

[5] Bryan to Wilson, May 29, 1915, with enclosures. Fuller was sent on April 29th. New York *Times*, April 30, 1915.

[6] *Foreign Relations*, 1915, pp. 472–475.

[7] To John Franklin Fort.

This was practically his final statement regarding Haiti for many months: his decision to use strong measures had been made. The desired treaty was signed September 16, 1915,[1] and American marines were long to remain in control.[2]

Conditions in the Dominican Republic were not quite so vicious as those in Haiti; the United States was from the first in a position, owing to the convention of 1907, to exercise more control. Jimenez, a fine type of man, had become president late in 1914 after a supervised election; and it was clearly understood that the United States would support him in maintaining order and constitutional authority.[3] Bryan optimistically believed that the situation had "cleared up" and that the American policy had been "vindicated by a fair election,"[4] but the American election commissioners warned that ". . . in case of any further revolutions it will be essential for us to go in and put them down with a strong hand. . . .

"One thousand troops or marines with machine guns . . . could control the situation."[5]

Outbreaks did indeed begin early in 1915, and the attempts by Jimenez to stamp them out were ineffective. Bryan telegraphed:

---

[1] *Foreign Relations*, 1915, pp. 448–451. Lansing proposed to the President, August 9th, that in regard to Mole St. Nicholas, assurances be given that the United States desired no Haitian territory but merely guarantees against cessions to any foreign government. The President was not prepared to do this. At his instruction, the wording of the telegram was changed to read: "The question of the cession of Mole St. Nicholas will be taken up later by the government of the United States along with the other questions to be submitted to the re-organized government with regard to its relations to the United States." (Benson to the Naval Commander at Port-au-Prince, August 9, 1915.) The treaty was made operative as a *modus vivendi* in November, ratifications being exchanged on May 3, 1916. *Foreign Relations*, 1915, pp. 459–460; *ibid.*, 1916, p. 328.

[2] Congress authorized this action in 1916. The American forces served under the government of Haiti, which paid the occupation expenses. *Cong. Rec.*, 64–1, pp. 7424–7429, 9168.

[3] *Woodrow Wilson, Life and Letters*, Vol. IV, *President*, pp. 448–449.

[4] Bryan to Wilson, December 12, 1914.

[5] *Foreign Relations*, 1915, pp. 279 *et seq.*

"This Government meant what it said when it declared that it would tolerate no more insurrections in Santo Domingo. . . ."[1]

The situation became increasingly grave: the opposition was irritated by the stern control, especially of finances, by the American authority. Wilson had considered these measures "disinterested" attempts "to aid Dominicans in the establishment of a government that will provide peace, individual guarantees, and opportunity for development, without which no true prosperity can come,"[2] and proposed to continue them.

Although the crisis was delayed more than three months, fighting broke out in the capital on May 5th, and on the 14th American troops occupied the city of Santo Domingo.[3]

Wilson had watched these developments anxiously, and approved from time to time, often by telephone or in conversation, all the significant instructions sent by the State Department, but unquestionably the use of American troops was distasteful to him.

"It is with the deepest reluctance that I approve and authorize the course . . . proposed, but I am convinced it is the least of the evils in sight in this very perplexing situation."[4]

It was thus, in spite of his high ideals and his ambition for coöperation with all these lesser nations, that he was compelled to resort to military control in the Dominican Republic as in Haiti and Nicaragua. It was to be many

---

[1]April 20, 1915. *Ibid.*, pp. 284–285.

[2]Wilson to Jimenez, January 15, 1916, revised form of draft made by the State Department on instructions from Wilson. (Wilson to Lansing, November 17, 1915.)

[3]*Foreign Relations*, 1916, pp. 224, 227.

[4]To Lansing, November 26, 1916. The occupation was announced November 29th. One of the reasons compelling this action was the economic crisis which had resulted from the withholding of funds from the government, by the receivership, due to revolutionary conditions. (Lansing to Wilson, November 22, 1916, with enclosures. *Foreign Relations*, 1916, pp. 240–242.)

years before the debate on this policy of government by marines was to die away.

Purchase of the Danish West Indies

A further development in the Caribbean policy at this period was more satisfactory to Wilson: the purchase of the Danish West Indies.

The World War had newly impressed upon Americans the lengths to which the nations of Europe with their gigantic naval power might go. There was, specifically, the rumour and the fear that Germany might secure control of the Virgin Islands, the chief port of which, St. Thomas, was the focal point for many of the important lanes of European and American traffic to the Canal and for some of the cable lines that linked the various Caribbean islands to the United States.

On more than one occasion in past years, Denmark had been willing to sell the islands, or the United States to buy them. Negotiations in 1902 had broken down in Denmark, due, it was thought at that time, to German influence.[1] The war wrought a sharp change in the status of the matter. Their continued possession by Denmark might conceivably encourage Germany to absorb Denmark by force or by "peaceful penetration," and thus by one move improve her position in Europe and gain the desired islands. There was reason to think that Denmark appreciated this risk.[2]

As a first definite move Lansing instructed Egan, June 16, 1915, to interview the proper Danish officials.[3] Egan's

---

[1] For other attempts to negotiate, see *Foreign Relations*, 1917, pp. 457 *et seq.*

[2] Robert Lansing, "Drama of the Virgin Islands Purchase," in the New York *Times*, July 19, 1931. A confidential report to Secretary Daniels from the General Board of the Navy, dated August 1, 1914, emphatically warned that the United States would have to be on guard against the serious possibility that changes in Europe by war might bring changes in the sovereignty of possession in this hemisphere. See, for Danish attitude, *Foreign Relations*, 1917, pp. 588–590.

[3] *Ibid.*, p. 591.

reports were encouraging.[1] While the Danish minister thought that "immediate action would seem strange in time of war," he believed that "an offer generously made safeguarding the interests of the inhabitants would be seriously considered."[2]

When reflection over the commercial advantages accruing from the Canal trade began to cool the desire of the Danish government to sell, Lansing informed the Danish minister in the United States "in a general way," that "under certain conditions the United States might find it necessary to occupy the islands in case Denmark should lose sovereignty over them." Apparently the Danish authorities were left in no doubt that the United States was determined to have the islands. Wilson gave his approval to Lansing's course, declaring that he was glad that the matter had been presented to Denmark so frankly.[3]

The amount of the purchase price gave Lansing some anxiety, but the President directed that negotiations were not to be held up "on a question of money";[4] and in mid-July 1916 he directed orally that the treaty text agreeable to the Danish minister should be promptly accepted. As part of the bargain Wilson also agreed that the United States "will not object to the Danish Government extending their political and economic interests to the whole of Greenland"[5]—a provision which seemed most unlikely to cause any stir in the world, but which years later caused something of a flurry in Scandinavian relations.

The Senate of the United States consented to ratifi-

---

[1]*Ibid.*, pp. 592–595.

[2]Egan to the Secretary of State, August 19, 1915. Transmitted to Wilson by Lansing, August 21, 1915.

[3]Wilson to Lansing, December 5, 1915.

[4]Wilson to Lansing, January 7, 1916, incompletely quoted in the New York *Times*, July 19, 1931. $25,000,000 was given by the terms of the treaty.

[5]Polk to Wilson, July 27, 1916.

cation in September 1916, but the ratification of the Danish government was delayed until December 1916.[1]

Negotiations with Nicaragua

These extensions of American control in the Caribbean naturally produced some anxiety in Latin America; American activity in Central America produced more; both made increasingly difficult Wilson's plans for a Pan-American pact. Negotiation for a treaty with Nicaragua providing for a protectorate, rights to an inter-oceanic canal, and a naval base on the Gulf of Fonseca, had from the first aroused a spirit of bitter contention among the neighbouring states of Costa Rica, Salvador, and Honduras.[2]

To the suggestion that American marines be withdrawn "in order that the people down there might have an insurrection and settle the question of government for themselves," Bryan answered: ". . . nothing is to be gained by throwing the country into chaos merely to see which faction can win in the fight that would ensue."[3] Bryan— although still the anti-imperialist!—was reluctant to give up the protectorate feature. The letter in which he gave his opinion to the President, June 12, 1914, is a commentary on the irony of fate and the power of circumstance:

"We cannot escape the responsibilities of our position, and this is an opportune time for us to secure the necessary treaty provision, as we can secure it at their request."[4]

After a study of the situation, Wilson also decided that

---

[1]*Foreign Relations*, 1917, p. 688.

[2]See *Woodrow Wilson, Life and Letters*, Vol. IV, *President*, pp. 434-440.

[3]Bryan to Wilson, July 8, 1914.

[4]The State Department desired to embody if possible our peculiar political relations with all of the Central American states in formal treaties, and thus clear up uncertainties. There was no question at the State Department but that, by necessity, this region was an American "sphere of our influence." (Solicitor Cone Johnson to Lansing, December 6, 1915.)

the treaty should be "fully sustained." He wrote Bryan, June 13th:

". . . I have not at all changed my attitude with regard to the treaty itself. I think with Mr. Lansing that we perhaps give more than we get and yet in spite of its generous character I think it a wise and indeed, in the circumstances, necessary agreement."

In spite of the bitter protests of various Central American states, ratifications were exchanged, and on June 24, 1916, the treaty was proclaimed.[1]

The protesting states were naturally offended, and the fulfillment of Wilson's larger policy of promoting friendship with Latin America was obstructed.

The President's programme was thus caught between the realistic demands upon the United States as a great power facing a world war, and the difficulties that Washington had always had in dealing with the Latin-American nations—the fears and jealousies of sensitive peoples having rigid conceptions of national dignity, and, in many of the smaller republics, the inability to maintain orderly and competent governments without help.

". . . during the last three years," wrote Wilson on September 14, 1916, "I have learned to be very careful and circumspect because of what I did not at first know or suspect, namely, the very complicated and many-sided jealousies existing amongst them."

Despite these setbacks, Wilson worked ceaselessly to bind the two Americas together "in the assertion of their common rights and interests."[2] In his public addresses he

---

[1] The proclamation included the declaration that, in view of the protests of Costa Rica, Salvador and Honduras, the United States Senate had ratified "with the understanding . . . that nothing in said Convention is intended to affect any existing right of any of the said named States. . . ." *Foreign Relations*, 1916, pp. 849–852.

[2] From Article VIII of one of the late drafts of the Democratic platform for 1916 (undated).

tried to eliminate the fear and suspicion that were delaying the Pan-American pact.[1] He supported efforts to establish a "more extensive and adequate and reliable system of interchanging news between the northern and southern continents."[2] And he tried to have the treaty with Colombia ratified so as to clear up old irritations:

"The main argument for the treaty . . . is, of course, that in it we seek to do justice to Colombia and to settle a long-standing controversy which has sadly interfered with the cordial relations between the two republics. In addition to that argument which should be conclusive . . . we need now and it is possible shall need very much more in the immediate future all the friends we can attach to us in Central America, where so many of our most critical interests center."[3]

While President Wilson's course throughout was guided by far-sighted intelligence, it was interrupted by violent contrasts and upheavals of opinion in the Latin-American states. His original pronouncements on policy in 1913 promoted a wave of good feeling. The occupation of Haiti and the Dominican Republic rekindled the flame of ugly apprehensions so prevalent during the mid-nineteenth century. The proposed treaty with Colombia again cleared the air; the treaty with Nicaragua definitely darkened it. The Tampico incident awakened the sharpest suspicions; the President's acceptance of mediation by the A.B.C. powers drew warm commendation. The Pershing expedition was roundly criticized, but the final avoidance of war with Mexico renewed good feeling. Throughout it all the evident sincerity of the President's efforts to secure a Pan-American pact helped greatly to swell the credit balance.

[1] *The Public Papers of Woodrow Wilson*, Vol. IV, p. 286; Vol. V, p. 227.
[2] Letter of introduction sent by Wilson to Roy Howard, June 27, 1916.
[3] Wilson to Senator William J. Stone, February 17, 1917.

Wilson firmly and deeply believed that "the real interests of all American countries lie together and not apart,"[1]
but at a time of many revolutions and a world war he had
only partly succeeded in translating his hopes into realities.
But the groundwork for a new understanding and a better
order in this hemisphere had been laid down by the end
of 1916—in itself a notable achievement.

His greatest disappointment had been the failure of the
Pan-American pact.

". . . I must admit that I was ambitious to have the
states of the two continents of America show the way to
the rest of the world as to how to make a basis of peace."[2]

Since the Western Hemisphere would not "show the
way" the United States must pioneer alone; the pact
negotiations had taught the President much about the
diplomacy of peace.

---

[1]Wilson to Señor Don Julio Betancourt, March 22, 1917.

[2]Address to a party of Mexican editors at the White House, June 7, 1918. *The Public
Papers of Woodrow Wilson*, Vol. V, p. 227.

CHAPTER IV

STRUGGLE FOR THE NEW FREEDOM

"... If I understand the life of America, the central principle of it is this, that no small body of persons, no matter how influential, shall be trusted to determine the policy and development of America."
Address in Philadelphia, June 29, 1916.

"When we are dealing with domestic affairs ... we are dealing with things that to us as Americans are more or less calculable."
Address in Washington, May 15, 1916.

I. CRITICAL DOMESTIC REFORMS

WILSON had entered the White House with a programme for domestic reform that touched every fundamental aspect of the nation's economic life. He had worked out the programme with a clear philosophy, the heart of which was to achieve the rights and welfare of all the people. He had declared:

"The government must employ its powers and spend its money to develop a whole people and a whole continent, and at the same time keep ... its eye always on the common use and purpose, its thought constantly of what will happen to the average man and of what will be prepared for the next generation. ... We must ... think at every turn of men and women and children, of the moral life and physical force and spiritual betterment of those, all of those for whom we profess to have set government up."[1]

The New Freedom!

His earlier triumphs, and he was always best in his

---

[1]Governor Wilson's address to voters, November 1912.

gallant initial attacks, have been fully recounted in earlier chapters of this biography.[1]

Reform of business had been the first great step, and he proceeded from victory to victory—the Federal Reserve Act, the Underwood Tariff reform, the Federal Trade Commission, and the Clayton Anti-Trust Act. Protection of the rights of labour had been begun in the Sundry Civil bill, the Clayton Act, and the Seamen's Act of March 1915. Great achievements, won against the tremendous opposition of entrenched interests!

All of this earlier harvest, however, had been in fields thoroughly cultivated by the sharp instrumentalities of public discussion and controversy; but Wilson, with his far-seeing mind, intended also to attack a series of problems more fundamental than any he had yet dealt with—for example, those relating to the control of the nation's natural resources, and, more drastically, with the relationships of capital and labour. In these fields he had no such dependable antecedent support as in the earlier campaigns: and his following in Congress, however much it might trust him and his leadership, was beginning to doubt the political practicability of some of his suggestions. He was repeating the old pattern of his campaign for educational reform at Princeton—he was beginning to drive too hard and too fast.

Other difficulties also assailed him, which, so far as his personal fortunes were concerned, may have been salutary, since they prevented the stormy reaction of entrenched conservatism, so evident in the mid-term campaign of 1914, which might have defeated him in the national field as he was defeated at Princeton in 1911. These crowding difficulties were, of course, the foreign problems which forced him to turn aside from his

[1]Cf. *Woodrow Wilson, Life and Letters,* Vol. IV, *President,* pp. 357–373, and Chapters III and IV.

domestic campaign—Mexico and the Caribbean in the earlier period, and afterwards the war in Europe.

But Wilson had many of the qualities of his Scotch-Irish forbears: an obstinate determination of purpose when his mind was definitely made up. In spite of wars on two continents, he never for a moment ceased to press for the domestic legislation he considered necessary—this to the not infrequent irritation of his supporters.

Problems of the American Farmer

In his efforts in behalf of the farmer, for example, the campaign which began in the first year of his presidency was not relinquished until the middle of 1916, when the storm of the European war blackened the entire political landscape.

He had, indeed, been long interested in the improvement of country life. To him the rural part of America was "the older America," where work "does not crowd out companionship," where "impulse is not instant, hot, insistent," but steady.[1] The movement of country people to the urban centres, which had not escaped his attention, was one of the most important sociological problems in modern America. In coöperation with Secretary Houston he had instituted many executive reforms—an office of Markets and Rural Organization, measures supervising cotton exchanges, setting fair prices for grain, and providing for better warehousing and roads. A highly significant provision for education in agricultural methods was provided in the Agricultural Educational Extension Act of 1914, which in time brought thousands of trained experts into this form of national service. One of the problems he regarded as of first importance, however—that of rural credits—was most baffling, and it took years of struggle,[2]

[1] Wilson, *Constitutional Government in the United States*, pp. 118-119.
[2] See *Woodrow Wilson, Life and Letters*, Vol. IV, *President*, pp. 364-365.

reaching down into the heat of the war, before he could achieve the desired results. It was not, indeed, until July 17, 1916, that he signed the Farm Loan Act. He was delighted over the passage of this particular legislation—the first for adequate farm credits ever approved by Congress. It provided for twelve land banks which would "introduce business methods into farm finance," reduce the cost of handling farm loans, and in other ways serve the interests of the farmer. It would, he felt, "result in making agriculture more profitable and country life more comfortable and attractive, and therefore insure the retention in rural districts of an efficient and contented population."[1]

Conservation of Natural Resources

Wilson was also deeply interested in the group of problems connected with the preservation of the nation's natural resources. We had settled a virgin continent and prospered by the reckless and wasteful exploitation of timber, coal, oil, water power, and even the generous soil of our fields. To the larger part of Congress and the general public, "conservation" had always seemed something vaguely desirable but easily put off, the more so because of the extreme difficulty of accommodating public and private interests.

Wilson had asked stoutly for legislation in his first annual message:

"We must use the resources of the country, not lock them up." They must be used, "but not destroyed or wasted"; used, "but not monopolized upon any narrow idea of individual rights as against the abiding interest of communities."[2]

The House had repeatedly passed water power bills

[1]Wilson to A. F. Lever, August 11, 1916. *The Public Papers of Woodrow Wilson,* Vol. IV, p. 263.

[2]*Ibid.,* Vol. III, p. 78.

satisfactory to Wilson, but each time the Senate failed to agree. The President's papers show how frequently the matter was before him, how many letters he wrote and conferences he held in behalf of the reforms he desired, and how carefully he tried to protect the public interest at all times. In the midst of problems absorbingly difficult —the war in Europe, difficulties in Mexico, and the beginnings of his own campaign for reëlection—we find him writing:

"The matter is giving me a good deal of anxiety."[1]

And to Senator Kern, April 21, 1916:

"I think you know how deeply I am concerned to see the Myers Water Power and Ferris Leasing Bills taken up in time to assure their passage at this session of Congress. It seems to me that this is not only necessary from the point of view of the credit of the party, but . . . from the point of view of the preparation of the country to use its resources as freely as possible, and for the general development. . . ."

However, as Kern replied, there was still "a lack of interest," and Western senators were unfortunately "divided in sentiment."[2] The President made a great many efforts to set the matter forward;[3] but it was June 1920 before a water power bill was presented for his signature.

The effort to conserve the nation's oil, since it involved vast, wealthy, and powerful private interests, proved even more difficult. It was no new issue. Taft had created two Naval Oil Reserves in California, and Wilson himself had approved a third one in 1915. This was the famous Teapot Dome Reserve in Wyoming, which under the next

---

[1]To Secretary Lane, March 9, 1916.

[2]April 30, 1916.

[3]On April 12, 1918, he wrote to Representative Scott Ferris, asking to know the prospects for the Water Power bill. "You know . . . how much I should like to help if there is any way in which I can help."

Republican administration became a symbol of the notorious abuses from which Wilson had tried to protect the public.

Wilson and Lane, his Secretary of the Interior, had met in conference with mining men and conservationists early in the administration and formulated a General Leasing bill, but here again the House acted and the Senate balked. Early in 1916, when comprehensive projects for military preparedness were in the air, the President brought a new and powerful argument to bear—the need of the American navy for its essential fuel must be safeguarded.

"May I not express the earnest hope that the general development bill . . . may get its place on the calendar of the Senate? . . . The shortage of gasoline has made the development of the oil resources very important; the potash is very much needed because of our dependence hitherto upon Germany for that product; and the phosphates are required as fertilizers for our western lands. The release of these resources would seem a necessary part of our plan of preparedness. . . ."[1]

The President was impeded by sharp disagreements in his cabinet. Daniels and, to a large extent, Gregory wanted to keep the Naval Oil Reserves wholly intact for naval uses. Lane, who was from California, where the private oil interests were powerful, endorsed what he considered proper conservation, but favoured a lenient interpretation of the rights of private operators. This difference confused and retarded legislation, and on May 17th Senator Tillman wrote to Wilson asking help in reconciling the views of the two Secretaries. Wilson replied: "I am very much concerned . . . and am going to try my best to carry out your suggestion. . . ."[2] The thorny question

---

[1]Wilson to Senator John W. Kern, April 12, 1916.
[2]May 22, 1916.

was thrashed out in cabinet, but with no perceptible results.

"I know," wrote the President to Lane, "that I showed
the other day in our discussion at the Cabinet how deeply
interested I am and how much perplexed I am about the
oil question and the naval reserve in California."[1]

As time went on, the President drew increasingly closer
to Daniels and Gregory. Lane, as Secretary of the Interior,
sent over many leases of oil lands to private companies
and the President steadily refused to sign them—one of
the causes that led eventually to Lane's resignation.[2]

In the end the comprehensive plans the President had
made to meet the problems of conservation were blotted
out by the whirlwind of the war; but here again he had
laid down sound principles of public interest and had
begun the struggle which would, in future times, be carried
forward. The nation and, perhaps, the world may yet
find itself tracing back to Wilson's prophetic spirit not a
few of its accepted ideals, and to his leadership the beginnings of new ways of life.

New Immigration Policies

Other important domestic problems also engaged Wilson's serious attention, and in one of them he found himself wholly out of agreement with his Congress. This was
the regulation of foreign immigration into America.

As already pointed out, Wilson had, in the beginning,
committed himself and his party, as far as he could, to a
liberal policy. What he had in mind was not so much
restriction as selection—keeping out the physically and
mentally unfit, welcoming those sound of body and mind.

---

[1] May 26, 1916.

[2] The wisdom of this refusal was amply proved when the scandals of the Harding
administration broke.

Early in 1914 the House passed the Burnett Immigration bill, providing a "literacy test" which would exclude all foreigners who could not read some language. Such a test did not, in Wilson's view, measure character or industry or physical fitness. He wrote at once to Senator E. D. Smith:

"I told you very frankly what position I would be obliged to take on the literacy test, and I have this suggestion to make . . . Could we not substitute for that provision a provision arranging for a careful inquiry by the Government, through some proper instrumentality, as to the best plans for effecting an economic distribution of our immigrants after they arrive in this country, so as to relieve the congestion in the cities, assist the industry in the rural districts, and relieve the many problems which associate themselves with the arrival and residence here of unskilled workmen? This matter of distribution has been very much on my mind for a great many years and seems to be one of the keys to this difficult subject."[1]

One or the other House of Congress had voted many times since 1896 for a literacy test, and Wilson was courting defeat by holding the ground he chose—but there he stood until swept away by a final flood of votes.

He was not alone. Franklin MacVeagh, Jacob H. Schiff, and Charles W. Eliot argued against the literacy test. Andrew Carnegie, that able son of Scotch immigrants, who had himself learned to read and write only because of "John Knox's law which . . . required all citizens of whatever station to educate their children," wrote a moving letter based on his own experience:

"There are some foreign countries in which education does not reach the children of the poor; but my opinion is that any family which has proved itself able to save sufficient to pay the cost of migration to our country may

[1]March 5, 1914.

safely be trusted to seek their children's education here without fail."[1]

When the bill finally passed in January 1915, the President vetoed it—one of the few important vetoes of his administration:

"In two particulars of vital consequence this bill embodies a radical departure from the traditional and long-established policy of this country. . . . It seeks to all but close entirely the gates of asylum . . . and it excludes those to whom the opportunities of elementary education have been denied, without regard to their character, their purposes, or their natural capacity. . . .

"If the people of this country have made up their minds to limit the number of immigrants by arbitrary tests . . . it is their right to do so. . . . Let the platforms of parties speak out upon this policy and the people pronounce their wish. The matter is too fundamental to be settled otherwise."[2]

He continued to be determined in his support of what he regarded as a fundamental American doctrine; and vetoed the bill again, January 29, 1917.

"It is not a test of character, of quality, or of personal fitness, but would operate in most cases merely as a penalty for lack of opportunity. . . ."[3]

But this time the majority behind the bill in each House was overwhelming, and it was passed over his veto.[4] Three months later, "all aliens over sixteen years of age" who could not read English or some other language or dialect

---

[1]Carnegie to Wilson, January 23, 1915.

[2]*The Public Papers of Woodrow Wilson*, Vol. III, pp. 252–254. The Democratic platform of 1916 made no reference to immigration.

[3]*The Public Papers of Woodrow Wilson*, Vol. IV, p. 420. An additional reason for the veto was the provision that exemptions from the test based on religious persecution in the country of last permanent residence "might lead to very delicate and hazardous diplomatic situations."

[4]February 5, 1917. *Cong. Rec.*, 64–2, pp. 2456–2457, 2629.

became, with certain exceptions, subject to rejection as immigrants.[1]

The Tariff Board

In what he considered a clear matter of principle—such as was involved in the immigration question—Wilson could be immovable. But where no real principle was at stake, his mind was often, as he himself put it, "to let." The demand which had grown up in the country for a tariff board to investigate facts regarding international trade in order to guide business during and after the war furnishes a case in point. Wilson at first opposed such a commission; it seemed to him unnecessary, and he feared also, because of the vast private interests involved, that it would become a political instrument.[2] But the persistence of the agitation set him to thinking. Secretary Houston advocated it, and in December 1915 Professor F. W. Taussig, whose judgment Wilson greatly respected, expressed his views in a long memorandum.[3] The various arguments were carefully studied by the President, and he was finally convinced that a tariff commission was really desirable.[4]

He announced his support in January 1916:

"... I have changed my mind.[5] ... There is going on in the world under our eyes an economic revolution. No man understands that revolution; no man has the elements of it clearly in his mind. No part of the business of legislation

---

[1]The bill was the forerunner of the more severe immigration measures of the 1920s.

[2]Wilson to M. A. Matthews, August 17, 1915; and Houston, *Eight Years With Wilson's Cabinet*, Vol. I, pp. 196–197.

[3]Sent by Taussig to Houston, December 17, 1915, thence transmitted to Wilson. Taussig did not advocate, however, "a brand new independent tariff commission," but rather the creation "within the existing framework" of a "body of permanent non-partisan . . . officials."

[4]Wilson to Kitchin, January 24, 1916.

[5]Certain Republicans of course did not overlook the opportunity to ridicule the President's shift of opinion. See, for example, *Cong. Rec.*, 64–1, pp. 10529 *et seq.*

with regard to international trade can be undertaken until we do understand it . . ."[1]

Congress enacted the measure for a Tariff Commission as a part of the Revenue bill, and Wilson signed it September 8, 1916.[2] He found difficulty, however, in securing the right men as members.

"I am a little at sea yet just where to turn for non-partisan members of the Tariff Board," he wrote.

"For I want *non*-partisan members if I can find them, rather than bi-partisan . . ."[3]

Professor Taussig was finally chosen as chairman;[4] and the work of the commission soon won Wilson's warm admiration.

In all these great measures Wilson's sound legal knowledge stood him in good stead; but he used that knowledge with a penetrating understanding of social change. He would make law "a rule, but not an interdict; a living guide, but not a blind and rigid discipline." Perhaps this view of law is one of the elements that has given such vitality to Wilson's ideas down the years.

The Adamson Act

Finally, reference must here be made to what was probably Wilson's most courageous handling of a profoundly difficult domestic problem. This was his method of dealing with the tremendous upheaval, during the crucial period of American neutrality, of railroad employees seeking an eight-hour day.[5]

---

[1] *The Public Papers of Woodrow Wilson*, Vol. IV, p. 10. He did not expect the tariff to be taken wholly out of politics by this expert commission, he told the author, May 11, 1916, because it was "a form of taxation." (Author's notes, made at the time.)

[2] *U. S. Statutes at Large*, Vol. 39, Pt. I, pp. 795–798.

[3] To Representative J. W. Alexander, August 10, 1916.

[4] Other members were Daniel C. Roper, vice-chairman, David J. Lewis, William Kent, E. P. Costigan, and W. S. Culbertson.

[5] A subject also treated in the chapter on the campaign of 1916, in which it played a considerable part. See this volume, Chapter VII, pp. 268–269.

Agitation by the railroad workers had begun in January 1916: by the middle of the summer, in the midst of Wilson's campaign for reëlection, the struggle between employers and employees had reached a deadlock.

In August the President called union leaders and railroad executives to confer with him in Washington. He proposed that the eight-hour day be substituted for "the present ten-hour day in all the existing practices and agreements"; and that other questions be postponed until a commission could study the subject and report to Congress, after which either side could terminate the agreement. The unions accepted; the executives refused. Wilson then reported to the public. The eight-hour day was "right," he said, and had "the sanction of the judgment of society in its favor."[1]

Ten days later, after a series of conferences, the executives confirmed their opposition. On the morning of August 29th a dramatic interview took place at the White House. Eight railroad presidents were there:

". . . they were shown into one of the long reception rooms which was darkened by the blinds being closely drawn to exclude the almost torrid heat of the sun. Suddenly at one end of the room a portiere was drawn back, disclosing the President standing in bright sunlight, clad in a summer suit of white duck."

The President, believing that "the whole spirit of the time and the preponderant evidence of recent economic experience spoke for the eight-hour day,"[2] and that the interests of society warranted it, made a speech lasting scarcely five minutes, in which he made it clear that he held the managers responsible for the tragedy that might

---

[1] Public statement, August 19, 1916. *The Public Papers of Woodrow Wilson*, Vol. IV, pp. 264–266.

[2] *Ibid.*, pp. 268–269.

result from a nation-wide tie-up. When they were alone, one of the dazed railroad men asked:

"What in hell does he mean?"

"I suppose," answered another, "he means it is up to us to settle the strike."[1]

Wilson left no doubt as to his determination. He went to Congress the same day, asking for the immediate establishment of an eight-hour day as the legal basis for work and wages on the railroads, and provision for "full public investigation of the merits" of such disputes in the future:

"These things I urge upon you, not in haste or merely as a means of meeting a present emergency, but as permanent and necessary additions to the law of the land . . . The time and the occasion only give emphasis to their importance."[2]

The result was the Adamson bill, signed just before the strike was to begin: September 3, 1916.

The championship of this advanced social legislation was one of the boldest acts in Wilson's career. His re-election was in fact jeopardized by the anger of business interests; but his stand was consistent with his personal belief: "Where the individual should be indomitable is in the choice of direction . . ."[3] Progress for labour lay in the direction of better working conditions. The President's policy was sound, not only in the light of later developments in the same direction, but in the support it received from the Supreme Court, which passed favourably on the law in March 1917.

Wilson was often and sharply criticized, in sponsoring such advanced legislation as this, for being a "radical"

[1]See the account in Winthrop M. Daniels' *American Railroads*, pp. 84–87. A nation-wide strike had been called, to begin in case of the failure of negotiations, on September 4th.

[2]*The Public Papers of Woodrow Wilson*, Vol. IV, p. 274.

[3]*Ibid.*, Vol. II, p. 185. (November 2, 1909.)

and seeking "radical changes." He met this criticism vigorously:

". . . I do not think that it can justly be said that the tendencies of the Democratic party are radical or that I have assisted in making them so. If by radical you mean that a constant attempt is being made on the part of Democratic leaders to keep the legislative action of the country abreast of the extraordinary changes of time and circumstance, I can only say that I see no other way to keep the law adjusted to fact and to the actual economic and personal relations of our society. But radicalism is a matter of spirit rather than form and I believe that the truest conservatism consists in constant adaptation.

"I am distressed that you should think that tendencies exist which you cannot acquiesce in."[1]

It will thus be seen that Woodrow Wilson pioneered, not only in the statement of principles, but in the effort to secure action regarding most of the great economic and social problems which have since shaken our institutions to their foundations, the solution of which is still upon the lap of the gods.

II. WILSON AND THE SUPREME COURT

Woodrow Wilson's appointment of Louis Dembitz Brandeis to the United States Supreme Court on January 28, 1916, was the occasion of one of the bitterest struggles for senatorial confirmation in the annals of American politics. It raised, if it did not settle, many of the vital questions concerning the powers of that exalted body and the relationships of its members not merely to the legal issues in question, but to the burning new problems of American economic and social progress.

Wilson had come to the presidency with settled con-

---

[1]Wilson to John B. Knox, October 30, 1916.

victions regarding the place of the Supreme Court in the
American system, and the kind of men who should be
chosen to exercise the vast power implicit in its decisions.
Much of his earlier academic life had been devoted to an
objective study of the historical origins of the Constitution
and the organization of the governmental institutions
which grew out of it. He had lectured and written for
many years upon these subjects and was recognized as one
of the foremost authorities in the field. The book in which
he finally drew together the results of his ripest thought,
Constitutional Government in the United States, was published in 1908, long before he entered the political arena.

In this treatise he declares that the courts are "the
instruments of the nation's growth." The interpretation of
the Constitution in its strict letter would prove "a strait-
jacket, a means not of liberty and development, but of
mere restriction and embarrassment." Judges must therefore be statesmen with "a large vision of things to come";
for "it is true," as he says, "that their power is political."

"The atmosphere of opinion cannot be shut out of
their court rooms"—but the judges must "prove themselves such men as can discriminate between the opinion
of the moment and the opinion of the age, between the
opinion which springs, a legitimate essence, from the enlightened judgment of men of thought and good conscience, and the opinion of desire, of self-interest, of
impulse and impatience."[1]

Wilson's first appointment to the Supreme Court Bench
was that of James C. McReynolds. McReynolds had been
Attorney General in his cabinet, appointed somewhat

[1]Pp. 167–168, 172. In an inscription which Wilson wrote for a presentation copy of
this book he says of the Constitution:
"The constitution of the United States, like the constitution of every living state,
grows and is altered by force of circumstances and change in affairs. The effect of a
written constitution is only to render the growth more subtle, more studious, more
conservative, more a thing of carefully, almost unconsciously, wrought sequences.
Our statesmen must, in the midst of origination, have the spirit of lawyers "

hastily, largely upon Colonel House's recommendation. He was known as an able lawyer and, because he had taken a notable part in the prosecution of the tobacco trust, had seemed to be a "progressive"—at that time the President's chief test in making his choices for office. Wilson had never known him personally. After serving for about a year and a half in the cabinet, Wilson appointed him to the Supreme Court, August 19, 1914, and he was promptly confirmed by the Senate, August 29th. He soon became a thoroughgoing strict constructionist, a conservative of the conservatives, and Wilson later considered that the appointment had been a great mistake.[1]

When it became necessary, after the death of Justice Joseph R. Lamar in January 1916, to appoint a new member of the Court, the President determined upon Louis D. Brandeis, who was a boldly constructive liberal in his views, with an unusual grasp of the economic problems that confronted the nation.

Brandeis' parents, who were Jewish in origin, had been among the choice group of refugees who had migrated to America because of the political oppression in Germany which culminated in 1848. They had settled in Louisville, Kentucky, where Brandeis was born in 1856. He was a brilliant student, graduating from the Harvard Law School so young in years that the rules were suspended to permit the granting of his degree. He had had a notable career both as a lawyer and as a student of affairs, with a statesmanlike interest in progressive legislation. He had demanded reforms in the control of transportation and public utilities and had been a consistent enemy of monopoly and "bigness." In his work as "the people's attorney" he had earned the bitter hostility of the so-called "privileged interests."

Wilson had early been strongly attracted to Brandeis.

---

[1] As he told the author.

They were kindred in spirit: both had constructive as well as critical minds, and both knew what it meant to be pilloried by relentless opponents. After he became President—and even before—Wilson had sought the counsel of Brandeis on trust legislation, currency, and labour problems.[1] In spite of bitter opposition, he had wanted him for his Attorney General in 1913, before McReynolds was appointed.[2]

When the nomination of Brandeis was announced, a cry of "radicalism" at once went up. Preposterous attacks were made, not only upon the candidate's record, but upon his personal honour. A Senate inquiry, which began hearings February 9th, lasted intermittently for months. Its reports contribute highly interpretive glimpses of the battleground in the American struggle for greater social justice: the bitterness of the opposing forces and the unscrupulous lengths to which some of the opponents of a liberal court were willing to go.[3]

The President, although great pressure was exerted upon him, never for a moment faltered in his support. He wrote to Senator Owen on February 7th:

"I believe the nomination was the wisest that could possibly have been made, and I feel that few things have arisen more important to the country or to the party than the matter of his confirmation."

In March ex-President Taft and six other former presidents of the American Bar Association, including Elihu Root and Moorfield Story, protested against the appointment.[4]

---

[1]See *The Life and Letters of Woodrow Wilson*, Vol. III, *Governor*, p. 398; Vol. IV, *President*, pp. 163, 357–358, 366.

[2]*Ibid.*, Vol. III, pp. 450–451.

[3]Vicious attacks in such a matter as this were, however, not unknown: witness the confirmations of Marshall, Story, Taney, and Matthews. *Cong. Rec.*, 64–1, pp. 9049–9050. Railroads, public service corporations and allied banking interests fought the appointment to the bitter end.

[4]New York *Times*, March 15, 1916.

The President entered more directly into the struggle in May by writing a vigorous letter to Senator Culberson defending Brandeis and urging his appointment.[1]

In this letter the President did not spare Brandeis' critics; he declared that the opposition had come "for the most part from those who hated Mr. Brandeis because he had refused to be serviceable to them in the promotion of their own selfish interests, and from those whom they had prejudiced and misled. . . .

"He is a friend of all just men and a lover of the right; and he knows more than how to talk about the right—he knows how to set it forward in the face of its enemies."

Not only was he, as Chief Justice Fuller had said of him, "the ablest man who ever appeared before the Supreme Court of the United States" and "absolutely fearless in the discharge of his duties"; he was a "friend of justice and of men."

Brandeis represented the "statesmanship of adaptation" which as a scholar, in earlier days, Wilson had considered necessary to the preservation of the Court,[2] and he hoped by this appointment to add to popular confidence in the Court through the liberalization of its decisions.

The struggle in the Senate resolved itself into a contest between conservatives and liberals. Similar opposition was going on at the same time to another of Wilson's liberal appointments. For a year and more he had sought to place George Rublee on the Federal Trade Commission.[3] The Senate had been against confirmation

---

[1]This letter throws so much light upon the controversy and is in itself so interesting as a disclosure of Wilson's character and thought that it should be read in full. It is printed in *The Public Papers of Woodrow Wilson*, Vol. IV, pp. 160–164.

[2]*Constitutional Government in the United States*, p. 168.

[3]George Rublee was an able and experienced lawyer whose independence of mind appealed strongly to Wilson. He served on the Federal Trade Commission, through a recess appointment, from March 5, 1915, to September 1916.

chiefly through the objection of one man, Senator Gallinger, a Republican from New Hampshire, a "dyed-in-the-wool conservative," who could not, as Wilson wrote on May 12th, "allege anything" showing unfitness for the position.

"Our whole fortune in the coming election depends upon whether we gain . . . the confidence of the independent voters, and I could not imagine anything that would be more likely to defeat us than the rejection of such nominations as this and that of Mr. Brandeis."[1]

Confirmation of Brandeis' appointment was finally voted on June 1st, more than four months after the submission, the Senate dividing closely upon party lines.[2]

Wilson was greatly pleased.

"I never signed any commission with such satisfaction . . ."[3]

And on June 7th he wrote exultantly to E. P. Davis:

"I am going to see the new Justice today and tell him how happy it makes me to see him on the great court."

Wilson was to make one more appointment to the Supreme Court, that of John H. Clarke on July 14, 1916. He chose him, as he wrote on July 18th, because he could be depended upon for a "liberal and enlightened interpretation" of the law.

When Clarke resigned in September 1922 to devote his life to forwarding the cause of world peace, Wilson wrote him a letter expressing his regret. It was after he had retired from the presidency and is significant in expressing prophetically his views, as an observer of unequalled experience, upon the dangers incident to the exercise of

---

[1] To Senator Atlee Pomerene.

[2] Newlands (Democrat) voted nay; La Follette, Norris, and Poindexter (Republican) voted yea. New York *Times*, June 2, 1916. But the confirmation of Rublee was lost. "I think his rejection," wrote Wilson to Norman Hapgood, "was one of the worst pieces of business the Senate has engaged in in our time . . ." (July 7, 1916.)

[3] Wilson to Morgenthau, June 5, 1916.

power confided by the American people to the Supreme Court:

"Like thousands of other liberals throughout the country, I have been counting on the influence of you and Justice Brandeis to restrain the Court in some measure from the extreme reactionary course which it seems inclined to follow. . . .

"The most obvious and immediate danger to which we are exposed is that the courts will more and more outrage the common people's sense of justice and cause a revulsion against judicial authority which may seriously disturb the equilibrium of our institutions, and I see nothing which can save us from this danger if the Supreme Court is to repudiate liberal courses of thought and action."

CHAPTER V

CRISIS IN WILSON'S LEADERSHIP

"I would a great deal rather know what they are talking about around quiet firesides all over this country than what they are talking about in the cloakrooms of Congress."

Address at a Gridiron Dinner, February 26, 1916.

"America ought to keep out of this war. She ought to keep out of this war at the sacrifice of everything except this single thing upon which her character and history are founded, her sense of humanity and justice."

Ibid.

"Valor is self-respecting. Valor is circumspect. Valor strikes only when it is right to strike."

Ibid.

I. EXPLORING THE POSSIBILITIES OF MEDIATION

IF IT is the genius of the astute statesman to seize the direction of movements he cannot prevent, Wilson had succeeded notably, during the winter of 1915–1916, in going to the country upon the preparedness programme. He had become its spokesman and leader—able to quiet extreme opposition and, by frank coöperation with Congress, to secure legislation that would be approved by the nation.

He was to find the problem of leadership in the peace movement, which in the fall of 1915 had begun to be widespread and clamorous, a far more difficult undertaking. Preparedness was as much a domestic problem as Federal Reserve legislation; he knew exactly how to handle it; but the problem of mediation in the bloody conflict in Europe involved vast issues, imponderable elements, wholly beyond the control of America. There was no ready political method of approach, no international congress in which to test the issue and pass the law. To meet such a situation there was need for a supreme display of all the resources of that statesmanship which functions in the inchoate field of diplomacy, wherein Wilson was as yet little skilled compared with the practised leadership of Europe.

He knew well that, if he did not lead, other agencies were determined upon action which might conceivably get out of hand and forestall or confuse a real opportunity for mediation.

In the spring of 1915, for example, a woman's peace organization had sent a delegation to Europe headed by Jane Addams, probably the foremost, certainly the best-loved, American leader in social reform. Bryan, wholly relieved of official responsibility, expanding in his own most effective field of evangelism, was not only carrying on a peace campaign in America, but was proposing to go to Europe. In December, Henry Ford's astonishing expedition sailed away, amid the jeers of critics, to "get the boys out of the trenches by Christmas."

These extremist movements were tempered by a far more constructive enterprise headed by President Lowell of Harvard and ex-President Taft. The League to Enforce Peace, organized at Philadelphia in June, began to awaken widespread interest and discussion.

Peace activities in general represented a tremendous weight of opinion, probably deepest seated in the West and South. Although in part emotional and ill-informed, the movement was sincere: and it had votes.

While the President had been drawn with reluctance into the campaign for preparedness, he was from the beginning ardently in sympathy with the spirit that actuated all of these peace movements. He longed to give

America the opportunity of being the "mediating Nation of the world."[1] In the days of his struggle for self-mastery after receiving news of the *Lusitania's* fate, he had said, in explaining his wish to avoid war:

"My earnest hope and fervent prayer has been that America could withhold herself . . . and at the right time offer herself as the only mediating influence to bring about peace."[2]

He had referred, in the "too proud to fight" speech, to peace as the "healing and elevating influence of the world."[3]

But the problem of the idealist in office, unlike the idealist at large, is forever one of method and of occasion. He cannot talk to the stars: he must work in harness. Every word is an act: every act a kind of destiny. From the beginning we have seen Wilson struggling with the hows and the whens of the great problem of mediation. In the first two days of the war there was sharp diversity of opinion among his advisers as to whether he should tender the good offices of the United States to the infuriated nations—and how and when. He tendered them immediately.

The same disparity of advice, as we have seen, had continued. One group demanded immediate, positive, and public action on the part of the United States either with or without the coöperation of other neutral nations. Bryan and many other sincere advocates of peace urged this course. The opposing group advised caution and preferred private negotiation. Colonel House and Secretary Lansing, who were the President's closest advisers, strongly supported this view. Page in London was opposed to any peace talk whatsoever.

---

[1] *The Public Papers of Woodrow Wilson*, Vol. III, p. 304.
[2] Joseph P. Tumulty, *Woodrow Wilson As I Know Him*, p. 234.
[3] *The Public Papers of Woodrow Wilson*, Vol. III, p. 321.

Wilson, guided from the beginning by his determination not to become involved in the war, and hoping that skillful negotiation would preserve our neutrality until the warring nations were ready for peace, tended to pursue the cautious course. He hoped to avoid what he considered the hasty decision which had driven Madison into the War of 1812.

In the meantime, as we have seen, our neutrality, however he might seek to base it upon legal sanctions, was proving to be unequal in its bearing upon the belligerents. We were attempting to hold Germany severely to the observance of traditional rules for the treatment of merchant ships in her submarine operations—by which she strove to retaliate against the blockade- -while tolerating with ineffective protests the violation of established rules by the British. On almost all questions of neutrality—sale of munitions and their carriage on passenger ships, loans and shipments of food—the rulings were to Germany's disadvantage. This course, dictated in part by uncompromising conceptions of American rights and in part by economic interests and compulsions, may have been inevitable; but it was slowly and surely, despite the President's determination to avoid entanglements, forcing the United States toward war with Germany.[1]

In this increasingly critical situation the President was not only recommending military preparedness: he was

---

[1] As a matter of fact, Wilson's policy of neutrality was never strictly legalistic. How could it have been with the antiquated international rules that had existed in 1914? He himself clearly recognized the situation. As he wrote to Bryan on April 5, 1915:

"We must compound policy with legal right in wise proportions, no doubt."

Where accepted sanctions did not exist, he had to feel his way. Writing to Lansing (September 10, 1915), he remarked that "what we are guided by is our sense of what is just and right and not our sensibility as regards what other nations think about us."

Where there was no organization or instrumentality for developing world opinion as to what was "just and right," judgment upon the part of any one nation, however disinterested, or any one leader, however prescient, was open to question. Savage, *Policy of the United States Toward Maritime Commerce in War*, Vol. II, pp. 293, 383.

more than ever seeking some new opening toward peace. Peace alone would solve all his problems.

But when and how?

In August a group of prominent pacifists, among whom were such well-known leaders as Jane Addams and Lillian D. Wald, presented a memorial to Secretary Lansing.[1] It was a demand for the immediate initiation of a peace movement by the United States as the natural leader of the neutral nations. An unofficial committee having the President's sanction should be instituted, which should make and revise propositions, "coming back again and again, if necessary, until a basis may be reached upon which actual negotiations looking toward peace could begin."

Lansing declined to make any comment upon the memorial, merely forwarding it to the President. Wilson returned it next day with a note saying:

"Have [you] . . . any opinion about this proposal that you would be willing to express to me? I ask because I know these good people are not going to let the matter rest until they bring it to a head in one way or another. I must, I suppose, be prepared to say either Yay or Nay."[2]

Lansing, in his reply, disagreed with the premises of the argument:

"I do not believe that it is true that the civil leaders of the belligerents would at the present time look with favor on action by the neutral nations; and, even if they did, the military branches of the belligerent governments dominate the situation, and, they favor a continuance of the war."

The Central Powers, he said, would demand territorial and financial compensation on the basis of their military

---

[1]August 6, 1915, by the hand of O. G. Villard.

[2]Written on the President's own typewriter.

success; while the Allies would hold out in the confidence of ultimately turning the tide. He concluded:

"Holding these views I would strongly favor discouraging any neutral movement toward peace at the present time, because I believe it would fail and because, if it did fail, we would lose our influence for the future."[1]

Wilson responded on August 19th:

". . . I entirely agree . . ."

The President, in short, considered that this direct and persistent approach was not the best method of reaching the ends which he himself desired quite as much as did the memorialists who signed the petition.

Colonel House, devoted to secret negotiation, had also douched the efforts of the pacifists with the coldest of cold water. After Jane Addams returned from Europe in July, House wrote the President scornfully:

"Jane Addams . . . has accumulated a wonderful lot of misinformation in Europe. She saw von Jagow, Grey and many others and for one reason or another, they were not quite candid with her so she has a totally wrong impression."[2]

Later in August the advocates of immediate peace activity tried to appeal to the President again through Professor Emily G. Balch and Dr. Aletta Jacobs, who were interested in a woman's peace conference at The Hague. Wilson referred them to Lansing,[3] who gave them an unsympathetic reception, and to House, who "tried to show them how utterly impracticable their plan was,

---

[1] August 18, 1915. This reason, which House and Lansing continually advanced—that we must keep our influence strong by never moving toward mediation until success was guaranteed—was throughout the basic cause for Wilson's hesitation in acting publicly for peace.

[2] July 17, 1915. But had Grey and others been "quite candid" with House? Only three weeks later he wrote to Page, virtually admitting that the British had been playing a game with him since the previous autumn by putting off American activity in behalf of peace. August 4, 1915. See *The Intimate Papers of Colonel House*, Vol. II, pp. 60–62.

[3] The President received Professor Balch on August 18th.

while evidencing the deepest sympathy with their general purpose."[1]

That scorn of any direct movement because of the opposition of the leaders of the warring nations was not wholly warranted appears in a letter from Grey to House on August 26th:

"I have said that no one could resent any efforts of neutrals which were impartial and independent to promote peace, but I did not think a Conference of neutrals would be of much use unless the United States was in it.

"If the end of this war is arrived at through mediation, I believe it must be through that of the United States."[2]

While it is clear that Wilson believed that the most hopeful approach was by diplomatic channels, wherein he agreed with House and Lansing, he gave indications of his impatience at the prolonged delay. A ray of hope in one of House's letters led him to write:

"How does his [Laughlin's] suggestion that you might get a readier hearing now than you got when you were over there before impress you?"[3]

In the meantime there was widespread discussion, growing out of the League to Enforce Peace movement, as to the ultimate terms of the peace. The idea of an organization or league of nations, which was nothing new, and which the President himself had envisioned much earlier, was advanced from various quarters.[4]

[1]Colonel House's diary entry, September 1, 1915. *The Intimate Papers of Colonel House*, Vol. II, p. 94.

[2]*Ibid.*, p. 88. We do not know, for certain, that this letter was forwarded to the President.

[3]August 25, 1915. Irwin Laughlin was Ambassador Page's secretary, a man of excellent judgment.

[4]Paul S. Reinsch, Minister to China, among some peace suggestions sent to Wilson on January 4, 1915, included the idea "that the organization of civilized society be strengthened by providing The Hague Court with an executive supported by the armies and navies of the Allied Powers." Wilson answered on February 8th that these suggestions "have made a permanent impression on me." The platform of the League to Enforce Peace, adopted June 17th, contained a clear-cut plank:
"We believe it to be desirable for the United States to join a league of nations . . ."

In a remarkable letter to House, written August 10th, Grey revealed that he was thinking of a league which would give the nations a tool for preventing future wars:

"My own mind revolves more and more about the point that the refusal of a Conference was the fatal step that decided peace or war last year, and about the moral to be drawn from it: which is that the pearl of great price, if it can be found, would be some League of Nations that could be relied on to insist that disputes between any two nations must be settled by the arbitration, mediation, or conference of others. International Law has hitherto had no sanction. The lesson of this war is that the Powers must bind themselves to give it a sanction. If that can be secured, freedom of the seas and many other things will become easy."[1]

This letter, while containing reservations regarding the settlement of the present war,[2] strongly arrested the President's attention. He was fully aware of the growing interest in America: here was the highest confirmation of similar thinking abroad. In his letter to House of September 22nd, Grey bluntly put the question as to how far the United States would go in this direction:

"... To me, the great object of securing the elimination of militarism and navalism is to get security for the future against aggressive war. How much are the United States prepared to do in this direction? Would the President

---

[1] Sent to Wilson on August 30th. Grey had prepared the way for such a suggestion by the following lines in his letter to House, July 14, 1915:

"I see that it will naturally take very great provocation to force your people into war. If they do go to war, I believe it is certain that the influence of the United States on the larger aspects of the final conditions of peace will prevail, and I am very doubtful whether anything short of being actually involved in the war will stir your people sufficiently to make them exercise, or enable the President to exercise, on the terms of peace all the influence that is possible. Personally, I feel that the influence of the President would be used to secure objects essential to future peace that we all desire." *The Intimate Papers of Colonel House*, Vol. II, p. 55.

[2] "... it is not a fair proposition that there should be a guarantee of the freedom of the seas while Germany claims to recognize no law but her own on land, and to have the right to make war at will."

propose that there should be a League of Nations binding
themselves to side against any Power which broke a
treaty; which broke certain rules of warfare on sea or
land (such rules would, of course, have to be drawn up
after this war); or which refused, in case of dispute, to
adopt some other method of settlement than that of war?
Only in some such agreement do I see a prospect of
diminishing militarism and navalism in future, so that no
nation will build up armies or navies for aggressive purposes. I cannot say which Governments would be prepared
to accept such a proposal, but I am sure that the Government of the United States is the only Government that
could make it with effect. . . ."[1]

It is difficult to make out from the documents exactly
what followed.[2] It appears that the President and House
discussed not merely Grey's proposal regarding an ultimate basis of settlement—at that time a more or less
academic subject, the discussion of which might easily
further the British policy of delay—but some early means
of stopping the war then raging. For the dangers were
steadily increasing: hatred, fanned by propaganda, was
everywhere spreading.[3] Not only were American pacifist
societies extremely active, but on September 2nd Wilson
had had a solemn visit from the foremost Catholic prelate
in America, Cardinal Gibbons, urging some peace movement. In October the German execution of the British
nurse Edith Cavell as a spy sent a shock throughout the
nation. In short, was not the time arriving when the
United States, which had hitherto merely offered its good

---

[1] *The Intimate Papers of Colonel House*, Vol. II, p. 89. Grey avoided the direct suggestion that the United States should enter such a league.

[2] President Wilson made no notes of the conversations with Colonel House. One
must usually depend upon the diary of Colonel House, naturally a report of but one
view of what occurred.

[3] Although ninety per cent of the people, wrote House to Walter H. Page on August
4th, wanted to stay out of the war.

offices, should *demand*, in the name of the neutral world and of humanity, that the war be stopped?

Accordingly, Colonel House drew up an encouraging reply to Grey's letter of September 22nd, which he submitted to Wilson on October 17th.

In this proposed letter he asserted that "the time may soon come when this Government should intervene between the belligerents and demand that peace parleys begin upon the broad basis of the elimination of militarism and navalism. . . ." He went on to express the idea that peace should be brought about by the Allies "with the aid of the United States." As for the programme, whenever Grey considered that the time was propitious for his mediation, he, House, was to propose it to the President, who might send him abroad to settle the details. After completing arrangements in England, he would go and notify Germany of "the President's purpose to intervene and stop this destructive war, provided the weight of the United States thrown on the side that accepted our proposal could do it." He would try to get Germany to accept by giving her to understand that the Allies would reject the proposed settlement, but if "the Central Powers were still obdurate, it would probably [this word was later inserted by Wilson] be necessary for us to join the Allies and force the issue."[1]

Here was a proposal, with a vengeance, for prompt action—even to the point, as the Colonel interpreted it, of carrying the United States into the war—to be worked out by secret diplomacy, with House himself the diplomat!

"I would not let Berlin know, of course, of any understanding had with the Allies, but would rather lead them to think our proposal would be rejected by the Allies."

---

[1] *The Intimate Papers of Colonel House*, Vol. II, pp. 90–91. House added: "I would have made this proposal to the President last autumn [1914], but you will remember that it was not agreeable to the Allies."

Obviously the President, who above everything in the world wanted peace, saw in the plan a method of exploring the possibilities of American mediation. He knew well enough that he alone could not promise to go to war upon any contingency whatsoever. He knew the immense preliminary preparation that would be necessary to secure acceptance of war by the American people or by Congress. He was even then beginning his struggle, which he knew would be difficult and protracted, for the mildest, most hesitant military preparedness. He knew, with the knowledge of the astute politician, the immense anti-war sentiment in America. Bryan and the pacifists were no joke!

In returning House's letter in which, as House remarks, he "seemed to acquiesce by silence"—after twenty minutes of discussion![1]—the President had inserted the one word "probably" which, although he called the change "unimportant," "verbal," profoundly changed the commitment.[2]

Undoubtedly he regarded House's private efforts at this time exactly as he had on previous occasions, as a legitimate exploration of possibilities. If House could really get definite and reliable proposals from either side—it did not matter much what they were—an opening toward mediation might be developed. He would then have something concrete to submit to his cabinet and to the experts of the State Department. After that he would have to prepare the country and Congress for such action as might be necessary. House could try out the situation,

---

[1]House himself observes that he "had no time to push it further," that "our entire conversation did not last longer than twenty minutes."

[2]Wilson's written response was as follows: "I have made one or two unimportant verbal changes in this, but they do not alter the sense of it. I do not want to make it inevitable quite, that we should take part to force terms on Germany, because the exact circumstances of such a crisis are impossible to determine. The letter is altogether right. I pray God it may bring results." (October 18, 1915.) The author is much indebted to Colonel House for a copy of this and numerous other private letters written by the President, of which no records were found among Mr. Wilson's own papers.

but his own action beyond mediation was to be governed by the potent word "probably."

Here, as with House's former "mission," there seems to have been no clear, sharp understanding between the two men. It was House's practice to approve everything, or almost everything, the President said: and Wilson assumed that House completely understood his mind. He could say that the letter House submitted was "altogether right" without any discussion whatsoever of the meaning of "intervention" or "force" or of the momentous change wrought by the insertion of his word "probably." And all along, as we shall see, there was a continual failure to secure a genuine and frank meeting of minds as to what was to be said or done. It was the fatal flaw in their relationship, and led to infinite confusion and thwarted effort. It was Wilson's lifelong error to suppose that men whom he accepted as his friends—sorely needed intimate friends—not only loved him, but understood completely his clear and swift-running mind, and agreed with him in all things. It had been the flaw in the friendship with Hibben at Princeton.

Apparently House saw the plan essentially as follows. In consultation with the British and French, he was to arrange a set of terms as a basis of peace parleys sufficiently restricted to appear moderate, yet sufficiently drastic to make Germany's acceptance practically a capitulation. If, as was to be expected, she refused to accept, the United States would join the Allies against her. Germany was to be consulted only after all the plans were complete. It was a scheme as different as possible from such proposals as those of Bryan, who would have appealed openly to both sides to lay their cards on the table, permit a comparison of their aims, and demonstrate their real willingness for a reasonable peace.[1] We were still

---

[1] In appealing to the belligerents for their peace terms on December 18, 1916, the President approached closely to the essence of Mr. Bryan's suggestion.

technically neutral, still supposedly seeking a just peace, and yet, under House's scheme, we were practically to conspire with one side to arrange terms that would mean defeat or at least a disadvantageous peace to the other side. Clear-headed Sir Edward Grey was in no doubt about the matter after discussing the specific terms with House. It was "certain," he wrote, "that Germany would refuse anything like the terms suggested."

"The American terms were, it is true, not the terms that the Allies would regard as those of victory, but for Germany they were the terms of positive defeat."[1]

One immediate result of House's proposal was to convince the Allied leaders still further of the favourable disposition of the Washington administration—and even that, sooner or later, we should be coming into the war on their side. And this, of course, tended to nullify the force of the President's arguments with Great Britain over any and all of the problems of blockade.[2]

House's letter of October 17th to Grey was so vaguely framed and so little an answer to Grey's of September 22nd proposing action regarding a league of nations that Grey cabled House on November 9th:

"What is the proposal of the elimination of militarism and navalism that you contemplate? Is it that suggested in fourth paragraph of letter to you of September 22nd?"

The paragraph referred to contained Grey's proposal regarding a league of nations. House suggested to Wilson that he reply:

"Yes, the proposal contemplated is broadly speaking

---

[1]Viscount Grey, *Twenty-five Years*, Vol. II, p. 134.

[2]The Germans, as we have seen, had hoped that our note of October 21st, regarding the British blockade, would result in some concessions by their enemies to counterbalance those which they had made. Bernstorff, with the clearing of the *Arabic* crisis, pressed for the exercise of America's good offices in advancing the ideal of the "freedom of the seas" which played such a part in his dealings with House and in the *Lusitania* correspondence. But when he called on House on October 30th he received no encouragement.

along the lines mentioned in fourth paragraph of your letter to me of September 22nd."

House concluded a further argument in favour of American participation in a league of nations with one of the ingratiating comments so familiar in his letters to Wilson:

"This is the part I think you are destined to play in this world tragedy, and it is the noblest part that has ever come to a son of man."[1]

Wilson replied in a telegram:

"Message approved. You might even omit words 'broadly speaking' and say merely 'along the lines of.'"

And the next day, the 11th, he wrote that the paragraph of Grey's letter under discussion "contains the *necessary* programme."

It was thus that the President, although the vision had long been in his mind, adopted the idea of a league of nations as a *policy* underlying any future programme of world peace; but there was as yet no specific mention of the entrance of the United States into such a league.

In these exchanges with Grey, it is to be noted, there was no reference at all to House's plan for forcing an immediate peace. Grey was enough concerned to telegraph regarding the plan for a distant league of nations, but he did not comment on the other proposals. His formal reply to the letter of October 17, 1915, was not received, indeed, until the latter part of November, and it appeared at once that he was not impressed by House's scheme of immediate action—at least not as it had been diluted by Wilson's qualification. He wrote:

". . . the situation at the moment and the feelings here and among the Allies, and in Germany as far as I know, do not justify me in urging you to come on the ground

---

[1]November 10, 1915. From original letter in Mr. Wilson's files. Also printed in part in *The Intimate Papers of Colonel House*, Vol. II, p. 92.

that your presence would have any practical result at the moment."

He was not to be convinced by large and vague proposals. His mind went straight to the vital point: the Allies must know exactly what was proposed, and particularly that "the United States of America were prepared to intervene and make it good if they accepted it."[1]

Here were frank realities: but instead of meeting them with equal frankness and clarity—finding out on the one hand exactly what terms Grey would demand, exactly how far Wilson would or could go, House attributed Grey's failure to grasp the favourableness of the proposed scheme to the bad feeling engendered in England by the blockade controversy and by our failure to break with Germany. He even tried to impress upon Lansing "the necessity of the United States making it clear to the Allies that we considered their cause our cause"[2]—a somewhat startling proposal, considering the fact that the official position of the American government was still neutral, and that the President was still protesting against the severities of the British blockade. And what *was* the "cause of the Allies" that we were to consider our cause? Did it mean the continuation of the war until the Germans were crushed? Did it mean the always vaguely stated public objectives of the Allies: or, by this blanket approval, were we also to accept the intensely practical and specific war aims set forth in secret treaties already ratified, or under consideration, of which Grey had not, so far as disclosed in any of the Wilson documents, informed House?[3] Certainly, if we had been even remotely serious

---

[1] Sir Edward Grey to Colonel House, November 11, 1915.

[2] Colonel House's diary entry, November 28, 1915. *The Intimate Papers of Colonel House*, Vol. II, p. 100.

Five days before this, Bernstorff had reported to the German Foreign Office: "Colonel House is at least absolutely neutral . . ." *Official German Documents*, Vol. II, p. 1279.

[3] Two most important secret treaties had already been signed: in March 1915 the treaty between Great Britain and France and Russia, in regard to the annexation of

in proposing to go to war we ought to have known—in detail and with indubitable clarity—what it was that we were fighting for. Lansing's clearer mind went instantly to the practical points. While House was proposing, with abounding good will, vast schemes for the "elimination of militarism, and . . . navalism,"[1] Lansing was commenting upon House's proposal, which Wilson had at length sent to him:

". . . there are so many problems connected with it—such as boundaries, colonial possessions and indemnities, that I hardly like to express an opinion until it takes more definite form."[2]

---

the Straits and Constantinople by Russia; and on April 26, 1915, the Treaty of London, giving Italy Trentino, Trieste, part of the Tyrol, etc.

No American diplomat seems to have learned anything about the first of these treaties at this time; at least no reports were made either to the President or to the State Department. As to the Treaty of London, no American diplomat had official and complete information, but several of them had learned of it by indirect means. Walter H. Page's information came through H. Wickham Steed, an editor of the London *Times*. Page's cablegram reported that Steed had told him "in strictest confidence that England, France, and Russia made a bargain with Italy . . . agreeing to cede to Italy very large parts of Austrian territory, some of which has a Slavic population, if Italy comes into the war within a month. This was done without consulting Servia and against her wishes." (May 8, 1915. *Foreign Relations*, Supp., 1915, p. 386.) And Thomas Nelson Page at Rome reported to the same effect. (May 12, 1915. *Ibid.*, p. 33.)

Ambassador Sharp had already reported to Bryan (May 1st), on authority which he believed "reliable," the signing of this treaty which he said was "supposed to accord guaranties of territorial extension to Italy in return for military support of cause of Allies." (*Foreign Relations*, Supp., 1915, p. 31.) The Italian note received May 26th offered the full background for this action. (*Ibid.*, pp. 36–39.)

And finally House wrote the President from London on May 14th:

"It may interest you to know that Italy has signed an agreement with the Allies to come into the war before the 26th. This agreement will be carried out unless the Italian Parliament refuses to sanction it. I have had this information for ten days or more, but have not written it because there seemed so many slips between the agreement and its completion."

This was sketchy but pointed information; but there is no evidence that it made any impression upon the President or the State Department, or that any attempt was made to follow it up.

Some weeks later, notice of territorial negotiations in connection with Bulgaria was also given to the President. House wrote to Wilson on July 13th that he had learned from Walter H. Page of the secret inducements made by Great Britain to Bulgaria to get her military support for the Allies, and the counter proposals of Germany. Wilson replied to House the next day that "It is painfully interesting." But he did not ask House to investigate further, nor did it seem to have occurred to House to ascertain the bearing of such territorial dealings upon the peace proposals he was making.

[1] In his letter to the President of November 19th.

[2] Lansing to Wilson, November 24, 1915.

In the meantime there were intimations that the Central Powers were ready for a more substantial peace movement. On November 10th Wilson wrote to House that a message had come in from Morgenthau saying that "the Turkish Secretary of War had sent for him to say that this was the time to move for peace, if we were ever going to move,—before Germany had broken through the Balkans, crushed the Allies at the Dardanelles and got in a position to dictate peace!" Wilson concluded that this intimation must have been inspired by the Porte's German advisers and that it "would look . . . as if it were possible that Germany were getting anxious to have someone say that the fight must stop."[1]

But House discouraged any attempt to follow up the suggestion.

"I do not believe that much can be done at the moment, or that the time is propitious for more than an understanding that is being arrived at through Sir Edward. If we can get that end of it properly buttoned up we can afford to wait until they consider the time opportune."[2]

House, like Page, was looking at everything through the eyes of the British.

But Wilson was not convinced. Pressure from the pacifists was increasing. On November 26th he received another delegation of the Woman's Peace Conference headed by Jane Addams, Mrs. Philip Snowden of England and Mme. Rosika Schwimmer, of Budapesth: and on the same day nearly 20,000 telegrams from various parts of the country urging a peace movement were de-

---

[1] Such an interpretation of the Turkish Minister's *démarche* may well have been incorrect; it might even have been due to Turkey's reluctance to see Germany in direct control of the Balkan situation.

[2] November 11, 1915. About a month later House sent the President a letter he had received from England, written by Wilson's old friend, James Bryce:

". . . there is not the slightest change in British sentiment regarding the duty and necessity of prosecuting the war with the utmost vigour, and listening to no suggestions for negotiations with the German Government." (November 26, 1915.)

livered at the White House.[1] And Ford's peace ship was making ready to sail for Europe—with Bryan's blessing—but accompanied by telegrams from the State Department instructing diplomatic officials to have as little as possible to do with it and to make clear that the government did not in any way endorse it.[2] There was, indeed, little to be expected of such an ill-organized adventure. It probably deserved much of the ridicule heaped upon it, and yet the fundamental concept behind the movement represented a large body of earnest, if naïve, American opinion—that practical yet high-minded American citizens, by talking common sense to the European leaders and peoples, could get them to perceive the error of their ways and cease their bloody folly. All that was best in House's efforts derived from the same source; but they brought to the task few qualifications besides good will; they were too confident that this was enough!

Having interested Wilson in his new plan of negotiation with the British[3] and discouraged other methods of approach, especially the faint intimations from Germany, House began to procrastinate, influenced, no doubt, by the dissuasive letter of November 11th from Grey:

"I am willing, of course, to go at any time, but I doubt the necessity for precipitate action."[4]

A week later, after talking with Sir Horace Plunkett, he wrote:

---

[1]Practically all worded alike: "We work for peace. The mothers of America pray for it." They were said to have been paid for by Mrs. Henry Ford. New York *Times*, November 27, 1915.

[2]*Foreign Relations*, Supp., 1915, pp. 78–79.

[3]In November, House discussed with Bernstorff the possibility of eliminating militarism and navalism. He told Bernstorff that the country would sustain Wilson if he "undertook to intervene upon these broad lines," and "left the impression . . . that there was danger of the Allies conceding what we desired first and getting the weight of our influence on their side." He vaguely intimated that Wilson would be supported "to any degree . . . necessary . . . to bring about peace along such lines." (House to Wilson, November 19, 1915.)

[4]House to Wilson, December 1, 1915.

"I feel sure it would be best to refrain from decisive action until the wearing down process has continued for some months longer."[1]

On December 12th he was "thinking of going to Texas in the early part of January for a few weeks."

Probably House felt, honestly enough, that the time for peace proposals, considering the attitude of Grey and other Englishmen, was unpropitious; nevertheless delay was still the dominant note of British policy. *They* wanted the "wearing down process" to go on; and House's policy for America was to consider "their cause our cause."

But the President was not so easily satisfied.

II. AMERICAN DIPLOMACY REDUCED TO FUTILITY

December 1915 had brought a new crisis: that following the sinking by a submarine of the steamer *Ancona*[2] with the loss of the lives of twenty Americans. The situation had suddenly become acute: with the possibility of a break with Germany at any time.[3]

Incidents such as these, one after another, were making it clearer every day to the President that if the United States was to keep out of the war, something must be done, and done immediately. Peace was now the only solution for the swelling dangers that confronted him. He had already sought every available opening toward mediation: all without the slightest encouragement.

Colonel House, as we have seen, had finally proposed the desperate last resort of *demanding* peace—but had

---

[1] December 7, 1915.

[2] On November 15th.

[3] There was a disturbing account sent in a mysterious way by Gerard of an interview he had had with the Kaiser. The Kaiser had said, Gerard reported, that he "would attend to America when this war was over; that President Wilson's attitude regarding Germany eliminated him from any possibility of acting as mediator." Gerard, *My Four Years in Germany*, p. 250 *et seq*; also *The Intimate Papers of Colonel House*, Vol. II, pp. 102–103.

met such prompt rebuffs from the Allies that he was preparing to drop the matter and go off "for a few weeks" to his home state of Texas.

Evidently the President, nonplussed as to which way to turn, or what to do, decided to give House and his plan one more serious trial. Something might possibly come out of it!

He evidently acted sharply, for by December 16th we find House busily preparing for his trip to Europe, getting assurances from Bernstorff that he would be welcome in Berlin, as he hoped to be in London. He was now proposing "general disarmament" and telling Bernstorff that "we were not concerned regarding territorial questions or indemnity, but we were concerned regarding the larger questions which involved not only the belligerents, but the neutrals also." He went on to explain lightheartedly to the President:

"The Allies will take care of the territorial and indemnity questions and we need not go into that at this time."[1]

In short we were to give the Allies blanket approval—without knowing what their demands, open and secret, really were.

The President himself was apparently giving no more real attention to the details of settlement than House; what he wanted, as his letters show, was an opening—almost any opening—that would enable him to begin mediation; he undoubtedly regarded the proposals of Grey relative to a league of nations as a hopeful method

---

[1]House to Wilson, December 22, 1915. The British had carefully implanted this idea in the mind of our ambassador at large. Grey wrote to House, August 26, 1915:

"If I could feel that your people were sure to say, sooner or later, 'though we have no concern with territorial changes between the belligerents themselves, who must settle things of that kind by themselves, there can be no peace till the cause of Belgium is fairly settled . . .' I should be content."

And he looked forward to the help of the United States "in those larger conditions of peace, which looking to the future, interest neutrals as much as belligerents. . . ." *The Intimate Papers of Colonel House*, Vol. II, pp. 68, 89.

of approach. He was confident as usual that House fully knew his mind.

"You need no instructions," he wrote on December 17th. "You know what is in my mind and how to interpret it, and will, I am sure, be able to make it plain to those with whom you may have the privilege of conferring."

A week later he sent a letter of instructions:

"You ask for instructions as to what attitude and tone you are to take at the several capitals. I feel that you do not need any. Your own letters (for example, this one in which you report your conversation with Bernstorff) exactly echo my own views and purposes. I agree with you that we have nothing to do with local settlements,—territorial questions, indemnities, and the like,—but are concerned only in the future peace of the world and the guarantees to be given for that. The only possible guarantees, that is, the only guarantees that any rational man could accept, are (a) military and naval disarmament and (b) a league of nations to secure each nation against aggression and maintain the absolute freedom of the seas. If either party to the present war will let us say to the other that they are willing to discuss peace on such terms, it will clearly be our duty to use our utmost moral force to oblige the other to parley, and I do not see how they could stand in the opinion of the world if they refused."[1]

All this was explicit enough so far as it went. But had Wilson himself thought the problem through? Was it possible to secure the "future peace of the world" and "have nothing to do with local settlements"? Such a position could only lead to serious trouble at a future peace conference—as proved to be the case. Moreover, it is to be noted that there was no suggestion whatever in Wilson's letter of adhering to the essential premise of House's plan, insisted upon also in Grey's letter of November 11th, that

---

[1]December 24, 1915.

America agree to intervene with *armed* force against Germany if she refused the proposals put to her. Quite the contrary. Wilson obviously meant mediation, not armed intervention; we were to use only "our utmost moral force" and appeal to the "opinion of the world." There was in this no plan of war.

One wonders sometimes, reading the documents, whether there was ever a real meeting of the minds of the two men: or whether there could have been a more slippery basis for effective diplomatic action. While House was envisaging his errand in England as a means of assuring the Allies that we considered "their cause our cause," Wilson added to this very letter of instructions a devastatingly clear reference to the demand in the Senate for "further, immediate, and imperative pressure" upon the British in the matter of their infractions of American neutral rights:

"The errand upon which you are primarily bound you understand as fully and intimately as I do, and the demand in the Senate for further, immediate, and imperative pressure on England and her allies makes the necessity for it the more pressing. About the possibilities in the direction of peace you need no further intimation than that given above. If any particular question arises I know that you will cable me fully, and I shall of course reply at the earliest possible moment."

Although these unresolved divergences of view were startlingly clear and extremely serious, House replied on December 26th, "I think we agree entirely"—and sailed away to Europe.

While it is possible here to set down the actual documents, it is impossible to reconcile this strange relationship, or this method, so full of portent for the nation. With all of its inertia, would it not have been safer for the President to trust his State Department? Here he would have had at least a background of method based upon experience, at least partially informed, at least equipped with a modicum of skepticism. The question occurs: what course of action would Wilson have initiated if Colonel House had not been at his elbow?

We have vivid evidence of how far the President was from any armed intervention in Europe, in a statement made by him while House was on the high seas. It concerned the sinking by a submarine of the British liner *Persia* with great loss of life.

"About ten minutes to ten o'clock this morning,"[1] Tumulty's notes read, "I had a very interesting conversation with the President at the White House . . .

" . . . it was plainly evident that the *Persia* affair rested heavily upon him. My attitude toward this matter was for action . . . This did not seem to meet with a very hearty response from the President. He informed me that it would not be the thing for us to take action against any government without our government being in possession of all the facts. . . . When I began to tell him about the attitude of the country and the feeling in the country that there was a lack of leadership, he stiffened up in his chair and said: 'Tumulty, you may as well understand my position right now. If my reëlection as President depends upon my getting into war, I don't want to be President. I have been away,[2] and I have had lots of time to think about this war and the effect of our country getting into it, and I have made up my mind that I am more interested in the opinion that the country will have of me ten years from now than the opinion it may be willing to express to-day. . . . I believe that the sober-minded people of this country will applaud any efforts I may make without the loss of our honour to keep this country out of war.'"[3]

[1] January 4, 1916.
[2] On his honeymoon in Hot Springs, Virginia.
[3] J. P. Tumulty, *Woodrow Wilson As I Know Him*, pp. 249-250. It is also worthy of comment that at this very time Wilson and Lansing were working upon well-con-

It is not necessary here to go into a full account of House's mission which was, of course, so far as any real approach to an opening toward peace was concerned, a total failure. But certain facts connected with it, since they tend to make clear the President's attitude, are worthy of comment.

Soon after he arrived in England, House reported to Wilson:

"Sir Edward Grey is now in favour of the freedom of the seas provided it includes the elimination of militarism, and further provided we will join in general court to sustain it."[1]

Here indeed were tremendous assertions! Exactly what did Grey, an Englishman, mean by being "in favour of the freedom of the seas": what was involved in the "elimination of militarism," and what obligations might be involved, for the United States, in joining a "general court"? Was House being led along through the discussion of grandiose schemes to prevent the "immediate, and imperative pressure on England and her allies" of which the President had spoken in his "instructions," and which Grey had persistently blocked?

House asked the President to cable some assurance of his "willingness to coöperate in a policy seeking to bring about and maintain permanent peace among civilized nations."[2]

As vague a request for a commitment as could have been worded! There was scarcely a man in America who would not have answered "yes" to such a pious and general proposal. Wilson cabled, on January 9th:

"Would be glad if you would convey my assurance that

---

sidered plans for a *modus vivendi* by which peace with both groups of belligerents would be encouraged. See this volume, p. 159 *et seq*.

[1]January 8, 1916. Code cablegram transcribed by the President on his own typewriter.

[2]*Ibid.*

I shall be willing and glad when the opportunity comes to coöperate in a policy seeking to bring about and maintain permanent peace among civilized nations."[1]

Both men were here dealing perilously in vague generalizations, the details and implications of which were loaded with dynamite.

A few days later House was explaining to Grey and Balfour that "you [i.e. the President] believed . . . it might be necessary to bring to bear all our power in behalf of peace and the maintenance of it."[2]

Here was no limitation to the "moral force" so clearly set forth in Wilson's letter of instructions. And it is not at all surprising to find the hard-twisted, if velvety-gloved, Englishmen immediately demanding to know "how far you [the President] would be willing to enter into an agreement concerning European affairs."

What they wanted, of course, was to know when American armies were to march. House reported his reply to the President: "I thought you would not be willing to do this at all, but you would be willing to come to an agreement with the civilized world upon the broad questions touching the interests and future of every nation. Such questions, for instance, as the general elimination, so far as practicable, of militarism and navalism."[3]

House comments in his letter: "We did not define, to the satisfaction of any of us, what would constitute a solution of these two fundamental questions"[4]—which reminds one of Boswell's famous remark after discussing with Johnson the resurrection of the human race: "He left the question in obscurity."

---

[1] From original in Mr. Wilson's files, written on his own typewriter.
[2] House to Wilson, January 11, 1916.
[3] *Ibid.*
[4] In a passage eliminated from the letter as printed in *The Intimate Papers of Colonel House*, Vol. II, p. 120.

Amembassy (House)

It now looks as if our
several difficulties with
Germany would be presently
adjusted. So soon as they
are the pressure _demand_ here especially from the Senate will be
imperative that we force England to make at least e-
qual concession to our unanswerable claims of right.
This is just at hand. I
send this for your information and guidance.

W.

39608 — 33391 — 37200 -

67906 — 32040 — 22114 — 52927

12726 — ZodAK — 65092 — 29004 — 72610

20885 — 68613 — 54058 — 43336 — 49674

46352 — 22643 — 65062 — 42217 — 17802

47156 — Zenobia — 36858 — 66908 — 49733

58436 — 17288 — 16137 — 59957 — 32756

24556 — 17503 — 39195 — 44120 — 42630

22662 — 17686 — 47124 — 41126 — 70104

44885 -

1 Co Rax Bl
745P

CABLE.

Amembassy, London.

Hagyzkedun – 39608 – 33391 – ~~30729~~ 37200 – 67906

32040 – 22114 – 52927 – 12726 – Zodak –
65092 – 29004 – 72610 – 20885 – 68613 –

54058 – 43336 – 49674 – 46352 – 22643 –

65062 – 42217 – 17802 – 47156 – Zenobia

36858 – 66908 – 49733 – 58436 – 17288 –

16137 – 59957 – *32* 28756 – 24556 – 17503 –

39195 – 44120 – 42630 – 22662 – 17686 –

47124 – 41126 – 70104 – 44885.

Wilson.

47—

Three documents showing President Wilson's method of communicating with Colonel House, in London. The message was written out in the President's own hand, and signed "W." It was then transferred into the complicated code figures and letters by Mrs. Wilson (the code word "Zadok" signifies Germany, and "Zenobia," England). The President then copied out the figures on his own typewriter, for transmission by the Department of State.

As a result of all these interesting discussions there was more delay—exactly what the British wanted.

On the very day that the Colonel was suggesting an "agreement with the civilized world upon the broad questions touching the interests and future of every nation," the President was cabling, sharply:

"It now looks as if our several difficulties with Germany would be presently adjusted. So soon as they are the demand here especially from the Senate will be imperative that we force England to make at least equal concessions to our unanswerable claims of rights. This is just at hand."[1]

Here was talk not of forcing Germany, but of forcing England!

Page found "a certain fierce, blue-bellied Presbyterian tone" in this telegram, which House showed him;[2] but it reveals the wide divergencies of view that separated the President and his confidential diplomat. It was at least an assertion of an independent American policy.

There is, of course, no doubt that the President's personal sympathies—as we have shown—were now strongly with the Allies, but he was still guided by his deep-seated basic purpose to keep out of the war. He wanted to maintain the official neutrality required to satisfy American complaints regarding the blockade, and to be in a position to mediate among the warring nations if any sort of opening could be found. A letter written just at this time to Dr. Charles W. Eliot, with whom he was invariably candid, expresses his determination to maintain a "policy of detachment."[3]

---

[1] January 11, 1916. From original document in the President's hand. In the version as received by House, the last quoted sentence reads: "This is just." See facsimile.

[2] *The Life and Letters of Walter H. Page*, Vol. III, p. 279.

[3] "I feel the force of what you say about the Republic of France and yet I cannot help feeling that it would hardly be consistent with the policy of detachment from the European struggle which I have hitherto so sedulously sought to maintain if I were to express a sympathy which, after all, would go to the very merits of the present struggle." (January 18, 1916.)

Whatever his hopeful dalliance with House's scheme as a means of exploring the possibilities in Europe, it is to be noted that he did not at any time change the broad objectives of his own policy. He never committed himself on the military interventionist aspect of the scheme, as the British clearly perceived, guarding his freedom of action even in this desperate bid for peace. The fatal defect of his method was in placing so much confidence in House's hopeless "missions," which did two things: favoured the British policy of delay until Allied victories should give terms satisfactory to the Allies, and prevented any attempt—for a year or more—to explore an open and direct approach to mediation. While this approach would probably have failed—as it did fail when Wilson really tried it in December 1916—it was not attempted.

While House thought he could smooth over the situation by his remark, "The United States would like Great Britain to do those things which would enable the United States to help Great Britain win the war,"[1] neither Grey nor Cecil, according to his own accounts, gave him any satisfaction that the blockade against which Wilson was protesting would in any way be modified. How could he have expected it, when he was giving such guileless assurances, far beyond the powers granted in his instructions, of American support of the Allied cause, *without inquiry as to what their objectives really were?*

At the end of January, House spent four days in Germany deciding that "the rulers of Germany were in no

---

[1]Colonel House's diary entry, January 11, 1916. *The Intimate Papers of Colonel House*, Vol. II, p. 124. By January 16th the emissary wavered, writing to Wilson that "it is best for all concerned for us to keep out, conserving our strength so at the proper moment, we may lead them out of their troubles.

"I am more and more certain that it would be a mistake from every viewpoint for us to come in, although we should be ready to throw our weight at the right time in the right direction for the good of humanity. We are growing stronger as they grow weaker, consequently our power is increasing in double ratio."

But this hesitation was quickly dropped. (For part of this letter, see *Ibid.*, pp. 133–134.)

mood to consider peace terms that would satisfy the Allies,"[1] but, from his reports to Wilson, apparently not even mentioning the two general peace terms which Wilson had instructed him to emphasize.

All he could recommend was further delay, but he continued to be hopeful of the great part that the President was destined to play—at some future time!

"I am as sure as I ever am of anything that by the end of the summer you can intervene."[2]

Returning to England by way of Paris, House paused to reassure Briand and Cambon:

". . . I again told them that the lower the fortunes of the Allies ebbed, the closer the United States would stand by them."[3]

Although he was ostensibly upon a peace mission, House was telling the Allies that if they went on fighting, and if worse came to worst we, the United States, would come in and help them out. Indeed, he seemed actually to have promised that the President would "intervene": "It was finally understood that in the event . . . that the tide of war went against them, or remained stationary you [the President] would intervene."[4]

"We had," House observed naïvely, "a complete understanding as to the immediate future."[5]

House seems, indeed, to have been skillfully led along

---

[1]Seymour, in *The Intimate Papers of Colonel House*, Vol. II, p. 141.

[2]House to Wilson, February 3, 1916.

[3]House's diary entry February 7, 1916. *The Intimate Papers of Colonel House*, Vol. II, p. 163.

[4]House to Wilson, February 9, 1916. This biographer has frankly been puzzled by some of the documents connected with these negotiations, but he here presents them fully for the judgment of the reader.

[5]Colonel House's diary entry, February 7, 1916. *The Intimate Papers of Colonel House*, Vol. II, p. 163. Page from the beginning was contemptuous of the whole scheme. He observed in a memorandum written at the time: ". . . the fatal moral weakness of the foregoing scheme is that we should plunge into the war, not on the merits of the cause, but by a carefully sprung trick." *The Life and Letters of Walter H. Page*, Vol. III, pp. 281-282.

by Grey and Balfour and Lloyd George, who were serving well their own objectives, getting what they wanted, and seeing that America did not get what the President wanted —neither an opening toward peace nor a modification of the blockade policy.[1]

Colonel House completed his preliminary negotiations at a dinner meeting in London, February 14th; specific peace terms dealing with territorial adjustments were discussed—"We all cheerfully divided up Turkey"—and it was agreed, as Lloyd George has put it, that there "were also to be guarantees" of permanent peace.[2] House noted in his diary: "... there was ... a common agreement reached in regard to the essential feature; that is, the President should at some time, to be later agreed upon ... demand a conference."[3] A few days later, the French ambassador asked Grey "how serious" he thought House's proposal was![4]

But even Colonel House was not wholly certain that the President would do all he had been "committed" to do; he "might agree, and I would cable as much to Grey; then something might arise to cause the President to change his mind ..."[5]

It appears that the President, during this period, was leaving the negotiations wholly in the hands of House. He cabled to him on February 12th:

"I have not replied to your messages merely because

---

[1]Years later, an English journal went straight to the point in its comments: "Sir Edward Grey seems to have been a better diplomat than most of us knew, for all talk of intervention was at that moment sheer nonsense, but Colonel House was allowed to suppose that he had made a deep impression and had even carried his point." *New Statesman*, March 13, 1926, quoted in Bausman, *Facing Europe*, p. 237.

[2]*The War Memoirs of David Lloyd George*, Vol. II (1915–1916), p. 138.

[3]*The Intimate Papers of Colonel House*, Vol. II, pp. 179–182.

[4]*Ibid.*, p. 195. Page utterly refused to attend this dinner discussion because he did not believe in what was being done (*The Life and Letters of Walter H. Page*, Vol. III, p. 282); and House did not report the details of the conference to the President in any known document.

[5]*The Intimate Papers of Colonel House*, Vol. II, pp. 194, 196.

they seemed to need no comment and the situation here in respect of our programme of preparation for national defense required my undivided attention. What you have done seems admirable and gives me lively hope of a development of events that may bring peace."[1]

House returned to America, having "buttoned up" his agreement with the British in the form of a "memorandum" written by Grey.[2] He lunched at the White House on March 6th and afterwards went to drive with the President and Mrs. Wilson. The automobile turned from the White House driveway, swung out upon open country roads, past the quiet houses where, Wilson had lately said, lived some of the people whose opinions he cared most of all to know, ordinary citizens at home.[3] He had talked with many of them on his recent preparedness tour: he knew well that, in vast majority, they did not want war.

House relates that he explained what he had done in Europe,[4] but it was not until late in the afternoon, at a second conference, that he presented the memorandum itself.[5]

---

[1]From original document.

[2]Dated February 22, 1916, and first published by Grey in his *Twenty-Five Years*, Vol. II, pp. 127–128.

[3]*The Public Papers of Woodrow Wilson*, Vol. IV, p. 126.

[4]We have no account of House's report beyond the statement in his diary that he had "outlined every important detail" of his mission. *The Intimate Papers of Colonel House*, Vol. II, p. 199.

[5]This document has been published before, but it is appended here to make clearer exactly what the President's agent had agreed to:

"Colonel House told me that President Wilson was ready, on hearing from France and England that the moment was opportune, to propose that a Conference should be summoned to put an end to the war. Should the Allies accept this proposal, and should Germany refuse it, the United States would probably enter the war against Germany.

"Colonel House expressed the opinion that, if such a Conference met, it would secure peace on terms not unfavourable to the Allies; and, if it failed to secure peace, the United States would ["probably" was added by Wilson] leave the Conference as a belligerent on the side of the Allies, if Germany was unreasonable. Colonel House expressed an opinion decidedly favourable to the restoration of Belgium, the transfer of Alsace and Lorraine to France, and the acquisition by Russia of an outlet to the sea, though he thought that the loss of territory incurred by Germany in one place would have to be compensated to her by concessions to her in other places outside

The President had sent his friend abroad to urge peace negotiations, with power to promise that we would throw our *moral force* against Germany if she refused to acquiesce.[1] House had returned with a proposed arrangement by which we "would probably enter the war against Germany" if she refused to negotiate or failed to accept peace terms satisfactory to the Allies.

It would be interesting to know what the President really thought upon reading this document. By this time he was probably as well informed as any American regarding the problems of Europe, and he must have seen at once how vague were the commitments of the British and French: Grey must consult the Prime Minister and his colleagues; he was not sure how the Cabinet "would probably feel"; he would be ready to "talk the matter over" with Briand if Briand desired it! And the peace terms for which we might be asked to fight were certainly as vague as they could well have been made.

"Colonel House expressed an opinion decidedly favourable to the restoration of Belgium, the transfer of Alsace and Lorraine to France, and the acquisition by Russia of an outlet to the sea, though he thought that the loss of

---

Europe. If the Allies delayed accepting the offer of President Wilson, and if, later on, the course of the war was so unfavourable to them that the intervention of the United States would not be effective, the United States would probably disinterest themselves in Europe and look to their own protection in their own way.

"I said that I felt the statement, coming from the President of the United States, to be a matter of such importance that I must inform the Prime Minister and my colleagues; but that I could say nothing until it had received their consideration. The British Government could, under no circumstances, accept or make any proposal except in consultation and agreement with the Allies. I thought that the Cabinet would probably feel that the present situation would not justify them in approaching their Allies on this subject at the present moment; but, as Colonel House had had an intimate conversation with M. Briand and M. Jules Cambon in Paris, I should think it right to tell M. Briand privately, through the French Ambassador in London, what Colonel House had said to us; and I should, of course, whenever there was an opportunity, be ready to talk the matter over with M. Briand, if he desired it.

[Initialled] "E. G.

"Foreign Office,
"February 22, 1916."

[1] *Ante*, p. 138.

territory incurred by Germany in one place would have
to be compensated to her by concessions to her in other
places outside Europe."

These terms, of course, did not begin to touch either the
aspirations or the actual purposes of the Allies as already
expressed in the secret treaties of which Wilson, at that
time, knew next to nothing at all. No mention of Poland,
nothing whatever about the Balkan states, no word concerning a possible league of nations. The partition of
Turkey is referred to only in a vague phrase regarding
Russia's outlet to the sea, and there is nothing about
the claims of Italy, although both of these fiery subjects
had already been determined by secret treaties concerning
which House had apparently never been informed. The
last qualification, to anyone who, even at that time, had
given it careful thought, touched absolute absurdity.
Exactly where and how was Germany to be "compensated . . . by concessions" outside Europe?

It is probable, however, that the President gave the
memorandum no searching examination whatever. All
along he had, however mistakenly, regarded the territorial
and other material terms in the European settlement as of
little importance to Americans. What he was seeking
earnestly was some opening toward peace negotiations:
any basis, even a flimsy one like this memorandum,[1] that
would start reasonable discussion. Undoubtedly he saw
how conditional and tentative were all the proposals.
There were already two safeguarding "probablys" in the
document and he promptly added a third, changing the
sentence in the second paragraph, "the United States
would leave the Conference as a belligerent on the side
of the Allies" to "the United States would *probably* leave
the Conference as a belligerent on the side of the Allies."

On March 8th House sent Grey a cablegram composed

---

[1] To which, indeed, he was to recur, as a possible approach, a little later.

by Wilson, agreeing to the memorandum, with the single change; and the matter dropped from sight for the time being.[1]

The whole affair, however looked at, gives the impression of complete unreality. At the very time, indeed, that the President was (according to House) accepting the memorandum "*in toto*,"[2] he was continuing his unremitting effort to keep the nation out of war. On March 13th he said to a visiting delegation of Scandinavians:

"I can assure you that nothing is nearer my heart than keeping this country out of war and doing anything that the United States can do to show its preference for peace . . ."[3]

Seen in retrospect, the plain fact of the matter seems to be that the cause of peace by negotiation was damaged by House's well-intentioned bungling. His confident secret assurances to the Allies of American support no doubt encouraged their relentless prosecution of the war, as a result of which the Germans, driven to desperation, were now considering extreme counter-action.

For a brief period in March, it had, indeed, appeared that Germany would keep her U-boat war within the limits demanded by Wilson. Admiral von Tirpitz, the leading advocate of extreme measures, was defeated in the Charleville conference and resigned; and Gerard reported that the German Chancellor seemed to welcome his intimation that the President was ready to mediate

---

[1] "At present," Grey observes in his book, "there was no use to be made of it." *Twenty-Five Years*, Vol. II, p. 128.

[2] As he wrote in his diary. *The Intimate Papers of Colonel House*, Vol. II, p. 200. He also wrote to Grey March 10th that the President's acceptance was "a complete approval of what had been done"—a letter to which Grey seems never to have responded.

[3] New York *Times*, March 14, 1916. And yet the President again expressed his warm appreciation of House's efforts; when his friend spoke of the pride he would have in the President if the plan were realized, Wilson answered:

"You should be proud of yourself and not of me, since you have done it all." *The Intimate Papers of Colonel House*, Vol. II, p. 200.

whenever invited.[1] But the war deepened: and America drifted nearer and nearer to the centre of the maelstrom.

In the midst of this rush of tremendous, confusing, hurrying events American statesmanship was baffled and hesitant, delaying where, possibly, in the afterlook, it might have been better to act, and acting where, perhaps, it might have been better to delay. While Wilson could still act with a modicum of freedom, Europe was already beyond reason: diplomacy was now dominated, not by statesmanship, but by military compulsion.

If there were ever a convincing argument that wars must be stopped before they begin, it can be found in the events set forth in this and following chapters.

III. THE REVOLT IN CONGRESS

No period of Woodrow Wilson's eight years of administration of the presidency involved a greater test of his political leadership than the first quarter of the year 1916. Strategic decisions were imperative as early as February as to his course in the party convention in June, where he would, presumably, be a candidate for renomination. His opponents, all along the line, were trying to establish a case against him which would be plausible to the electorate. Diversities in his own party were even more troublesome. Some of the most powerful Democratic leaders feared he was going too far toward military preparedness: Garrison, his Secretary of War, resigned because he was not going far enough.

Mexican affairs were again disturbing. In March,

---

[1]Bethmann-Hollweg even spoke of sending a special ambassador to the United States to improve relations. *Foreign Relations*, 1916, Supp., pp. 207–208. House brushed the report aside as merely "an additional proof that Germany desires to cash in while she is ahead of the game." (House to Wilson, March 22, 1916.) When Bernstorff had interviewed House on March 12th, eager to know whether Wilson would soon demand peace negotiations, House told him "the English would resent our interference." House added, in his report to Wilson the same day: "This is true, but of course, it was given to him for a purpose."

American troops were crossing the border in pursuit of Villa. Senator Fall had demanded an investigation,[1] and Theodore Roosevelt seized upon the occasion for a new assault on Wilson's policy of watchful waiting.[2]

All these difficulties, however perplexing, were mere political pinpricks compared with the looming black cloud of the European war. With Germany sinking or capturing ships, and the Allies interfering to the point of exasperation with American commerce—with the war in February in furious concentration at Verdun—the President well knew that if he could satisfy the nation with his European policies everything else would take care of itself.

The real difficulty was that he was not satisfying the people upon this main issue. They were becoming thoroughly alarmed: they could not discern just where he stood, or what he was going to do. His formula from the beginning had been simple, and he had held to it with tenacity: keep out of the war, explore every opening toward mediation. It had generally satisfied the American public.

With the passage of the months, however, and the war growing steadily more intense, with less hope of any mediation, a tremendous new reality had begun to intrude itself upon the popular mind: that the United States might, no matter how hard the President turned and twisted and struggled, be forced into the conflict. The President himself, by demanding military preparation, however he might explain it, contributed to the awakening alarm.

When Congress met for the winter session on December 6, 1915, it mirrored perfectly this public confusion and anxiety. Every new Congress comes back to Washington

[1] On January 6th.

[2] In an interview at Oyster Bay, January 13, 1916. New York *Times*, January 14, 1916.

convinced that everything has gone wrong during its absence: that the President is on the verge of ruining the country. In this instance senators and representatives had been at home, fuming with impatience, for nine months, at a time when the world was literally on fire. No one of them knew comprehensively what the situation really was: they were determined to find out instantly—and change everything! Resolutions were at once introduced seeking embargoes on the export of munitions, providing for the control of armament manufacturers, pressing for peace conferences, asking for investigations of everything under the sun.[1]

Senator Stone, of Missouri, wise old politician, who by the attraction of opposites had surprisingly become Wilson's friend, wrote that senators were "quite seriously disturbed" by the diplomatic situation.[2] Everything indeed seemed going at loose ends. The *Lusitania* case, now seven months old, was still hanging fire, and there had been several alarming incidents since—the *Arabic*, the *Hesperian*, the *Ancona* and others—involving American interests. The British were interfering with commerce in the precious product of the South—cotton—and the precious product of the West—wheat.

In the midst of all this ferment, on December 30th, came the news of the sinking of the British liner *Persia*, with great loss of life.[3]

At this time the President and Mrs. Wilson were snatching a few days of honeymoon and holiday at Hot Springs in Virginia, taking long tramps, climbing Warm Springs Mountain by way of Delafield Trail.[4] But the din

---

[1] *Cong. Rec.*, 64–1, *passim*. (December 6–10, 1915.)

[2] December 13, 1915.

[3] An American consul, R. N. McNeelly, was among those lost.

[4] New York *Times*, January 3, 1916. They had been married about two weeks. On the day before the sinking of the *Persia* he was writing to his daughter Jessie (Mrs. Sayre): "These are blessed days for Edith and me. She is beyond all measure lovely and

of events in the far-away world penetrated even these Elysian fastnesses. On January 2nd Wilson was telegraphing anxiously regarding the *Persia*, and Lansing the next day expressed his fear of the effect of the popular excitement upon Congress. "Personally, I am very much alarmed . . ."[1] The President and Mrs. Wilson at once hurried back to Washington and on Tuesday morning, the 4th, he was again at his desk at the White House, facing one of the sternest struggles of his career.

Congress was openly in revolt: a revolt begun by members of his own party, eagerly seized upon by opponents who were looking forward to the coming presidential campaign. Nothing could have served Wilson's political enemies better than a row between the President and his party followers in Congress.

On January 5th a number of senators engaged in an acrimonious debate on permitting Americans to sail on belligerent ships, and Senator Gore, after consultation with Mr. Bryan, widened the breach in the Democratic ranks by introducing a bill "to prohibit the issuance of passports for use on the vessels of a belligerent country . . ."[2] The next day the President's bitterest partisan enemies in the Senate, Lodge and Fall, made an attack upon his Mexican policy:[3] and a week later senators were trying to force his hand by demanding armed intervention in Mexico.[4]

In short, a struggle between Congress and the President, not unfamiliar in our history, was developing over the

---

delightful and we dread to see these blissful days of quiet and seclusion come to an end."

[1]Telegram, Lansing to Wilson, January 3, 1916.

[2]*Cong. Rec.*, 64-1, p. 495. On the same day Senator Gore also introduced a bill "to prohibit belligerent vessels from transporting American citizens as passengers to or from ports in the United States, and to prohibit American and neutral vessels from transporting American citizens as passengers and contraband of war at one and the same time."

[3]*Ibid.*, p. 589 *et seq.*

[4]January 12, 1916.   *Cong. Rec.*, 64-1, p. 942 *et seq.*

control of foreign relationships, wherein a vital prerogative of the presidency was involved. John Sharp Williams, of Mississippi, who was one of the ablest members of the Senate, saw the situation clearly from the first. He said on January 6th:

"All these questions are in the field of diplomacy now, and the President of the United States has very wisely attempted to keep them within the field of diplomacy. . . . I think the management of our diplomatic affairs would have been more wisely handled by a man long visioned and deep visioned and tender visioned than they are apt to be when they are made a game of battledore and shuttlecock on the floor of these two Houses . . .

". . . I, for one, decline to bring a great international question down into the dust and sweat and turmoil of political discussion."[1]

It was, of course, entirely legitimate to seek information: it was indeed essential to the democratic process: but crude, impetuous, piecemeal legislation based upon wholly inadequate knowledge might easily destroy national unity, to say nothing of plunging the administration into diplomatic chaos. Violent action might even force us into a war which both Congress and the President were earnestly seeking to avoid.

Woodrow Wilson never exhibited his powers of persuasive and patient leadership to better advantage than in this crisis. He had returned from his vacation in unusually vigorous health, and in high spirits.[2] Much depended, during all of Wilson's life, upon the state of his health: the elasticity and fervour of his mind. Moreover, as he told Tumulty, he had had, during his vacation, "time to think about this war and the effect of our country

---

[1]Speech in the Senate. *Ibid.*, p. 602.

[2]"A fine mood," says Tumulty. Joseph P. Tumulty, *Woodrow Wilson As I Know Him*, p. 249.

getting into it." When his secretary, seeking to "bring to him the atmosphere of Washington," urged drastic action, the President made it indubitably clear as to where he stood:

". . . I will not be rushed into war . . ."[1]

His task was now twofold: he must subdue the mutiny in his own political camp at home; he must maintain the patient and difficult negotiations with the intractable belligerents of Europe.

The President and his Secretary of State had, indeed, just begun working hopefully on a *modus vivendi* for presentation to the belligerents, which by regulating the German submarine on the one hand, and the Allied practice of arming merchant vessels on the other, would, it was hoped, remove one of the chief dangers to neutral rights and ease our own position. The problem precipitated by the sinking of the *Persia* and brought to a head by the arrival of Italian liners bristling with guns, had long worried the President.[2]

"It is hardly fair to ask Submarine commanders to give warning by summons if, when they approach as near as they must for that purpose they are to be fired upon."[3]

Lansing's proposal to the ambassadors of the Allies[4]—a remarkable document, considering the conditions in Europe—asked that the armament of merchant vessels be wholly discontinued in consideration of the full compliance by submarines with the rules of visit and search.[5]

Here was an effort based solidly upon reason to "bring submarine warfare within the general rules of international

---

[1] *Op. cit.*, p. 250.

[2] "It is a question of many sides and is giving Lansing and me some perplexed moments." (Wilson to House, October 4, 1915.)

[3] *Ibid.*

[4] January 18, 1915.

[5] This would have included the safe removal of all persons before sinking the ships in compliance with the old rules for destruction of prizes at sea.

law and the principles of humanity without destroying its efficiency."[1] But it was like trying to make new laws during a riot! How talk reason to hard-pressed fighters who stood with their weapons poised? Both sides, indeed, were being asked to forego important naval advantages in order to solve certain dangerous American problems. Such a proposal, however logical in itself, was not likely to be approved by either belligerent. The British, highly disturbed, thought the proposal unfair in itself: and besides, why ease America's controversies with Germany when a submarine incident might, any day, bring America into the war against Germany?[2]

But if reason could not be made to prevail abroad, if coöperation was becoming wholly impossible, statesmanship within America urgently demanded both reason and coöperation as the price of internal unity of action. Wilson therefore set himself at once to the reëstablishment of party discipline, so violently shaken by the revolt in Congress. Even before leaving Hot Springs for Washington, he had telegraphed to his secretary:

"Please consult Secretary of State and if he approves request Senator Stone to meet me tomorrow morning at the White House at ten bringing with him such other Senators as he thinks it wise and best to bring."[3]

---

[1] There was more than a hint of stern action by America in the concluding paragraph of the note:

"I should add that my government is impressed with the reasonableness of the argument that a merchant vessel carrying an armament of any sort, in view of the character of submarine warfare and the defensive weakness of undersea craft, should be held to be an auxiliary cruiser and so treated by a neutral as well as by a belligerent government, and is seriously considering instructing its officials accordingly." *Foreign Relations*, Supp., 1916, pp. 146–148.

[2] Lansing was much irritated by Page's handling of the proposal in London. He wrote to Wilson on January 27th:

"I must say that I am very considerably disturbed as to Mr. Page's attitude on all subjects which in any way affect the policies of Great Britain. He certainly is influenced very strongly by the atmosphere in which he is and I frequently doubt whether he urges the cases involving American rights with the force and vigor which he should as American Ambassador."

[3] January 3, 1916.

He followed this up with many other conferences with senators and representatives in which he laid the situation before them with great frankness: always urging unity of action.[1] He consulted with opposing partisans who showed signs of supporting any part of his programme—Lodge, for example, on January 20th.[2] He was assiduous in recognizing and encouraging his supporters, both in Congress and in the country.

"May I not send you at least a line of warm and sincere thanks for your editorial, 'Stand up for the President'? It has made my heart very warm."[3]

On the other hand he did not abate his pressure for any element in his well-considered programme. He continued with good-humoured inflexibility to demand preparedness, starting his "swing-around" through the country on January 26th—in itself a method of going to the people over the heads of Congress. He nominated Louis D. Brandeis for the Supreme Court (January 28th) even though he knew it would cost him a hard struggle in the Senate. There was something in him—something of the fibre of his Scotch-Irish ancestors—which seemed to fling out a flag, march more boldly, in the face of danger. He loved a good fight.

Wilson returned to Washington from his campaign

---

[1]During one morning, January 24th, he conferred with Senator Poindexter, Representative Linthicum and a committee, Representative Barnhart, Representative Garner, Representative Edwards, Senators Stone and Reed, Senator Thomas, Senator Kern and Dr. McKelway, Senator Tillman and the South Carolina delegation, and Senator Martin and a committee. In the afternoon of the same day he conferred with Representative Flood, Representative Stephens, Representative Page, Representative Lever, Senator Hitchcock.

[2]Lodge reports in his book, *The Senate and the League of Nations:*

"As I turned to go, he [the President] said, greatly to my surprise, that he wished to thank me for having advised with Mr. Lansing. I said I was very glad if I could be of service on any international question. I then talked with him about embargo and investigation by committees of Congress on pending negotiations in [the] same vein as I had with Lansing. He said he fully agreed with me on both points and that 'there must be no embargo in any form.'" (p. 69.)

[3]Wilson to the editor of the Chicago *Record-Herald*, January 13, 1916.

through the West on February 4th. He had been immensely reassured and fortified by his reception: he felt that the people generally trusted him.[1] His instinct for understanding people in the mass being of a high order, he had learned what was being said "around quiet firesides all over this country," which he regarded as better guidance than talk in the "cloakrooms of Congress."[2]

It was well that he felt himself so fortified, for he returned to find affairs at Washington in the wildest confusion. The foreign situation was growing steadily worse: the newspapers were full of disturbing rumours. Colonel House was cabling:

"I doubt whether a crisis with Germany can long be avoided."[3]

A few days later (February 10th) the Germans were finally and forcefully overthrowing the last hope of any *modus vivendi* regarding the use of submarines. They issued a memorandum that "enemy merchantmen armed with guns no longer have any right to be considered as peaceable vessels of commerce. Therefore the German naval forces will receive orders, within a short period, paying consideration to the interests of the neutrals, to treat such vessels as belligerents."[4]

The ominous attack on Verdun was beginning, with the world holding its breath over the outcome: and Page, expressing his own anxiety and alarm, was demanding immediate severance of diplomatic relations with Germany (February 15th).[5]

---

[1]See this volume, p. 31.

[2]Address at the Gridiron Dinner, February 26, 1916.

[3]Probably on February 2nd. From the President's translation of House's code telegram, written on his own typewriter.

[4]*Foreign Relations*, Supp., 1916, pp. 163–166. Received in Washington on the afternoon of February 11th.

[5]And in private denouncing Wilson and Lansing. House wrote in his diary of a talk with Page on February 9th:

"My entire evening was spent in listening to his denunciation of the President and

All these rumours, combined with the President's increasingly confident demands for American armament—which, his Secretary of War Mr. Garrison was telling the committees, were quite inadequate[1]—tended to increase the all but panicky alarm in Congress.[2]

There is no doubt that the President himself was profoundly disturbed. A dinner guest on February 15th—Miss Ida M. Tarbell, one of the faithfulest of observers and reporters—remarked that it was an anxious time.

"No one," answered the President, "can tell how anxious it is. I never go to bed without realizing that I may be called up by news that will mean that we are at war. Before tomorrow morning we may be at war."

He said that his "great duty was not to see red."[3]

It seemed that a head-on collision between Congress and the President had become inevitable, and at a moment when, as the President said, anything might happen. On February 16th Lansing was issuing his "circular telegram" —the reply to the threatening German declaration of February 8th—in which he declared that although the United States felt that the "rule of international law

---

Lansing, and of the Administration in general. He thought the State Department should be 'cleaned out from top to bottom.'" *The Intimate Papers of Colonel House*, Vol. II, p. 177.

[1] Garrison resigned in the midst of this crisis, February 10th.

[2] Uncertainty and anxiety were indeed widely prevalent throughout the nation— even among the President's friends. The author wrote in his journal on February 16th:

"It is difficult, at a time when the country is crying out for strong and definite leadership, to find out where Mr. Wilson is going, or what he wants done. Recognizing the vast difficulties he is meeting, and the wholly unorganized state of public opinion, still, among men like myself, who desire to see him succeed . . . he ought to make it indubitably clear where he stands and what he is trying to do. . . .

"The attacks upon him here in the East are very bitter. . . . The whole situation in America at the present time is most disturbing to thoughtful people. . . . With this uncertainty is the consciousness of vast material benefits and prosperity due to war orders. We are making billions out of the sufferings of other nations and seem to think only of still further extending our greedy trade. . . ."

[3] Memorandum prepared by Miss Ida M. Tarbell and published by William Allen White in his *Woodrow Wilson*, p. 290.

permitting belligerent merchant vessels to arm ought to be changed," nevertheless we would hold Germany fully responsible for the loss of American lives through the action of German submarines.

This was sufficiently alarming—might it not mean actual war?—but he added, in order to keep the American case firmly based upon legal grounds, that "there was no present intention to warn Americans to refrain from traveling on belligerent merchantmen armed with guns solely for the purpose of defense. . . ."[1] At this very moment powerful forces in Congress were seeking the passage of legislation designed, exactly, to defeat this presidential policy.[2] Jeff McLemore, of Texas, presented his first resolution on February 17th,[3] and this was followed within a week by a barrage of attacks in both Houses. All these legislative proposals involved not only the question of American rights on the high seas, but the President's initiative in foreign policy, and his leadership of the Democratic party.[4]

It was a crisis that had to be promptly and vigorously

---

[1] *Foreign Relations*, Supp., 1916, p. 170. On the same day the President made another hopeless appeal for reason to the British, in a cablegram to House:

". . . Germany is seeking to find an excuse to throw off all restraints in under-sea warfare. . . . If the English will disarm their merchant ships she will be without excuse and the English will have made a capital stroke against her. We are amazed the English do not see this opportunity to gain a great advantage without losing anything."

[2] There were three main lines of attack: (1) Forbid issuance of passports; (2) Forbid clearances of armed vessels; (3) Warn passengers off belligerent ships.

[3] *Cong. Rec.*, 64–1, p. 2756.

[4] There was much to be said for such laws, as well as legislation regarding embargoes and loans of money—if they could have been made a part of the neutrality policy of America at the beginning of the war. Thrust forward at a moment of tremulously delicate negotiation, in the midst of hair-trigger events, they were as ill timed as they were dangerous. They would have destroyed utterly any unity of diplomatic action; they might easily have precipitated the war they were designed to prevent. But they represented the not unfamiliar attempt of an irritated Congress to solve grave problems by panicky legislation. As Wilson wrote to Congressman Barnhart regarding one of these resolutions:

"I can assure you from abundant knowledge of the circumstances that it would be distinctly hurtful to the cause we all have at heart and not helpful. It would be a serious embarrassment just now." (February 17, 1916.)

met. The President called a conference at the White House on February 21st, late in the afternoon, of the chairmen of the committees on foreign affairs of both Houses, Stone of the Senate and Flood of the House. Kern, floor leader of the Senate, accompanied them.[1] The President laid the situation before them with perfect clarity, possibly imparting also some of his own anxiety, as he had done a few days before in talking with Miss Tarbell. We are fortunate in having a report of the conference in a letter of Senator Stone to the President, written three days later. Confessing, in this remarkably able, frank, and withal loyal letter, that he was "more troubled than I have been for many a day," and was being besieged by "inquiries from my colleagues," he set down what he understood to be the President's position, as stated at the conference:

"That while you would deeply regret the rejection by Great Britain of Mr. Lansing's proposal for the disarmament of merchant vessels of the Allies" with the understanding that Germany and her allies would conform to the accepted legal forms, "you were of the opinion that if Great Britain and her allies . . . insisted upon arming her merchant ships she would be within her right under international law."

Then he added the decisive words:

"Also . . . that you were not favorably disposed to the idea of this Government taking any definite steps toward preventing American citizens from embarking upon armed merchant vessels. Furthermore, that you would consider it your duty, if a German war vessel should fire upon an armed merchant vessel of the enemy upon which American citizens were passengers, to hold Germany to strict account."[2]

---

[1]Representative Kitchin was also invited, but was unable to attend. Arnett, *Claude Kitchin and the Wilson War Policies*, p. 159.

[2]From original in Mr. Wilson's files.

Stone warned the President that members of both Houses felt "deeply concerned and disturbed" and voiced their fear that Wilson may have pressed his programme of preparedness because of such a crisis as this.

"I have counseled all who have talked with me to keep cool; that this whole business is still the subject of diplomacy and that you are striving to the utmost to bring about some peaceable adjustment, and that in the meantime Congress should be careful not to 'ball up' a delicate diplomatic situation by any kind of hasty and ill-considered action."

Stone's own attitude showed the conflict present among some members on the Hill:

". . . I find it difficult from my sense of duty and responsibility to consent to plunge this nation into . . . this world war because of the unreasonable obstinacy of any of the Powers upon the one hand, or, on the other hand, of fool-hardiness, amounting to a sort of moral treason against the Republic, of our own people recklessly risking their lives on armed belligerent ships."

There is no doubt that the President's position had been clearly explained to members of Congress by Stone and Kern and Flood, but it seemed only to make the revolt more determined. On February 22nd McLemore introduced his second resolution in the House,[1] and there was little doubt that the members were at the moment overwhelmingly in favour of its passage. It was reported in the press that "leaders of the House of Representatives virtually served notice on President Wilson this afternoon that unless within forty-eight hours he agreed to warn American citizens that they must not take passage on armed belligerent merchant ships . . . the House by an

---

[1]*Cong. Rec.*, 64–1, p. 2958. McLemore had the strong support of Bryan and his following. Bryan sent a telegram to Representative W. W. Bailey, endorsing the McLemore resolution. New York *Times*, February 26, 1916.

overwhelming majority would issue the warning in the form of a resolution."[1]

The House was in a panic. "A member of many years' experience in the House said that not since the Spanish War crisis had there been such a feeling of uneasiness."[2] The situation in the Senate, though calmer, was still deeply disturbed; but the odds and the opposition seemed only to arouse Wilson's fighting spirit.[3]

He was fresh from his appeal to the people—always with him a sovereign source of confidence—and he felt that he could count upon their support. Several wise friends, among them Newton D. Baker,[4] assured him that the country was with him.[5] His secretary, Mr. Tumulty, looking at the situation from its political aspects, as always, considered it a move to weaken the President's leadership, and also advised fighting.

The President immediately wrote a strong letter to Senator Stone, working it out carefully first in shorthand —an evidence of the importance which he attached to it. It is here set forth in full:

February 24, 1916.

MY DEAR SENATOR:

I very warmly appreciate your kind and frank letter of today, and feel that it calls for an equally frank reply.

You are right in assuming that I shall do everything in my power to keep the United States out of war. I think the country

---

[1]New York *Times*, February 24, 1916 (date line February 23). For a competent survey of this state of affairs, see the New York *Times*, February 24, 1916. Representative Fuller introduced a similar resolution on February 22nd. And on February 24th Representative Hilliard presented another. *Cong. Rec.*, 64–1, pp. 2958, 3110.

[2]New York *Times*, February 24, 1916.

[3]Senator Keller had an interview with the President on the 25th, at which Mr. Wilson spoke of the matter indignantly: "And it is with such a ―― outfit as that that I am supposed to act and achieve nationally for America." (Kent E. Keller to Ray Stannard Baker, June 5, 1929.)

[4]In a telegram of February 24, 1916.

[5]There were also strong expressions in the press. "The President has need of all his firmness, all his power, all his great authority, to circumvent the men who are plotting

will feel no uneasiness about my course in that respect. Through many anxious months I have striven for that object, amidst difficulties more manifold than can have been apparent upon the surface; and so far I have succeeded. I do not doubt that I shall continue to succeed. The course which the central European powers have announced their intention of following in the future with regard to undersea warfare seems for the moment to threaten insuperable obstacles, but its apparent meaning is so manifestly inconsistent with explicit assurances recently given us by those powers with regard to their treatment of merchant vessels on the high seas that I must believe that explanations will presently ensue which will put a different aspect upon it. We have had no reason to question their good faith or their fidelity to their promises in the past, and I, for one, feel confident that we shall have none in the future.

But in any event our duty is clear. No nation, no group of nations, has the right while war is in progress to alter or disregard the principles which all nations have agreed upon in mitigation of the horrors and sufferings of war; and if the clear rights of American citizens should ever unhappily be abridged or denied by any such action, we should, it seems to me, have in honor no choice as to what our own course should be.

For my own part, I cannot consent to any abridgment of the rights of American citizens in any respect. The honor and self-respect of the nation is involved. We covet peace, and shall preserve it at any cost but the loss of honor. To forbid our people to exercise their rights for fear we might be called upon to vindicate them would be a deep humiliation indeed. It would be an implicit, all but an explicit, acquiescence in the violation of the rights of mankind everywhere and of whatever nation or allegiance. It would be a deliberate abdication of our hitherto proud position as spokesmen even amidst the turmoil of war for the law and the right. It would make everything this government has attempted and everything that

---

against him in and out of Congress. It is with no friendly intent that bills are drawn and plans hatched to palsy the arm with which he directs the country's foreign policy. The conspirators are not so much enemies of his policies as of himself. The influence of the implacable and vindictive Bryan is at work. . . ." New York *Times*, February 24, 1916.

The *Times* also quoted a number of other New York newspapers, most of which upheld the President's position. *Ibid.*, February 26, 1916.

it has achieved during this terrible struggle of nations meaningless and futile.

It is important to reflect that if in this instance we allowed expediency to take the place of principle, the door would inevitably be opened to still further concessions. Once accept a single abatement of right and many other humiliations would certainly follow, and the whole fine fabric of international law might crumble under our hands piece by piece. What we are contending for in this matter is of the very essence of the things that have made America a sovereign nation. She cannot yield them without conceding her own impotency as a nation and making virtual surrender of her independent position among the nations of the world.

I am speaking, my dear Senator, in deep solemnity, without heat, with a clear consciousness of the high responsibilities of my office, and as your sincere and devoted friend. If we should unhappily differ, we shall differ as friends; but where issues so momentous as these are involved we must, just because we are friends, speak our minds without reservation.

Faithfully yours,
WOODROW WILSON

HON. WILLIAM J. STONE,
United States Senate.[1]

It was a letter at once so clear and so bold that it attracted the widest attention and approval. But it had come too late to head off the revolt in the House. On the afternoon of the 24th, Speaker Clark telephoned to Tumulty that "the Speaker, Leader Kitchin, and Chairman Flood would like to call on the President as soon as possible to discuss with him the state of affairs"[2] in the House. The President made an appointment for them on the following morning, February 25th, at nine o'clock.[3] It was an uncommonly early hour for official Washington in winter; but Wilson wished to have the conference out of the way before the cabinet met at eleven o'clock.

---

[1] From copy in Mr. Wilson's files; published in the New York *Times*, February 25th.
[2] New York *Times*, February 25, 1916.
[3] According to both the White House usher's diary and the executive office diary.

The three congressmen were plainly greatly disturbed. They knew that the President was considering a fight to the finish on the McLemore resolution; they knew also the temper of the House. The Speaker, Mr. Clark, told the President that he thought the resolution would command a majority of two to one of the membership: others thought it would carry by three to one.[1]

Considering the strong impression it made upon the three congressmen, the conference must have been one of fire and power. We are fortunate in having a statement made immediately afterward by Speaker Clark as to what was said:

"The sum and substance of the conference, outside of an explanation made as to the temper of the House regarding the diplomatic situation with Germany and some argument on both sides, is fully set out in Senator Stone's letter to the President and the President's letter to Senator Stone. . . .

"At the conclusion of the conference it was very clear to all that the President stands on his letter to Senator Stone."[2]

---

[1]Speaker Clark's statement in the New York *Times*, February 26, 1916.

[2]Out of these events grew the legend of the "Sunrise Conference" embodied by Gilson Gardner in an article in *McNaught's Monthly* for June 1925 which was afterwards exploited by several writers as proof that Wilson was all along decided upon leading the country into war and only concealed his intentions for some time longer in consequence of the demonstration against him at this juncture. The article is based upon no substantial documentation, and is full of inaccuracies. It is even vague as to the date of the conference, placing it "early in April" and to make it sensational, setting the hour at "sunrise." The connection of the conference with the *Sussex* crisis, alleged in an editorial note to Gardner's article, wholly breaks down, since the *Sussex* was not sunk until March 24th, a month after the conference took place.

Professor A. M. Arnett, in his book on Claude Kitchin, brings out the fact that Kitchin, at least, did feel that Wilson wanted war with Germany at this period. Kitchin's letter to C. H. Claudy, quoted by Professor Arnett, is as follows:

"Champ Clark, Flood, and myself did have, early one morning, between seven and eight o'clock, such a conference with the President. At that time he seemed anxious to go to war with Germany immediately. This was in April 1916. Champ Clark, Flood and myself have talked about the matter dozens of times and our recollection as to just what was said exactly coincides."

The date of the conference given here (which Professor Arnett accepts, although with an implication that there is room for doubt) is April 1916. All the evidence in

The visitors departed feeling hopeful that Germany would "postpone enforcement of the new Admiralty order."

"This," said Speaker Clark, "will give more time for consideration of this matter. We told the President that in the event of such a postponement all action in Congress certainly would be postponed. Meantime these resolutions would remain where they are."[1]

After the cabinet meeting, which immediately followed the conference, the President talked with Burleson, shrewd politician, who was his dependable adviser as to developments on Capitol Hill. Burleson was for having an immediate "showdown"; he advised demanding a vote in the House. While they were talking, Attorney General Gregory, and later Secretary McAdoo, came in: and both agreed with Burleson.[2] This advice was, in fact, merely

Mr. Wilson's files points to the date as February 25, 1916. It will be noticed that Kitchin's letter to Mr. Claudy is dated April 2, 1921, five years after the event, and shortly before Mr. Kitchin's death. Arnett, *Claude Kitchin and the Wilson War Policies*, pp. 188–190. And Mrs. Clark's letter, printed in Gardner's article and written eight years after the conference when all three of the conferees were dead, is, of course, at second hand.

The real genesis of the legend is to be found probably in a speech by Senator Gore on March 2nd—about a week after the famous conference, in which he referred to "a report" that in a recent conference the President clearly intimated that if Germany "insisted upon her position," war would probably result and that this would not of necessity be an evil since our entrance would bring the war more swiftly to a close, to the benefit of civilization. *Cong. Rec.*, 64–1, p. 3410.

Flood, who attended the actual conference on February 25th, denied the whole story *at the time:*

"I have heard the President say nothing to indicate that war with Germany might not be a bad thing for this country or that he desired war. On the contrary, the President told us that he was working night and day to keep this nation out of war." New York *Times*, March 3, 1916.

And the White House, learning of the charge, immediately issued a reply:

". . . the President authorized an unqualified denial of any utterance to which any such meaning could be attached." *Ibid.*

Wilson also wrote to Representative William Gordon on March 2nd:

". . . [I] am glad to have an opportunity of assuring you that the report that you say was current that I was trying in some way to bring on war was too grotesquely false to deserve credence for a moment. If anybody ever strove harder to preserve peace than I have striven and am striving, I wonder who and what he could have been."

[1]Speaker Clark's statement in the New York *Times*, February 26, 1916.

[2]From memorandum of a conversation of A. S. Burleson with the author, March 17, 1927; also Burleson to the author, February 25, 1931; also T. W. Gregory to the author March 5, 1931.

confirmatory and reassuring, since the President had already made up his mind.

But the battalions on the Hill were already moving. That very afternoon Senator Gore continued the attack by introducing another resolution—that American citizens should "forbear to exercise the right to travel as passengers" on armed belligerent ships[1]—with Senator Lodge, Wilson's sharpest Republican opponent, supporting the administration.

On the following morning, the 26th, information as to the President's fixed determination having no doubt been widely circulated on the Hill by Stone and Clark and Kitchin and Flood, the two generals-in-chief of the revolt began to hesitate. There was a sudden easing away, an effort now to save face by avoiding a direct clash. Both authors of the resolutions publicly stated that they desired, as McLemore said, to delay the vote until the President could "try out his policy and arrive, if possible, at a definite conclusion," or unless the gravest crisis seemed at hand, as Senator Gore intimated.[2]

That evening Wilson cleared his mind in a speech at the Gridiron Club. He began with a biting reference, which everyone understood, to the events of the moment:

"I find that I am seldom tempted to say anything nowadays unless somebody starts something . . ."—observing that "it is very difficult to think while so many people are talking, and particularly while so many people are talking in a way that obscures counsel and is entirely off the point."

He put his views in rather happier form than in the letter to Senator Stone:

"America ought to keep out of this war . . . at the sacrifice of everything except this single thing upon which

---

[1]*Cong. Rec.*, 64-1, p. 3120.
[2]New York *Times*, February 27, 1916.

her character and history are founded, her sense of humanity and justice."[1]

If the revolters on the Hill thought that they could, by easing the situation along, continue to hold the club of their threatened resolutions over the President's head, they did not know their man. He deemed it necessary to know exactly where he stood diplomatically; and the sooner Germany realized the folly of counting on division in America, the sooner she might be induced to recall or modify her Admiralty order on armed ships.

On February 29th the President moved to an attack which was as disconcertingly bold and dramatic as it was unprecedented. He wrote a letter to Representative E. W. Pou, then ranking member of the House Committee on Rules, asking for an early vote on the Gore and McLemore resolutions so that our foreign relations might be "once more cleared of damaging misunderstandings."

"The report that there are divided counsels in Congress in regard to the foreign policy of the Government is being made industrious use of in foreign capitals. I believe that report to be false, but so long as it is anywhere credited it cannot fail to do the greatest harm and expose the country to the most serious risks."[2]

In taking this action the President disregarded all known precedents of communication between the Executive and Congress. He sent no message to Congress. He did not communicate directly with the Committee on Foreign Affairs in charge of the resolution; he went straight to the committee that in emergencies is expected to produce a special rule for prompt action.[3] But, precedents or

---

[1] *The Public Papers of Woodrow Wilson*, Vol. IV, pp. 125–128.

[2] From copy in Mr. Wilson's files; also *The Public Papers of Woodrow Wilson*, Vol. IV, p. 129.

[3] The New York *Times* of March 1, 1916, reported much surprise, and a feeling of "puzzled resentment" in the House, as a result of the President's letter to Representative Pou.

no precedents, the great public outside was left in no
doubt as to where he stood or what he intended to do,
which was exactly what he desired.[1]

The downfall of the revolt was as swift as it was ignominious. On March 3rd Gore's resolution, by now con-
fusingly amended, was tabled by the Senate and, on the
7th, McLemore's, by the House—both quite safely, with
the mass of Democrats supporting the administration,
the Republicans dividing almost equally.[2]

From the President's point of view it was a glorious victory: he felt himself again dominant in his party leadership, and newly confirmed in his prerogative in the conduct
of foreign affairs. But the revolt, while momentarily sub-
dued, still smouldered, and the victory itself had its fateful
aspects. We were now still further committed to the policy
of holding Germany to the observance of rules for the
treatment of merchantmen which exposed submarines
to risks in a manner admitted by Wilson to be "hardly
fair." The Allies could now (March 23rd) formally reject
Lansing's *modus vivendi* without fear of unpleasant con-

---

[1]Evidences began immediately to accumulate that the backbone of the revolt was
broken. There were letters of approval or explanation or apology from various members
of the Senate and House to which Wilson responded in terms of the most generous
confidence and appreciation. To Senator Stone he wrote:

"Your generous letter of February twenty-eighth has warmed my heart and I want
to send you my affectionate thanks for it. I understand your attitude perfectly and
you may be sure have not the slightest doubt as to the spirit in which you are acting. . . .

"I want you to feel, my dear Senator, that your affection is sincerely reciprocated
and that it is a matter of real distress to me to find myself differing with you in any
matter of importance. Pray take care of your health and be sure that nothing will ever
mar our delightful relationship." (February 28, 1916.)

And to Representative Pou he wrote:

"Your letter of February twenty-fifth to Mr. Tumulty has cheered me mightily.
In fact, I am always cheered when I deal with you in any way, because your straight-
forward manliness about anything reassures me even when others have discouraged
me. Your letter brings me assurances which strengthen my heart and I thank you for
it most warmly." (February 29, 1916.)

[2]*Cong. Rec.*, 64–1, pp. 3463–3465; 3689 *et. seq.* Republican support in this crisis was
an important element in Wilson's victory. Ex-President Taft, in a conversation with
reporters in Boston, said: "We must stand by the President. This is an international
question, and we must stand behind the President in all matters of this kind." New
York *Times*, March 5, 1916.

sequences, although Lansing did not acknowledge the finality of their rejection until April 7th.[1] On the other hand the demonstration of Wilson's strength, giving an impressive sense of unified diplomatic control, no doubt tempered extreme action for the time being on the part of the Germans. But the whole situation, as we shall see later, was in a state of perilous uncertainty, with the nation reduced to bickering argument—while drifting onward toward war.

For the time being a new feeling of confidence and co-operation between Congress and the President resulted in steady progress in the passage of the preparedness legislation which Wilson was seeking. On March 23rd the House approved the Hay Army bill,[2] but it was not until June 3rd, after exhaustive discussion, that the President signed the National Defense Act.

It had been a hard struggle: but there are evidences throughout the documents that Wilson not only met it calmly and with assurance, but that he actually enjoyed it. There is a total absence in his letters of the misanthropic note which sometimes marked his comments on earlier struggles. His letters to friends have an unaccustomed buoyancy, an unusual warmth of feeling. Many deep elements in his character contributed to this steadiness and confidence. He was functioning in the field of domestic leadership where he was at his best; and having in a direct appeal to the people gone "back to the fountains of American action,"[3] he could employ his genius for political guidance and control to the uttermost. Another important element was the notable change that had come into the atmosphere of his home life, animated by

[1] *Foreign Relations*, Supp., 1916, pp. 211–212; 223–224.

[2] *Cong. Rec.*, 64–1, pp. 4696 *et seq.*

[3] As he said in his address on February 26th at the Gridiron Club, referring, no doubt, to his recent campaign throughout the West for preparedness.

the buoyancy, the humour, the radiant health of the new mistress of the White House. The daily records show that the President and Mrs. Wilson were inseparable.[1] Every day they rode out together, played golf or tramped together, read aloud to each other, and later they worked together many long hours, Mrs. Wilson, in addition to her multitudinous social duties as the "first lady," helping with the laborious coding and decoding of secret cablegrams from Europe. Often they spent the week ends cruising down the Potomac or out to sea on the *Mayflower*. The importance of this new element in the President's life, healing a loneliness and discordance that had rent his peace of mind, enabling him to devote all his powers to the problems that confronted him, can scarcely be overestimated. It was to continue to the end of his life.

---

[1]"After his second marriage it was the President's custom to be called at six o'clock in the morning. On a little table outside of his bedroom door there would be put, the night before, a small plate of sandwiches and a thermos bottle of coffee. The President would have a cup of coffee and a sandwich and then hurry off with Mrs. Wilson and a secret service man or an aide for an hour of golf. Then he would return and dress and at eight o'clock have breakfast with Mrs. Wilson . . ." (Mrs. Elizabeth Jaffray, at that time housekeeper in the White House, in the *Cosmopolitan*, February, 1927.)

CHAPTER VI

FACING EUROPE: MAY, 1916

"... we cannot forget that we are in some sort and by the force
of circumstances the responsible spokesmen of the rights of humanity,
and that we cannot remain silent while those rights seem in process
of being swept utterly away in the maelstrom of this terrible war."
Address to Congress, April 19, 1916.

"Our own rights as a Nation, the liberties, the privileges, and the
property of our people have been profoundly affected."
*Address before the League to Enforce Peace,
Washington, May 27, 1916.*

"... the peace of the world must henceforth depend upon a new
and more wholesome diplomacy."
Ibid.

I. THE "SUSSEX" CRISIS: A DECISIVE GERMAN PLEDGE

EVENTS in the spring of 1916 came to a crisis, one of
the sharpest during the period of American neutrality,
with the torpedoing of the unarmed French steamer *Sussex*.
Though less ghastly than the *Lusitania*, the tragedy burst
upon America at a moment of emotion and anxiety. It
capped a long accumulation of grievances and broken
pledges. It recalled the still festering *Lusitania* controversy.

For the first time Americans were beginning to realize
clearly and with a sense of shock that we might ourselves,
despite everything the President might do or say, be
drawn into the war. We scanned the newspapers daily for
news of battles on blasted fields and ridges at Verdun, war
on the eastern front, war in the Holy Land. We read of the
fate of ships mined or torpedoed in the gray waters of the

Atlantic. We counted the staggering totals of men under arms; estimated the dead and the wounded; calculated the stupendous costs of war. For the first time our imaginations began really to grasp the horrifying portent of it all. Wilson's demand for military preparedness was forcing upon our century-old isolation a new fear of world entanglements.

News of the torpedoing of the *Sussex* appeared in the newspapers on the morning of Saturday, March 25th. The ship was a cross-channel ferry, known to be unarmed; yet no warning had been given. The explosion had killed or injured a large number of the passengers and crew.[1] The long-expected submarine crisis had come.

Two of the President's advisers made ready at once to guide him into war: Lansing and House.

Lansing was thoroughly angry, insisting "that something should be done . . ."

". . . the time for writing notes discussing the subject has passed . . . the present method of submarine warfare can no longer be tolerated."

He recommended an ultimatum; the Germans must give up their present methods, admit "the illegality of submarine warfare in general," and pay a just indemnity for Americans killed or injured. If the terms were not met, we must sever relations.[2] He knew well that this course "might possibly" lead to war.

In New York, Colonel House was writing in his diary: "It looks as if we should have to act this time without

---

[1] New York *Times*, March 25, 1916. *Foreign Relations*, 1916, Supp., p. 214. It became known much later that no Americans had been killed, but the President believed during the crisis, and indeed until February 1917, that American lives had been lost. The principle at stake was of course the same whether Americans were injured or killed. American lives were jeopardized, also, in the sinkings of the *Berwindale* and the *Englishman*, March 16th and 21st, but authentic information was evidently not received until after the news of the *Sussex*. *Ibid.*, pp. 215–216, 219.

[2] Lansing to Wilson, March 27, 1916. Savage, *Policy of the United States Toward Maritime Commerce in War*, Vol. II, pp. 468–470.

further parley. . . . I am afraid he [the President] will delay and write further notes, when action is what we need."[1]

He hurried uninvited to Washington, where he found Wilson so busy that a detailed discussion had to be postponed.

". . . from the way he looked at me, I am inclined to believe that he intends making excuses for not acting promptly . . ."[2]

But the President, as habitually when facing a crucial decision—how often Wilson faced the question of war!—went driving in the country; thinking. He, if anyone, must hold steady. What was necessary? What was right? He must act upon facts and far-reaching policies, not upon impulse and emotion. He, if anyone, must think of America's obligation to civilization. It was three days before he answered Lansing's angry letter.

"My impressions," he wrote, "are not quite the same. The proof that the disaster was caused by a torpedo seems to me by no means satisfactory or conclusive. And, if it was caused by a torpedo, there are many particulars to be considered about the course we should pursue as well as the principle of it . . . if we are to keep clearly and indisputably within the lines we have already set ourselves."[3]

On the same day, House reports in his diary with a shade of exasperation:

"He was afraid if we broke off relations, the war would go on indefinitely and there would be no one to lead the way out."[4]

Unable to convince the President by talking about German attacks upon our rights, House chose a more ingen-

[1]March 27, 1916. *The Intimate Papers of Colonel House*, Vol. II, p. 226.

[2]March 28, 1916. *Ibid.*, p. 226.

[3]Wilson to Lansing, March 30, 1916. Savage, *Policy of the United States Toward Maritime Commerce in War*, Vol. II, pp. 470–471.

[4]*The Intimate Papers of Colonel House*, Vol. II, p. 228

ious method. His proposals were that Bernstorff should be given his passports, that the President should "make a dispassionate statement of the cause of the war and what the Allies were fighting for"[1]—and perhaps by midsummer, should send him (House) to Holland, where, after a conference with the Allies and with their consent, he could "open negotiations directly with Berlin, telling them upon what terms we were ready to end the war."[2]

It was strange that the President should have listened with patience to such utter nonsense.[3] But he did, for he had to winnow out such help as he could from the endless suggestions of his advisers. In this case, he was willing to go so far as to threaten a break: and he authorized House to see Bernstorff and say that, unless Germany made a decisive change in her submarine policy, we would surely be forced into the war.[4]

This did not look at all like the immediate break that his excited advisers were urging. It was clear, indeed, that Wilson was pursuing his usual course with imperturbable patience; he was doing his best to avoid war; and he was determined to give Germany a chance to mend her ways, if she would. He wrote specifically:

"The German submarine policy is making an extremely complicated and difficult situation for us, and sometimes there seems to be little prospect of extricating ourselves

[1] Surely a most extraordinary proposal—as if either the President or House knew what the Allies, who were even then tied up with secret treaties of which they knew almost nothing, were really fighting for. And what a course for the head of a nation trying desperately to maintain its neutrality!

[2] The President should preside over the peace conference, House added.

[3] "Not even good nonsense," as House himself confessed years later—to his credit. *The Intimate Papers of Colonel House*, Vol. II, p. 228, footnote.

[4] We are here, however, compelled to rest for authority, as in so many other cases, upon House's uncorroborated diary notes—notes no doubt honestly set down, but by an adviser who may have interpreted his instructions as more drastic than they actually were, since he was trying to force the President into war. What a godsend to the historian of later years if there could have been a really accurate stenographic report of some of these conversations!

House did not see Bernstorff for more than two weeks after the *Sussex* incident.

from it without serious conflict, but we are still hoping that it will be possible."[1]

He was guiding his course by two convictions: that the American people did not want war with anybody; and that a permanent settlement could be won only when battles stopped, by the insistent "opinion of mankind."[2] Bryan would have endorsed both views, for the two men still differed, in the main, only on method—but it was not he who was at Wilson's elbow. Colonel House wrote to the President on the 3rd of April that unless the Germans discontinued their present policy, a break seemed inevitable, and made a further suggestion of which he also later repented:

"Before it comes do you not think it would be well to cable Grey telling him the status of affairs and asking him whether or not it would not be wise to intervene now rather than to permit the break to come?"

He had in mind, of course, intervention with a demand for peace negotiations backed up by an assurance that we would (probably) go to war against Germany if she refused to negotiate or if she refused to agree to terms satisfactory to the Allies—in short, a recurrence to the plan suggested in the House-Grey memorandum.[3]

There was, indeed, appalling support for the belief that a break could not now be avoided; for it had become certain that the *Sussex* had been destroyed by a German submarine.[4]

Too eager for the fray to await a reply to his letter of the 3rd, House posted back to Washington, where he found Lansing busily at work upon tentative instructions

[1]Wilson to Thomas Nelson Page, March 31, 1916.

[2]Address in New York, June 30, 1916. *The Public Papers of Woodrow Wilson*, Vol. IV, p. 219.

[3]See this volume, pp. 150–151.

[4]The report of the French authorities was received from the French ambassador on the 5th. *War Memoirs of Robert Lansing*, p. 135.

to Gerard designed to break relations. This evidently led him to believe that Wilson leaned toward immediate action, for when he talked with the President on April 6th he showed hesitation in supporting his proposal for intervention.

But the President was still seeking any loophole—even the most unlikely—that would lead to peace negotiations. In spite of desperate and bloody battles the war was at a dead centre of exhaustion: neither side, of its own will, could end the tragedy. He was even willing, since there was some faint evidence that Germany really wanted peace, to explore again the flimsy possibilities of the House-Grey memorandum. Accordingly he typed out a dispatch for House to send to Grey:

"Since it seems probable that this country must break with Germany on the submarine question unless the unexpected happens, and since, if this country should once become a belligerent, the war would undoubtedly be prolonged, I beg to suggest that if you had any thought of acting at an early date on the plan we agreed upon, you might wish now to consult with your allies with a view to acting immediately."[1]

Of course the effort was abortive. A public demand for peace might possibly have brought the Allies around; a secret appeal was, in any case, a mistake.[2] Grey had fully understood a month before that the President had no intention of committing the United States without reservations to war on the side of the Allies. Why, therefore, should he help the United States to keep out of the war when the submarine issue was irresistibly driving us into it? This was precisely what the British hoped for! Instead of coöperation, therefore, Grey's reply to House showed

---

[1] April 6, 1916. *The Intimate Papers of Colonel House*, Vol. II, p. 231.

[2] As House himself afterwards admitted. *The Intimate Papers of Colonel House*, Vol. II, pp. 231–232, footnote.

that he actually hoped the crisis would lead to war. He intimated that a peaceable solution would invite the contempt of the Allies:

"If the United States Government takes a strong line about [the submarine incidents] . . . it must I suppose become more difficult for it to propose a conference to Germany; if on the other hand it passes them over the Allies will not believe that the United States Government will at a conference take a line strong enough to ensure more than a patched up and insecure peace."[1]

In fact, there was no ground in Europe on which the dove of peace could alight. Von Bethmann-Hollweg addressed the Reichstag on April 5th, discussing some of the better-known demands of the Allies in a scalding temper, ruinous to every thought of a conference. He curtly proclaimed that the disposition of Belgium and occupied parts of France could be decided only with full guarantees for German security, and that the question of Poland would be settled by Germany and Austria alone. Neutrals would have to recognize the right and duty of Germany "to wreak retaliation with all the means in her power against the starvation policy" of England.[2]

Asquith answered him five days later, in a speech charged with emotion:

"The German Chancellor wants us to assume the attitude of a defeated to a victorious adversary. But we are not defeated. We are not going to be defeated."[3]

Nevertheless Wilson refused to give up hope. On the 6th—the very day on which he had framed the message

---

[1]Grey to House, April 7, 1916, sent to Wilson April 19, 1916. Grey would not discuss the memorandum with French statesmen. The French felt that "war must yet continue to have any chance of securing satisfactory terms from Germany." And the English felt "it was not a time when we could ask the French Government to consider a conference. . . ."(Grey to House, telegram, April 8, 1916, forwarded to Wilson the same day.)

[2]Digest sent by Gerard. *Foreign Relations*, 1916, Supp., p. 23; New York *Times*, April 6, 1916.

[3]*Ibid.*, April 11, 1916.

to Grey—he began work on a note to Germany, keeping
it before him for several days. We find him conferring at
weary length with members of his cabinet.[1] Having worked
painstakingly over Lansing's harsh proposals, he finally
drew up a new note himself. While not designed, as were
the Secretary's drafts, to lead to the immediate breaking
of relations, it was an unsparing indictment of the German
submarine policy, recurring to the original American
contention that it was wholly illegal and should be abandoned. Where he differed from his warlike advisers was in
refusing to close, finally, the pathway to peace. There was
not lacking some ground for hope that a break might be
avoided. Bernstorff had made a visit to House on the 8th,
of which House reported:

"He said a break must not occur and that he would
immediately get busy."

Indeed the German ambassador had notified his government of the seriousness of the situation and asked "instructions on the basis of which I can pacify the Government here."[2]

On April 13th, however, the crisis was intensified by the
arrival of the German explanation of the *Sussex* tragedy.
It was a marvel of stupidity. The case was treated with
what appeared little less than cynical levity; the note
maintaining that the only ship torpedoed on March 24th
in the locality where the *Sussex* was attacked was "a long
black vessel" whose stern did not look like that of the
Sussex. Hence, ran this astonishing chain of reasoning,
the ship torpedoed by the submarine could not have been
the *Sussex*. However, in case of a difference of opinion,
Germany would arbitrate.[3] Bernstorff, with a restraint

---

[1] The discussions held the cabinet for unusual hours on April 11th and 14th. New
York *Times*, April 12, 1916; April 15, 1916. *Cf*. also, *War Memoirs of Robert Lansing*,
pp. 133 *et seq*.

[2] Bernstorff, *My Three Years in America*, p. 245.

[3] *Foreign Relations*, 1916, Supp., pp. 227–229.

demanded by the proprieties of his position, later expressed his belief that this was "probably the most unfortunate document" ever sent from Berlin to Washington:

"Mr. Wilson thought he detected a direct untruth . . ."[1]

It is remarkable that the President did not break with Germany then and there. His first public statement touching upon the situation shows that he was not far from it. It was made on the evening of April 13th, after a crowded day of conferences, letter writing, and study of the Mexican problem. The occasion was the annual Jefferson Day dinner. He had had almost no time to prepare his address, for, as he wrote to Page on that very day:

"My task . . . is to go breathlessly through innumerable tasks whose pace constantly makes me fear that I am going too fast to exercise wise and deliberate judgment."

On that evening the President plainly believed that the crisis might mean war:

"God forbid that we should ever become directly or indirectly embroiled in quarrels not of our own choosing, and that do not affect what we feel responsible to defend; but if we should ever be drawn in, are you ready to go in only where the interests of America are coincident with the interests of mankind . . .

"These are solemn days, when all the moral standards of mankind are to be fully tried out."[2]

Grave words. Men who listened were to feel their dramatic effect grow more intense as they looked back upon that evening. As he finished, one of those present

---

[1]Bernstorff, *My Three Years in America*, pp. 247–248. Writing to House, April 14th, Bernstorff, on instructions from Berlin, tried to soften the crisis by defending Germany's good faith in desiring peace in Europe and friendship with America. On his own initiative, he expressed hope that no formal note would be sent to Germany. The publication of those notes, he wrote with the air of a person impatient with the law of gravity, "always causes irritation." *The Intimate Papers of Colonel House*, Vol. II, pp. 237–238.

[2]*The Public Papers of Woodrow Wilson*, Vol. IV, pp. 145–146.

said to another—expressing, it seemed, the general thought:

"I like his spirit, but what is he going to do?"[1]

Many there were at this time who wanted Wilson to *lead*, to act, but they would not at all have agreed to what end. Some demanded immediate war: others were desperately crying peace: and between these extremes were hurrying and excited advocates of this or that fantastic mediatory policy. It was indeed a moment when statesmanship faced its supremest tests: tests not only of intellect and emotional stability but, above everything else, of character.

Through it all the President adhered steadily, patiently, to his fundamental purpose—to keep the peace if the peace could be kept. His letters of the time show his purpose clearly. On the day following his address he wrote: "Our desire for peace I need not expound to you."[2]

"I entirely concur," he wrote on the 17th, "with your view as to what is the sober, though perhaps as yet silent, judgment of the country and I am trying to serve that judgment, not the judgment of some parts of the country that are hysterically vocal."[3]

House had returned to Washington on April 11th to discuss the President's draft. Seeing that it did not sever relations as he had hoped, he bowed with easy pliancy: but criticized the concluding paragraph which read:[4]

"If it is still the purpose of the Imperial Government to prosecute relentless and indiscriminate warfare against vessels of commerce by the use of submarines without regard to what the Government of the United States must consider the sacred and indisputable rules of international

---

[1]The author was present: his notes were written immediately after the dinner. See further comment upon this address in Chapter VII of this volume, pp. 234–237.

[2]To Professor Benjamin F. Battin.

[3]To J. W. Harriman.

[4]Taken from Wilson's original copy.

law and the universally recognized dictates of humanity, the Government of the United States is at last forced to the conclusion that there is but one course it can pursue. Unless the Imperial Government should now immediately[1] declare its intention to abandon its present practices of submarine warfare and return to a scrupulous observance of the practices clearly prescribed by the law of nations, the Government of the United States can have no choice but to sever diplomatic relations with the German Empire altogether. [It will await an early announcement of the future policy of the Imperial Government in the earnest hope that this unwelcome course will not be forced upon it.]"[2]

House thought that this last paragraph as it stood would open up "the entire question for more argument. . . ."

". . . it would give Germany a chance to come back with another note asserting she was willing to make the concessions he demanded, provided Great Britain obeyed the letter of the law as well."

To this the President did not agree, as House reports, but he did consent to add the word "immediately" and he cut out the last sentence.

House reports in his diary account:

"I urged him to say if Germany declined to agree immediately to cease her submarine warfare that Ambassador Gerard was instructed to ask for his passports."[3] Wilson, however, refused to make the ultimatum absolute.

The last paragraph of Wilson's draft also troubled Lansing.

"I have been going over the ending of the instruction to Gerard in the submarine matter," he wrote, "and I am

---

[1]"Immediately" was added at House's suggestion.
[2]The bracketed material was crossed off at House's suggestion.
[3]*The Intimate Papers of Colonel House*, Vol. II, pp. 235–236.

more and more convinced that the formula which you propose in your redraft, beginning—'Unless the Imperial Government should now, etc.' raises some serious objections.

"In the first place, the phrase—'return to a scrupulous observance of the principles clearly prescribed by the law of nations'—offers an opportunity to raise the question as to what are the clearly prescribed principles. . . . In addition to this, the whole question of the treatment of armed and unarmed merchantmen will be raised. . . . I am afraid if we employ that language that we will be involved unavoidably in a discussion of that question, which I assume we both wish to avoid. Any phrase which raises a reasonable difference of opinion invites discussion, and the word 'immediately' would be nullified.

"If we are to follow substantially the language of the redraft, I would suggest its amendment as follows:

"'Unless the Imperial Government immediately declares that it abandons its present method of submarine warfare against passenger and freight-carrying vessels, the Government of the United States can have no choice but to sever diplomatic relations with the German Empire.' . . ."[1]

This suggestion the President accepted; the note as finally sent followed Lansing's proposed paragraph almost verbatim.[2] Lansing was relieved at the change.

"It was in the nature of an ultimatum for which I had so earnestly pressed," he wrote afterward, "though it lacked the force of the one contained in the note which I had originally drafted."[3]

---

[1]*War Memoirs of Robert Lansing*, pp. 138–139.

[2]See *Foreign Relations*, 1916, Supp., pp. 232–237. A concluding sentence was added, presumably by the President: "This action the Government of the United States contemplates with the greatest reluctance but feels constrained to take in behalf of humanity and the rights of neutral nations."

[3]*War Memoirs of Robert Lansing*, p. 139.

Nevertheless the note, in its basic policy, represented Wilson and not his Secretary of State, and not his confidential adviser.[1] As a disclosure of Wilson's thought in April 1916 it has enormous significance. While sternly critical of the Germans he was not ready to go to war with them, if war could possibly be avoided; nor was he committed to the Allies; he was even considering compulsion if they failed to observe American rights. His efforts indeed all along had been to be as impartial as possible. As he wrote to a friend:

". . . it would be a mistake to think that we are not exerting as much pressure in the case of our rights in the one direction as in the other."[2]

That Wilson fully intended to carry out his threat if Germany refused his demands is indicated by a telegram to Page instructing him to inquire, confidentially, the wishes of the British government, "in regard to British representation in Berlin in the event of a severance of relations between the United States and Germany."[3]

On the 19th the President went before Congress to report upon his course of action and to ask approval and support. The seriousness of the crisis was everywhere recognized, and every seat on the floor and in the galleries was occupied; high dignitaries even stood or sat in the aisles. The diplomatic gallery was filled—but the Central Powers were not represented. Just before one o'clock, the President entered the room, walking quickly to the rostrum as the audience stood and applauded. He read his address.

Germany, he said, was placing no check upon her sea weapon; shocking results were following, week after week.

[1] And yet House, while disagreeing basically with the President, could write to him concerning the note: "It marks an epoch in American history." *The Intimate Papers of Colonel House*, Vol. II, p. 277.

[2] To H. A. Garfield, March 7, 1916.

[3] April 25, 1916. *Foreign Relations*, 1916, Supp., p. 241.

He had declared that unless Germany ceased that kind of warfare diplomatic relations would be severed: he was speaking for the rights of mankind as well as for our own.

". . . we are in some sort and by the force of circumstances the responsible spokesmen of the rights of humanity. . . ."

No man could know the probable outcome. He could express his solemn hope, however: that Germany might "recognize the justice of our demands and meet them in the spirit in which they are made."[1]

He was not elated by the applause. He had told Senator Stone that morning, after outlining in advance to members of the Senate and House committees on foreign relations what he planned to say:

"You look as sad as I feel."[2]

The majority of the senators and representatives generally supported the President's moderate course; and the country at large, when the reports came in, seemed to be equally favourable.

". . . diplomacy has many resources and they have not been exhausted."[3]

Largely, no doubt, as a result of the President's frank and luminous discussions of the problems involved—his insistence upon knowing the facts before he acted, his steady devotion to the highest ideals of national responsibility—it is clear from the comment of the time that our people were thinking of international relationships with a greater degree of maturity than they ever had before. If the nation was forced, finally, into the war, Wilson was determined that it should be with eyes wide open and minds made up. One of the notable aspects of Wilson's

---

[1]*The Public Papers of Woodrow Wilson*, Vol. IV, pp. 153–159.
[2]New York *Times*, April 20, 1916.
[3]Pittsburgh *Dispatch*, quoted in the New York *Times*, April 20, 1916.

career, through all of these stormy years, was the way in which he continued to justify his leadership and maintain his secure hold upon the people.

The note opened the eyes of the German government to the gravity of the situation. Von Jagow received it from the hands of Ambassador Gerard with the feeling that a break was certain.[1] And yet at the first intimation, through Bernstorff, that Germany might suspend submarine operations in order to negotiate a settlement, the President indicated his readiness to open discussions. He asked Lansing to prepare "a statement of what we hold we have a right to demand," and send it to House as a basis for negotiations with Bernstorff.[2]

"I think it right," he telegraphed House, "to discuss with the German Government any accommodation it may suggest provided their maritime warfare is entirely stopped during the discussion."

While House plaintively repeated his warnings that "we would lose the friendship and respect of the Allies,"[3] he undertook the task.

Placing the negotiations in the hands of House made for unnecessary irritation and delay, since there seemed to be no proper coöperation between him and Lansing. Gerard, who would naturally have been instructed by the State Department, was given no adequate information. Moreover, since the German Foreign Office could not send secret cable or wireless messages to Bernstorff owing to British control of all the lines of communication not strangled by the censorship or by American neutrality

---

[1]*Foreign Relations*, 1916, Supp., p. 239. All German ships sheltered in American ports were ordered, in case the break came, to be disabled. Bernstorff, *My Three Years in America*, p. 250.

[2]Wilson to House, telegram, April 21, 1916, after a telephone conversation in the afternoon. (Copy written by the President on his own typewriter.)

[3]April 19, 1916, enclosing a letter from Grey dated April 7th, which intimated such a view.

regulations, there was left only the formal exchange of letters and notes.[1] This was as irritating a handicap as was conceivable in a diplomatic crisis where minutes were days.

Lansing, however, gathered the correct impression that Germany would try to gain a strategic advantage by compromise; and urged that a statement of the American position on armed merchant ships be published. Wilson agreed at once.[2]

In fact, Germany wished assurances on more than rules; acting on instructions April 25th, Bernstorff asked House the question: If we accede to your demands, will the American government "bring pressure upon Great Britain in regard to the blockade?"

House pointed out the "difficulty" of such a course and wrote to Wilson immediately afterward that Bernstorff "will impress upon his Government the impossibility of our forcing Great Britain to modify her blockade." He went on to acknowledge coolly, without apparently perceiving the irony of his comments, the inequality of American pressure on the two groups of belligerents:

"He [Bernstorff] is advising his Government that the position we take regarding submarine warfare is a forerunner to the freedom of the seas which Germany so much desires for it looks to the protection of commerce.

"As a matter of fact, it is the freedom of the seas for England, as far as I can see, not freedom for Germany, for it would merely restrict depredations by submarines, and the nation that controlled the seas would destroy commerce with their other war ships."[3]

The President felt the difficulties of the prolonged con-

---

[1] Gerard to Lansing, April 25, 1916, reporting the complaints of the German Chancellor. *Foreign Relations*, 1916, Supp., pp. 243–244.

[2] Lansing to Wilson, April 25, 1916; statement published April 26th. New York *Times*, April 27, 1916; *Foreign Relations*, 1916, Supp., pp. 244 *et seq.*

[3] From original, House to Wilson, April 25, 1916. Printed in part in *The Intimate Papers of Colonel House*, Vol. II, p. 239.

flict intensely. He afterward described these troubled days:

"There were multitudes of messages from the country, offering all kinds of suggestions, but always they ended: 'We will stand by what you think it best to do.' The awful and overwhelming thought was that the country trusted me."

He had refused to be hurried into action, or excited:

"I made it a point not to read the details of what was happening, in instances of personal suffering and what seemed individual outrage. . . . I feared to be overwhelmed by a storm of feeling."[1]

In the midst of the suspense incident to those negotiations the British ineptly sent over their long-delayed reply to the note in which America had protested the abuses of the Allied blockade. Dignified, immaculate, nervous, Sir Cecil Spring Rice dutifully mounted the steps of the State Department building, April 24th, and formally presented the document.[2] The American argument had been delivered November 5, 1915—five and a half months before. Already, in March, Wilson had grumbled about such delay, writing that correspondence with Great Britain moved "as slowly as cold molasses."[3] But this moment—April 24th—was a thoroughly inopportune time to try to refute our arguments and to deny all wrongdoing if Britain had any hope of gaining American aid—which she had. As Sir Horace Plunkett cabled to House, April 20th:

"Should this [American entrance into the war] come to pass the President may rely on a cordial welcome as an ally and on the full appreciation of the high motives which determined his action."[4]

[1]Ida M. Tarbell, "A Talk with the President of the United States," in *Collier's Weekly*, Vol. 58, p. 6 (October 28, 1916).

[2]*Foreign Relations*, 1916, Supp., pp. 368–382.

[3]Wilson to H. A. Garfield, March 7, 1916.

[4]Sent to Wilson April 21, 1916.

Well enough; but it was premature at this moment to talk of welcoming us to the battlefields. The longer the decision with Germany was postponed—a month had passed since the torpedo had been sent crashing into the bow of the *Sussex*—the more stoutly opinion supported Wilson in his efforts to maintain peace. The feeling spread that he would win out, and the public began to have a renewed feeling of safety and confidence in him.[1]

The President's letters were filled with gratitude for these evidences of approval. He wrote of his "genuine appreciation" to Taft, whose attitude manifested both largeness of spirit and understanding.[2] And to his old friend, Dr. M. W. Jacobus, he confessed how very much he needed from him "the blessing of clear thinking and high feeling in the midst of confused counsels and many petty things which obscure the whole face of policy."[3]

Some of his friends, however, despite their personal warmth of feeling, materially differed with him. President Garfield of Williams College touched a sore spot when he doubted whether the inhumanity of the blockade could be distinguished from that of the submarine. Wilson, however, would not argue the point.

". . . it seems to me that the blockade and the submarine matter stand on different grounds."[4]

Near the close of April, since the controversy was still unresolved, Wilson began to consider precautionary measures. The navy received instructions for activity in case of mobilization.[5] Gerard was informed what to do if relations were broken.[6]

---

[1] Author's notes, April 27, 1916.
[2] April 25, 1916.
[3] April 26, 1916.
[4] Garfield to Wilson, April 24, 1916; Wilson to Garfield, April 27, 1916.
[5] April 27, 1916. Daniels, *Our Navy at War*, pp. 9–10.
[6] April 28, 1916. *Foreign Relations*, 1916, Supp., pp. 249–250.

Bernstorff reported to House on the 26th that the most Berlin could offer by way of concession was a promise to conduct submarine warfare according to the rules of international law for cruiser warfare.[1] A temporary abandonment would be "unacceptable to public opinion in Germany." "The chief thing for the moment," he wrote, "is to know whether a declaration of my Government in this sense would avert a break, as this is the object I want to attain."[2]

It seemed to offer a way out of the crisis; but was it a solution of the problem? Could the submarine really fight within the rules? Experience spoke against it.

Gerard had visited the Kaiser's field headquarters at Charleville on April 28th. There he had argued the American position with the Kaiser and the Chancellor for three days—indeed, they discussed the whole conduct of the war, dumdum bullets, Henry Ford's peace expedition, the Allies' use of American ammunition, and why "we had done nothing with England." The question was asked: Would America try to bring peace if Germany met the demands? Gerard was encouraging.[3]

While these conversations were taking place in Germany, Wilson's feeling, intensified by the irritation of the delay, began to break through his restraint. In a conversation with House on May 3rd, he spoke far more emotionally than was his custom, discussing Germany's responsibility for the war, and expressing his opinion that those

---

[1] As laid down in the German notes and memoranda on the *Frye* and the *Persia*.

[2] Transmitted to Wilson April 27, 1916. By the time the letter reached Wilson he had already requested Lansing to inform Gerard what we considered to be the applicable rules of international law. *Foreign Relations*, 1916, Supp., p. 252; and Wilson to House, April 29, 1916.

[3] Gerard to Lansing, sent May 3rd, received May 4th. *Foreign Relations*, 1916, Supp., pp. 253–255. See also Gerard, *My Four Years in Germany*, pp. 336–345. The Germans also displayed a desire to consider peace mediation, which under the circumstances was suspect because it seemed mere bargaining. (Gerard to Lansing, cablegram, May 2, 1916, received May 3rd.) Lansing wrote to Wilson May 3rd: ". . . I confess to be very skeptical . . ."

guilty should have personal punishment. For the moment he felt that if war were at last forced on us, it would not be completely an evil.[1]

The answer which the Germans finally made on May 4th was a prickly document—a concise, hard statement of the German position, not without telling counter-demands and thrusts of defiance. It discounted the American plea of humanity: was the United States also concerned regarding the deprivations of Germans threatened with starvation by Great Britain? While repudiating the charges of unrestrained conduct of submarine operations, it did agree in the future to give warning and protect lives in accordance with American demands—unless the ships should "attempt to escape or offer resistance." In short, it conceded our minimum demands.

Germany hoped that the United States would now proceed to restore the "freedom of the seas"; and insist that Britain forthwith observe international law regarding the blockade. If this object were not attained, "the German Government would then be facing a new situation in which it must reserve itself complete liberty of decision."[2]

Wilson was meeting with the cabinet when the advance press version of the note reached him. He held a general discussion immediately,[3] and then consulted House by wire. The German concession seemed to be acceptable, but not so the comments and conditions.[4] Germany dictating what the United States must do to Great Britain!

---

[1] From an incomplete account in *The Intimate Papers of Colonel House*, Vol. II, pp. 239–240. Whether he qualified these statements in his conversation cannot be learned from House's diary notes as published.

[2] *Foreign Relations*, 1916, Supp., pp. 257–260.

[3] New York *Times*, May 6, 1916.

[4] House's reply, sent the same day, suggested that the answer should express general satisfaction at the concession made, but should add that the United States government "would exercise its own judgment in regard to negotiations with other belligerents who infringe upon our rights." (House to Wilson, May 5, 1916.) Lansing feared the concession was a "gold-brick swindle" and thought it necessary to "weigh every portion with care." (Lansing to Wilson, May 6, 1916.)

The country was hopelessly divided in opinion on the note: it averted a calamity; it meant a break; it was evasive; it was satisfactory; it placed the future in grave doubt![1] But congressional opinion, if it might be taken to reflect the main trend in the country, was strongly in favour of remaining at peace.[2]

There was no longer any reason to hope for "friendly" relations except in a formal sense. Both nations were irritated. As to a break—the decision rested with the President. Every American citizen waited anxiously to see how the die was to be cast. "If he accepts the note as a compliance," wrote the editor of the New York *Times*, "we are sure he will have the country's devout prayers that his decision may be justified by its results."[3]

". . . the pressure on me," Wilson was hurriedly writing, "instead of growing less, grows greater from day to day, and I cannot find hours enough in the twenty-four. . . ."[4]

He was now being advised by House to make no formal reply; Lansing, thought House, should simply make a public statement that we would deal with other belligerents "as we see fit." While House did not see how we could "break with Germany on this note," he urged that the German government be told, through Gerard and Bernstorff, that "the least infraction would entail an immediate severance of diplomatic relations."[5]

The President drafted a short reply accepting the abandonment of the illegal submarine policy "with satisfaction," but asserting that the United States could not entertain any suggestion that American rights should "in

---

[1] Quotations of editorial opinion, New York *Times*, May 6, 1916.

[2] According to a journalist's poll, only one senator and three representatives believed that Germany had given the United States sufficient cause for war. New York *Tribune*, May 6, 1916, quoted in M. E. Stone, *Fifty Years a Journalist*, p. 311.

[3] New York *Times*, May 6, 1916.

[4] Wilson to C. R. Macauley, the cartoonist, May 5, 1916.

[5] House to Wilson, May 6, 1916.

any way or in any degree be made contingent upon the attitude or action of any other government . . .

"Responsibility in such matters is single, not joint or conditional; absolute, not relative."

This draft he read to Lansing on the 7th. After some discussion Lansing asked if he might take it home with him for further study, and the President assented.[1] The next day Lansing returned the draft with a number of changes and suggestions which showed clearly his conviction that "we should omit any expression of relief on having avoided a break with Germany."[2] The President replied at once:

"You are probably right about cutting out all 'satisfaction', and I am quite content to have the note go as you have amended it."

On the same day, May 8th, the message was sent.[3] The stroke was audacity itself. By snatching the concession free from its restrictions, the Germans were manœuvred into an unconditional acceptance of his demands. Bargaining was adjourned.

Bernstorff was not surprised,[4] nor, probably, were the diplomats at Berlin, who in making their demands had their eyes on their own public feeling. It was a bitter pill for Germany to swallow, but the government of Bethmann-Hollweg, bent now upon avoiding trouble, gulped it down.

It had been a difficult and prolonged struggle: and for Wilson, considering his objectives, a great victory. He had

---

[1] *War Memoirs of Robert Lansing*, p. 143.

[2] Lansing to Wilson, May 8, 1916.

[3] *Foreign Relations*, 1916, Supp., p. 263. On its way the note passed another message from Germany admitting liability for the *Sussex* attack and offering indemnity. *Ibid.*, pp. 265–266.

[4] It was Bernstorff's opinion, indeed, that American commercial, financial and industrial interests would never permit any effective action against England.

won it by consummate patience and skill, by adhering, against all opposition, to his own principles. He had kept the peace.[1]

Nevertheless the situation was left fundamentally precarious. Unless the British weakened their blockade, or unless peace should come quickly, Germany in desperation must eventually forego her pledge to limit the use of the dreaded submarine. In all probability war would follow. American neutrality was at the mercy of the British and German struggle to control the seas. American freedom of choice and action was now marked out in inflexible lines: spring 1916 pointed to spring 1917.

II. WILSON LAUNCHES HIS CAMPAIGN FOR A LEAGUE OF NATIONS

Wilson was vastly eased and relieved by the hard-won German pledge to restrict submarine warfare. For weeks the tension had been merciless; he had now won a magnificent diplomatic victory. The war he dreaded had at least been postponed: he had secured a respite, however brief it might prove, in which to seek again the supreme objective to which he had committed himself: the opportunity and the glory on behalf of his countrymen of becoming peacemaker to the world. He longed to lift "some sacred emblem of counsel and of peace, of accommodation and righteous judgment before the nations of the world."[2]

There remained, indeed, certain difficult problems connected with Allied blockade restrictions—the British were seizing neutral mails, blacklisting our ships and even in-

---

[1]The relative lull in diplomatic activity which followed was to have a profound effect upon the presidential campaign of 1916, then just beginning. See Chapter VII, this volume, pp. 242 *et seq.*

[2]Address at Charlotte, North Carolina, May 20, 1916. *The Public Papers of Woodrow Wilson*, Vol. IV, p. 183.

terfering with efforts of the Red Cross to transport hospital supplies—but these, while increasingly irritating, did not, at the moment, seem critical.[1]

Even though Congress might explode with exasperation[2] no one could quite forget that American war trade with the Allies had now become the bulwark of our economic prosperity. While we believed and charged that the blockade and the black list were illegal, no one could see—at this stage in the war, at any rate—how they could be broken without involving grave danger to the United States. If we laid embargoes on our shipments or closed our ports, what would become of American industry and finance?[3] Wilson himself, as an historian, was vividly conscious of the results of such a drastic course in the past. Embargoes, as he had written to a critic, might be "much more hurtful to us than to the countries against which they were aimed."[4]

It was thus, in early May (1916), that there came a moment of relief, as rare as it was unexpected, from the burden of anxiety connected with the war. The President and Mrs. Wilson deliberately and with delight planned a celebration. They motored to a Virginia golf course in the afternoon hours of May 8th, and in the evening, joined by relatives and friends, went to the circus! The President was in a holiday mood. Passing one of the rings, he took

---

[1]Since the British "Trading with the Enemy Act," December 1915, American trade had been constantly hampered. The black list (or list of firms or ships suspected of having trade relations with the enemy) began to include American ships in April. The British were seizing mail wholesale from neutral ships as early as December 1915. *Foreign Relations*, 1916, Supp., pp. 591, 595–602 (mails), 361, 363–364 (black list).

[2]For example, see *Cong. Rec.*, 64–1, pp. 138–145, 1295–1311, 1671–1679.

[3]What might conceivably have been done in 1914 if there had been foreknowledge of what the war was to become, and the part that America must necessarily play in it— if there had been sufficient courage and self-control!—had become a practical impossibility in 1916. Any attempt to readjust our complicated economic relationships, even if objections at home could have been overcome, would have involved a real risk of war with the now desperate Allies.

[4]Wilson to William Bayard Hale, March 31, 1915.

off his hat and made a gesture as if to throw it in, the crowd cheering until the tent shook.[1]

The next day might possibly have offered some further relaxation, since there was a garden party at the White House—one of the functions that a democracy seems to require—except for the fact that the President had to shake hands with 1,364 guests! He decided on the spot to take a week-end cruise "down the river."

". . . this is my only chance to get away for an absolutely needed rest . . ."[2]

A few days later he told his friends at the National Press Club:

"If I did not go off at week ends occasionally and throw off, as much as it is possible to throw off, this burden, I could not stand it. This week I went down the Potomac and up the James and substituted history for politics, and there was an infinite, sweet calm in some of those old places . . ."[3]

But the President's "rests" throughout his life seldom meant idleness. What he really wanted was to get away from people, from crowding appointments and unceasing talk, where he could look calmly at the questions confronting him, think them through without interruption. From such excursions he returned always with his vision clarified, his determination reënforced.

Many problems were demanding immediate consideration. Major measures—the Shipping bill, Defense bill, Tariff Commission bill, Brandeis' appointment, conservation bills—moving sluggishly through the legislative mill, required his unremitting attention. Mexican relations were highly critical—no one could tell from day to day what might happen—and the Pan-American pact, upon which

---

[1] New York *Times*, May 9, 1916.
[2] Wilson to R. Heath Dabney, May 10, 1916.
[3] *The Public Papers of Woodrow Wilson*, Vol. IV, p. 177.

he had set his heart, had encountered rough going. In addition to all of these complications, the Democratic national convention, in which he was to play the dominant part, was scarcely a month away.

And yet it is clear that the chief problem in his mind during the voyage down the river concerned his duty in connection with the European war.

"No one feels the burden of the present time more than I do, or more profoundly longs for peace, and you may be sure upon the slightest opening I will act."[1]

It seems, indeed, to have been the first time that he had turned his entire attention, devoted his whole mind, to the subject. He had desired peace and discussed it, he had offered good offices, he had sent Colonel House on secret exploratory trips to Europe, but to none of these projects, astonishing as it may appear, does he seem to have given his undivided attention.

It was becoming clearer to him, and to America generally, that unless some way toward peace could be speedily developed, the United States would inevitably and probably soon be drawn into the war. Discussion in Congress was rapidly increasing: all sorts of proposals were being wishfully advanced. Hold an international conference of neutrals? Urge the President to act at once? Offer a specific programme of territorial terms to induce the belligerents to discuss peace?[2]

The President himself felt a new and insistent pressure for action. On May 8th the analytical editor of the Springfield *Republican*,[3] asked whether the President was "obliged to await definite assurances from each coalition that it would welcome an offer from him?"

---

[1]Wilson to Dr. M. A. Matthews, May 8, 1916.

[2]Types of resolutions presented from late February to May 15, 1916. *Cong. Rec.*, 64–1, pp. 3221, 6476 *et seq.*, 7840, 7958.

[3]Waldo L. Cook.

"He is to consider whether new conditions have not arisen which entitle him to propose peace negotiations even regardless of a possible reluctance of certain belligerents to listen to him. The danger that the United States will be drawn into the war has become very real and menacing."[1]

This comment the President read with care, passing it on to House on May 9th:

". . . I want you to see and digest this editorial . . . as soon as possible. The peace intimation contained in the German note seems now to be holding the attention of the country, and it is my prediction that it is going to be increasingly difficult to keep off the insistent demand that I act."

On the quiet voyage down the Potomac in the *Mayflower*, the President considered all of these things. Conditions in Europe were drifting from bad to worse. The belligerents were hopelessly deadlocked; their antagonism had become automatic, insensate. Now, if ever, a definite basis for peace must be proposed, and the thinking initiative must come from some power not directly involved, and not exhausted by war.

When he returned it was with an entirely new programme of action. He had been content with haggling secret conferences: he would have no more of them. He was suspicious (as House tells us) of the peace terms of the Allies; he wished to promote the general good of mankind,

---

[1]Springfield *Republican*, May 8, 1916. Wilson also gave especial attention to an article in the *New Republic*. He pencilled double lines opposite the suggestion of making a call for a peace conference in which Germany was to agree "to evacuate Belgium, France, and Serbia, to indemnify Belgium, and to accept the principle that in the future all nations shall use their resources against the Power which refuses to submit its quarrel to international inquiry." A large question mark was placed beside the suggestion that if Germany accepted, we would, among other actions, accord to Germans "equal rights with Americans in all American protectorates" and refuse to furnish aid to any Power which did "not apply the open door" in its protectorates, etc. *New Republic*, April 22, 1916.

not the territorial aspirations of France and Russia or the naval and commercial ambitions of Great Britain.[1]

The cablegram which he immediately directed House to send to Grey gives striking evidence of this new course of action:

"I believe the President would now be willing to publicly commit the United States to joining with the other powers in a convention looking to the maintenance of peace after the war, provided he announced at the same time that if the war continued much longer, he purposed calling a conference to discuss peace."

As to the league plan here suggested there were two main elements: the signatory nations were to "pledge themselves to side against any power breaking a treaty," and "against any nation refusing in case of dispute to adopt some other method of settlement than that of war." Rules were to be formulated for "limiting armaments both on land and sea" and for making warfare "more humane to those actually engaged and safe-guarding the lives and property of neutrals and non-combatants."[2]

While these ideas, and the general conception of a league of nations, had been long in the air and widely discussed, the President's proposals, so far as responsible statesmanship was concerned, were radically new. Wilson was here demanding that a dream of the poets and the prophets be made the practical objective of international statecraft.

He himself, indeed, had been one of the prophets. As early as 1887 he had believed that the rapid developments of modern politics would ultimately lead to a "confederation" of nations. He had realized, as soon as the world proportions of the war had been disclosed in August 1914,

---

[1]The exact diary sources for the summary of House's impressions at this period (May 3rd to May 8th) have not been made available. *The Intimate Papers of Colonel House*, Vol. II, p. 250.

[2]Sent as a cablegram, May 10, 1916.

that out of it must come "an association of the nations, all bound together for the protection of the integrity of each, so that any one nation breaking from this bond will bring upon herself war; that is to say, punishment, automatically."[1] He had written, January 4, 1915, to his college friend, Heath Dabney, that he was "very much interested" in creating a world federation, although he "could not venture" just then to give public sanction to the idea:

"It is imperative that I should stand aloof at present for fear of seeming to press a matter which must be handled with the utmost delicacy and can be carried only the first practicable step."[2]

However prophetic his vision, Wilson would never have committed himself to such a radical step as he was now proposing, if he had not believed that the moment for action in the field of practical statesmanship had arrived. There was, indeed, much evidence that Americans were beginning to realize acutely how fully they were involved economically and morally in world affairs, and how necessary it was to take part in keeping the world at peace. Bryan had stated, when the war was barely two months old, that in "this age our interests are so entwined with the interests of those who reside in other lands that no nation can live or die unto itself alone," and that America must help the world toward "enduring" peace.[3] Henry Cabot Lodge went even further in June 1915 when at

---

[1] See *Woodrow Wilson, Life and Letters*, Vol. V, *Neutrality*, pp. 74–75.

[2] Dabney had written a letter explaining the ideas of Raleigh C. Minor, who had prepared and sent to the President on January 1, 1915, a manuscript constitution for such a federation.

Wilson also wrote a similar letter to Minor after seeing the manuscript, January 5, 1915. Dabney pressed the matter again during the *Lusitania* crisis, already drawing the conclusion that if we had to go into the war, one of the compensations would be that we could assist in carrying "the human race toward the goal of a universal federation of the world" for peace, with the liberty-loving democracies of the United States, Great Britain, France, and (perhaps) Russia at the head of it. (Dabney to Wilson, May 11, 1915.)

[3] Prayer Day address, October 4, 1914.

Union College he declared: "Nations must unite as men unite in order to preserve peace and order."[1] Theodore Roosevelt thought Lodge's speech "admirable," "capital," "in your best style."[2] The other living ex-President, Taft, was president of the League to Enforce Peace. The evidence seemed to justify Wilson's assumption that America was now prepared to take a more active and practical rôle in encouraging a new world organization.

On the other hand it is to be noted that nearly every major argument in the later League fight was advanced *before* Woodrow Wilson spoke in favour of any League!

Bryan, close to the people throughout his active political career, was strongly opposed to an organized league which involved the use of force to keep the peace. Speaking May 18, 1916, at the very moment when Wilson was preparing the crucial address to be delivered before the League to Enforce Peace, he set forth his objections: it would involve us in "entangling alliances with Europe," it would break down the Monroe Doctrine and permit foreign nations "to assist us in maintaining peace" in our hemisphere; it would vest the power of Congress to declare war in "a council controlled by European nations"; and finally, "when we turn from moral suasion to force, we step down and not up."[3]

Curiously enough, Lansing, while agreeing with Bryan in little else, was thinking along the same lines, though, characteristically, stressing legal rather than idealistic arguments. Writing to the President on May 25th, he maintained that an organization such as the League to Enforce Peace would infringe upon "our national sovereignty and national interests." It would "limit our

---

[1]Lodge, *War Addresses, 1915–1917*, p. 41.

[2]Roosevelt to Lodge, August 4, 1915. *Selections from the Correspondence of Theodore Roosevelt and Henry Cabot Lodge*, Vol. II, p. 460.

[3]*Report of the Twenty-Second Annual Lake Mohonk Conference on International Arbitration*, May 17, 18, and 19, 1916, pp. 144–147.

independence of action . . . to the will of other powers beyond this hemisphere." The only alternative to using force beyond the seas would be the repudiation of our treaty obligation. "Neither our sovereignty nor our interests would accord with such a proposition . . ." And "popular opinion as well as the Senate would reject a treaty framed along such lines." He suggested that "the use of force might be avoided by outlawing the offending nation." He thought the world was so bound together in economic dependence that such outlawry would be effective. Interdict trade and even communication—"make that nation a pariah" until it was willing "to perform its obligations." The use of physical force was not "practical or advisable."

Strong arguments, destined to outlive their authors, for they marked permanent divisions of opinion.

But Wilson had thought his position through and was prepared to take his stand. As much an idealist in his vision of the ultimate goal as Bryan, as sensitive to the dangers involved as Lansing, he was a realist as to facts. Against Mexico, and in the Caribbean, he had used force —both physical and economic. Lansing's distinction between the two was one of degree, not of kind, for economic pressure, often as cruel as war itself, passes quickly into actual fighting, as any extended labour strike or international embargo has plainly shown. Bryan and Lansing had both admitted that the world was newly bound together by economic and other non-political ties; our freedom of action was obviously already limited. America, as the chief creditor for all the world, had certainly as great a stake in world peace as any other nation. Furthermore —it was one of Wilson's deepest convictions—America should serve the world with her power, her ideals, her example, and her leadership. America—and America alone —could lead the way to peace and progress. Our participation in a league of peace was at once a moral responsibility to the world and a means of protection to ourselves.

There is no doubt, also, that the idea of future security for all nations loomed large in Wilson's mind, not only as an ultimate objective, but as an immediate influence in bringing about peace negotiations. The promise of such future security might induce the belligerents to modify their immediate material demands. Grey undoubtedly favoured the proposal partly in alarm at the territorial scramble which he saw ahead, just beyond the war, in which Great Britain, as the greatest of colonial powers, might lose more than she gained.

Force, then, was implicit in the plan the President was now proposing, and he accepted it frankly.

"In the last analysis," he told a pacifist delegation on May 8th, "the peace of society is obtained by force . . ." It was true that "when action comes,—it comes by opinion," but back of the opinion was "the ultimate application of force."

"If you say, 'We shall not have any war,' you have got to have the force to make that 'shall' bite."[1]

A further significant letter from House to Grey on the 11th was approved by Wilson:

"If we should get into the war . . . It would probably lead to the complete crushing of Germany; and Russia, Italy and France would then be more concerned as to the division of the spoils than they would for any far-reaching agreement . . . looking to the maintenance of peace in the future and the amelioration of the horrors of war."

There was here no mention of England's material desires—but the disapproval which was expressed for the appetite of her allies indicated in general the attitude of the United States.

---

[1] Interview with a group from the American Union Against Militarism. See the *Independent*, May 22, 1916, p. 264.

The letter struck also at the idea, often advanced by the British, of winning conclusive victories before talking peace:

"The wearing down process, as far as Germany is concerned, has gone far enough to make her sensible of the power we can wield. This . . . will help in the final settlement."

The British were, indeed, warned outright against refusing to support this move for peace:

"Her statesmen will take a great responsibility upon themselves if they hesitate or delay, and in the event of failure because they refuse to act quickly, history will bring a grave indictment against them."

These were bold challenges: and Grey's response was thoroughly weak and wholly disappointing. He said he would not be able to discuss peace; his colleagues and the Allies would be sure to say that a conference was "premature, especially after the German Chancellor's last speech of which both the terms and tone were resented by the Allies."[1]

As to the terms suggested, Grey wrote:

"The President's suggestion [of] summoning a peace conference without any indication of a basis on which peace might be made . . . would be construed as instigated by Germany to secure peace on terms unfavourable to the Allies while her existing military position is still satisfactory to her."

From Grey's viewpoint, there had been a decided retrogression in American proposals since February, when he had been pleased with House's unauthorized talk of material peace terms which Germany might be *forced* to accept. In May, dealing directly with the President, he was being offered genuine mediation in the interest of the

---

[1]Grey to House, cablegram, May 12, 1916; received May 13th and sent by House to Wilson, May 14th.

world's future peace and stability. He hesitated even as to the league idea. Except for the direct limitation of armaments—which he questioned—he was, he wrote, still personally in favour of a league. But he could not "guarantee how others would receive it." ". . . as to the desirability of it now and with a summoning of a peace conference I cannot express an opinion beyond what I have stated above." This was evasive enough!

In the meantime there was no slackening of peace talk from other sources. The King of Spain had information that Germany would favour a peace movement. Ambassador Willard telegraphed from Madrid that the King had said he was ready to act with President Wilson, and that the Pope would also coöperate.[1] Gerard reported from Berlin that Bethmann-Hollweg believed that "if in four or six weeks nothing is done by us to enforce international law against England," there would be such a clamour in Germany for unrestricted submarine warfare that opposition to it would be useless.[2] Gerard himself added: "There is in my opinion no doubt whatever but that he is right. . . . The only other alternative in my opinion is for the President to demand a general peace." Page was quite wrong; the Germans had not been "bagged" by the *Sussex* pledge.[3]

The President was meanwhile earnestly debating two questions:

"When is the time to offer our good offices?

"Shall I outline tentatively some plan at the dinner of the League to Enforce Peace . . . the latter part of this month?"[4]

He spoke to the Press Club on Monday, the 15th:

"There are two reasons why the chief wish of America is

---

[1] May 11, 1916. *Foreign Relations*, 1916, Supp. pp. 28–29.

[2] *Ibid.*, p. 267.

[3] Walter H. Page to Wilson, May 12, 1916.

[4] As he put his problem to the author at a conference, May 11, 1916. From the author's notes.

for peace. One is that they love peace and have nothing to do with the present quarrel; and the other is that they believe the present quarrel has carried those engaged in it so far that they cannot be held to ordinary standards of responsibility . . ."

Even though the rest of the world was mad, we could not in the future isolate ourselves. We must use our moral influence even to the point of disciplining those who refused to heed it.[1]

". . . the great burden on my spirits, gentlemen, has been that it has been up to me to choose when that time came."

Although this use of force might become necessary at any time, he stressed the importance of "keeping out of the present war," if it were possible to do so. If somebody did not keep "the processes of peace going" and his passions disengaged, "by what impartial judgment and suggestion is the world to be aided to a solution when the whole thing is over?"[2]

It was characteristic of Wilson that he should have spoken so frankly. He was thinking aloud, revealing his mind with that vividness and warmth which a sympathetic audience so often aroused in him. It aided him no doubt in the momentous decisions of the next twenty-four hours.

He had now before him Grey's unsatisfactory, even alarming, letter, and the draft of a response that House was proposing.

"It is not intended that the President's statement regarding the calling of a peace conference should be definite. It would be scarcely more than an intimation in order to satisfy the growing insistence that he take some action.

[1] A direct illustration occurred the day before he spoke, when American marines entered the capital city of the Dominican Republic to compel order.

[2] The address was by agreement not to be reported textually, but the President later consented to revise the transcript of it for publication. *The Public Papers of Woodrow Wilson*, Vol. IV, pp. 171–173.

"His proposal for a league of nations would be definite. The cause of the Allies is at high tide here, but if there comes a recession it would not be possible to do the things that would now be approved."[1]

But Wilson was unwilling, now, to follow the mollifying House, or to soothe Grey's fears by backing away from the proposals he had made. Instead he moved forward to a new position, setting forth his views in one of the most vigorous and decisive letters of his career. He himself considered it a "turning point." It contained, indeed, in essence, the things he was to say in one speech after another from this time on:

Washington.
16 May, 1916.

MY DEAREST FRIEND,

I have been giving some very careful thought to your question how we should deal with Sir Edward and his Government at this turning point,—for it really is that.

It seems to me that we should really get down to hard pan. The situation has altered altogether since you had your conference in London and Paris. The at least temporary removal of the acute German question has concentrated attention here on the altogether indefensible course Great Britain is pursuing with regard to trade to and from neutral ports and her quite intolerable interception of mails on the high seas carried by neutral ships. Recently there has been added the great shock opinion in this country has received from the course of the British Government towards some of the Irish rebels.

We are plainly face to face with this alternative, therefore. The United States must either make a decided move for peace (upon some basis that promises to be permanent) or, if she postpones that, must insist to the limit upon her rights of trade and upon such freedom of the seas as international law already justifies her in insisting on as against Great Britain, with the same plain speaking and firmness that she has used against Germany. And the choice must be made immediately.

---

[1] Quoted entire. Sent by House to Wilson, May 14, 1916.

Which does Great Britain prefer? She cannot escape both. To do nothing is now, for us, impossible.

If we move for peace, it will be along these lines 1) Such a settlement with regard to their own immediate interests as the belligerents may be able to agree upon. We have nothing material of any kind to ask for ourselves and are quite aware that we are in no sense parties to the quarrel. Our interest is only in peace and its guarantees; 2) a universal alliance to maintain freedom of the seas and to prevent any war begun either a) contrary to treaty covenants or b) without warning and full inquiry,—a virtual guarantee of territorial integrity and political independence.

It seems to me to be of imperative and pressing importance that Sir Edward should understand all this and that the crisis can not be postponed; and it can be done with the most evident spirit of friendliness through you. Will you not prepare a full cable putting the whole thing plainly to him? We must act, and act at once, in the one direction or the other.

With affectionate messages from us all.

Faithfully yours,
WOODROW WILSON.

MR. EDWARD M. HOUSE,
115 East 53rd Street,
New York City.[1]

House immediately drafted a new message to Grey on the basis of this letter, secured the President's approval, and sent it off on the 19th. As might have been expected, House diluted the President's sternness by saying that there was no intention of calling a conference "immediately," so that the Allies would have "ample" time to test out the endurance of the Germans; and by repeating Bernstorff's words of the day before that German public

---

[1]Examined in retrospect, after seeing what happened at the Paris peace conference, Wilson's statement regarding the settlement of the material demands of the belligerents, on the basis of what they "may be able to agree upon" seems a feeble solution, but under the circumstances of the moment, May 1916, with the war in deadlock, and each side strong enough to prevent the imposition of too drastic terms, the suggestion was sound enough. Wilson not only expected at that time a settlement by negotiation, but he always underestimated the importance of lands, goods, chattels!

opinion "would not at present tolerate the President as a mediator." The most astonishing paragraph in House's cable to Grey is that in which House flatly states that if "England is indeed fighting for the emancipation of Europe, we are ready to join her . . ." Nevertheless the British were given to understand that if peace discussions were not "soon" begun, the Allies might expect to have their interferences with American rights challenged as Germany's had been.[1]

The American public, indeed, was now vociferously declaring its opinion that British invasions of American trade rights were both illegal and intolerable and must be stopped.[2] The State Department was sharpening its demands; Page was ordered to bring to the attention of the British government complaints against the "black-listing" of various American ships.[3] An investigation was started to determine just how much legitimate trade we were entitled to have with the neutral nations of northern Europe.[4] On the 24th a note was sent to the British and French ambassadors in Washington which branded the seizures of American mail as "lawless" and stated that only a "radical change in the present British and French policy, restoring to the United States its full rights as a neutral power, will satisfy this Government."[5] Such a display of

---

[1]*The Intimate Papers of Colonel House*, Vol. II, pp. 286–287.

[2]*Cf.* Senator Paul O. Husting, a defender of the administration, to Wilson, May 16, 1916. America was also distinctly anxious about the peace negotiations that failed month after month to materialize. A peace rider was attached to the Naval Appropriation bill pending in Congress, authorizing the President to call a conference "not later than the close of the war in Europe" to make recommendations, (a) for an international organization providing for a peaceful settlement of disputes, and (b) for disarmament; and setting aside $200,000 for this purpose! Introduced by Representative W. L. Hensley, of Missouri, and ultimately passed. *U. S. Statutes at Large*, Vol. 39, Pt. 1, p. 618.

[3]*Foreign Relations*, 1916, Supp., p. 392.

[4]*Ibid.*, p. 395.

[5]*Foreign Relations*, 1916, Supp., pp. 604–608. The original intention was to send the note only to Great Britain, but a minor storm of last-minute negotiations caused a change. Grey, in a state of excitement, cabled a long protest insisting that the French

cold thinking and hot feeling did stir the British: but not to the point of making a "radical change." Ambassadors Spring Rice and Jusserand expressed themselves as disappointed in the tone of the note, parts of which would, they thought, make "for bad feeling instead of good," but as to the issue itself, "there was no conflict of principle that could not be met."[1] In other words, to the Allies the criticism was deplorable, and the issue not vital.

Page in London gave so little support to the efforts of the administration that Lansing and Wilson became thoroughly disgusted. They considered having him come home for a few weeks in order to gain a better understanding of American opinion and policy.[2]

Back of all the discussions and negotiations, one brutal fundamental fact had constantly to be recognized. This was the vast web of commerce and finance in which belligerents and neutrals alike were now hopelessly entangled. Trade between the United States and the Allies had become the great artery which, flowing westward, fed American war prosperity, and flowing eastward, sustained the life of the Allied armies and populations. Diplomats and statesmen alike dreaded any policy that threatened to contract that life-giving stream. Even the boldest pronouncements and demands of the President fell short of being vital. Nevertheless, there was always the danger, which the diplomats of the belligerent nations had to watch narrowly, that some outrage would prove a breaking point, or that this strange President with his ideals and his

be included so as to cushion the blow against England. *The Intimate Papers of Colonel House*, Vol. II, pp. 308–309.

[1] Quoting House's summary of Captain Gaunt's report, House to Wilson, May 26, 1916.

[2] Wilson to House, May 17, 1916. *The Intimate Papers of Colonel House*, Vol. II, p. 269. House perhaps inflamed this attitude by his letters at this time. A letter to Wilson dated May 10th undermined Page by charging that Page had felt so "offended" at the presence of House on his former mission that he would probably resign if House were sent again; and by remarking Page's hostility to Wilson's policy. Page was called home only later, in mid-summer.

moral convictions might—there was horror in the thought
—bring his vast nation into the war on the wrong side!

The President kept daily contact with all the negotiations and with the dispatches to and from the State Department, sometimes remaining at his desk until past
midnight.[1] His main effort, during these difficult weeks,
however, was in behalf of his peace plans, which he carried
forward practically without reference to Lansing.

By the middle of May he had decided to take the leadership of the important and rapidly growing American
movement in behalf of a world league for peace. He had
declined, on April 14th, an invitation to speak at a great
meeting of the League to Enforce Peace: but he recon-
sidered, and accepted on May 18th, regarding it then,
apparently, as an opportunity to drive home his convictions as to American responsibility in world affairs.

Washington.
18 May, 1916

DEAREST FRIEND:

I am thinking a great deal about the speech I am to make on
the twenty-seventh, because I realize that it may be the most
important I shall ever be called upon to make, and I greatly
value your suggestion about the navy programme.[2]

Would you do me the favour to formulate what you would
say, in my place, if you were seeking to make the proposal as
nearly what you deem Grey and his colleagues to have agreed
upon in principle as it is possible to make it when concretely
formulated as a proposal? Your recollection of your conferences
is so much more accurate than mine that I would not trust
myself to state the proposition without advice from you,
though it may be wise to strengthen and heighten the terms a
little.[3]

---

[1]According to Mrs. Wilson, who frequently assisted him.

[2]House had written on the 17th: "If we are to join with other great powers in a
world movement to maintain peace, we ought to immediately inaugurate a big naval
programme."

[3]He asked Colonel House for this information believing—probably mistakenly—that
House had thoroughly discussed the league idea with Grey.

Why do you say so confidently that it is idle to hope that the European nations will at this time consider the establishment of some such tribunal as the programme of the League to Enforce Peace proposes?[1] It is a body only to inquire and report and is given no right of decision. How else can we secure the deliberate consideration of all situations that may threaten war and lay a foundation for the concerted action of nations against unjustifiable breaches of the peace of the world? The only inducement we can hold out to the Allies is one which will actually remove the menace of Militarism.

Affectionately yours,
WOODROW WILSON.

The President also began to bring together suggestions bearing upon his proposals. He kept these clippings and his own notes in shorthand close beside him in his study, in confidential folders which not even a secretary was permitted to touch. Among them were selections from the *Independent*, including an editorial, "The Time Has Come"[2]; sheets from the *New Republic* carrying James Bryce's article, "America's Traditional Isolation"[3]; an

---

[1] The League's proposals were as follows:

"*First:* All justiciable questions arising between the signatory powers, not settled by negotiation, shall, subject to the limitations of treaties, be submitted to a judicial tribunal for hearing and judgment, both upon the merits and upon any issue as to its jurisdiction of the question.

"*Second:* All other questions arising between the signatories and not settled by negotiation, shall be submitted to a council of conciliation for hearing, consideration and recommendation.

"*Third:* The signatory powers shall jointly use forthwith both their economic and military forces against any one of their number that goes to war, or commits acts of hostility, against another of the signatories before any question arising shall be submitted as provided in the foregoing.

"*Fourth:* Conferences between the signatory powers shall be held from time to time to formulate and codify rules of international law, which, unless some signatory shall signify its dissent within a stated period, shall thereafter govern in the decisions of the Judicial Tribunal mentioned in Article One."

House wrote Wilson May 9th: "You cannot form 'immediate judicial tribunals for hearing and judgment upon the merits of international issues.' Nor can you now get the great powers to submit differences . . . to a council of conciliation." In his reply to Wilson's letter of the 18th, however, House agreed that the tribunal could be "worked out" after the powers were committed to the general idea of a league.

[2] May 22, 1916, written by Hamilton Holt.

[3] May 20, 1916.

editorial from the Baltimore *Sun* urging an immediate conference of neutrals to offer to the belligerents a peace programme that would, by requiring of the great world powers the surrender of a little independence, guarantee an international system of keeping peace.[1] And there, too, were quotations from the speeches of English statesmen since the beginning of the "Time of Troubles"—Asquith, Grey, Lloyd George, Balfour.[2]

Wilson also clarified his thought in another notable public address. He spoke May 20th at Charlotte, North Carolina, near Davidson College, where he had once been a student, interested already in the drafting of constitutions.[3] The boy of 1873 had now become a world leader and was thinking about the greatest of all constitutions, a new world order.

Nations, he was thinking, have been finding their lives in recent years more and more interrelated—the world a kind of melting pot, unifying hopes and thoughts. The great war itself was "the tremendous—I had about said final—process by which a contest of elements may in God's process be turned into a co-ordination and co-operation of elements."

America, with her experience in bringing men of different races together in liberty and coöperation, had been "a sort of prophetic sample of mankind." "Now ... every nation [is] face to face with this question, 'What are you going to do with your power? Are you going to translate it into force, or are you going to translate it into peace and the salvation of society?'"[4]

---

[1]May 20, 1916.

[2]Given to Colonel House by Norman Angell, and sent by House to Wilson, May 19, 1916. Asquith's speech at Dublin, September 25, 1914; Lloyd George's speech at the Queen's Hall, July 28, 1908; Grey's dispatch to Sir E. Goschen, July 30, 1914, and Grey's interview with Edward Price Bell, May 13, 1916; also excerpts, London *Times* editorials: this, "a war against war," August 16, 1914; the great objectives, to crush the German brand of "international morality" and militarism, September 5, 1914.

[3]*Woodrow Wilson, Life and Letters*, Vol. I, *Youth*, pp. 75-76.

[4]*The Public Papers of Woodrow Wilson*, Vol. IV, pp. 178-183.

Upon his return to Washington, he began at once to prepare his address, deciding that, in view of the antagonistic attitude of the Allies, suggestions for immediate peace moves should be made cautiously.[1] On May 24th, indeed, Grey made an impromptu speech in the Commons, declaring—to the accompaniment of "Hear, Hear's"—that the time had not come to make speeches about peace. ". . . the Allies are not beaten, and are not going to be. The first step towards peace will be when the German Government begins to recognize that fact."[2] The English public, Page wrote the next day, responded to Grey with the will to "fight to a finish." "The more sensational press intimates that any Englishman who uses the word 'peace' ought to be shot."[3] The war creed —ancient and still blind! Even Grey, "the most gentle of all the Cabinet,"[4] was opposing Wilson's peace hopes!

The President, however, let nothing interfere with the main part of his address, his declaration in behalf of a league of peace.

He made his great commitment on May 27th. A distinguished audience of some two thousand, gathered in the New Willard Hotel in Washington, heard the address. Senator Henry Cabot Lodge had preceded him:

"The limit of voluntary arbitration has, I think, been reached . . . the next step is . . . to put force behind international peace. . . .

". . . I do not believe that when Washington warned us against entangling[5] alliances he meant for one moment

---

[1]"Signs multiply," he wrote to House, May 22nd, "that the Allies are becoming alarmed at the possibility of our making a move for peace." See also *The Intimate Papers of Colonel House*, Vol. II, pp. 294-295.

[2]*Parliamentary Debates*, House of Commons, Fifth Series, Vol. LXXXII, p. 2203, May 24, 1916.

[3]*The Life and Letters of Walter H. Page*, Vol. II, p. 158.

[4]*Ibid.*

[5]The word was, of course, Jefferson's. Washington said "permanent" alliances in his Farewell Address.

that we should not join with the other civilized nations of the world if a method could be found to diminish war and encourage peace."[1]

So thought the bitterest American opponent of a league of nations—before it had become a political and partisan issue!

The President began and ended his address with a calm discussion of America's relation to the war:

"It is right that I, as spokesman of our Government, should attempt to give expression to what I believe to be the thought and purpose of the people of the United States . . ."

The great war had "affected us very profoundly."

"With its causes and its objects we are not concerned. The obscure fountains from which its stupendous flood has burst forth we are not interested to search for or explore. . . .

"We . . . are quite aware that we are in no sense or degree parties to the present quarrel."

He made one observation, however, concerning the outbreak of the war:

"It is plain that this war could have come only as it did, suddenly and out of secret counsels, without warning to the world, without discussion . . . It is probable that if it had been foreseen just what would happen . . . those who brought the great contest on would have been glad to substitute conference for force. If we ourselves had been afforded some opportunity to apprise the belligerents of the attitude which it would be our duty to take, of the policies and practices against which we would feel bound to use all our moral and economic strength, and in certain circumstances even our physical strength also, our own contribution to the counsel which might have averted

---

[1]*Proceedings of the First Annual National Assemblage of the League to Enforce Peace,* May 26–27, 1916 (Washington), pp. 165–166.

the struggle would have been considered worth weighing . . ."

The lessons of this war, then, were that "a new and more wholesome diplomacy," the governing of nations "by the same high code of honor that we demand of individuals," and a reliable assurance of peace must be brought about.

Having surveyed the scene, and shown that we "are participants, whether we would or not, in the life of the world," with obligations and interests in all that "affects mankind," Wilson spoke directly of his great plan.

The thought of world statesmen, he declared, had been set ahead "a whole age" by the war and had reached the following conclusions:

". . . that the principle of public right must henceforth take precedence over the individual interests of particular nations, and that the nations of the world must in some way band themselves together to see that that right prevails as against any sort of selfish aggression . . ."

In the midst of the dark prejudices and animosities of the war he could see a bright hope for a world community and for coöperation to do justice and keep the peace:

"The nations of the world have become each other's neighbors. It is to their interest that they should understand each other."

What should be the charter for this neighbourhood world?

"We believe these fundamental things: First, that every people has a right to choose the sovereignty under which they shall live. . . . Second, that the small states of the world have a right to enjoy the same respect for their sovereignty and for their territorial integrity that great and powerful nations expect and insist upon. And, third, that the world has a right to be free from every disturbance of its peace that has its origin in aggression and disregard of the rights of peoples and nations."

The crucial declaration followed:

". . . the United States is willing to become a partner in any feasible association of nations formed in order to realize these objects and make them secure against violation.

"There is nothing that the United States wants for itself that any other nation has. We are willing, on the contrary, to limit ourselves along with them . . ."

He faced the final implications, the danger and the importance of which he knew well: this league must be enabled to maintain peace by "coercion" if necessary.

". . . some common force will be brought into existence which shall safeguard right . . ."

He spoke for immediate peace guardedly, but offered a clear-cut plan. He said that he would be glad to initiate a peace movement:

". . . First, such a settlement with regard to their own immediate interests as the belligerents may agree upon. . . . Second, an universal association of the nations to maintain the inviolate security of the highway of the seas for the common and unhindered use of all the nations of the world, and to prevent any war begun either contrary to treaty covenants or without warning and full submission of the causes to the opinion of the world—a virtual guarantee of territorial integrity and political independence."

He hoped negotiations could begin soon:

"God grant that the dawn of that day of frank dealing and of settled peace, concord and coöperation may be near at hand!"[1]

The immense significance of his address was at once understood in America: it marked "the opening of a new period of history and the ending of our deepest tradition"; the President had grasped the "supreme opportunity"; he

[1] *The Public Papers of Woodrow Wilson*, Vol. IV, pp. 185–188.

had chosen "the noble part" on the chief issue of modern life.[1] It was hoped that Europe would make "a sympathetic response."[2]

It was inevitable, of course, that opposing opinion should also find immediate and vigorous expression—its chief tenet being, of course, that the United States dare not forget the historic injunction against alliances.[3] Wilson met this criticism promptly and frankly:

"I shall never myself consent to an entangling alliance, but I would gladly assent to a disentangling alliance—an alliance which would disentangle the peoples of the world from those combinations in which they seek their own separate . . . interests and unite the people of the world to preserve the peace of the world upon a basis of common right and justice."

The President was himself confident that the country would agree:

". . . America is roused, roused to a self-consciousness and a national self-consciousness such as she has not had in a generation.

"And this spirit is going out conquering and to conquer. . . ."[4]

The President had tried to put his proposals "in a way that it would be very hard for the Allies to reject, as well as for Germany."[5] However, neither of the two European coalitions reacted favourably. British and French editors pounced angrily upon the so-called "unfortunate phrase" about the war: "With its causes and its objects we are

---

[1] *The New Republic*, June 3, 1916 (editorial).

[2] Springfield *Republican;* quotations from the press, New York *Times*, May 29, 1916.

[3] Pittsburgh *Gazette*, May 28, 1916; New York *Times*, May 29, 1916.

[4] Address at Arlington, May 30, 1916. *The Public Papers of Woodrow Wilson*, Vol. IV, pp. 195, 196. As will be shown later, he wrote the proposal into the Democratic platform in order to have the party responsibly committed and thus give opportunity for a public endorsement or rejection by the only direct method available in American government: the automatic four-year election.

[5] Wilson to House, May 29, 1916.

not concerned." They scorned the plea for peace. In Germany newspaper editors found interest only in the mention of peace, for which, in general, there was approval even though they were sensitive on the subject of mediation.[1] And the whole Reichstag, excepting only the Socialists, applauded a speech by Delegate Stresemann indignantly rejecting the thought of mediation by Wilson.[2] Bernstorff was officially ordered to block any such attempt by the President.[3]

Only the Liberal press in England sympathetically understood the immense significance of Wilson's proposal of a league. Most of the British papers were infected with virulent suspicion of a league having as one of its objects to make the seas secure "for the common and unhindered use of all the nations."[4] German editors thought—or at least said—very little about the league. Only the European neutrals praised the whole address, seeing in it a hopeful step toward making a sound world peace.[5]

The attitude of Great Britain was the determinative factor in realizing any hopes for either the league or peace. Without support from her, the belligerent with whom America had the closest ties, further progress was impossible. Page's letters soon conveyed the discouraging fact that the British public generally regarded the President as hopelessly ignorant of the meaning of the war and as a meddler in trying to make peace. They even ques-

---

[1]"We must . . . make it clear that he who desires to mediate a peace must confine himself exclusively to broaching and starting the discussion." *Vossische Zeitung*, quoted in the New York *Times*, May 30, 1916. "President Wilson and the Peace of Europe," pamphlet collection of European press comment, published by the Neutral Conference for Continuous Mediation (Stockholm, 1916), No. XII, pp. 26–47.

[2]*Foreign Relations*, 1916, Supp., p. 33.

[3]*Official German Documents*, Vol. II, pp. 976–978.

[4]A. G. Gardiner, the able Liberal writer for the London *Daily News*, expressed in a letter to House, June 15th, the regret of the more understanding Englishmen "that the response has not been more enthusiastic in some of the English journals." (Sent by House to Wilson, June 27, 1916.)

[5]"President Wilson and the Peace of Europe," pp. 13–26.

tioned whether he might not be merely electioneering![1]
Sir Horace Plunkett cabled that the "announcement of
unconcern with the causes and with the objects of this
war has shocked those who only entered the war to defend Belgium."[2]

The British attitude was in turn shocking to this government. Grey's reply to the urgent cable of May 19th was
at last sent on the 29th. Its tone was especially unfortunate. A league of nations, asserted Grey, should be founded
upon a peace favourable to the Allies! As to calling a peace
conference, he suggested that if "the President desires the
Allies to be consulted he should, if he does not wish to
approach them all simultaneously, take the French
Government at any rate into his confidence as directly as
he has taken us. The French Government in this way may
be sufficiently impressed with his real intentions and
good will."

Grey denounced the whole idea of a negotiated peace.
He pointed out that there was "real danger that if Germany succeeds in obtaining terms of peace satisfactory
to her ... militarism in Germany will remain the dominant
force, and will render ineffective and insecure any convention for maintaining future peace.

"The terms must be sufficiently favourable to the Allies
to make the German people feel that aggressive militarism
is a failure."

The Foreign Secretary even intimated that Wilson was
interfering with the territorial changes which the Allies
wished to settle among themselves, though Wilson had
said as plainly as possible that "our interest is only in
peace and its future guarantees."

"The best chance" for the President's "great scheme"

---

[1]See, for example, the London *Times*, May 29, 1916, and the *Morning Post*, May 30,
1916 (clippings enclosed, Page to House, May 30, 1916, transmitted to Wilson June
14th; Page to Wilson, June 1, 1916).

[2]Plunkett to House, May 29th, transmitted to Wilson June 1, 1916.

lay in that kind of peace, Grey concluded, not even hesitating to add that it was "obtainable with American aid." "The worst chance" would be to propose his league in connection with an "inconclusive or disastrous peace accompanied, perhaps promoted, by diplomatic friction by the Allies and the United States over maritime affairs!"

This remarkable and revealing letter ended on a note of warning: ". . . a premature announcement of intervention by the President . . . would be interpreted as meaning that he desired peace on a basis favourable to Germany and for the reasons above stated. No such peace could secure a reliable and enduring international organization of the kind he contemplates."

This left the British attitude in no doubt whatever. But House transmitted the message to the President on the 31st of May without a hint of dissatisfaction except that it should have arrived earlier. "I shall talk freely with Jusserand tomorrow as Sir Edward suggests," he wrote.

The 31st of May was also the day on which Wilson received Carranza's impertinent note impugning our good faith and intentions, which, however, Arredondo presented with the remark that it was "not an ultimatum, but merely a continuation of the diplomatic discussion."[1] The chief contrast was that Grey's note abruptly suspended all discussion.

The President was thoroughly exasperated. During the following three weeks he became sterner, more determined to force the issue. At last he wrote to House, a letter marked by decision and a full realization of the tremendous struggle he was facing:

"The letters and the glimpses of opinion (official opinion) from the other side of the water are not encouraging, to say the least, and indicate a constantly narrowing, instead of a broad and comprehending view of the situa-

[1] Polk to Wilson, May 31, 1916. See this volume, Chapter III, p. 75.

tion. They are in danger of forgetting the rest of the world, and of waking up some surprising morning to discover that it has a positive right to be heard about the peace of the world. I conclude that it will be up to us to judge for ourselves when the time has arrived for us to make an imperative suggestion. I mean a suggestion which they will have no choice but to heed, because the opinion of the non-official world and the desire of all peoples will be behind it."[1]

Wilson had now taken the measure of the opposition which had constantly thwarted his moves for peace. The fact marked a great change in him. In May he had assumed, with a masterful initiative, the leadership of the world forces for peace; and in June he became the aggressive fighter for the new order—the League of Nations—for which his name was henceforth to stand.

This assumption of strong leadership on the part of the President, with his clear programme of what ought to be done, served at first to increase the distrust between the Allies and the United States. The French feared that our peace efforts would result in detaching one or more of their allies, leaving France in dire need.[2] Jusserand tried to bring pressure upon Wilson by informing House that Russia, Japan, and Germany would, in his opinion, drift together in an alliance after the war and attack the United States. Then he coolly "hinted we would have no sympathizers in our [hour] of trouble unless we more actively took the part of the Allies."[3]

"In reply to this," House reported, "I said, we could take care of ourselves for within a few years we would probably have a navy large enough to withstand both

---

[1] June 22, 1916. That the French and British *people* were in large part for peace was admitted even by Jusserand. House to Wilson, June 10, 1916.

[2] Polk to Wilson, June 6, 1916, reporting a conference with Jusserand.

[3] House to Wilson, June 1, 1916.

Germany and Japan." House thereupon advised Wilson again to build up the navy: "If we do not, some such trouble may come. . . .

"If after all the warning we have had, trouble should follow this war, the people would feel that their interests had not been properly protected."[1]

As for the British, determination to stiffen the blockade remained the keynote.[2] House tried—on the whole quite unfortunately, and without warrant from the President— to smooth the stormy waters. Writing to Grey June 8th he sought to explain away Wilson's "minor"[3] phrase about unconcern with the war's causes, and to argue that the peace Wilson had in mind would be favourable to the Allies' territorial ambitions—about which he offered certain suggestions. They were surprisingly elementary: France might "perhaps" receive Alsace and Lorraine, Germany get compensation "perhaps in Asia Minor," Russia "get a warm seaport and Italy what she is entitled to"! "The world at large . . . might have something akin to permanent peace."

Falling in with Grey's pointed advice, he wrote in conclusion that there was "nothing" for us to do but to "rest content" if the Allies preferred to gamble for military victory rather than accept Wilson's mediation on the basis of a league.[4]

As has been seen, the President was anything but willing

---

[1]*Op. cit.* On September 24th, however, House wrote: "It was my opinion that the real difference with Great Britain now was that the United States had undertaken to build a great navy . . ." and he warned Wilson of grave danger of trouble regarding it. *The Intimate Papers of Colonel House*, Vol. II, pp. 316–317.

[2]Lloyd George, then British Minister of Munitions, wrote: "Only a crushing military victory will bring the peace for which the Allies are fighting, and of which Germany will understand the meaning. That victory we shall have; it will be complete and final." (Letter to Robert Donald, June 8, 1916, published in *Current History*, July 1916, p. 733.)

[3]House to Wilson, June 10, 1916.

[4]From original in Mr. Wilson's files; Grey's answer was sent June 28th, but House's letter transmitting it on July 12th was never opened by the President.

so to "rest content." But he yielded in the face of violent Allied opposition. Even Germany, while still desiring peace negotiations,[1] discouraged his mediation.

By this time, the war had reached a hopeless deadlock; men blinded to all save the mechanical, haggard, bloody quest for victory. The tragedy of Verdun had been played through; the terrifying scene was shifting to the Somme. Momentarily, the talk of peace died away: became a vision and a dream. Indeed, diplomatic controversy during the next few months was to settle into a state of unexpected quietude that was to have a notable effect upon the American political campaign of 1916, in which Wilson was a candidate to succeed himself.[2] There were still minor excursions and alarms, but nothing at all approaching, for example, the crisis of the *Sussex*. When confidential telegrams brought reports of the agreements being negotiated at the Paris Economic Conference, June 14th to June 17th, the State Department became exceedingly apprehensive. The more Lansing thought about the matter the more positive he was that the Allies were deliberately making encroachments upon the rights of neutrals under the guise of measures against Germany. He warned the President, June 23rd, that the results of the Paris pacts might be "very far reaching on the commerce and trade of the whole world after the war is over."

"The drastic measures against the enemies of the Allies . . . purpose to prevent as far as possible the rebuild-

---

[1]Gerard was informed that in spite of the intemperate remarks in Reichstag debates, Wilson should not feel himself unwelcome as "mediator." (Gerard to House, thence to Wilson, June 28, 1916.) This was really an effort to encourage Wilson to make a move to bring about negotiations, without interfering with the terms. Neither side ever desired true "mediation" by Wilson.

Bernstorff wrote to House, June 16th, that according to "advices received from Berlin today they are getting impatient there. Our Navy is exerting continual pressure on the Government, and it will be difficult to keep their party quiet, if nothing is done against the British blockade or for the purpose of promoting peace." (Copy sent by House to Wilson.)

[2]See Chapter VII, this volume, pp. 242 *et seq.*

ing of their industries and commerce after the war . . . the knowledge of this intention to continue the war industrially . . . will cause the central Powers to hesitate in taking steps toward a restoration of peace. . . .

"In view of these possibilities . . . would it not be well to consider the advisability of holding a Congress of Neutrals to . . . determine upon ways and means to relieve the present situation and to provide for the future. . . .

". . . the best way to fight combination is by combination."

The same fears cropped out in a Senate resolution, offered by the alert Senator from Missouri, Stone, inquiring of the President what was the "character, form, and full purpose" of this new action by the Allies.[1]

The matter finally merged into a further blockade controversy which began to develop in July, and must be considered in a chapter devoted to the group of fateful foreign problems which the President and the nation were now confronting: preparedness, new trade restrictions by the British, and the continued failure of peace hopes. But first the campaign and election of 1916 must be considered. Would Wilson's course be approved by his own people? Would he himself be returned to power to carry his bold programme into action? Indeed, the warring nations of Europe were watching the election with scarcely less anxiety than the Americans themselves: for they could not know until November what party, what programme, what manner of man, would command the power and the resources of the greatest of neutral nations—the nation, indeed, upon which their own future depended.

---

[1] June 29, 1916. The President complied July 10th, giving the recommendations of the economic conference. *Senate Document*, No. 490, 64–1, "Trade Agreements Abroad."

CHAPTER VII

WILSON'S CAMPAIGN AND ELECTION IN 1916

"I am not interested, and I beg that you will believe me when I say that I never have been interested, in fighting for myself, but I am immensely interested in fighting for the things that I believe in, and so far as they are concerned I am a challenger to all comers."

Address in Philadelphia, June 29, 1916.

". . . I am willing, no matter what my personal fortunes may be, to play for the verdict of mankind. Personally, it will be a matter of indifference to me what the verdict on the 7th of November is, provided I feel any degree of confidence that when a later jury sits I shall get their judgment in my favor."

Address in New York, June 30, 1916.

I. PRE-CONVENTION STRATEGY

NO AMERICAN political campaign can be regarded as properly launched until that decisive moment in the prodigious party ritual when the candidate throws his hat in the ring.

"While I am entirely unwilling," wrote Wilson on February 14, 1916, "to enter into any contest for the presidential nomination of the Democratic party, I am willing to permit the use of my name that the Democrats in Ohio may make known their preference in regard to that nomination."[1]

Although there had been uncomfortable reminders regarding the one-term plank that Bryan and others had written into the Democratic platform in 1912—which no one had taken seriously as referring to the next campaign —and although Wilson himself said repeatedly, then and

---

[1]Wilson to Charles Q. Hildebrant, Secretary of State of Ohio.

later, that he had, personally, no desire for a second term, there was never any doubt that he would be the candidate in 1916.[1]

Many of the President's political advisers seem to have been alarmed by the outlook in the early months of that year.

"William G. McAdoo told me frankly of his intention shortly to resign from the Cabinet and return to private business. Josephus Daniels spoke hopelessly of the political outlook."[2]

The prestige of the administration, shaken by the revolt in Congress over foreign policy—the Gore and McLemore resolutions[3]—and with the entire nation confused by the President's demand for military preparedness, was just then at its lowest ebb, with Wilson under attack from many quarters.[4] As an American historian he was probably well enough aware of that period of low barometer in most

[1] As if in preparation for the presidential announcement of February, Wilson's famous letter of February 5, 1913, to A. Mitchell Palmer, regarding a second term for presidents, had been given to the press on January 10, 1916. The plank in the 1912 platform had read:

"We favor a single presidential term, and to that end we urge the adoption of an amendment to the constitution making the president of the United States ineligible for re-election and we pledge the candidate of this convention to this principle."

It was a subject to which Wilson, in earlier years, had given much thought, and he expressed his convictions in the letter to Palmer—an interesting and thorough discussion in which, a month before he entered the White House, he commented upon the functions and powers of the presidency, and suggested again his favorite reform: the adoption in the American system of "responsible government." He also said:

"Four years is too long a term for a President who is not the true spokesman of the people, who is imposed upon and does not lead. It is too short a term for a President who is doing, or attempting a great work of reform, and who has not had time to finish it." *The Public Papers of Woodrow Wilson*, Vol. III, p. 22.

[2] Henry Morgenthau, *All In a Life-Time*, p. 235.

[3] See this volume, pp. 154 *et seq.*

[4] E. S. Martin, of *Life*, a shrewd observer, wrote on March 2, 1916:

"Mr. Wilson's unpopularity seems to be growing. He is unpopular just now with M. Clemenceau in France, whose speciality is demolishing statesmen, with *Punch* and others in London who think him too patient, with Germans, Austrians, and Turks pretty generally we fear, with Mr. Root, Mr. Roosevelt, and most of the other Republicans and Progressives who are getting ready to nominate someone for President, with some Democrats who don't know what they want but are conscious of a suspicion that they are not getting it, with pacifists like Mr. Bryan and Mr. Villard, with militarists generally and especially the Continental army and universal-compulsory-service

administrations, toward the close of the third year, when the opposition, planning the strategy of a new campaign, seeks to test the defenses of the party in power. It is, indeed, easy enough to attack an administration when all of its accumulated mistakes and weaknesses are nakedly exposed, before there is either an alternative programme or an opposition candidate to present to the people. It is one of the major sports in a democracy to bethwack the party in power—so long as there is none of the sobering responsibility of choosing a new one.

Theodore Roosevelt's broad sombrero was in effect flung into the ring on March 9th with a statement full of characteristic invective. "Nothing is to be hoped from the present administration . . ."[1] That high priest of Republicanism, Elihu Root, was vigorously attacking the President's "bankrupt diplomacy,"[2] and Senator Lodge was calling the Wilson administration the worst in the history of the country with the exception of Buchanan's.[3] We have records of a luncheon[4] of the Sanhedrin of the opposition—Roosevelt, Lodge, Root, Bacon, and General Leonard Wood—easily sensationalized in the press as bringing together the Republican and the Progressive parties to defeat Wilson. Roosevelt, upon this occasion, indicated his approval of Wood as a candidate.[5]

---

kind, with Col. George Harvey, with a large company of dislikers of Josephus Daniels, and with everybody who ever bet a cent on the business future of Mexico.

"If Mr. Wilson was malfeasant, incompetent, cowardly, vacillating, and insincere in the degree that all these detractors, between them, aver, the wonder would be that he had managed to shuffle along three years in office with such immense defects without having a committee appointed to be answerable for his behaviour." *The Diary of a Nation*, p. 240.

[1]Though he refused to "enter into any fight" for the nomination. New York *Times*, March 10, 1916.

[2]*Review of Reviews*, March 1916.

[3]Springfield *Republican*, March 17, 1916.

[4]March 31, 1916.

[5]In his diary account of the luncheon, Wood wrote: ". . . Roosevelt said to me in the presence of Root that he would be for me in case things went right . . ." Hagedorn, *Leonard Wood*, Vol. II, p. 183.

It is clear, however, that the rank and file of the opposition appreciated the strength of the President's position. No matter how much Roosevelt might bluster and Root criticize, the country did not want war. It was doubtful even of the administration's plans for preparation, which were in Wood's opinion disgracefully insufficient. Moreover, the country was still "progressive" if not "radical" in its attitude toward social and economic problems. A soldier in the presidency was anathema: so was a candidate fully approved by conservatives like Lodge, Root, and Bacon.

One of the great determining moments in Democratic presidential campaigns is the Jefferson Day dinner on April 13th. Here the candidate or candidates are presented to the party leadership, and here are set forth the dominating policies, later to be hewn into planks for the platform.

The dinner of 1916 was held in the vast ballroom of the Willard Hotel, at a moment ominous with doubt and fear. The gloomy background of the World War, now threatening to engulf us also in the chaos of its passion and its anarchy, had just been made momentarily darker by a new involvement in Mexico, where American forces, led by the redoubtable Pershing, were already engaged. As the guests were gathering, boys on the dark streets of Washington were crying, "Extra! Extra!"—our soldiers had been fired upon.

The President had doubted the wisdom of making any speech whatsoever at the dinner. Events were too menacing. That very day he had been considering what must be said to the Germans regarding the tragic sinking of the *Sussex:* "this terrible business"[1] which threatened our entire policy of neutrality. If he carried his problem to Congress,[2] demanding restraints upon submarine activity,

[1]Wilson to Walter H. Page, April 13, 1916.
[2]As he was to do on April 19th.

VANCE C. McCORMICK (*right*), CHAIRMAN OF THE DEMOCRATIC NATIONAL COMMITTEE IN 1916; AND CARTER GLASS, OF VIRGINIA (*left*), SECRETARY.

would it mean war? He seemed to doubt where his oratory, which was never at its best unless he disclosed his entire mind, might, at such a moment, carry him.

He came into the banquet hall plainly worried and irritated. He feared the pliant atmosphere of an after-dinner audience, remarking to the toastmaster, Robert Woolley, that it was difficult to talk seriously to such a gathering.

"They all agree with me!"

Woolley smilingly replied that there was one man present of whom that could not be said.

"Who is it?" asked the President.

"George Harvey."

The tensity of Wilson's mood expressed itself irritably.

"How did he get in?"—adding grimly: "All holds must go if he qualifies as a Democrat!"

Upon such occasions Wilson always wished to speak last. He liked to feel the pulse of his audience: he liked to watch the effect of earlier speakers. In this case, it was fortunate, the opening address was made by Carter Glass of Virginia, one of the President's warmest friends, himself a notable orator. It was a glowing outline of one of the principal achievements of the administration—the Federal Reserve Act, in which he himself had played a distinguished part. Wilson listened intently, turning his chair gradually toward the speaker. Sincere oratory always fired him: and when Glass sat down the President leaned forward and said:

"That's one of the greatest speeches I ever listened to."[1]

The President had prepared carefully in advance. His notes show that he intended to adhere sternly to more or less academic general principles—chiefly harmless lessons

---

[1] Robert Woolley to the author.

from the career of Thomas Jefferson. But the inevitable
happened, as it must happen, upon such an occasion,
with any true orator. He must pour forth unreservedly
what he has in his soul. No powerful effect is ever produced unless the personality becomes knit into an intense
unity, seeking to deliver itself of convictions passionately
held. He knew well, as he said, that "these are days that
search men's hearts"—he had been searching his own. He
had been oppressed by the consciousness of the enormous
power of the American people—and his own responsibility,
as their President, for using it. It was a power that might
easily carry us into the war: or, with restraint, it might
conceivably bring peace to the suffering nations.

"How are we going to use this power?"

It must not be used selfishly, it must not be dictated by
partisan purposes: it must truly serve the "welfare of
the world."

It was noted by those who had long known the President
that when he rose to speak upon such an occasion his
whole manner changed. His face became suddenly alive,
his eyes glowed, and as he spoke his entire body, even his
restrained gestures, seemed to register the intensity of his
emotion. His speech, wholly devoid of flamboyance, instead of rising to oratorical flights, seemed to deepen into
a penetrating seriousness.

Leaning forward across the table and looking into the
eyes of his fascinated auditors,[1] he demanded in words
of solemn import:

"Are you ready for the test?"

He paused: there was not a sound in the crowded room.

"God forbid that we should ever become directly or
indirectly embroiled in quarrels not of our own choosing,
and that do not affect what we feel responsible to defend;

---

[1] The author was present upon this occasion.

but if we should ever be drawn in, are you ready to go in only where the interests of America are coincident with the interests of mankind and to draw out the moment the interest centers in America and is narrowed from the wide circle of humanity?"

Again he paused: one who was there could never forget that moment of intense suspense. Here stood speaking the man in all the world whose words carried farthest: whose acts at that time were charged with the greatest potentialities. He was asking, probably, the most important question then confronting the world. What should America do?

"Are you ready for the test? Have you courage to go in? Have you the courage to come out according as the balance is disturbed or readjusted for the interest of humanity?"[1]

It was a speech that made a never-to-be-forgotten impression—not only for the poignancy of its stabbing queries, but for the sense of a great personality, a great leader, torn with anxiety, wrestling with responsibility too great for him or for any man, and here revealing the gravity and perplexities, the seriousness of his own moral purposes.[2]

An address such as this, however it may have impressed those who heard it, could have had little political value. What a campaign requires is not honest doubt, the faithful expression of a soul torn by a sense of moral responsibility; it demands happy assurances, a definite and simplified programme of action. Many Democrats high in the

---

[1] *The Public Papers of Woodrow Wilson*, Vol. IV, pp. 140–152.

[2] Mrs. Wilson had come in with the ladies of the cabinet at the close of the dinner and taken her place on a raised platform opposite the speakers' table. It was one of the earliest important public occasions, since her marriage in December, upon which she had appeared. A dark, handsome woman, with an air of poise and distinction, she attracted every eye. There were those who caught the wireless messages of solicitude and confidence which passed across the crowded room between the President and his bride.

councils of the party were more or less openly critical. Secretary Lane, for example, was impatient with the President's hesitation. He wanted vigorous action, and wanted it immediately, even to the point of war with both Germany and Mexico.

"Only strong leadership will reëlect him."[1]

But it was probably this honest hesitation, the struggle to avoid a crisis, the continued and determined efforts for peace, which in the end reëlected the President. For Wilson, in these agonized questionings, was expressing the mind of a large proportion of the American people.

So far as his personal predilections were concerned, the President would probably have been willing to lay down these all but intolerable problems and anxieties. It would be a "delightful relief," he told Colonel House in May, "if he could conscientiously retire."

He knew well enough, however, that no escape was possible; a successful general might as well try to resign from his army in the midst of a battle, as a political leader in such a crisis.

"You wanted to be nominated in 1912," argued wise old Burleson, "and you needed the party to nominate you. This time the party needs you. You are the only Democrat who can be elected."[2]

The President not only assumed all along that he was to be renominated, but to an unusual degree directed every phase of the pre-convention campaign. Even before any public announcement of his candidacy was made, we find him writing to his old friend Judge Wescott, of New Jersey, "on the assumption that I am to be nominated again for the Presidency":

"It does my heart good to think how loyal and generous a friend you have been and I should consider it a great

---

[1] Lane's conversation with the author at luncheon, April 14, 1916. From diary notes.
[2] A. S. Burleson to the author.

honor if you would renew the endorsement you gave me in your first nominating speech."[1]

He concerned himself in succeeding days with the selection of a temporary chairman of the convention and the important choice of a man to head the National Democratic Committee—and even arranged, in some cases, for chairmen to preside over crucial state conventions.[2] The record shows the overwhelming prestige of his leadership in his party. No one seemed willing to move, either in the matter of appointments or in drafting the provisions of the platform, without his approval—a dependence reaching such a point that we find him protesting on June 7th in a personal memorandum for his secretary, Mr. Tumulty:

"Please say to Doremus[3] what I said to you the other day, that I do not feel at liberty to suggest *everything* about the convention, and that it has been the immemorial custom, so far as I can learn, to leave the naming of those who shall second the nomination to the several delegations."

Woodrow Wilson, beyond any other recent President— beyond any, perhaps, since Thomas Jefferson—was a thinking leader. In former volumes this biographer has pointed out some of the special difficulties which confront the thinker as statesman; the temptation to think too deeply, the occasional impatience with intractable reality. His belief in the power of thought, of reason, of well-considered ideals, was profound. In the notes which he made for an address before the American Bible Society on May 7th we find this paragraph:

"Weave the world together in ideal, thought, and principle and you have woven it together in action. Thought the real amalgam."

---

[1] May 2, 1916.

[2] As when he sent Newton D. Baker, his Secretary of War, to Ohio.

[3] Representative Frank E. Doremus.

Again and again in his addresses, as when he was appealing for cool judgment in the Mexican crisis, we find him emphasizing the immense importance of thought:

"Thoughts may be bandits. Thoughts may be raiders. Thoughts may be invaders. Thoughts may be disturbers of international peace; and when you reflect upon the importance of this country keeping out of the present war, you will know what tremendous elements we are all dealing with."[1]

We find him, then, in these tempestuous months of the spring of 1916, when facing problems as critical as any ever presented to an American President—desperate war in Europe, an armed American expedition in Mexico, a bitter political campaign in process of development—we find him endeavouring, by the disclosure of his own perplexities, literally by a process of thinking aloud, to encourage reason, steadiness, moral courage among the people.

Through it all shines his longing to make America the disinterested moral leader of humanity, "lifting some sacred emblem of counsel and of peace, of accommodation and righteous judgment before the nations of the world."[2]

He would have the nations in the future "governed by the same high code of honor that we demand of individuals"[3]—an idea also advanced by that apostle of British liberalism, Gladstone, but far yet from being realized anywhere in this world.

It was in this time of turmoil, doubt, anxiety, that we find him also, as the thinking leader, expressing faith in the sublimest ideals known to our race, and what is more astonishing, presenting them as practical policies of action,

---

[1]Address before the National Press Club, Washington, May 15, 1916. *The Public Papers of Woodrow Wilson*, Vol. IV, p. 173.

[2]Address at Charlotte, North Carolina, May 20, 1916. *Ibid.*, p. 183.

[3]Address before the League to Enforce Peace, Washington, May 27, 1916. *Ibid.*, p. 186.

as when he committed himself to the idea of a league of nations.

"We are participants, whether we would or not, in the life of the world. The interests of all nations are our own also. We are partners with the rest. What affects mankind is inevitably our affair as well as the affair of the nations of Europe and of Asia."[1]

It is not inexpressive of his character, with its deep religious foundations, that his league of nations address closed with what was almost a prayer:

"God grant that the dawn of that day of frank dealing and of settled peace, concord, and co-operation may be near at hand!"[2]

The necessary corollary of service to the world implied in this idealistic programme was American unity of thought and of action. Just as individual morality depends upon inner unity of purpose, so the high quality of national morality that he was demanding must rest upon a clear inner understanding and unity. We find the President, therefore, centring upon the "fine gold of untainted Americanism"[3] as the most important objective, the most necessary plank in the platform, on which he was to stand in the forthcoming campaign. What he seemed to fear most were the hyphenated groups, "influences which have seemed to threaten to divide us in interest and sympathy."[4]

He made it clear, moreover, in this series of addresses, that he was no doctrinaire pacifist. War at times was necessary and beneficial. "The Union was saved by the processes of the Civil War," and America, while passionately desirous of peace, might have to fight again.

---

[1] *The Public Papers of Woodrow Wilson*, Vol. IV, p. 185.
[2] *Ibid.*, p. 188.
[3] Address at Charlotte, North Carolina, May 20, 1916. *Ibid.*, p. 180.
[4] As he said in his Flag Day proclamation of May 30, 1916. *Ibid.*, p. 189.

"We are not only ready to co-operate, but we are ready to fight against any aggression, whether from without or from within. . . . We are ready to fight for our rights when those rights are coincident with the rights of man and humanity."[1]

This, however, was wholly different from "militarism," of which, as he told the graduating class at West Point, he could discover "no taint" in America.[2]

Such was the man who was about to become a candidate for reëlection to the presidency. Such were the ideals and the purposes to which he was now devoting every energy, seeking a renewed vote of the country's confidence.

One element or condition of the approaching campaign which was of the utmost importance ought to be here considered: this was the relative lull in American diplomatic activity which began in May, before the conventions, and continued until after the elections in November. It applied not only to Europe but to Mexico. For five months, while there were indeed irritating controversies, especially with the British regarding the black list, no really acute foreign crisis disturbed American life or influenced American opinion. It is only in the after-look that the immense political importance of this fact can be fully recognized. The campaign, so far as the slogan "He kept us out of war" was concerned, largely turned upon it.

Various influences, elsewhere presented, contributed to produce the lull; one of the chief of which was the President's fortunate, as well as astute, handling of the *Sussex* crisis, by which the Germans pledged themselves to refrain from unrestricted submarine warfare. This proved to be a diplomatic victory of the first magnitude. It quieted, if it

---

[1]Address at Arlington, May 30, 1916. *The Public Papers of Woodrow Wilson*, Vol. IV, p. 194.

[2]June 13, 1916. *Ibid.*, p. 203.

did not fully satisfy, the British, since it crippled the use, for the time being, of the Germans' most effective weapon; and by allowing the enormous Allied trade in supplies and munitions with America to continue without too much interruption, served also to quiet American industrial and banking interests. When coupled with the peace plans which Wilson was urgently considering—including the proposals for a league of nations—it tended temporarily to quiet the Germans. The President's vision of peace with ultimate security, indeed, soon became alluring to the people of all the war-weary nations. With the powerful aid of the American President and the coöperation of the American people, might it not be realized?

There were dangers, of course, in a period such as this of deceptive lull that settled nothing; it meant protraction of the agony, an increase in the slaughter and destruction, swelling grievances and hatreds that would make a fair settlement, when the time came, more difficult to attain: and in the end, possibly, aggravate the influences that were dragging America also into the war. But what could be done with these "incalculable forces," as Wilson called them? To him the only sensible policy seemed to be to keep out as long as possible, seek always some opening toward mediation, and point the way toward a league of nations that would assure permanent future peace in the world.

Previous to his somewhat unexpected victory in the *Sussex* case, the President had plainly intended to rest his case in the campaign for reëlection largely upon the record of his administration in the domestic field, which was truly notable. The *Sussex* victory, to which the party could now "point with pride," made it clear to many of the party leaders that the emphasis should be shifted to foreign affairs. The German pledge served immediately to minimize the possibility of American involvement in the war. It might, really, lead on to peace negotiations. At any rate it was not only vastly encouraging to the millions of Americans who wanted no entanglements with European quarrels; it also stopped the mouths of some of the President's sharpest critics. In short, Wilson was keeping us out of the war; and at the same time American industry and finance, fattening upon trade with the Allies, were undisturbed.

It was, of course, a fact—an entirely legitimate claim—that Wilson had avoided war. On several occasions war would probably have been the easiest way of meeting a situation. Going to war, especially at the beginning of the political campaign, might even have been the surest means of securing his reëlection. Vance McCormick says that Lansing came to him greatly worried about the "kept us out of war" appeal, arguing, what was perfectly true, that a shocking submarine incident at any time might put us into it. McCormick replied with true insight that nothing, politically speaking, could be better; if we were forced into war on such an issue, all question of Wilson's reëlection would disappear. The country would rise immediately to his support.[1] But Wilson was earnestly and honestly seeking to keep out of the war. He had indeed been gradually forced to let American neutrality, through the want of any dependable international sanctions, take on a one-sided bearing, but he was pinning his faith on two possibilities—perhaps, as events were now shaping themselves, even probabilities—one, that the war could be stopped by immediate peace negotiations, which Germany seemed even then willing to consider; and the other, that the world could be guided into a permanent peace, through a league of nations, which was everywhere being hopefully discussed.

Nevertheless the President, while doing his best to avoid

---

[1] Vance C. McCormick to the author.

war, never lost sight of the possibility that we might have to go into it. He was convinced "that the people of the country, the mass, wanted peace, not war, but also that if war came, after every effort had been made to avoid it, we should go into it sadly but vigorously."[1]

By early June, even before the Republican and Progressive conventions had met, the two broad policies for appealing to the people in the campaign had been fairly well settled by the Democratic leaders. They believed that the country was still strongly progressive: they would offer the record of the Wilson administration in progressive legislation, and Wilson himself would continue to push forward to completion still further items in his programme. They believed that the country was opposed to war: and they would offer the record of the administration in keeping out of it.

II. THE CONVENTION AT ST. LOUIS

A strong President, as a candidate for reëlection, not only dominates the convention of his own party, but sways that of his opponents. This was peculiarly true in 1916. Wilson was the vital force that shaped action in both Republican and Progressive conventions. He was the enemy: he must be beaten.

While the Progressive movement had lost the aspects of a crusade which animated it in 1912, there remained a nostalgic adoration for their spurred and booted chief. The bare mention of the name of Roosevelt produced a reminiscent storm of applause; but a "sense of futility" in reality pervaded the convention, two balconies in the great auditorium being wholly empty.[2] However the delegates might flinch at a union with the "crooks" and

---

[1] From notes of an interview with Wilson, by the author, on May 11, 1916.
[2] New York *Times*, June 8, 1916.

"porch-climbers" of 1912, the leaders, at least, knew well enough that it was the prime objective of their meeting. Their only effective strategy was to force the nomination of their hero by the Republicans through the threat of a third-party candidacy,[1] and then join in electing him.

The real struggle at Chicago took place behind the scenes in smoky hotel rooms where the leaders of the two parties wrestled mightily for a working agreement.

"Let us forget the differences," Senator Harding had pleaded in his keynote speech.

It was no accident that their conventions were staged in the same city at the same time. The Progressives stood obstinately for Roosevelt: the Republicans utterly rejected him. Most of a long night they were at it. At two o'clock on Saturday morning, the 10th, Nicholas Murray Butler called Roosevelt, who was keeping vigil at Oyster Bay, on the telephone, and gave him what must have been one of the bitterest messages of a career which in its earlier phases had been all triumph and, in its later, all defeat—that he could not and would not be nominated by the Republicans. Whom would he suggest?

Roosevelt's two greatest friends in public life were General Leonard Wood and Senator Henry Cabot Lodge. He first suggested Wood, as a man to whom he would give his support.

"But we will not nominate a soldier," Butler declared.

After further conversation Butler came back to the

---

[1]Bainbridge Colby, who made the speech placing Roosevelt in nomination, says in a memorandum written for the author:

"Before the convention week was far advanced, it was evident that the strategy of Colonel Roosevelt and his close advisers, such as the late George W. Perkins, Frank Munsey and others, was to hold the threat of his nomination by the Progressive party over the Republican convention, in the hope that the latter would make Colonel Roosevelt its nominee.

"There was evidently some working understanding between Colonel Roosevelt and the managers of the Republican convention. . . .

"As a part of this understanding, he was to be nominated in the Republican convention and given a chance to develop his full strength in the Republican convention."

conference with the astonishing news that the Colonel would support Henry Cabot Lodge as a compromise.[1]

Nothing could have been better calculated to infuriate Roosevelt's own following, which looked upon Lodge as the arch-type of all that was reactionary. The feeling was so strong that the Progressive delegates summarily refused to consider an endorsement of Justice Hughes, of the United States Supreme Court, whose nomination by the Republicans was then momentarily expected, and in great excitement chose their hero by acclamation.

Hughes was the logical Republican candidate. He had had no part in the schism of 1912. Sitting high in the Supreme Court, above the dust and clamour of partisan feuds, a distinguished and dignified figure with a fortunate record of mild liberalism, he was the ideal candidate to unite the torn opposition and defeat Wilson. His peculiar availability from the beginning was that he most nearly resembled Wilson.

"What, then," asked one of the shrewdest of American political observers, "is the purpose of nominating Justice Hughes? To continue the Wilson administration under Republican auspices? To replace a Democratic Wilson with a Republican Wilson?"[2]

Roosevelt, keenly aware of the situation, dubbed Hughes the "whiskered Wilson."

As a matter of fact the rejection of Theodore Roosevelt and his deputy, General Wood, meant the refusal to meet the only vital issue, capable of clear statement, that the opposition really had. Roosevelt stood for immediate and extensive military and naval preparation and for prompt military action: a soldier in the White House. If he had

---

[1]Hagedorn, *Leonard Wood*, Vol. II, pp. 189–190; also *Selections From the Correspondence of Theodore Roosevelt and Henry Cabot Lodge*, Vol. II, pp. 486–489, for Roosevelt's letter, June 10th, to the conferees of the Progressive party.

[2]Frank I. Cobb, in the New York *World*, April 2, 1916.

been selected there would have been no confusion of issues: but the Republican leaders, quite as well as the Democratic, knew the temper of the country, and they wanted a candidate, not to stand for clear issues, but to defeat Wilson. No higher tribute could have been paid to the President's genius for leadership, as expressed by his hold upon the country, than the nomination of a candidate so nearly like himself. However grudgingly, his opponents came near an express approval of the policies of his administration.

It is not necessary here to recount the pathetic story of Roosevelt's refusal of the Progressive nomination: or the gloom and disillusionment that descended upon his delegates. He too was actuated by the incontrovertible political fact of Woodrow Wilson's power in the nation: and he knew well enough that the only hope of defeating him lay in the unity of the opposition. It was a bitter dose to swallow Hughes, but he did it.

Roosevelt's surrender was received by the Progressives with "anger, derision and groans." They felt that they had been used "as a stalking horse for his personal ambitions."[1] The entire episode demonstrated again the futility of personal leadership, however magnetic, as the basis of a great permanent political movement.

The Democratic convention which met at St. Louis on June 14th was little more than a colossal ratification meeting. In contrast with both the conventions at Chicago, it was ardently enthusiastic, with a sense of unity that presaged victory in November. Its chief purpose was to extol the achievements of its leader and adopt the platform he was proposing.

A Democratic convention is never as easily regimented as a Republican. It is more likely to do the impulsive and unexpected thing: there is a touch of wildness in its

---

[1] From memorandum written by Bainbridge Colby for the author.

blood. It had been quite soberly planned—and it was Wilson's idea—that the keynote emphasis of the convention was to be upon Americanism: the patriotic unity of the nation in meeting the stresses imposed upon it by a foreign war in which the sympathies of so-called hyphenates were so keenly aroused. Demonstrations were to hinge upon nationalism and the flag. The music of "Dixie," the classic rouser of Democratic conventions, was to be subordinated to the "Star-Spangled Banner." And it was no mere coincidence that the opening of the convention was set for June 14th, which the President had already designated for the annual celebration of Flag Day. The fact that the Republican convention at Chicago had also laid great stress upon the same issue no doubt added to the energy with which Wilson and his friends prepared for the occasion.

A tremendous parade was planned for Washington. All the federal offices were closed, and all places of business; the President himself and members of his cabinet marched on foot as far as the stand in front of the White House and there dropped out to review the parade. It took five hours for the marchers, sixty thousand of them, to pass the stand. In the afternoon the President spoke before a vast throng at the Monument: the note was "our country," the whole of it. Back of the sincerity and power of the address lay deep the President's own memories of the disruption and desolation caused by the lack of national unity which resulted in the Civil War. "A whole generation following that great struggle" was "bitter and sore." In the present crisis—and the President was here speaking out of his own anxiety over the propagandist activities of "hyphenated groups" in America—every effort must be exerted to secure unity of opinion as a basis for unity of action.

"There is disloyalty active in the United States, and it

must be absolutely crushed. It proceeds from a minority, a very small minority, but a very active and subtle minority. It works underground, but it also shows its ugly head where we can see it; and there are those at this moment who are trying to levy a species of political blackmail, saying, 'Do what we wish in the interest of foreign sentiment or we will wreak our vengeance at the polls.'"[1]

It was for these reasons Wilson thought that the keynote of the convention should be Americanism. He wrote the plank himself, and Newton D. Baker took it with him to St. Louis.

But the convention had been in session scarcely an hour before the real feeling of the delegates, lately from home, began to assert itself. It was not that they did not approve Wilson's views upon Americanism—they adopted his plank unanimously—but what stirred them to the depths was Wilson's course in keeping America out of the war. They knew what they wanted as a keynote!

It was the speech of Martin H. Glynn, former Governor of New York, whom Wilson had chosen for temporary chairman, that fired the fuse.[2]

At the outset Glynn defined the avoidance of war as "the paramount issue": and his argument was designed to prove that Wilson's determined adherence to neutrality was the traditional American policy. It was based upon historical precedents—always, with Wilson, a compelling excellence; and the essence of it, as of most keynote speeches, was to "point with pride" to the achievements of their leader and the party. Neither Glynn nor the President seems to have had any idea of the possible reaction of the delegates to the speech.

But Glynn was a born orator with the imagination and

---

[1] *The Public Papers of Woodrow Wilson*, Vol. IV, p. 209.

[2] He had drafted it well in advance, and the first half had been sent to Wilson who, after slight changes, had approved it.

OLLIE M. JAMES

JOHN W. WESCOTT

MARTIN H. GLYNN

HENRY MORGENTHAU

Leaders active in President Wilson's campaign for reëlection in 1916: Ollie M. James of Kentucky, permanent chairman of the Democratic Convention at St. Louis, who also presided at the ceremonies at Shadow Lawn, Long Branch, New Jersey, September 2, 1916, when President Wilson was notified of his nomination; John W. Wescott, of New Jersey, who made the nominating speech at St. Louis; Martin H. Glynn, of New York, temporary chairman of the convention, whose fiery speech stirred the delegates and who was more than any other man responsible for the origin of the phrase, "He Kept Us Out of War"; Henry Morgenthau, chairman of the Finance Committee of the Democratic National Committee.

temperament of the Celt. He began at once to feel the rising pulse of his audience.

"If Washington was right, if Jefferson was right, if Hamilton was right, if Lincoln was right, then the President of the United States is right today . . ."[1]

The case for the amicable settlement of violations of American rights was equally justifiable in the light of precedent:

"When Grant was President, during the war between Spain and the Spanish West Indies, a Spanish gunboat seized the vessel 'Virginius,' flying the American flag, and a Spanish commandant in cold blood shot the captain of the 'Virginius,' thirty-six of the crew and sixteen of the passengers.

"But we didn't go to war. Grant settled our troubles by negotiation just as the President of the United States is trying to do today."

The convention burst into wild applause.

The orator cited cases of violations under Harrison and Lincoln:

"But we didn't go to war."

He paused for the roar of approval.

"And so goes our history. I don't want to take too much time to enumerate——"

But the great throng, thrilled and excited, was not to be denied.

"Go on, go on—give it to them."

It was such a moment as comes rarely in any orator's life.

"All right, I'll hit them again——"

He cited precedents under Pierce, Van Buren, Jefferson, Adams, Washington:

"But we didn't go to war."

The crowd was delirious with joy. Their faith in their

---

[1] Wilson's copy of the *Official Proceedings*.

chief and his course of action was being completely justified.

"Go it, Glynn. Give them some more!"

One auditor, in the press gallery, the "peerless leader," William J. Bryan, was weeping with emotion at this recital of the victories of peace: but the party leaders who had wanted to stress Americanism were aghast. The convention was getting wholly out of control. It looked like a demonstration for pacifism. Senator John Walter Smith of Maryland rushed to the platform to confer with McCombs. Something must be done to check the stampede. McCombs hastily scrawled on a sheet of paper, "but we are willing to fight if necessary," and passed it over to Glynn, who was waiting for the delirium to subside.

"I'll take care of that," he called back—and, intoxicated with his own oratory, roused to a still higher pitch the ardour of his vast audience.

"In the face of this record, do Republicans realize that when they arraign the policy of the President of the United States today, they arraign the policy of Harrison, of Blaine, of Lincoln and of Grant? For the pleasure of criticizing a Democratic President, are they willing to read out of the Republican party the greatest men the Republican party ever had? . . .

"This policy may not satisfy those who revel in destruction and find pleasure in despair. It may not satisfy the fire-eater or the swashbuckler. [Laughter and applause.] . . . this policy does satisfy the mothers of the land, at whose hearth and fireside no jingoistic war has placed an empty chair. . . . It does satisfy the fathers of this land and the sons of this land, who will fight for our flag, and die for our flag——"

The crowd was completely intoxicated.

"Repeat it . . . Say it again!"

"All right. Give me a chance——"

". . . when Reason primes the rifle, when Honor draws the sword, when Justice breathes a blessing on the standards they uphold."

It was grand old-fashioned oratory! If it left no doubt as to the temper of the convention, and dismayed many of the party leaders, the worst was yet to come. On the second day Senator Ollie James, of Kentucky, was made permanent chairman: a man of gigantic physique, with a stentorian voice. He had "the face of a prizefighter, the body of an oak, and the voice of a pipe organ," and he had "all the tricks of the orator at the tip of his tongue."[1] James knew well what the convention wanted and played upon it again with tremendous effect.

"Four years ago they sneeringly called Woodrow Wilson the school teacher; then his class was assembled within the narrow walls of Princeton College. They were the young men of America. Today he is the world teacher, his class is made up of kings, kaisers, czars, princes, and potentates. [Applause.] The confines of the schoolroom circle the world. [Applause.] His subject is the protection of American life and American rights under international law [applause], the saving of neutral life, the freedom of the seas."

He touched the heights in a final flight:

"Without orphaning a single American child, without widowing a single American mother, without firing a single gun, without the shedding of a single drop of blood, he wrung from the most militant spirit that ever brooded above a battlefield an acknowledgment of American rights and an agreement to American demands."

The crowd roared with delight. "Repeat it, repeat it!"

When the orator ceased, the cheering was tumultuous and long continued. Nor was there anything bogus about it. Every delegate was on his feet: the Marylanders in the

---

[1] New York *Times*, June 16, 1916.

front row stood on their chairs: and women as well as men paraded in the aisles.

Nothing could better have expressed the deep feeling of the delegates than the shout that went up from every part of the great auditorium for "Bryan, Bryan!" They wanted still more oratory on the peace theme: and they wanted it from the silvery tongue of the Old Warrior. It was not, however, until the evening session that Bryan could be heard:

"My friends, I have differed with our President on some of the methods employed, but I join with the American people in thanking God that we have a President who does not want this nation plunged into this war."

His address, which reassured the unity of the party, was received with a magnificent tribute of respect and affection.

Wilson was renominated by Judge John W. Wescott, of New Jersey, who had so eloquently presented his name at Baltimore in 1912.

There could be no possible doubt of the responsive enthusiasm of the delegates. A huge banner bearing Wilson's likeness was unfurled from the roof, and the convention, in its ecstatic cheering, its tumultuous parades, the blaring of its band half smothered by the universal din, gave every conventional evidence of its complete approval.

In the meantime, during these fevered hours, the President and Mrs. Wilson remained quietly at the White House. Part of the time they listened, by means of special wires, to the proceedings. Early in the evening, despite a driving rain, they took a walk through the Washington parks.

Having heard their candidate nominated, and seconded by Harmon and Stuart, the delegates were impatient of any further speeches.

"Vote, vote!" they cried.

Senator Hughes moved that the rules be suspended and the nomination be made by acclamation. A single voice—from Illinois—was opposed. A storm of "ayes" followed the motion.

Senator James, the chairman, boomed the result:

"I therefore declare Woodrow Wilson nominated for President by the vote of 1092 to 1."

The convention followed precedent in making short work of the nomination for the vice-presidency. There had been talk of shelving Marshall and choosing a stronger candidate, like Newton D. Baker. When Wilson was consulted he wrote:

". . . I do not feel that I have any right to suggest anything on this head. The attitude of Mr. Marshall towards the administration has been loyal and generous in the extreme. He has given me every reason to admire and trust him."[1]

It was as good as an order, and Marshall was renominated by acclamation.

At one o'clock in the morning of June 16th the President received the news. His only comment was:

"I am very grateful to my generous friends."[2]

Discussion of the platform gave rise to real divergencies of opinion, though nothing that in the least disturbed the general spirit of unity.

Wilson himself had drafted many of the proposed planks. It is surprising, indeed, in examining the documents, to discover the amount of time and energy he had expended in defining the issues he wished discussed. From his early youth such work—the drafting of political

---

[1] Note attached to a letter of June 2nd from Governor Fielder.

[2] New York *Times*, June 16, 1916. Marshall telegraphed a characteristic message: "In the fight which you are to win I am always yours to command." The President replied: "It is a real pleasure to look forward to being associated with you again in the political campaign, and also, I hope and believe, in another four years of the administration of the Government."

principles, the outlining of constitutions—had been congenial to his spirit. He loved the exact word. In making his preparation, he had welcomed suggestions from cabinet members, senators, and others. A large envelope among his papers contains letters from Senators Walsh (of Montana), Simmons, Hollis, Underwood, Stone and others. Burleson and McAdoo were consulted, and there were many letters from other advisers.

What he wanted most, as already indicated, was an unequivocal plank on Americanism. He regarded pro-foreign influences in America—the widespread and subtle propaganda of both groups of belligerents—possibly too strongly, as a menace in itself: and he was determined to serve notice on the opposition that any party seeking to appeal for support to such "disloyal groups" deserved unmeasured condemnation. To many of the platform committee the approval accorded Glynn's and James's references to the President's peace policies made it more than ever necessary to support Wilson's plank. The Democratic party must not be represented as favouring peace at any price. Williams of Mississippi, a strong supporter of the President, Husting of Wisconsin, and later Carter Glass of Virginia, though not a member of the committee, strongly urged a ringing denunciation of hyphenism. The President himself, by telegraph from Washington, urged the adoption of his plank.[1]

With the plank that represented the strong peace feeling of the convention, Wilson personally had nothing whatever to do. He had considered it unbecoming for him to draft the plank which was to give him and his administration the unreserved approval of the delegates. It was, indeed, hardly more than a *pro forma* procedure, familiar in every convention.

---

[1] There was even an unconfirmed rumour that he would hasten to St. Louis and demand it of the convention. New York *Times*, June 16, 1916.

"We unreservedly indorse our President and Vice President Woodrow Wilson of New Jersey, and Thomas Riley Marshall of Indiana, who have performed the functions of their great offices faithfully and impartially, and with distinguished ability."

But a sentence was added—by whom written, no one seems to know—expressing the real and strong feeling of the convention: a sentence containing the phrase upon which the entire campaign was to turn:

"In particular we commend to the American people the splendid diplomatic victories of our great President, who has preserved the vital interests of our Government and its citizens, and kept us out of war."[1]

Several persons had used somewhat similar expressions in preparing platform data,[2] and Glynn and James had played upon the theme with magnificent oratorical effect, but no one of them seems to have hit upon the actual wording. It was undoubtedly added as a mere statement of fact, with no thought of its ultimate importance in the campaign.

It was certainly never the President's intent to rest the most important recent phase of his record—his attitude toward the European war—upon the naïve generality that he had kept us out of war (with the implication that he would continue to do so). There are, indeed, many evidences that he did not like the phrase, even though he

---

[1] *Democratic Text-Book*, p. 25.

[2] As appears in the documents retained by the President. The author has probed energetically for the origin of this exact phrase. Vance McCormick writes: "I thought that expression originated in our Publicity Department which was under the charge of Robert Woolley . . ." (McCormick to the author, 1928.) Woolley writes that the phrase was "not in the draft which Newton Baker brought to St. Louis." He says that the genesis of it was in a slogan he himself prepared for the 1914 *Democratic Text-Book:* "War in the east, peace in the west; thank God for Wilson." (Woolley to the author, 1928.) Newton D. Baker, who probably knew more of the origin of the platform than any other delegate, writes: "The phrase 'He kept us out of war' was put in by the Resolutions Committee, by which member I do not know. I myself always regarded it as a product of the Glynn speech." (Baker to the author, 1928.) In this opinion Baker is supported by Secretary Burleson. (Burleson to the author, July 14, 1928.)

could not object to it, since it was a plain statement of fact. He told Secretary Daniels:

"I can't keep the country out of war. They talk of me as though I were a god. Any little German lieutenant can put us into the war at any time by some calculated outrage."[1]

Yet he plainly recognized the tremendous popular force of the appeal. He wrote to Glynn on June 22nd, expressing appreciation of his speech and commenting on its "extraordinary and deserved success," and the "most unusual acknowledgment" it had received from the convention. He concluded:

"It was and I am sure will remain one of the notable things of a campaign which . . . should stir to the very bottom the conscience and thought of the United States."

His real attitude toward foreign relationships was indicated in the carefully considered plank—one of the longest in the entire platform—in which he set forth the constructive proposals to which he wished to commit his party and the nation. His references in this plank to the maintenance of our traditional neutrality—so powerfully stressed by the orators of the convention—are hardly more than casual. What he wanted was to emphasize America's changed position in the world and her duty to use her immense power—a favourite theme with him— "in the interest of humanity, to assist the world in securing settled peace and justice." He closed his draft with a ringing statement of a belief which committed him, and he hoped would commit his party, to an advanced stand in the moral leadership of the world:

". . . the time has come when it is the duty of the United States to join with the other nations of the world in any feasible association that will effectively serve these

---

[1]Josephus Daniels to the author, 1929.

must show itself, not a nation of partisans, but a nation of patriots.

VI.   Along with the proof of our character as a nation must go the proof of our power to play the part that legitimately belongs to us. The people of the United States love peace.   They respect the rights and covet the friendship of all other nations.   They desire neither any additional territory which cannot be acquired by honorable purchase, nor any advantage which cannot be peacefully gained by their skill, their industry, or their enterprise.   But they love and insist upon having absolute freedom of national life and policy, and feel that they owe it to themselves and to the role of spirited independence which it is their sole ambition to play that they should render themselves secure *and to be able to protect their just rights upon the seas or in any part of the world.* against the hazard of interference from any quarter, We, therefore,

favor the maintenance of an Army fully adequate to the requirements of order, *and of the protection of the nations rights* and safety which are constantly liable to disclose themselves even in times of settled peace; of an adequate reserve of citizens trained to arms and prepared to safeguard the people and territory of the United States against any danger of hostile action which may unexpectedly arise; *fixed policy for the continuous development* and of a Navy worthy to support the great naval traditions of the United States and fully equal to the international tasks which the United States hopes and expects to take a part in performing. *The plans and enactments of the present Congress afford substantial proof of our purpose in these exigent matters.*

VII.   The ~~present~~ *Democratic* administration has throughout the ~~present~~ *present* war scrupulously and successfully held to the old paths of neutrality and of the peaceful pursuit of the legitimate objects of our national life which statesmen of all parties and creeds have prescribed for themselves in America since the beginning of our history.   But the circumstances of

The platform for the Democratic national convention, held in June 1916, was to a large extent drafted by President Wilson. This page of his preliminary notes is especially interesting because it sets forth his attitude regarding peace. It is corrected in his own handwriting.

principles, to maintain inviolate the complete security of the highway of the seas for the common and unhindered use of all nations, *and to prevent any war begun either contrary to treaty covenants or without warning and frank submission of the provocation and causes to the opinion of mankind.*"

The words substantially as quoted appear in all the drafts of the plank kept by Wilson: but when it emerged from the committee, the final clause (here in italics) was omitted. No doubt the cautious leaders at St. Louis feared that it committed the party, with its fervid devotion to peace, too far.

One other statement on foreign policy remains to be noted. It occurs in the plank dealing with the protection of American citizens abroad and originated with influential Jewish leaders. It is as follows:

"At the earliest practicable opportunity our country should strive earnestly for peace among the warring nations of Europe and seek to bring about the adoption of the fundamental principle of justice and humanity, that all men shall enjoy equality of right and freedom from discrimination in the lands wherein they dwell."

It was submitted by Louis Marshall on June 7th, and although not included in Wilson's draft[1] it was adopted by the convention. It was to have far-reaching effects: for Wilson was thus pledged, as early as 1916, not only to strive to bring about an early peace—which he meant to do anyway—but to include in the treaties the religious-racial equality and minority rights clauses which were to give so much trouble three years later at the Peace Conference.

In his draft upon military preparedness, which was adopted practically as Wilson wrote it, he left no doubt as

---

[1]We know, however, that he approved and supported it. (Wilson to Herman Bernstein, June 16, 1916.)

to his belief in an army ". . . fully adequate to the requirements of order, of safety and of the protection of the nation's rights . . ."

On a few other points there were divergencies of opinion between the President and the members of the platform committee. He had thought it unnecessary to include a detailed plank regarding Mexico: the committee insisted upon a frank exposition of the party's position, since they felt it to be creditable.

The President also put a prompt quietus on a move to insert in the platform a condemnation of Mr. Hughes for "dragging the Supreme Court into the mire of politics" by resigning his justiceship of the Supreme Court to become a candidate.[1]

Probably the most acrimonious debate of the convention centred upon woman suffrage. Large numbers of representatives of women's organizations, bedecked with bright yellow sashes, ribbons, and parasols, filled the galleries, vociferously demanding a sweeping declaration of approval of their plank. The issue reached the floor of the convention, where it was hotly debated. Wilson had prepared a statement which expressed his long-held view that suffrage was a matter for state action:

"We recommend the extension of the franchise to the women of the country by the States upon the same terms as to men."

When the substitute plank favoured by the women's organizations was put to a vote, it was rejected, $181\frac{1}{2}$ to $888\frac{1}{2}$, and the Wilson plank was adopted.[2]

The convention closed as it had begun, with a triumphant sense of unity and absolute confidence in the leadership of Woodrow Wilson.

---

[1] New York *Times*, June 14, 1916.

[2] *Ibid.*, June 17, 1916. The Republicans in their platform had taken substantially the same position.

III. THE BATTLE OF 1916

Wilson's situation as commander-in-chief of the Democratic host at the beginning of the campaign of 1916 was by no means an easy one. However brilliant his leadership had been, however devoted his following, he could not now rely upon a divided opposition, as in 1912. It must not be forgotten that he had been elected to the presidency by a minority of the popular vote: he had polled some 1,300,000 fewer ballots than the total given to Taft and Roosevelt. His extraordinary record for progressive legislation, so confidently approved by his own party, had aroused the bitter animosity of the opposition, especially in the East, where conservative moneyed interests felt the challenge to their power, the threat to their profits. They had now succeeded in manœuvring the Progressive party and its candidate out of the field, and they stood, a united Republican army, with a popular following normally greater than that of the Democrats. They were, of course, strongest in the populous East, where their disapproval of so-called radical legislation was augmented by no inconsiderable discontent with Wilson's patient, if not pacifistic, attitude toward the war.

Wilson and the Democrats had two clear lines of strategy: they must capture the progressive West to reenforce the assured support of the solid South; they must win the independent vote which was largely opposed to war. Wilson saw the problem with the utmost clarity. To capture the West he had already to his credit a record of "the most important program of progressive domestic legislation ever enacted by a single administration since Washington's."[1] And with Congress in session he was driving steadily forward to the completion of his programme. As Congressman Pou wrote him:

[1] Editorial in the New York *World*, June 16, 1916.

". . . the House is now working like a well oiled machine. We shall put through your program sooner than some suppose."[1]

He had the vast advantage of a President in power over an opponent seeking to unseat him. He could act: he could keep the eyes of the country constantly upon him.

It was easier, indeed, to win the Progressive vote, since it was interested chiefly in domestic affairs, than that of the independents, who were disturbed by our foreign relationships. The former he could convince by action: the latter he must reach largely by argument and promises: in the upshot, the foreign issue was to prove, politically, more important.

Wilson gave much thought to the choice of a field marshal to conduct the campaign. He wanted a man of courage, energy and independence, above all, one who was free from entanglements with the old-school politicians. McCombs, who had been chairman of the Democratic National Committee since the campaign of 1912, in which his management had been as much of a liability as an asset, was obviously disqualified.

He considered Newton D. Baker for the post and even offered it to his friend Colonel House—"Could you possibly act yourself?"[2]—but finally settled upon Vance C.

---

[1]June 12, 1916. Wilson's record for progressive legislation during that hot and hectic summer was as extraordinary as it was comprehensive. In his speech of acceptance Wilson could well say:

"We have in four years come very near to carrying out the platform of the Progressive Party as well as our own; for we also are progressives." *The Public Papers of Woodrow Wilson*, Vol. IV, p. 280.

There was no doubt that this record did much to attract and hold the following of the defunct Progressive party. A few days before election, eleven of the nineteen members of the platform committee of the Progressive party convention of 1912 endorsed Wilson and called upon all members of the party to support him. They declared:

"Of thirty-three planks in the Progressive platform of 1912, twenty-two have been wholly or partly enacted into laws. Of eighty propositions embodied in these planks, more than half have been carried out by administrative acts or by laws." New York *Times*, November 1, 1916.

[2]Telegram to House, June 10th. House in these busy days was of great assistance to the President in ways in which he had real capability, that is, in exploring political

McCormick, of Pennsylvania. McCormick was then forty-four years old, an accomplished man of business, a first-class organizer and administrator.[1] He had worked zealously in Wilson's behalf in the Baltimore convention and could be counted upon to carry on an aggressive, honest and resourceful fight for a Democratic victory in 1916. While his appointment caused some heartburn in the ranks of the professional politicians of the party, it was widely approved in the country, and interpreted as an astute move by the President to secure progressive support.

It was characteristic of Wilson that, once he trusted a man, he trusted him utterly. He was soon speaking of McCormick as a "steam-engine in boots": and providing for regular Monday-evening conferences which sometimes lasted so late that the new chairman spent the night at the White House.[2] While Wilson was a consummate master of the larger strategies of politics, he doubted his capacities —and probably with warrant—for the lesser but highly important tactics of campaigning.

"To tell the truth," he himself wrote, "I am not fertile as a suggester of campaign methods."[3]

---

situations, making inquiries regarding leaders, and reporting faithfully to his chief, who had neither the time nor the temper for securing this necessary information. Wilson was warmly appreciative, writing to House on June 22nd: "I have treated you shamefully in the matter of letters of late, but, thank God, you understand and are generous enough to forgive.

"Meanwhile you have sent me no end of useful matter and have filled my thoughts with many suggestions that are of the highest value to me, and promptly become part of my thinking after I have read your letters. I thank you with all my heart!"

[1]He had inherited a fortune and added to it by publishing successfully two Democratic newspapers in the heart of a Republican state. He had been elected mayor of Harrisburg at the age of twenty-nine and was credited with being the best mayor the city ever had. In 1914 he was the Democratic candidate for governor, but also enlisted the support of the Progressives owing to his brilliant fight against the old machine elements. Theodore Roosevelt stumped the state in his behalf, and while not elected, McCormick's campaign was strong, clean and thoroughly progressive.

[2]A number of years later Mrs. Wilson, writing to say that the President wanted to have a talk with McCormick, added: "Come to lunch and have some 'Popovers' as in the good old fighting days." (January 14, 1920.)

[3]Woodrow Wilson to Theodore Wright, June 21, 1916.

before the conventions, which he would rather meet in the campaign, Roosevelt or Hughes, he responded:

"It matters very little. We have definite and constructive things to do and we shall go ahead and do them. Roosevelt deals in personalities and avoids arguments upon facts and conditions. One does not need to meet him at all. Hughes is of a different type. If he is nominated, he will have to be met."[1]

It is a truly remarkable tribute to the President's skill and patience, in these troubled times, that he was able to turn both of his chief problems of the summer, which might so easily have had disastrous results, to his political advantage. The Mexican situation, with American soldiers on Mexican soil and Carranza demanding, bluntly, their withdrawal, might easily have developed into war. Our own press was boiling with sensational news. Hughes was denouncing Wilson's "vacillation,"[2] and demanding a "new policy," without specifying what it should be. Roosevelt was even more violent.[3]

On July 10th the President was saying in answer to the criticisms:

"All along my motto has been 'Help Mexico,' but—— Some would help her by first fighting her and increasing her distrust and hostility. . . ."[4]

But in the end his patience and his magnanimity of purpose were rewarded. Early in September a distinguished joint commission[5] was meeting at New London,

---

[1] Notes made by the author of an interview with the President, May 11, 1916.

[2] As in his speech of acceptance, July 31st. New York *Times*, August 1, 1916.

[3] He wrote to Senator Lodge: "I agree with you; it is dreadful to think that some millions of Americans will vote for Wilson—including men like ex-President Eliot. They can't so vote without incurring moral degradation." *Selections from the Correspondence of Theodore Roosevelt and Henry Cabot Lodge*, Vol. II, p. 492.

[4] Wilson's notes for an address before the Salesmanship Congress, Detroit, Michigan, July 10, 1916. He actually said in the address: "I hear some gentlemen say that they want to help Mexico, and the way they propose to help her is to overwhelm her with force." *The Public Papers of Woodrow Wilson*, Vol. IV, p. 230.

[5] Secretary Lane, Judge George Gray, and John R. Mott represented the United States.

Connecticut, to discuss the problems involved, thus removing one dangerous issue from the arbitrament of the
campaign.

The President was equally successful in preventing the
threatened railroad strike[1] which would have affected
250,000 miles of trackage and 400,000 men, and disorgan-
ized utterly the economic life of the nation.

A timid leader might have dodged such a contentious
issue in the midst of a presidential campaign. A leader less
moved by deep convictions of what he considered right
and just might have compromised. Wilson boldly forced
the fighting, making clear his position not only in Congress, where it gave convincing evidence of the continued
power of his leadership, but in the country at large. The
highly controversial Adamson Act quickly passed both
Houses,[2] and the President signed it at once.

The Act was bitterly attacked by the conservatives,
alienating certain influential journals and driving no inconsiderable number of voters, especially in the East, who
had previously supported Wilson, into the Hughes camp.
Wilson had insisted upon this course of action in spite of
the advice of certain of his political friends, and the campaign management at once felt the reaction. Money practically stopped coming in, and "the fight had to be made
all over again." "It was one of the most courageous things
the President ever did."[3] The President wrote to one of
his old friends who was highly critical:

"The answer to those who wonder why I 'allowed myself to be coerced' in regard to the eight-hour law is that
I was not coerced. Neither the railroad presidents nor the
representatives of the brotherhoods desired legislation. I
took the matter into my own hands because I was deter-

---

[1] See this volume, pp. 108 *et seq.*
[2] Many Republicans joined the Democrats in supporting it.
[3] Robert Woolley to the author.

mined to save the country from a great disaster, and I recommended the terms of the Adamson Bill because I thought they were just and right, as I do now. The whole thing has been so systematically and deliberately misrepresented that there is no use trying to alter at this stage of the campaign the impressions which have been created. I am sure the right impressions have been made upon the vast majority of our fellow-citizens.

"Some of these days I will tell you all about the circumstances that preceded the Adamson law and you will be amazed at the new and overwhelming evidence of the continued existence of what we must set our faces like steel to correct."[1]

These weeks in the torrid summer of 1916 were difficult and wearing upon the President. He might demand and secure an eight-hour day for railroad workers: there was no such thing for a President of the United States. He and Mrs. Wilson during August were called, much of the time, as early as five or six o'clock in the morning: and his days were unbelievably crowded—often until late at night. The chronicle of a single blistering summer day—August 29th—as gathered from the White House diaries and other records, will give a vivid picture of the pressure he was under:

The President and Mrs. Wilson were called at six o'clock. After breakfast Senator Newlands arrived for a conference; and half an hour later, at ten o'clock, one James Kelley. At 10:30 Mr. Wilson walked over to the Executive Office where, surrounded by committeemen from both Houses, by army and navy officers, and by moving picture and camera men, he signed the Army and Navy Appropriation bills, the Philippine bill and the New Uniform Bill of Lading bill. In a few words he expressed his gratification at "so many pieces of useful and public-spirited legislation," and he added smilingly, as his eye fell upon the camera men:

[1] Wilson to Lawrence C. Woods, October 17, 1916.

"I am not accustomed to the kind of spotlight to which we have just been subjected, but I am very glad to have been caught at such acts."[1]

The committee of eight men, representing the railroad presidents (already referred to), had assembled meanwhile at the White House to discuss the threatened railroad strike.

After this dramatic episode, the President hastened to the cabinet meeting; and from that to luncheon. Two ambassadors were among the guests—Walter H. Page, home on a visit from his post in London, and William G. Sharp, Ambassador to France, who was also in Washington for a short time. Mrs. Hugh Wallace was another guest, as were the Misses Smith of New Orleans, old and dear friends of the President, and Mrs. Wilson's brother, Mr. Bolling. The Misses Smith remembered long afterward the brilliant talk about the table, though matters of especial interest to Page and Sharp were carefully avoided.[2] Page's sole comment upon the luncheon, made soon afterward in a memorandum, was that there was "not one word about foreign affairs."[3]

At 2:15 Wilson left for the Capitol, where he made his address to Congress on the critical railroad situation. Mrs. Wilson and their guests had preceded him, and were seated in the gallery when the President entered the House chamber. His address was business-like and straight to the point. When he had finished, he shook hands with the presiding officers, and left the room. Representative Adamson was waiting for him outside.

"I immediately told the President his proposition would not work, that we had no time to arrange for commissions and arbitration now before the strike . . . The President then said, 'Come down to the White House tonight and go with me up to the Capitol and we will have an interview with the leading members of the House on the subject.' I said, 'I will do that provided you will let me invite the leading Republicans as well as the leading Democrats.' He agreed to that . . ."[4]

Page, returning to the White House a little later, with the

---

[1]New York *Times*, August 30, 1916.

[2]The Misses Lucy and Mary Smith to the author, March 1927.

[3]*The Life and Letters of Walter H. Page*, Vol. II, p. 172.

[4]W. C. Adamson to the author, February 9, 1927.

other guests, inquired as to whether he was expected to see the President again, to say good-bye. He was not; and he departed, somewhat disgruntled, to comment in his memorandum on this unfortunate "lone-hand way of playing the game."

In the meantime the President himself, and Mrs. Wilson, drove to the Kirkside Club for their daily game of golf.

Adamson arrived at the White House after dinner, as Wilson had suggested, and they went together to the Capitol where, in the Speaker's Room, the conferees had assembled at Adamson's invitation—Clark, Kitchin, Sims and Adamson, Democrats; Republican floor leader Mann, and Esch and Hamilton, Republican members of the Committee on Interstate and Foreign Commerce.[1] After a two-hour conference, during which the whole thorny subject of the railroad crisis was discussed, the President returned to the White House accompanied by Adamson, who continued the discussion to the last.

It is scarcely surprising that a writer who was a close observer of the President's activities should ask, "How does he stand it?" and report:

"The President's eyes were blood-shot; his face was drawn and haggard. He had been up most of the night working on his message to Congress . . ."[2]

Indeed we are hardly surprised to find Wilson himself writing on one occasion:

"I have not been very well for the past week or two,—Since I came back from Detroit. My digestion has been upset in some way. But I am slowly getting it in shape again, I believe, the undeniable truth being that a rest, a real rest, has been now a long time overdue. I wish I were in better trim for the campaign. All join me in affectionate messages."[3]

Some day a necessary book will be written upon the health of the Presidents and its effect not only upon their

---

[1] List given to the author by Adamson, February 9, 1927. The list as given in the New York *Times* was: Clark, Adamson, Kitchin, Mann, and Sterling.

[2] David Lawrence, *The True Story of Woodrow Wilson*, p. 113.

[3] Wilson to House, July 23, 1916.

lives but upon their records as executives. In the case of President Wilson, physical health, especially later in his career, played a vast part.

In addition to all the other momentous occupations of this feverish summer, essential to the welfare of the nation, the merciless demands of visitors upon the President's time were never more overwhelming. We find him writing, despairingly, to many friends, trying to make them understand why he could not see them:

"I have received with interest through Mrs. Wilson your letter about child labor conditions, and thank you for it.

"I am sincerely sorry to hear of your experiences at my office, but I beg that you will not draw the conclusion that I am not democratic. If you could really see the amount of work which it is necessary for the President to do every day, you would see that if he made himself available for callers, it would be necessary for him to do the real work of the Government late at night when his wits were at their worst, and that the public would suffer more that way than by his denying himself the pleasure of seeing friends when they call."[1]

Under such pressure the President had to postpone his active participation in the political campaign—to the growing concern of his managers. His speech of acceptance was delayed to September 2nd—partly in the hope that Congress, by that time, would have adjourned.

The President and Mrs. Wilson had taken a house on the New Jersey shore near Long Branch. It was called Shadow Lawn: a huge, hotel-like place, surrounded, however, by spacious and attractive grounds. A wide veranda

---

[1] Wilson to Lillian E. A. Heath, July 24, 1916. But he remembered again and again, however great the pressure, those who were nearest to him. A letter to his daughter, Mrs. Sayre, brought this response: "How sweet and adorable of you, in the midst of all this dreadful business, to think of your little daughter's birthday! I could almost have cried when your telegram came, with its loving message . . ." (August 30, 1916.)

extended entirely around the house. There was a great Pompeian dining room and a hall with built-in bookcases all about, but without books, some "awful statuary" and a golden piano.[1] The Wilsons were able to escape from Washington and reach this hoped-for haven only the evening before the widely expected ceremony of acceptance. It was raining on the morning of the 2nd, but after luncheon the sun came out and over twenty-five thousand people swarmed around the eight thousand chairs provided and filled the grounds in all directions.

Senator James, of Kentucky, with his mighty, rolling voice, performed the ritual of "notification"—not unlike a coronation in England months after the King has begun his reign. The President's response was mainly a review of his administration:

". . . the Democratic Party has . . . merely done its duty."[2]

He placed especial emphasis upon its progressive policies:

"The Republican Party is just the party that *cannot* meet the new conditions of a new age. It does not know the way and it does not wish new conditions. It tried to break away from the old leaders and could not. . . . A new age, an age of revolutionary change, needs new purposes and new ideas."[3]

In the important international issues which a large number of doubters were narrowly watching, he defined his position with a clarity that is better perceived a score of years later than it was at the time. He avoided any reference whatever to the slogan of the campaign that "he kept us out of war" or any implication whatsoever that he could keep out in the future, though he made it clear that many leading Republicans wanted war and that he did

---

[1] Mrs. Wilson to the author, December 1925.
[2] *The Public Papers of Woodrow Wilson*, Vol. IV, p. 276.
[3] *Ibid.*, p. 281.

not.[1] And he asserted more sharply than ever the impossibility of American isolation in the world:

"There must be a just and settled peace, and we here in America must contribute the full force of our enthusiasm and of our authority as a nation to the organization of that peace upon world-wide foundations that cannot easily be shaken."[2]

The implication of such a position was that we could not "any longer remain neutral as against any wilful disturbance of the peace of the world." In short, we might have to go to war.[3]

Even after the acceptance speech, the President continued to torment his campaign managers. Both he and Mrs. Wilson resented personal publicity. When the American Press Association wished to have special photographs of President and Mrs. Wilson taken, "with a view to showing the simplicity of their personal lives in the White House," Wilson's comment was brief: "I know Mrs. Wilson would not be willing to do this at all. I am willing to do anything reasonable." Some of the innocence of his earlier campaigns seemed still to cling to him: the hope that he could really avoid personalities and keep the campaign on a plane of high reason and the clear consideration of issues.[4]

---

[1] *The Public Papers of Woodrow Wilson*, Vol. IV, pp. 330, 331.

[2] *Ibid.*, p. 287.

[3] It is clear enough that he was here looking squarely at the realities of the situation; but he never for a moment gave up his hope of securing peace without war. Three weeks after this speech (September 23rd) he was telling Page that he meant to support a German proposal of an armistice looking toward a negotiated peace, if it were made.

On the other hand there might have to be "radical changes of policy," as he wrote the next week (September 27th), in a letter to the Women's Democratic Club of Portland, Oregon, regretting the partisan use of the suffrage issue "at a time so critical as this when the question is about to be determined whether we shall keep the nation upon its present terms of peace and good will with the world or turn to radical changes of policy which may alter the whole aspect of the nation's life."

[4] ". . . I hope it goes without saying, so far as I am concerned, that there will be no descent to personalities or to anything unworthy of the dignity of the nation." (Wilson to W. L. Spencer, August 7, 1916.)

He even thought he could get along without making any campaign tours whatever. Were not his record and his clear statement of his position sufficient to convince the voters? He was confirmed in this opinion by the feebleness of the Republican campaign: and by the speeches of Mr. Hughes.

"I am inclined," he wrote to B. M. Baruch, "to follow the course suggested by a friend of mine who says that he has always followed the rule never to murder a man who is committing suicide, and clearly this misdirected gentleman is committing suicide slowly but surely."[1]

As late as September 19th he was issuing a denial from the White House:

"The President has no intention of making any campaign tour. He does not intend to change the program already agreed upon by those in charge of his campaign to accept invitations to discuss public questions only from non-partisan organizations."[2]

During all of these weeks he had been under extremely heavy pressure. On September 4th he delivered the address at the dedication of the new memorial at Lincoln's birthplace at Hodgenville, Kentucky, from which he returned "utterly worn out."[3]

---

[1]August 19, 1916.

[2]New York *Times*, September 20, 1916.

[3]It may be observed in passing that the Lincoln address was one of the most finished literary productions of his presidency, resembling, in the loving care bestowed upon it, his earlier and more studied essays. It may be read also because of its intimate self-revelation, disclosing Woodrow Wilson's deep love and admiration for Abraham Lincoln. He said:

"I have read many biographies of Lincoln; I have sought out with the greatest interest the many intimate stories that are told of him, the narratives of nearby friends, the sketches at close quarters, in which those who had the privilege of being associated with him have tried to depict for us the very man himself 'in his habit as he lived'; but I have nowhere found a real intimate of Lincoln's. I nowhere get the impression in any narrative or reminiscence that the writer had in fact penetrated to the heart of his mystery, or that any man could penetrate to the heart of it. That brooding spirit had no real familiars. I get the impression that it never spoke out in complete self-revelation, and that it could not reveal itself completely to anyone. It was a very lonely spirit that looked out from underneath those shaggy brows and comprehended men

When Congress, at length, adjourned on September 8th, the President having returned to Washington to sign several important bills, the way seemed clear for a period of rest with some attention to the campaign. But on the 11th he and Mrs. Wilson were called suddenly to New London, Connecticut, by the last illness of his sister, Mrs. Howe.[1]

It was not, then, until September 23rd that he made what may be called the opening address of the political campaign, speaking from the broad veranda of Shadow Lawn to an audience of some two thousand business men and others.

In the meantime the Republicans had been carrying forward their campaign throughout the country with assiduity on the part of Mr. Hughes and with ferocity on the part of Mr. Roosevelt.

Hughes's speech of acceptance, delivered weeks previously (on July 31st) had been distinguished by its "dead levelism."[2] It was critical and non-constructive, characterized by "no passion . . . for democracy in government, either in the United States or Mexico."[3] He adhered to the good old Republican doctrine of tariff protection and favoured "adequate national defense," without defining what he meant by "adequate."

A few days after his acceptance Hughes had set out on a speaking tour that took him to the Pacific Coast. To those who remembered his forcible and effective campaigning in 1908, his speeches were disappointing. They had expected to hear bold and powerful arguments; he was merely an "itinerant fault-finder." He dwelt much on petty ques-

---

without fully communing with them, as if, in spite of all its genial efforts at comradeship, it dwelt apart, saw its visions of duty where no man looked on." *The Public Papers of Woodrow Wilson*, Vol. IV, p. 295.

[1] They left for Columbia, South Carolina, where the funeral was to be held, on September 17th.

[2] As Newton D. Baker characterized it in a letter to the President, August 4, 1916.

[3] Comment in the Springfield *Republican*, August 1, 1916.

tions, criticized certain removals of government employees, and accused the administration of being sectional. It is a lesson which candidates seem never to learn, that the American people have never liked or followed mere fault-finders.[1]

Of course the Republicans were in a difficult position. They had no real or strong issues.[2] Most of the accomplishments of Wilson's administration, particularly in the domestic field, were beyond dispute, as the opposition itself admitted by its silence.[3]

When the President signed the highly explosive Adamson eight-hour law (on September 3rd) the Republicans seized thirstily upon it as the paramount issue of the campaign. "Transcending every other issue is the issue that has just presented itself—whether the Government shall yield to force."[4]

Charging that Wilson had surrendered to party expediency, Hughes declared:

"I would not surrender to anybody in the country. . . .

"I stand for two things: first for the principle of fair,

---

[1]". . . we shall learn after the election if it pays to measure out full-strength unmitigated damnation to the opposition," commented the St. Paul *Pioneer Press*, a Republican paper. Quoted in the New York *Times*, August 21, 1916.

[2]New York *Times*, August 19–21, 1916. It is probably not too much to say that on the woman suffrage question alone was Hughes's position effective. At the beginning of the campaign he announced that he favoured the submission and ratification of an amendment to the federal constitution granting the franchise to women on the same basis as to men. *Ibid.*, August 2, 1916. Throughout the campaign the President on his part adhered with good-humoured inflexibility to the position he had always held. ". . . if I should change my personal attitude now, I should seem to the country like nothing less than an angler for votes, because . . . my attitude in this matter has again and again been very frankly avowed . . .

"I have all along believed, and still believe, that the thing can best and most solidly be done by the action of the individual states, and that the time it will take to get it that way will not be longer than the time it would take to get it the other way." (Wilson to Mrs. E. P. Davis, August 5, 1916.)

[3]"Now the astonishing fact is that, with the exception of the Democratic tariff revision and the new army law, Mr. Wilson's opponents in this campaign offer practically no condemnation of this long list of constructive measures . . . they would have the voters forget entirely the very exceptional record of what he has actually done for the American people." Springfield *Republican*, September 3, 1916.

[4]Hughes's address September 7th. New York *Times*, September 8, 1916.

impartial, thorough, candid arbitration; and, second, for legislation on facts according to the necessities of the case. And I am opposed to being dictated to, either in the executive department or in Congress, by any power on earth before the facts are known, and in the absence of the facts."[1]

This attack, however it might please the conservatives, increased Hughes's difficulties with the Progressives. Even here he was in an awkward position, for he dared not oppose the general principle of an eight-hour day; and he was not allowed to forget the fact that seventy members of his own party in the House had joined with the Democrats in passing the bill.[2]

At one point Hughes's criticism, in the light of subsequent events, had some justification—that is, in the matter of preparation for possible war. Holding to the old Jeffersonian views, and supported by public opinion, neither party had ever in the past advocated real military preparation in time of peace. No war in our national history has ever found us prepared. The failure of the McKinley administration to make ready for emergencies resulted in the deplorable disease and death in the mobilization camps in 1898, but at the close of the war and throughout the Roosevelt and Taft administrations no adequate steps were taken to rear safeguards against a repetition of these conditions. Had they been taken there would have been less occasion to condemn the Wilson administration for the situation that existed in the two years before our entrance into the World War.[3]

---

[1]New York *Times*, September 5, 1916.

[2]*Ibid.*, September 2, 1916. ". . . it is idle to say that Congress was clubbed by labor unionism into this legislation. The Senate could never have been driven into passing such a measure within two or three days, almost without debate, unless an irresistible public opinion, concerned first of all with a paramount public interest, had demanded instant action." Springfield *Republican*, September 3, 1916.

[3]In the case of the navy, there was little or no ground for criticism and little was offered. The President had looked upon the navy as our chief arm of defense. More

While there had been widespread criticism of Hughes's campaign of fault-finding and of his failure to take unequivocal positions on the outstanding questions of the time, the September elections encouraged him to hold to his course. In Maine the Republicans made a clean sweep of federal and state offices, and the exultant politicians rang the changes on the old saw: "As Maine goes, so goes the Nation." Two weeks later the Wilson forces suffered a severe repulse in the New Jersey primary, where Senator Martine defeated Judge Wescott, the man who had twice nominated Wilson for the presidency. Martine polled a heavy German-American vote because of his pronounced anti-British views, and his assertion that he was "tired of going to the White House for orders"[1]—this in spite of the fact that he owed everything, politically, to Wilson's earlier support.

In the populous and more conservative East, Hughes seemed to be gaining—even to have a good chance of victory—as the hard-driven Democratic managers began to be well aware. Reports from the West, however, were far more favourable to Wilson,[2] and every effort was made to assure a sweeping victory there in the hope of overcoming the hostility in the East. Leading Democrats began in October to bring renewed pressure upon the President to make a real stumping tour across the country.

---

than twice as much money had been expended or appropriated for naval vessels in the first three and a half years of the Wilson administration than from 1901 to 1913. (Information taken from a chart which Secretary Daniels sent to the President, August 21, 1916.) The naval bill, passed in August 1916, backed by Wilson in the face of opposition from members of his own party, promised to give the United States a fleet second only to that of Great Britain. In signing it, the President said:

"Never before by one single act of legislation has so much been done for the creation of an adequate navy." New York *Times*, August 30, 1916.

[1]New York *Times*, September 28, 1916.

[2]When Wilson visited Omaha two weeks later he received a great ovation. It was estimated that from 150,000 to 200,000 persons turned out to greet him, and the auditorium where he spoke in the evening, normally accommodating 10,000 people, was packed to the doors. New York *Times*, October 6, 1916.

"Dignity is all right, but it will not in this instance compensate for defeat. . . . The leader must lead."[1]

Wilson finally agreed to make two addresses at Omaha on October 5th, three at Indianapolis on October 12th, three at Chicago on October 19th, and four at Cincinnati on October 26th. These were all highly successful, attracting large audiences and giving remarkable evidence of his power of appealing to the people.

No one reading the speeches delivered during the spring and summer of 1916 and comparing them with those of the campaign of 1912 can fail to be impressed by the growth in the power, the depth, the skill—even the humour—of Wilson's appeal. Four years of bitter struggle, triumph and defeat, four years of discipline—to a man of Wilson's temperament and background—in meeting, dealing with, and dominating the strongest men in public life, had left their purifying mark. He himself clearly recognized it:

"I have come through the fire since I talked to you last. Whether the metal is purer than it was, God only knows; but the fire has been there, the fire has penetrated every part of it, and if I may believe my own thoughts I have less partisan feeling, more impatience of party maneuver, more enthusiasm for the right thing, no matter whom it hurts, than I ever had before in my life."[2]

There continued to be the familiar inspirational quality and the moral fervour, enhanced now by the largeness of view, the sureness of touch, the knowledge of facts, that only experience could have given; but there was also a new sense of ease, and an aptness of humour:

"Now, I have found a few disinterested men. I wish I had found more. . . . There never was a time in the history

[1]Senator Stone to Tumulty, October 1, 1916.

[2]Address before the National Press Club, May 15, 1916. *The Public Papers of Woodrow Wilson*, Vol. IV, pp. 174-175.

of the world when character, just sheer character all by itself, told more than it does now. A friend of mine says that every man who takes office in Washington either grows or swells, and when I give a man an office, I watch him carefully to see whether he is swelling or growing. The mischief of it is that when they swell they do not swell enough to burst. . . .

"I remember when I was president of a university a man said to me, 'Good heavens, man, why don't you leave something alone and let it stay the way it is?' And I said, 'If you will guarantee to me that it will stay the way it is I will let it alone; but if you knew anything you would know that if you leave a live thing alone it will not stay where it is.'"[1]

Again and again he emphasized the need of noble men, defining the noble man as one "who has some margin of energy outside the little circle of his own self-interest to spend for the benefit of his fellow-men,"[2] and the power of moral force—"I have not read history without observing that the greatest forces in the world and the only permanent forces are the moral forces."[3] And more and more he emphasized his belief in the worth of the common man: and in the superiority of the democratic system:

"The principle of the life of America is that she draws her vitality, not from small bodies of men who may wish to assume the responsibility of guiding and controlling her, but from the great body of thinking and toiling and planning men from whom she draws her energy and vitality as a nation. I believe, and this is the reason I am a Democrat, not merely with a big 'D' but with a little 'd'

---

[1] *Ibid.*, pp. 174-175.

[2] Address at Washington, July 20, 1916. *The Public Papers of Woodrow Wilson*, Vol. IV, p. 256.

[3] Address before the Press Club of New York, June 30, 1916. *Ibid.*, p. 219.

. . . in the patriotism and energy and initiative of the average man."[1]

It is impossible in any short space to give more than glimpses of Wilson's power as an orator; this writer, who heard many of his addresses during this hard campaign, believes that their influence was based far more upon the popular belief in the President's sincerity, his faith in democracy, the moral fervour of his convictions, than upon the exposition of his record and his programme. After all, the great mass of people cannot know or understand all the complex problems that a government faces, but they have an unerring instinct for sincerity, for character, and for the leadership that upon the whole satisfies their own ideals and desires. Thomas A. Edison who, outside of his own special field, was a type of the ordinary American, in announcing his support of Wilson (on September 3rd) exactly expressed this common reaction: "They say he has blundered. Perhaps he has. But I notice that he usually blunders forward."[2]

In short, to read the speeches of this period is to look into the soul of a devoted, clear-thinking, far-seeing statesman, interested in broad principles and high ideals, and never, at any time, whatever the provocation, descending to crude trivial personalities.

Another developing quality of the President may here well be emphasized since it, also, had an undoubted effect upon the campaign. One of the stock criticisms of him as a man had been that he "could not work with people," that he had to "dominate or ruin." But the records of this period are full of incidents showing how he bound his associates to him not only by his own staunch loyalty and support, but by a certain delightful courtesy of apprecia-

---

[1] Address before the Associated Advertising Clubs, Philadelphia, June 29, 1916. *Ibid.*, p. 214.

[2] New York *Times*, September 4, 1916.

PRESIDENT WILSON DELIVERING HIS ACCEPTANCE SPEECH AT
SHADOW LAWN, LONG BRANCH, NEW JERSEY, SEPTEMBER 2, 1916.

tion. If a friend in whom he believed was under attack no one could stand more immovably in his defense than Woodrow Wilson. This was well illustrated in the case of Secretary Daniels. In spite of the provisions made to develop the navy and the testimonials of such distinguished authorities as Admiral Dewey as to its excellent condition, there was a vicious conspiracy of attack upon the Secretary which, in the after-look, seems singularly unjust. There must always, perhaps, in every administration, be some such a scapegoat! Widespread demands were made for his removal, in which even one close to the President in the summer of 1916 played a part. He asked McCormick to talk to Wilson about it, suggesting that McCormick himself should be appointed to succeed Daniels.[1]

"Wilson ought to get rid of Daniels, and you should be appointed in his place."

Had the President yielded to the pressure for Daniels' dismissal, much of which came from interests which were disturbed by Daniels' uncompromising attitude in regard to oil leases, he might have eased off some of the criticism levelled at him, but the President neither budged nor doubted, supporting Daniels straight through to the end.[2]

Another man much under attack was Burleson, and here again Wilson's loyalty did not falter.[3] The President

---

[1]McCormick did not, of course, follow the suggestion. In fact, he had from the beginning refused to accept any other appointment from the administration, although twice offered a place in the cabinet, and once an ambassadorship. (Vance C. McCormick to the author.)

[2]Furthermore, had Daniels been displaced the political results might have been damaging during the campaign, for it later developed that when moving pictures were used to illustrate the achievements of the various government departments, the cabinet officer and the Department that the theatre crowds applauded most generously were Secretary Daniels and the Navy. (Vance C. McCormick to the author, 1937.)

[3]Here is a letter written by Burleson to Wilson on June 8th: "When I reached home yesterday afternoon I found the beautiful flowers and your highly appreciated note. I feel that it was well worth while to live fifty-three years in order to receive such commendation."

was extremely fond of Newton D. Baker, who was also severely criticized, and whom the President again and again stoutly defended.

"He is one of the most genuine and gifted men I know, and I am sure that the better he is known the more he will be trusted, not only, but loved and admired."[1]

In a letter written in July he referred to "Gregory . . . whom I love and trust more than ever."[2] And in spite of former differences and rivalries Wilson and William J. Bryan, who was still a power in the party, remained upon a footing of genuine respect and coöperation, and Bryan was of the greatest service in the campaign.[3]

As a result of this coöperation and eager helpfulness, the bickerings and difficulties incident to the campaign of 1912 were wholly absent. Never was a candidate more wisely and unselfishly served than Woodrow Wilson in 1916. One of the great elements was McCormick's good sense, geniality and high efficiency:

"I cannot tell you how satisfactory the campaign has been from start to finish. From McCormick down to the most insignificant worker there has been unity of purpose without bickering or fault-finding of any sort whatsoever.

"Woolley, Roper, Wallace and some of the others have done really brilliant work and . . . the early hours of the morning have often found them still at it."[4]

And the President was prompt and generous in his acknowledgments:

[1]Wilson to General W. F. Sadler, Jr., May 19, 1916.

[2]Wilson to Colonel House, July 23, 1916.

[3]Wilson wrote Bryan on September 27th: "I cannot refrain from dropping you at least a line to express my admiration of the admirable campaign you are conducting. It is, of course, nothing novel to see you show your strength in this way, but I feel so sincerely appreciative of your efforts in the interest of what we all feel to be the people's cause that I must let you know with what deep interest I am looking on."

[4]E. M. House to Wilson, November 4, 1916.

November 13, 1916.

MY DEAR McCORMICK:

The first letter I write from my desk here must be to you. It makes me deeply glad to think how the whole country has seen and appreciated your quality. You have won the admiration and affection of all Democrats not only, but the sincere admiration of all parties. No campaign, I think it can be said, was ever conducted with such a combination of harmony and vigor and system as this one from your headquarters and the headquarters at Chicago, and you were throughout the moving and guiding spirit. It must be a source of deep satisfaction to you that you should have won this admiration by an unselfish service of the first magnitude.

May I not say for myself how entirely I have had my trust in you confirmed, and how throughout these trying months my genuine affection for you has grown and strengthened? My own sense of obligation and gratitude to you is immeasurable.

Mrs. Wilson and all my household join me in sending you the most affectionate greetings and congratulations.

Always

Affectionately yours,
WOODROW WILSON

HON. VANCE C. McCORMICK,
Harrisburg, Pennsylvania.

A disgraceful feature of the campaign was the circulation of scandalous stories regarding the President's private life. Such dastardly "whispering campaigns" have been one of the familiar and disheartening aspects of American politics—a last effort to destroy a candidate who cannot be met upon the high ground of reason and argument. While it had been impossible for Wilson's most vicious enemies to get any facts that they dared publish, evidence exists that the scandals were circulated by deliberately organized effort, for example by a number of women in Chicago who used the telephone. The President felt himself helpless in meeting them.

"I had a talk with the President the other day which was very touching. He made reference to the infamous stories that are being circulated regarding him with such indignation and pathos that I felt really very sorry for him. . . . there is no truth in them and yet a man can't deny them."[1]

In June, Wilson wrote to a friend:

"I do not know how to deal with the fiendish lies that are being invented and circulated about my personal character other than to invite those who repeat them to consult anybody who has known me for any length of time. . . .

"Poison of this sort is hard to find an antidote for."[2]

The indignant denials of intimate friends of the family, like Dr. Henry Van Dyke of Princeton—and there were many such—could not overtake the lies. It was still being charged that the grave of the first Mrs. Wilson at Rome, Georgia, was neglected—a story that circulated everywhere—although actual visitors constantly denied it and at that very time one of the most famous of American sculptors[3] was engaged in making an appropriate memorial. By October this whispering campaign had gained such headway that Professor Stockton Axson, brother of the first Mrs. Wilson, wrote an article entitled "The Private Life of President Wilson," which was published in scores of newspapers and afterwards largely circulated in pamphlet form. This helped, but it did not wholly kill the pestiferous falsehoods.

Hughes and the Republicans from the beginning made every effort to capture the elusive Progressive vote. They finally dramatized their purpose by a "feast of unity"[4] in New York. "Bolters" and "burglars" were to join

[1]Franklin K. Lane to F. J. Lane, June 6, 1916. *The Letters of Franklin K. Lane*, p. 211.

[2]Wilson to Sylvester W. Beach, June 26, 1916.

[3]Herbert Adams.

[4]October 3, 1916.

hands. Roosevelt and Taft were both there, to symbolize the occasion, but the coldness of their greeting—they shook hands with ill-concealed hostility—revealed the depth of the scar that still remained. The campaign was marked by a steady accession of former Progressive leaders to Wilson's support. John M. Parker, their vice-presidential candidate, bitterly attacked Roosevelt for returning to a Republican party more reactionary than ever before. Bainbridge Colby campaigned for Wilson. Victor Murdock, of Kansas, came out for Wilson on October 22nd, and Gompers joined with the vice-president and secretary of the American Federation of Labor in a statement which was strongly favourable to the Democrats.[1]

It was remarkable, indeed, how widely the thoughtful and independent leadership of the nation sided with the President. Former President Eliot, of Harvard, whose influence was pervasive, wrote a strong article for the *Atlantic Monthly*.[2] Miss Jane Addams and Miss Ida M. Tarbell were vigorous advocates: the two principal liberal journals, the *New Republic* and the *Nation*, while non-partisan early in the campaign, showed a decided swing toward Wilson in October,[3] and the New York *Evening Post* came out for the President on November 1st.[4]

---

[1]New York *Times*, October 22, 1916.

[2]October. He said: ". . . President Wilson has proved himself a party leader of unusual power; and . . . the party thus led has done much more for the country than the Republican party accomplished in five times as many years." Wilson wrote to Eliot: "I want to express to you my really very profound gratitude for the article in the Atlantic Monthly. There is no man in the country whose praise I more desire or whose approval gratifies and strengthens me more than yours." (October 2, 1916.)

[3]The *New Republic* came out for Wilson, October 28, 1916.

[4]It set forth its reasons: "From Mr. Hughes we hoped for an exhilarating campaign, with far-reaching and constructive policies, discussed in an appealing manner and on a high level. He has sorely disappointed all who expected this. His attacks upon Mr. Wilson have been far too sweeping and without a particle of generous recognition. We agree with Professor Bliss Perry in what he has lately written:

"'I like fair play. Having known Woodrow Wilson for nearly twenty-five years as a high-minded gentleman of absolute integrity, of stubborn Scotch-Irish courage, and of passionate devotion to his country, I resent the wilful misrepresentation and

As the campaign advanced, the foreign policy of the administration became more and more important as an issue. Roosevelt's attacks were violent and persistent; he characterized the statement, "He kept us out of war" as "an utterly misleading phrase, the phrase of a coward," and by implication distorted it into a promise that under no circumstances would we go to war.[1] He declared that if he had been President when the *Lusitania* was sunk, he would have seized every German vessel interned in American waters.[2] Vance McCormick challenged Hughes to endorse the Colonel's position,[3] and when a heckler put the question to him point-blank: "What would you have done when the *Lusitania* was sunk?" Hughes answered:

". . . when I said 'strict accountability' every nation would have known that that was meant; and, further, when notice was published with respect to the action (the action threatened), I would have made it known, in terms unequivocal and unmistakable, that we should not tolerate a continuance of friendly relations through the ordinary diplomatic channels if that action were taken, and the *Lusitania* would never have been sunk."[4]

This was the one important respect in which Hughes avowed that he would have taken a more advanced step than the President.

---

malignant disparagement which characterize the campaign against him.' In this respect, Mr. Hughes has been the President's best campaigner.

"Meanwhile, Mr. Wilson has in his speeches shone by contrast. He has known how to be dignified while forcible. And the increasing emphasis which the whole drift of the campaign has placed upon the President's highest service to the country—his maintenance of peace with honor—has been unmistakable." (Quoted in the New York *Times*, November 2, 1916.)

And there were a few prominent business men who also came to the President's support, notably Henry Ford, Robert S. Lovett, of the Union Pacific Railroad, F. D. Underwood, president of the Erie Railroad, and Roger W. Babson.

[1] New York *Times*, October 11, 1916.

[2] *Ibid.*, October 1, 1916.

[3] *Ibid.*, October 3, 1916.

[4] *Ibid.*, October 13, 1916.

Hughes was, indeed, in an impossible situation. He knew as well as Wilson what the sentiment of the country really was: that it did not want war. How could he, then, or the Republican managers, approve the fire-eating proposals of Roosevelt, who was going up and down the country insisting that "the time for the ostrich policy, the time for the head-in-a-hole policy, in America is past"?[1] Hughes declared, indeed, a few days before the campaign closed:

"A vote for me is not a vote for war. It is a vote for lasting peace. It is a vote for the maintenance of American rights on land and sea, throughout the world."[2]

On the issue of "black-listing" and the violation of property rights, Hughes, despite his criticism of Wilson's methods, was in accord with him. Speaking on October 9th he declared:

"I do not put life and property on the same footing. . . . We do not propose to tolerate any improper interference with American property, with American mails, or with legitimate commercial intercourse. No American who is exercising only American rights shall be put on any black list by any foreign nation."[3]

Another weakness in Hughes's position was the temporizing attitude of the party toward what was known as "hyphenism." Both the candidate and the Republican managers guarded carefully against alienating the support of the German-Americans or the Irish element that was hostile to Great Britain.

In marked contrast to Hughes's policy were the out-

---

[1]Statement published by Theodore Roosevelt, October 10th. New York *Times*, October 11, 1916. The Colonel undoubtedly did the Republican cause more harm than good. His hatred of Wilson led him into undignified outbursts and to extremities of statement that were irritating and embarrassing to Hughes and his managers. House wrote Wilson on October 5th: "I am told by newspaper men that Hughes is becoming more irritable and that it is caused largely by Roosevelt's speeches."

[2]New York *Times*, November 1, 1916.

[3]*Ibid.*, October 10, 1916.

spoken declarations of Wilson. As we have seen, in his Flag Day address he had exclaimed that disloyalty "must be absolutely crushed," and later in the campaign, when Jeremiah A. O'Leary, president of the American Truth Society, an Irish anti-British organization, sent an impudent telegram to Wilson, he responded immediately with a telegram that dripped vitriol:

"I would feel deeply mortified to have you or anybody like you vote for me. Since you have access to many disloyal Americans and I have not I will ask you to convey this message to them."[1]

And Hughes, sensing the political influence of this outright defiance, was forced into weak explanations.

"I don't want the support of anyone to whom the interest of this nation is not supreme."[2]

Two events in October somewhat disturbed the Democratic party managers—the appearance in American waters of the German submarine *U-53* and the charge made by Senator Lodge that a qualifying postscript had been added to the first *Lusitania* note of May 13, 1915, minimizing its strong phrases. Lodge asserted that the postscript had been withdrawn only when members of the cabinet threatened to resign, and that the withdrawal had resulted in Bryan's resignation.[3] Neither of these incidents, however, seems to have had any perceptible influence on the campaign.

---

[1]September 29, 1916.

[2]New York *Times*, October 25, 1916. "He speaks too late," said the *Times*, "and makes the fatal mistake of saying in a weaker way what his opponent and men of sturdier courage in his own party long ago said with full sincerity and sledge-hammer emphasis." *Ibid.*, October 26, 1916.

[3]See *Woodrow Wilson, Life and Letters*, Vol. V, *Neutrality*, pp. 339–341. The President promptly denied the charges, and Senator Lodge issued this statement: "The President of the United States has denied that there was any postscript to the *Lusitania* note and we are all bound, of course, to accept the President's denial just as he makes it." Lodge, *The Senate and the League of Nations*, p. 44.

Efforts of the Republican party to make an issue of Wilson's foreign policy collapsed by the end of October; and the Grand Old Party had to fall back upon the perennial tariff issue, with the argument that high wages and prices were dependent upon high tariffs, to which the Democrats responded with statistics showing the abundant existing prosperity of the country.

In spite, however, of what seemed the strength of Wilson's position, and the futility of Hughes's campaign, it began to look in October as though Hughes would win.[1] Many of the prophets so predicted, and the Wall Street betting, at the last, usually based upon shrewd judgment, was 10 to $8\frac{1}{2}$ in Hughes's favour. Wilson himself began to be doubtful. He wrote to his brother on October 16th:

"I hear all sorts of reports, most of them encouraging ... but I never allow myself to form confident expectations of any kind. I believe that the independent vote, the vote of the people who aren't talking and aren't telling politicians how they are going to vote, is going to play a bigger part in this election than it ever played in any previous election, and that makes the result truly incalculable."

He began also to consider the contingencies incident to his defeat—especially what might happen in the interim between the election and Hughes's inauguration in March —four months at a time when the world was literally on fire. He knew well as an historian how this period of Buchanan's discredited administration had affected critical problems of state. He had often reflected in the past as

---

[1] The author wrote in his diary on November 3rd: "The election is still doubtful. I have a strong feeling, based upon what seems good grounds, that Wilson will win. All the enthusiasm of the forward-looking and positive forces is on his side, but there is a great inert, critical, selfish, prejudiced weight of numbers on the other side. There is absolutely no enthusiasm for Hughes nor any real interest in what he says or does. It is 'anything to beat Wilson.'"

to what the duty of American Presidents might be in such an emergency. He discussed the matter with Colonel House, and later with Secretary Burleson and was prompted by the Colonel in a letter of October 20th. On the day before election he wrote this extraordinary letter to Secretary Lansing:

SHADOW LAWN, New Jersey,
5 November, 1916.

MY DEAR MR. SECRETARY,

There is a matter which has occupied my thoughts throughout the campaign and which I want to lay before you before the election, while I can discuss it without any touch of feeling as to the result.

Again and again the question has arisen in my mind, What would it be my duty to do were Mr. Hughes to be elected? Four months would elapse before he could take charge of the affairs of the government, and during those four months I would be without such moral backing from the nation as would be necessary to steady and control our relations with other governments. I would be known to be the rejected, not the accredited, spokesman of the country; and yet the accredited spokesman would be without legal authority to speak for the nation. Such a situation would be fraught with the gravest dangers. The direction of the foreign policy of the government would in effect have been taken out of my hands and yet its new definition would be impossible until March.

I feel that it would be my duty to relieve the country of the perils of such a situation at once. The course I have in mind is dependent upon the consent and cooperation of the Vice President; but, if I could gain his consent to the plan, I would ask your permission to invite Mr. Hughes to become Secretary of State and would then join the Vice President in resigning, and thus open to Mr. Hughes the immediate succession to the presidency.

All my life long I have advocated some such responsible government for the United States as other constitutional systems afford as of course, and as such action on my part would inaugurate, at least by example. Responsible government means government by those whom the people trust, and trust at the time of decision and action. The whole country has long perceived, without knowing how to remedy, the extreme disadvantage of having to live for four months after a[n] election under a party whose guidance had been rejected at the polls. Here is the remedy, at any rate so far as the Executive is concerned. In ordinary times it would perhaps not be necessary to apply it. But it seems to me that in the existing circumstances it would be imperatively necessary. The choice of policy in respect of our foreign relations rests with the Executive. No such critical circumstances in regard to our foreign policy have ever before existed. It would be my duty to step aside so that there would be no doubt in any quarter how that policy was to be directed, towards what objects and by what means. I would have no right to risk the peace of the nation by remaining in office after I had lost my authority.

I hope and believe that your own judgment will run with mine in this critical matter.

Cordially and faithfully Yrs.
WOODROW WILSON

P.S. I beg that you will regard this as in the strictest sense confidential until I shall have had an opportunity to discuss it with you in person, should circumstances make it a practical problem of duty.

W.W.

THE SECRETARY OF STATE.[1]

There is no doubt that he would have carried out his purpose of resigning in case Hughes had been elected.

The campaign closed with the customary blaze of ora-

---

[1]This letter was handed to Secretary Lansing by Frank Polk, when Lansing arrived in New York on election day, after voting at Watertown. "It was enclosed in a wax-sealed envelope addressed in Mr. Wilson's handwriting and marked 'most confidential' and to be opened by no one except myself." Lansing comments, in his *Memoirs:* "The letter shows very clearly that Woodrow Wilson had first in mind the welfare of the United States and the purpose to conform to the will of the American people at once without awaiting for his presidential term to expire. He did not think of himself but of his country. . . . No better evidence can be offered to prove the high type of Mr. Wilson's statesmanship and the purity of the motives which inspired him in the conduct of his great office. He considered this proposed action a public duty, not a personal sacrifice." *War Memoirs of Robert Lansing*, pp. 165–166.

tory. In the last days the Republicans lavished large sums for advertising.[1] The Democrats countered with a last-minute appeal to the people:

> "YOU ARE WORKING;
>   —NOT FIGHTING!
> ALIVE AND HAPPY;
>   —NOT CANNON FODDER!
> WILSON AND PEACE WITH HONOR?
> HUGHES WITH ROOSEVELT AND WAR?"[2]

Wilson made two addresses in Buffalo on November 1st, three in New York City on the 2nd. The plans for the final address at Madison Square Garden in New York City—which has become a part of the ritual of presidential campaigns—had been made without fully consulting the President. He was intensely irritated, arguing that the meeting was sponsored by Tammany Hall, the leaders of which were opposed to him, and that his voice would not carry effectively for such a large audience. Nevertheless, he finally yielded, and the meeting was staged according to the best technique of the time. Thirty thousand enthusiastic Democrats, with Sheriff Alfred E. Smith as marshal, marched in the President's honour, the Garden was packed to the roof, and a crowd of twenty-five thousand milled around outside in the streets. So congested were the entrances that the presidential party was obliged to enter by means of a fire escape. A deafening demonstration that lasted for half an hour or more, brass bands, and the roaring of the crowd greeted the President. No one apparently cared what he said or even heard it:[3] but

---

[1] Contributions to the Republican campaign fund totalled $2,445,421. The total campaign fund of the Democrats was $1,584,548. *American Year Book*, 1916, p. 46.

[2] New York *Times*, November 4, 1916.

[3] The writer, who sat on the platform, not far removed from the speaker, could get only part of the address.

any real understanding was not a necessary part of the ritual.[1]

The President returned to Shadow Lawn, made a brief speech there on November 4th, and waited, with a tranquillity surprising to his friends, the great arbitrament of the ballot boxes.

IV. ELECTION AND AFTERMATH

The President and Mrs. Wilson left Shadow Lawn early on the morning of election day and drove to Princeton, where, about nine o'clock, the President voted. They spent the remainder of the day quietly at home; Mr. Tumulty, who had an office at Asbury Park, reported only the most important bulletins.[2]

Many of the early reports came, of course, from the East and showed a strong trend to Hughes. Before ten o'clock on election night Republican leaders were jubilantly proclaiming a victory. New York had swung into the column by an undoubted majority—and when had a presidential election been won without New York? Extras soon appeared on the streets announcing Hughes's election, and the *Times* searchlight, which was looked upon as final authority, presently flashed the same news. An enormous electric sign on the roof of the Hotel Astor, where the Republican candidate and his family were stopping, blazoned the signal word "Hughes" to the crowds in the square below: and about eleven o'clock a thousand triumphant members of the Republican and

---

[1]Roosevelt made an address on the same evening to an enthusiastic audience in Cooper Union, who called for "Teddy" again and again, but did not mention Hughes! He said in part: "There can be no greater misfortune for a free nation than to find itself under incapable leadership when confronted by a great crisis. . . . He [Wilson] has made our statesmanship a thing of empty elocution. He has covered his fear of standing for the right behind a veil of rhetorical phrases. He has wrapped the true heart of the nation in a spangled shroud of rhetoric." (New York *Times*, November 4, 1916.)

[2]Sometime before the returns were all in, the President made a number of tally sheets. For a facsimile of one of these sheets, see p. 297.

Union League Clubs, preceded by two bands, marched to the hotel to greet their champion.

Hughes, however, was cautious, refusing to issue a statement until further returns had come in:[1] and the President, at Shadow Lawn, concealed his anxiety—if he had any.

It is clear, from his letters and the evidence of friends, that his defeat, so far as his personal feelings were concerned, would not have been unwelcome. He "talked like a man from whose shoulders a great load had been lifted."[2] When Dr. Grayson, who spent the evening with the President, remarked that "four years from now the people will demand your return to the White House," the President held up his hand and said with a twinkle in his eye:

"No, Grayson, I'm something like the Confederate soldier who returned to his home after Lee's surrender. He looked over his farm. The buildings had been burned, the stock run off and the fences demolished. Then he looked at his bleeding feet and at his wounded arm, and said:

"'I'm glad I fought. I'm proud of the part I played. I have no regrets, but—I'll be damned if I ever love another country!'"[3]

And he confessed to a friend a few days later that he "went to bed that night feeling a great burden lifted. . . . Now the burden upon me is heavier than ever. If we can escape entering the war and bring about a rational peace, it is something worth living and dying for, and I believe

---

[1]But the impetuous Colonel at Oyster Bay was not so cautious. About ten o'clock he issued a statement: "I am doubly thankful as an American for the election of Mr. Hughes. It is a vindication of our national honor.

"Because of some charges that have been made, I wish to state now that I will not, under any circumstances, make any recommendations to Mr. Hughes with reference to appointments or to his legislative policy." New York *Times*, November 8, 1916.

[2]J. P. Tumulty, *Woodrow Wilson As I Know Him*, p. 218.

[3]Rear-Admiral Cary T. Grayson to the author.

```
                              266
10  So. States   114          114          12
                              152           9
                  Arg.    3                 20
                  Cal.   13                 10
                  Col.    6                 10
                  Ky.    13                 12
                  Mo.    18                  9
                  Mon.    4                 20
                  Ohio   24                 12
                  Okl.   10         152     114
                  Tenn.  12         103      217
                                     49

Ks.   10          Daks.  10
Ill.  29          N.Y.   45
Ind.  15          Ia.    13
Md.    8          Mich.  15
Neb.   8          N.J.   14
Ore.   5          A. Dee.  5
Wis.  13          Wash.   7
Wy.    3                  99
      81      2          8 80
```

One of the tally sheets made by President Wilson in November 1916, before all the election returns were in.

the country feels that way or it would not have re-elected me."[1]

Even though from the point of view of public service he had a keen desire to win, his calmness in the face of apparent defeat was wholly in consonance with the nature of the man. Many years before he had written to Ellen Axson Wilson:

"I've never been sanguine. Things hoped for have never been real enough to me to build upon with confidence."[2]

Leaders of the Democracy were pessimistic. A large dinner party on the evening of election day, given by Henry Morgenthau and including cabinet members and party managers, held at the Biltmore in New York, was intended to be a jubilee, and the evening began with merry-making, but when the returns began to pile up, silence and then gloom spread over the gathering. A veritable Belshazzar's feast![3] Even when Robert Woolley appeared late in the evening with the assurance, "We've won: we have elected our man," the gathered Democrats could not be convinced.

By morning the papers were confessing that the election was in doubt. As the day advanced, the President's strength gradually increased. Forty-eight votes were in doubt. California, New Mexico, Minnesota, North Dakota, New Hampshire and Oregon were the most uncertain, but McCormick now began to be confident that the Democrats could beat any combination.

Although the strain must have been severe, Wilson remained calm and cheerful throughout the day. After a time he went for a game of golf with Dr. Grayson.[4]

---

[1] To Edith G. Reid.

[2] January 28, 1895.

[3] Henry Morgenthau, *All In a Life-Time*, p. 246.

[4] A friend who met him on the links called out: "How is your game today, Mr. President?" Mr. Wilson waved his hand and responded:

"Grayson has me three down, but I don't care; I am four states up on yesterday's election." David Lawrence, *The True Story of Woodrow Wilson*, p. 129.

Writing to George Foster Peabody the next day, the President said:

". . . the results of the election still remain in doubt, but I cannot believe that the hopes of the last forty-eight hours will be defeated."

They were not. During the day New Mexico and North Dakota swung into the Wilson column by narrow margins, adding eight votes to his total, and by evening the Republican state chairman in California conceded the state with thirteen electoral votes to the President.[1]

By the afternoon of the 9th the result seemed well assured, and the President and Mrs. Wilson, with Miss Margaret Wilson and the President's cousin, Miss Helen Bones, boarded the *Mayflower* at Atlantic Highlands and sailed up the Hudson River, on their way to Williamstown, Massachusetts, to attend the christening of the President's first grandchild, Francis Sayre.

While the electoral vote gave the President a narrow majority, his total popular vote of 9,127,695 exceeded that of Hughes by 594,188. His gain over the vote given him in 1912 was nearly three million,[2] and his 1916 strength outstripped the party ticket everywhere. It was in every sense a personal victory, a vote of confidence. He proved himself to be stronger than his party, for the Democrats lost their majority in the House.

The President could speak from his heart when he said in a brief address at Williamstown:

"I am glad that the political campaign is over and that we can settle down in soberness and unity of spirit to work for the welfare of the country, without thinking of the advantage of parties."[3]

Mr. Hughes met defeat with the quiet dignity that

---

[1]Robinson gives the final vote as 277–254. *The Presidential Vote*, p. 402.
[2]*Ibid.*, pp. 17, 46.
[3]New York *Times*, November 11, 1916.

might have been expected of him: but it was not until November 22nd, when the returns were all in, that he sent a congratulatory message to his victorious opponent:

"Because of the closeness of the vote I have awaited the official count in California and now that it has been virtually completed, permit me to extend to you my congratulations upon your re-election. I desire also to express my best wishes for a most successful administration."

Wilson said in reply:

"I am sincerely obliged to you for your message of congratulation. Allow me to assure you of my good wishes for the years to come."[1]

Wilson's reëlection was received in the characteristic American way. It had been a long and acrimonious struggle,[2] but when it was over, the results were quietly, even generously, accepted by the defeated voters, and the country prepared to go forward again with its usual affairs.[3]

---

[1] The Vice President had sent a delightfully characteristic message: "'Tis not so deep as a well nor so wide as a church door; but 'tis enough, 'twill serve!"

[2] The President himself expressed his feelings regarding it in a letter to Garrett Droppers, minister to Greece, on December 12th: "The campaign was indeed one of the most virulent and bitter and, I must believe, one of the most unfair on the part of the Republican opposition that the country has ever seen, but I think that very circumstance worked to my advantage. I think the country resented the methods used, and that a very strong resentment was felt which was characterized by strong and generous feeling.

"The results show themselves more truly in the popular vote than in the electoral vote, and I am heartened by the feeling that it can no longer be said that I represent a minority of the nation."

[3] Even the financial interests, or some of them, were reconciled. Theodore H. Price commented on November 3rd in *Commerce and Finance:*

"To us his election seems a distinct triumph of idealism over materialism and of liberalism over a conservatism that spells reaction. As such we believe it will result in the fresh sublimation of our national life by the same noble purpose that inspired us to free Cuba, abolish slavery and make the Declaration of Independence a human document rather than an abstraction. . . .

"As to the economic significance of the election we cannot see that it has any. The people have rejected the appeal that was made to their self-interest in the attempt to revive the tariff issue and have shown themselves confident of their ability to meet the future without the protection which will only prevent Europe from paying her debt to us in merchandise which we can use instead of gold which we do not want."

From *Woodrow Wilson's Scrapbook*, Vol. I, p. 125, prepared by John Randolph Bolling —an invaluable collection made available to the author by Mr. Bolling.

The President's correspondence of the time shows that he approached the responsibility of another four years at Washington with profound humility. He knew better than anyone else the difficulties and dangers he must face:

"The re-election seems to me to impose an additional responsibility upon me, and I am not at all sure that I can rise to it. I only know that I shall try with all my might."[1]

From Williamstown the Wilsons returned directly to Washington, arriving on the evening of November 12th. The excitement, turmoil, and strain of the campaign was over, and the President plunged at once into accumulated business.

To Senator Stone he wrote on the 15th:

"I have piles of papers around me so high that I am invisible below the eyes . . ."

A new peace move, which he had for some time been contemplating, he now took up in earnest. The sinking, without warning, of the *Marina*, a British vessel, on October 28th, resulting in the loss of American lives, and the destruction of other vessels without warning early in November, seemed to indicate that a resumption of ruthless submarine warfare, in disregard of the *Sussex* pledge, was about to begin. It was evident that the nation was heading for a new crisis unless the President's peace efforts met with a cordial response.

---

[1]Wilson to W. B. Kennedy, his nephew, November 16, 1916.

CHAPTER VIII

GROWTH OF ENTANGLEMENT IN THE WAR

".... it is our duty to prepare this Nation to take care of its honour and of its institutions."
Address in New York, June 30, 1916.

".... I have been a persistent friend of peace and ... nothing but unmistakable necessity will drive me from that position."
Address at Toledo, Ohio, July 10, 1916.

"No nation stands wholly apart in interest when the life and interests of all nations are thrown into confusion and peril."
Address at Shadow Lawn, New Jersey, September 2, 1916.

I. PROGRESS OF MILITARY AND NAVAL PREPARATION

SPRING 1916 brought to America, including the American President, a vividly increasing sense of entanglement in the World War: fears not yet clearly defined: anxiety that was not quite alarm. The February "revolt" of a panicky Congress, demanding drastic peace legislation, gave clear evidence of the changing feeling: the narrow escape from an actual break with Germany, following the torpedoing of the *Sussex*, added to it. We were isolated, but were we really safe? The President himself, as early as February, was expressing it:

".... circumstances ... make it only too evident that our country is not safe from disaster if it should be attacked ...."[1]

In January and February, as we have seen, he had made his famous "swing around," demanding that the nation

---
[1] To Herbert Myrick, February 15, 1916.

support him in an enlarged programme for military and naval preparedness.[1] He had returned feeling that the people generally, while fearful of "militarism," approved his proposals;[2] but the actual progress of legislation, in spite of his constant prodding, had been distressingly slow. Bryan and the other pacifist and peace workers campaigned unflaggingly against it; and the agitation and resistance were reflected in long-drawn-out debates in Congress.

The President, having made up his mind, never for a moment abated his steady pressure for action. He had the patience that goes with a consummate historical knowledge of the democratic process, how slowly it works, gaining majority agreement through persuasion, and moving to decision only in response to stubborn argument and pressing facts. It was a process he profoundly believed in and was prepared to work with.

We find him, then, in the spring of 1916, however absorbingly engaged upon other momentous problems—war in Europe and in Mexico, and a burgeoning political campaign—seeking the facts and supplying the arguments that were needed to bring conviction. He appealed to business men to coöperate with the Preparedness Committee of the Naval Consulting Board by supplying a "confidential industrial inventory"[3]; accepted the offer of the National Academy of Sciences to organize a National Research Council;[4] coöperated with the Secretaries of War and Navy and a committee of American physicians on medical provision for the new forces.[5] He early took

---

[1] See this volume, Chapter I, pp. 26–31.

[2] ". . . the chief thing that is holding many people back from enthusiasm for what is called preparedness is the fear of militarism." (Address at West Point, June 13, 1916. *The Public Papers of Woodrow Wilson*, Vol. IV, p. 203.)

[3] Wilson to the business men of America, April 21, 1916.

[4] April 26, 1916. Report of the Organizing Committee of the National Research Council, August 1916. The members of the Council were appointed August 5th.

[5] Wilson to Dr. William J. Mayo, May 8, 1916.

steps toward determining the location and character of a government-owned nitrate plant.[1] And he pressed for the development of the aviation service.[2]

Despite all these efforts, however, there was some feeling in the spring of 1916 that Wilson's interest had waned. He had, as always, however keen his political sense, too little flare for publicity. He did not create any such furore as the more dramatic Theodore Roosevelt was capable of doing, nor did he try, like Major General Wood, to arouse emotions of warlike patriotism. His chief interest, all along, while demanding preparation, was to secure peace; he wished to avoid anything that would arouse a "militaristic spirit"[3] or stimulate excesses of emotion that might interfere with possible proposals for mediation.

America presented in the spring of 1916, indeed, strange parodoxes of opinion: a double-mindness that paralyzed vigorous action. We wished to be somewhat prepared, but, hoping to avoid war, wished to avoid the cost and the danger of a really adequate military establishment. We wished to maintain national honour (all rights of travel), and prosperity (all trade rights), and still not be enmeshed.

Wilson himself was not free from these contradictions. His system of legal neutrality was to a degree unneutral in its results and directly endangered the peace he hoped for. In his earlier demands for preparedness, the programme he approved was at best only a strong gesture. Yet he was declaring at that very time that America must be made safe "against interference from the outside" and that preparedness was more than an empty threat designed to ward off war:

[1]Wilson to Senator B. R. Tillman, May 22, 1916; Wilson to Representative Carl C. Van Dyke, June 8, 1916. Authorized in the National Defense Act, *United States Statutes at Large*, 64th Cong., Vol. 39, Pt. I, p. 215.

[2]Wilson to Secretary Baker, July 13, 1916.

[3]Wilson to H. S. Kraft, September 15, 1916.

". . . mankind is going to know that when America speaks she means what she says."[1]

"We are ready to fight for our rights when those rights are coincident with the rights of man and humanity."[2]

Neutrality in modern times is in fact an inherently intolerable condition in which no consistent course can be chosen; and Wilson, like most Americans, was caught in a welter of doubt, hesitation, contradiction; for while we were out of the war, we were in a fashion in it, too.

Nevertheless the President pressed steadily for a larger army and navy. His analysis of the two bills sent to him in April by Representative Hay shows his directive influence and his comprehension of the military details involved:[3]

I think Mr. Hay will agree with me that the situation of the country in regard to its foreign relations has changed so much since the House Bill was passed as to make it admissible to reconsider the question of the numerical strength of the army.

The *peace* strength provided for in the Senate Bill seems to me much too large; but I [am] not sure that it would not be wise to come somewhere very near its figures in the number of units its [sic] creates. (Mr. Hay will remember that I have all along been keen on this point of the number of units, and have desired, in particular, as many officers as I could get authorization for.) The number of engineering units seems to me especially important, and the number of units of field artillery more important than the number of units of infantry.

What I hope is, that the measure can be so framed as to give us an ample skeleton and unmistakable authority to fill it out at any time that the public safety may be deemed to require it.

W.W.

---

[1]Address at West Point, June 13, 1916. *The Public Papers of Woodrow Wilson,* Vol. IV, pp. 202–203.

[2]Address at Arlington, May 30, 1916. *Ibid.*, p. 194.

[3]Memorandum written April 19, 1916. "Mr. Wilson during the whole progress of the legislation showed himself to be open to suggestion, was never impatient, and never dictatorial, and to his wisdom must be attributed the passage of a measure which is confessed to be the basis of all military legislation since enacted." (James Hay, in a memorandum written for the author.)

The National Defense Act took shape, indeed, in the face of a steady stream of criticism, not only the protestations of the pacifists at one extreme, but the far more pointed objections of the students of military affairs. The President knew he could not wholly satisfy either group.

"The truth must be admitted that not all of the country feels alike upon the questions of detail involved. . . . No doubt we are all going to be more or less disappointed but I believe that a reasonably satisfactory bill will be worked out in the long run."[1]

It was not until June that the first great measure was completed and passed. While providing for what Secretary Baker optimistically called "a considerable increase" in the size of the army, it proved to be painfully inadequate, a year later, when we went to war. Probably it was as large an increase as the American public would at that time agree to: certainly it was shocking to some of the peaceful-minded, even after the *Sussex* crisis and the Mexican imbroglio had revealed most disquieting possibilities. The actual strength of the Regular Army, June 30, 1916, was 101,856 officers and enlisted men, an increase during the second year of the World War, and the worst year of the Mexican difficulties, of but 227 officers and 1,248 men![2] The new provisions enlarged the Regular Army to a peace strength of approximately 223,580, and a war strength of 298,000.[3] We had no conception of the fantastic expansion that was yet to be![4]

---

[1]Wilson to Charles A. Munn, May 12, 1916. Major General Wood regarded the Defense Act as a "dangerous menace" because of the smallness of the army authorized. (Wood to House, April 17, 1916, in Mr. Wilson's files.)

[2]"Report of the Secretary of War," November 20, 1916. *War Department Annual Reports*, 1916, Vol. I, p. 26.

[3]*Ibid.*, pp. 27, 28. The army, June 30, 1917, numbered only 250,157, excluding the National Guard of 111,123 men. *Ibid.*, 1917, Vol. I, p. 12.

[4]The Act conferred upon the President the power in time of war to "draft" a sufficient number of the "unorganized militia into the service of the United States" to keep the reserve battalions at prescribed strength. Upon receiving sharp protests from Amos Pinchot and other pacifists, the President, who had not, in common with a

The next step was to pay for the new army and navy. On August 29th Wilson signed the necessary appropriation bills. A huge financial reservoir was created for the development of these two branches and a new one, a green and tender shoot as yet—aviation. The President himself believed that the navy should remain the chief reliance for defense, and Congress agreed with him. All through Wilson's administration, despite the unending patter of criticism—unjust criticism—against the competence of Secretary of the Navy Daniels, the navy had improved in organization and effectiveness. Admiral Dewey was so impressed with the progress that he remarked in 1916 that the past three years had been "wonderful years."

". . . both in material and personnel, we are more efficient today than ever before."[1]

Wilson was especially pleased with the new navy bill, with its enlarged programme,[2] including the establishment of a Naval Reserve Force.[3]

"Never before by one single act of legislation has so much been done for the creation of an adequate navy."[4]

considerable number of Congressmen, realized that the Act had approved the principle of conscription, began to study into the interpretation of the clause. (Wilson to Henry Morgenthau, September 22, 1916.) He concluded that it applied only to those who had "received military training with the assistance of the Government," and was therefore a draft in "the more limited sense of the term." (Wilson to Pinchot, August 11, 1916.) The chairman of the House Committee on Military Affairs reported to the President that it was his interpretation that it applied only in time of war, and then to "all of the members of the unorganized militia between the ages of eighteen and forty-five years," and that it made "no difference" whether or not they had received military training. The President evidently read the handwritten letter too hastily, for he considered that their views "exactly" agreed. (Hay to Wilson, August 14, 1916; Wilson to Hay, August 16, 1916.) There the matter rested, but it was a long step toward the act which a year later broadened the draft and fixed it as a precedent to be used when America goes to war: an inescapable compulsion inherent in the modern conception of the state and the nature of recent wars. Another war, if we get into it, may very well see us carrying the doctrine of compulsion to extremes never realized even in the World War!

[1] Quoted, Daniels, *Our Navy at War*, p. 18.

[2] By an addition of $139,345,287. *United States Statutes at Large*, Vol. 39, Pt. I, p. 617.

[3] *Ibid.*, pp. 587 *et seq.*

[4] *New York Times*, August 30, 1916. Wilson had thrown his support in June to the completion of Daniels' five-year naval programme in three years. *Ibid.*, June 27, 1916.

While the appropriations made for the army were so moderate as to draw—and perhaps merit—sharp criticisms, they were in line with traditional American restraint regarding armament. What was more important as an element in the army bill, since the President and the American people were awakening as never before to the immense importance of controlling the economic forces of the nation—food, clothing, ships, machinery—was the setting up, for the first time in our history, of a Council of National Defense. The President had been deeply interested in such a provision—radical though it seemed at the time—since early December 1915, when he had urged upon Congress "the creation of the right instrumentalities by which to mobilize our economic resources in any time of national necessity." He saw the immediate necessity of coördinating American transportation and securing, even by compulsion, the coöperation of manufacturers. There must be complete integration of industrial and military activities.[1]

This tremendously important new council—so necessary to modern war—was composed of the Secretaries of War, Navy, Interior, Agriculture, Commerce, and Labor, but the principal responsibility and labour rested upon a commission of seven men with expert knowledge in special fields.[2] The President even foresaw that such a Council might become an important adjunct in the development

---

[1] *The Public Papers of Woodrow Wilson*, Vol. III, pp. 425–426.

[2] Houston, *Eight Years With Wilson's Cabinet*, Vol. I, pp. 183–184. The original members were with one exception Republicans, indicative of the liberal spirit of the President who appointed them. Daniel Willard, transportation and communication; Bernard M. Baruch, metals, minerals, and raw materials; Howard E. Coffin, munitions, manufacturing, and industrial relations; Dr. Franklin H. Martin, medicine and surgery; Samuel Gompers, labour; Dr. Hollis Godfrey, engineering and education; and Julius Rosenwald, supplies. An admirably able group, as the test of the war was to prove. In his war appointments throughout the President was insistent, always, upon securing the most competent men—never serving any partisan ends. It was one of the elements which contributed to the remarkable spirit of American coöperation after we entered the war. Clarkson, *Industrial America in the World War*, p. 29.

of American efficiency during peace times. He told the members when he appointed them that their work was to unite the forces of the country "for the victories of peace as well as those of war."[1]

To the President personally no development of the preparedness programme could have been more gratifying than the final victory for his long-continued and bitterly contested demand for the development of a government-owned American merchant marine. For two years, as we have seen,[2] he had been striving for it against the powerful opposition of private interests and their political connections. With war as an active threat, Congress had at length yielded.

The creation of the United States Shipping Board, September 7th, to regulate American sea transportation and develop a naval auxiliary and a merchant marine,[3] practically completed the organization with which America was preparing itself to face war, if war should come.

The sweep of the President's campaign for preparation had been substantial and impressive; it solidified and implemented his leadership; it increased his power and his responsibility. Terms such as these, the President "is empowered" or "may authorize," appeared again and again in the measures as they came from Congress, and they applied not merely to the appointment of national boards and other general powers, but even to the details of placing orders for the production of goods. It was the development of the familiar process by which democracy goes to war: momentarily setting up a kind of dictatorship. The President was soon to become, by virtue of the immense potentialities of the American people, their numbers, their institutions, their resources, the most

[1] New York *Times*, December 7, 1916.
[2] See *Woodrow Wilson, Life and Letters*, Vol. V, *Neutrality*, pp. 107 *et seq.*
[3] *United States Statutes at Large*, Vol. 39, Pt. I, pp. 728–738.

powerful executive in the world. Well may he have expressed, as he did repeatedly, his sense of profound humility in the presence of such vast responsibilities.

The promptitude and confidence of such grants by Congress of all but regal power to the President were something more than the mere recognition of the necessity in time of crisis of trusting the Executive; it was a tribute to Wilson personally. It never would have come so promptly, so completely, with so little obstruction, if the President had not commanded the confidence and admiration not only of his own party supporters, but of the opposition. His ability, his character, the transparent integrity of his intentions had, after three years in the presidency, been thoroughly tested. Wilson himself knew well that a President's power always reflects his personality. It is not his position that makes him great!

"His office is anything he has the sagacity and force to make it,"[1] he had written long before he himself had dreamed of being President. Some Presidents are leaders, and some are not. "It depends upon the man and his gifts."[2]

He had also referred to the increase of presidential power in moments of emergency.

". . . times of stress and change must more and more thrust upon him the attitude of originator of policies.

"His is the vital place of action in the system . . ."

And when foreign questions become the "leading questions," the President must by necessity be "at the front of our government."[3]

Such vast responsibility might have destroyed a weaker man; Wilson hardened, developed, under the challenge; he met every duty demanded of him. Yet he knew well the

---

[1] Wilson, *Constitutional Government in the United States* (1907), p. 69.
[2] *Ibid.*, p. 77.
[3] *Ibid.*, pp. 59, 73.

PRESIDENT WILSON MARCHING IN PREPAREDNESS PARADE IN
WASHINGTON, JUNE 14, 1916.

merciless exactions of such a position upon the physical and nervous energy.

"Men of ordinary physique and discretion cannot be Presidents and live, if the strain be not somehow relieved."[1]

During the *Sussex* crisis he wrote: ". . . I am carrying a killing load and I have the most intense human sympathy for other men who are doing the same. . . . I sometimes wonder if anybody outside of this place knows what the load is."[2]

But he had come of strong old stock, as sound as any America has produced, and he bore the heavy burden with astonishing steadiness and courage. He wrote, September 7, 1916—the preparedness programme just completed, the eight-hour law won, the political campaign in full swing, and European problems still in a critical stage:

"These have indeed been days to try one's soul . . . but I am still fit . . . A kind providence is taking care of me. . . ."[3]

Only a few intimates at the time realized the tremendous strain upon him, or guessed the ultimate cost.

II. RENEWED CONFLICTS WITH THE BRITISH: BLOCKADE AND TRADE RIGHTS

It had seemed to the President after the acute *Sussex* crisis, when the Germans, with unexpected restraint, had agreed to curb the ruthlessness of their submarine warfare, that a period of relative quiescence in his struggle to maintain American neutrality might really be at hand. It was a deeply comforting thought. He seized ardently upon the opportunity to seek some new peace formula, beginning,

---

[1] *Ibid.*, p. 79.
[2] To Rev. John Fox, April 12, 1916.
[3] To Cleveland H. Dodge.

as we have seen, with a vigorous campaign to promote his plans for a league of nations.

But it was not to be. Throughout the entire period of our neutrality, if controversy with one belligerent died down, it was sure to flare up with another. If the Germans momentarily ceased to shock us by the bloody violence of their submarine attacks or their warfare in Belgium, the British and French straightway infuriated us with attacks upon our trade rights, or the pinprick seizures of our mails. There was no rest for the neutral!

In July, Wilson was writing one of the angriest letters of his career: and it referred to the British:

"I am, I must admit, about at the end of my patience with Great Britain and the Allies. This black list business is the last straw. I have told Spring Rice so, and he sees the reasons very clearly. Both he and Jusserand think it a stupid blunder. I am seriously considering asking Congress to authorize me to prohibit loans and restrict exportations to the Allies. It is becoming clear to me that there lies latent in this policy the wish to prevent our merchants getting a foothold in markets which Great Britain has hitherto controlled and all but dominated. Polk and I are compounding a very sharp note. I may feel obliged to make it as sharp and final as the one to Germany on the submarines. What is your own judgment? Can we any longer endure their intolerable course?"[1]

The next day he openly told callers at the White House that the black list "had got on his nerves."[2]

The President had long been irritated by the exactions of the British, never before so fully aroused. The effect had been cumulative. For two years the British had been interfering with American commerce; delaying their replies to our protests; refusing to meet our demands with ap-

---

[1] To Colonel House, July 23, 1916.
[2] New York *Times*, July 25, 1916.

propriate modifications. They were capturing our ships and taking them into British ports. There was even a suspicion, not so ill-founded, that they were agreeing with their allies for economic coöperation *after* the war that might seriously threaten American commerce.[1] Early in July, also, they had wiped out the last feeble vestiges of the poor old Declaration of London by a notification that American rights of trade with European neutrals near to Germany had become incompatible with the blockade except under more sweeping restrictions—meaning that neutral trade, including American, was to suffer still further disadvantages.[2]

These were major irritations: but there had been minor ones scarcely less offensive. The Allies, especially the British, were, as we thought, lawlessly seizing our mails. Many American business men were convinced that their trade secrets and confidential dealings with European neutrals were becoming known to British officials and being used for the advantage of British traders. Actual proof seemed to be lacking, but certainly the long delays incident to the search of the mails worked to the benefit of British merchants.[3] The State Department was so aroused by the discourteous delay in responding to our protest (made in May) that Polk at last ordered Page, on July 19th, to "press for an immediate reply."[4]

The President himself had another, more particular, cause of irritation. The British had for two years discouraged all his plans for peace mediation, at the same time

---

[1] The President on July 10th transmitted to Congress Lansing's report on the Allied Economic Conference held at Paris in June. The agreement, Lansing had pointed out, anxiously, proposed "to continue the war industrially after actual warfare ceases," and he drew the conclusion that it would "cause the Central Powers to hesitate in taking steps toward a restoration of peace." (Lansing to Wilson, June 23, 1916.)

[2] July 7th. *Foreign Relations*, 1916, Supp., pp. 413–415.

[3] *War Memoirs of Robert Lansing*, pp. 125–126.

[4] *Foreign Relations*, 1916, Supp., p. 612.

that they were demanding and securing every financial and commercial advantage, even to the point of regulating American trade with the neutral nations of Europe. Of course, all of these impositions were defended by the British either on grounds of international law or "military necessity"—just as the Germans were defending their impositions—but this did not in the least abate the real and sharp provocation that resulted.

The "last straw" which had provoked the President's letter of July 23rd was the news, falling like a thunderbolt on July 19th, of the wide extension of the British black list —"85 concerns domiciled in the United States" were now included.[1] It seemed a new and virulent kind of invasion of American rights. It was like the shock that comes home to us with the actual list of the wounded and dead in a battle—especially if some of them happen to be our friends and neighbours![2]

It was no wonder that the President was angry: according to this pronouncement British officials were in effect to be judges over the private business of American firms residing inside the borders of the United States. The whole country was stirred. On July 28th Polk wrote Lansing that the past week had been "absolutely hideous" because of this "extraordinarily stupid" black list.[3] The New York *Times*, always friendly to the Allies, described the black list as "the most tactless, foolish and unnecessary act of

---

[1]Skinner, at London, telegraphed the news to the Department of State on July 19th; the message was received early in the morning and was published in the newspapers the same day. *Foreign Relations*, 1916, Supp., p. 411. The black list itself, sent by mail, did not arrive until the 31st of July. *Ibid.*, pp. 423–424.

[2]The State Department knew before this that a number of American firms were being *confidentially* blacklisted, but no official notice had been given to this government. *Ibid.*, pp. 423–424, 428–429. Frank L. Polk, of the State Department, wrote to Colonel House, July 22, 1916, after the statutory black list was published: "It is nothing new and if the British Government would only keep quiet it could have been handled comparatively easily . . ." *The Intimate Papers of Colonel House*, Vol. II, pp. 312–313.

[3]*Hearings, Senate Munitions Investigation*, 73–2, Pt. 28, pp. 8660–8661.

the British Government during the war."[1] Other papers felt "amazement"; some declared that the indirect effect would be even worse than the interdict itself, since fear of being themselves blacklisted would keep many a customer from trading with a firm on the list.[2]

In Congress Representative Gallivan introduced a resolution to sever relations with Great Britain; another representative charged that "the commercial flag of Great Britain floats to-day from the Rio Grande to the North Pole . . ."[3] And Senator Stone, with the skeptical and independent spirit of a Missourian, painstakingly marshalled his facts and started preparations to have Congress take defensive action against the Paris Economic Pact, the broadest of the Allies' trade policies affecting America.[4] Even Walter Page thought the British had made a "gross" mistake.[5]

The State Department acted vigorously. Polk conferred with Spring Rice, explaining the injustices of the new declaration and asking for modifications, but the result was negligible:

"What the Ambassador said shows a friendly disposition, but does not materially change the question of principle involved."[6]

Polk then prepared a draft for a formal protest, of which Lansing said: "It could not be much stronger and be polite . . ."[7]; but House was at hand urging the President not to ask Congress for authority to prohibit loans and restrict

[1]July 20, 1916.

[2]*Literary Digest*, Vol. 53 (July 29, 1916), pp. 235–236.

[3]August 2nd and 8th. *Cong. Rec.*, 64–1, pp. 12013, 12331.

[4]Senator W. J. Stone to Tumulty, July 21, 1916. Stone conferred with the President on July 25th and 26th.

[5]*Foreign Relations*, 1916, Supp., p. 412.

[6]Polk to Wilson, July 25, 1916.

[7]Reluctant to press the British too hard, Lansing added: ". . . and of course we must observe our manners." C. C. Tansill, "American Neutrality 1914–1917," reported in the *American Historical Review*, Vol. XLI (April 1936), p. 442.

exports until the British and French ambassadors had been informed of what, unless some change were made, he intended to do.[1] Polk had, however, already given warning.

"It was evident to Polk when he last saw Spring Rice," Wilson wrote to House on the 27th, "that the British Government was not a little disturbed (and surprised, poor boobs!)"

Wilson was determined to express American indignation: to inform the British publicly and curtly that "undesirable results . . . might ensue" and that "serious consequences to neutral rights and neutral relations" would be necessarily involved.

This threat, which was not, finally, as sharp as Wilson intimated it might be, was dispatched on the 26th. The note argued that the black list was unfair and arbitrary. It pointed out "in the gravest terms" the serious effect upon neutral rights, and declared that it was "manifestly out of the question" for the United States to acquiesce in British punishment of American citizens, but it stopped short of the declaration that a continuance of the policy would raise "a presumption of unfriendliness on the part of the British Government." There was no stern or immediate summons to respect American rights such as had been addressed to Germany. Polk observed while the note was being prepared, "If they refuse to yield, then a stronger note could follow this."[2]

It was a weakness in the American position that the

---

[1] House to Wilson, July 25, 1916. *The Intimate Papers of Colonel House*, Vol. II, p. 315. House also wrote to Polk the same day, remarking that the President seemed "inclined to take drastic measures. . . ." With customary reluctance to see forthright expression of American rights directed against the Allies, the Colonel hoped for some kind of accommodation "without taking such a positive stand publicly." He advised that they be informed "confidentially" of our position, after which he expected that "they would try to meet it." *Ibid.*, Vol. II, pp. 314–315.

[2] Polk to Wilson, July 24, 1916. For the note itself, see *Foreign Relations*, 1916, Supp., pp. 421–422. The note was a composite work of the President and Polk, assisted by Cone Johnson and William Phillips.

black list, however unjust, could not be attacked as a direct violation of international law; Great Britain had the sovereign right to prevent her own subjects from trading with anybody, anywhere. Neutrals had no rights in the matter, therefore, except such as they were willing to *compel* belligerents to respect. And in America, there was then no unanimity in public opinion on using compulsion against either belligerent to the point of a severance of relations. The black list, after all, affected only a narrow interest, and in the public mind it seemed in some instances to have a measure of justification.[1] The note was therefore no ultimatum.

It was strong enough, however, to encourage the moderates in Germany, who were watching anxiously. Bernstorff informed House that the political pressure on the Chancellor had been "somewhat relieved by the black-list controversy."[2]

The British did not seem greatly exercised over the protest; and as usual there was an unconscionable delay in replying. Five weeks elapsed without a word; then the information was ventured that a reply might soon be expected. Five more weeks passed before the note was sent![3]

Meanwhile, Congress was discussing retaliatory legislation. It was a prickly subject. An embargo on loans and supplies was an action this government had repeatedly declared to be, in its international results, an unneutral course of action. Moreover, domestic repercussions might prove utterly devastating to industrial, commercial, and financial interests which now relied upon our inflated and expanding foreign trade.

---

[1]*Literary Digest*, Vol. 53, pp. 235–236 (July 29, 1916).

[2]Quoted by House, letter to Wilson, August 6, 1916.

[3]*Foreign Relations*, 1916, Supp., pp. 462–465. While it was dated October 10th, it did not actually arrive until the 24th.

After much discussion the President was empowered, by a provision in the Revenue bill then pending, to retaliate against a country which, in time of war and contrary to "the law and practice of nations," forbade the importation "into their own or any other country" of any product grown or manufactured in the United States and not injurious to "health or morals" by similar prohibitions of importation from the offending nation into the United States.[1] This was recognition, with a vengeance, of the use of the vastly potent weapon of economic reprisal; and if vigorously employed, it would have affected vitally the whole British blockade. Nevertheless it fell short of actually imposing an embargo on necessary loans or military supplies, which alone could have broken the blockade. With the British as with the Germans we stopped short of the irretrievable ultimatum.[2]

The President never used the authority he was given. We know that he was fundamentally opposed to any such desperate action, for he had rejected a plan offered more than a year before by William B. Hale to eliminate the interferences of both coalitions with American rights on the seas:

". . . the suggestion is in effect a suggestion of reprisal and I should be very loath to see this nation, which at present stands for peace not only, but for the use only of just and reasonable methods, adopt a policy which would seem to be in imitation or retaliation of anything proposed on the other side of the water. I really think we should cultivate a different spirit in the matter. We are detached

---

[1] *United States Statutes at Large,* Vol. 39, Pt. I, p. 799.

[2] Provisions of the same bill and of the Shipping Act authorized that vessels of a nation discriminating in any way against American firms or citizens or ships should be denied clearance. *Ibid.,* pp. 738, 799–800. An amendment to the Revenue bill, passed by the Senate but lost in conference, sought to empower the President to deny the use of American mails, cables, and telegraphs to any government or country which during wartime did not accord to us facilities of commerce, "including the unhampered traffic in mails." *Cong. Rec.,* 64–1, p. 13794.

and can keep our minds clear of any sort of feeling that might mislead us."[1]

A considerable part of Wilson's lack of enthusiasm for retaliation, despite the fact that he seemed temporarily ready to resort to it in midsummer, 1916, undoubtedly lay in the feeling that it might prove vastly expensive and that, economically, if hastily employed, it might drive us into a course that we should forever repent. He could not forget what happened, under somewhat similar circumstances, in 1812.[2]

There was another reason that had still deeper roots: drawing its vigour from his cultivated sympathies, from that sense of moral responsibility which, as an unusually civilized human being, he felt more deeply, probably, than most of his contemporaries.

"What would happen," he asked earnestly, "if no nation stood ready to assist the world with its finances and to supply it with its food? We are more indispensable now to the nations at war by the maintenance of our peace than we could possibly be to either side if we engaged in the war . . . by the same token there is a moral obligation laid upon us to keep free the courses of our commerce and of our finance, and I believe that America stands ready to vindicate those rights.[3]

A final and determining factor was, perhaps, the fear of jeopardizing his hope for a new order of world peace when the war was over. This hope from the beginning was, as he clearly recognized, largely contingent upon British and French support. A year earlier House had written that if we pressed hard enough, the British would go to almost

---

[1]April 5, 1915.

[2]He had written, years before, of the ruinous effects of the retaliatory embargo which preceded the War of 1812: "The States themselves suffered from the act more than the nations whose trade they struck at." *A History of the American People,* Vol. III, p. 194.

[3]February 2, 1916. *The Public Papers of Woodrow Wilson,* Vol. IV, pp. 90-91.

any limit rather than break with us, but "we would gain their eternal resentment . . . and our action would arise to haunt us—not only at the peace conference, but for a century to follow. . . ."[1]

Wilson had agreed, and had asked advice from House and Lansing as to "a line of action at once practicable and effective which would escape the consequences you (and I) would dread and deplore."

He went on to say, definitely:

"We cannot long delay action. Our public opinion clearly demands it."[2]

The British attacked the newly delegated presidential powers of retaliation on September 17, 1916, by a forceful argument that if the United States should try to force the Allies to trade with persons helping their enemies, and to prevent the Allies from bringing every possible pressure against commerce with Germany, it would present "an inconceivably invidious contrast" to our failure to protest during the past several months against the growing German submarine warfare.[3]

In short, here again was the familiar pattern of defense used by both belligerents in responding to our complaints: that we were not protesting against worse offenses by the enemy!

The clarity of the issue was also gradually dimmed by certain mollifying actions by the British. They displayed a willingness to examine specific cases with a view to removing names unjustly put on the black list, and they apologetically conveyed the feeling—no doubt genuine— that they had, in the words of a report from Page, "made a bad tactical error."[4] Only "tactical"—not a legal error,

---

[1] July 22, 1915. *The Intimate Papers of Colonel House*, Vol. II, p. 58.

[2] July 27, 1915.

[3] *Foreign Relations*, 1916, Supp., pp. 445–446.

[4] July 25, 1916, after talking with Lord Robert Cecil. *Foreign Relations*, 1916, Supp., p. 420.

not a real invasion of rights! And the State Department, by falling in with the suggestion that individual cases be studied, further compromised the American position—however much Lansing might protest that he did not admit "the correctness" of the British action.[1]

There should have been an opportunity to arrive at a clearer understanding of the elements of the controversy when Ambassador Page arrived in August. For a long time his dispatches had been showing such extraordinary ignorance of conditions at home and such querulousness in criticism, that Wilson felt that he should "get back a little way at least to the American point of view about things."[2] Page himself, not unaware of the wide divergences of understanding, suggested early in July that his secretary be sent home to explain the situation in London; and was pleased when he himself was summoned.

But the visit was in every way disappointing. Page had a genius for friendship, with powerful sympathies easily stirred. Even before the war he had come to know and deeply admire the English character: the charm of it, the cultivation of background, the intellectual maturity, the moral assurance. When all is said, there are few more civilized human beings on this planet than the best of the British race. Page himself, deeply conscious of his own English origins, felt that blood, after all, was thicker than water. When the war broke, the British had responded exactly as he expected them to respond: as he would, personally, have wished them to respond. He had by now met and made friends with scores of the finest living Englishmen and their families: he saw what the war meant to them: the losses of sons and brothers they bore without flinching, the grim purpose to fight to the last man. He

---

[1] Lansing to Laughlin, August 18, 1916. *Ibid.*, p. 435. *Cf.* also p. 440.
[2] Polk to Wilson, July 11, 1916; Wilson to House, July 23, 1916.

gave his heart utterly![1] He gave it to the point of capitulation to the British point of view on almost all the points of controversy between them and his own people.

The President received the ambassador on August 19th, affably, like the old friend he was, as though there were no differences between them.[2] He seems to have made no effort to impress upon Page the American attitude toward the issues raised by the war; and he gave his visitor no opportunity at that time to present his side of the case. No doubt the President, overburdened with vast problems and responsibilities, felt that Page would readily gather full knowledge of the situation from other sources. In matters of such consequence, however, where utter clarity of understanding was indispensable, it was a mistaken course. Page, knowing at first hand the struggles and sufferings of Europe, might have contributed largely to the President's knowledge: and Wilson, on his part, might have made Page see more clearly the peculiar problems that confronted the American administration. If such a complete understanding of their divergences of opinion had not resulted in a new and clear agreement as to policy— for Page was the President's indispensable representative at the Court of St. James's—the ambassador should have resigned, and the President should have found some other man who could and would faithfully express his views. But Wilson was here following, as men must, the inevitable pattern of his character. He dreaded argument or controversy with friends whom he trusted or admired or loved; he feared the emotional strain, shrank from the break that might follow. Making new human relationships had, from his youth upward, been difficult for him: he preferred to

---

[1]The writer was in London during much of the last year of the war and will never forget the power and the eloquence of Walter Page's accounts of what the war meant to the English people.

[2]White House Diary. For Page's brief memorandum of the luncheon conversation, see *The Life and Letters of Walter H. Page*, Vol. II, p. 171.

continue to work with men whom he knew, however unsatisfactory they might be, rather than to choose new
ones. He got along for years with Lansing without coming
to a real understanding with him, knowing that Lansing
had no fundamental sympathy with many of his projects.

This characteristic of the President had proved disastrous in his relationship at an earlier time with Hibben at
Princeton, and it was the worst flaw in his friendship with
House. He seems never to have known that felicity of
complete understanding and confidence which follows a
fiery struggle with a true friend. Perhaps such unguarded
and generous relationships are denied to those in high
places! If Wilson and Page, both men of the highest
ideals, could have come to a complete understanding at
their first meeting there in Washington in August 1916, it
might have eased the burden of both of them and contributed to better relationships between the American and
British nations.

When Page again met the President at luncheon at the
White House on August 29th—Ambassador Sharp, recently arrived from Paris, being also a guest—there was
the same irritating evasion of foreign affairs; but, a month
later, Page having made a direct appeal, Wilson invited
him to spend a night at Shadow Lawn (September 22nd),
where he and Mrs. Wilson had sought respite from the
heat of Washington and found only the confusion and
turbulence of an awakening presidential campaign.

Page arrived exasperated with delay, bringing with him
a bulky dossier of confidential messages, personal and
official, from English statesmen, and a lengthy statement
of his own. He was intensely earnest, he was eloquent, he
was bitter. He displayed with indignation the German
medal commemorating the sinking of the *Lusitania*. He
argued the British version of the war and America's duty
to help the Allies win it; he demanded that Bernstorff

be sent home. A folder remains in Wilson's files containing all the papers he left, marked by the President in pencil, "Left by Page on furlough."[1]

It was an unfortunate moment for such a discussion—since the American press was just then expressing its furious indignation over British interference with American trade; and the President, not less than his visitor, was at his wit's end to know what to do.

Moreover, Wilson evidently felt himself upon the defensive. He reminded the ambassador that Americans were irritated by the arbitrary course of the British and complained of their delays in responding to American protests. He told the pained ambassador that one of the causes of the war was "England's having the earth and of Germany wanting it." The German system might be "directly opposed to everything American," but this was no reason for war. As to retaliation, his declaration must have had a grain of comfort for Page—somewhat dashed by a threat as to the future:

"He said that he wouldn't do anything with the retaliatory act till after election lest it might seem that he was playing politics. But he hinted that if there were continued provocation afterward (in case he were elected) he would."[2]

When the two men shook hands in parting, their minds had drawn no nearer together. Wilson's irritation indeed seemed to have been deepened by Page's emotional reports and by resentment at what he considered the attempt of the Allies to exercise an improper influence upon Page.[3] Nevertheless when the ambassador, after Wilson's

---

[1] Page's reports on conversations with Grey, Bryce, and Asquith, contained in the dossier left with the President, are published in *Foreign Relations*, 1916, Supp., pp. 40-46.

[2] *The Life and Letters of Walter H. Page*, Vol. II, p. 186.

[3] *War Memoirs of Robert Lansing*, pp. 170-171.

reëlection in November, tendered his resignation in a long letter reiterating his creed that the war was a struggle between democracy and autocracy in which the United States should immediately declare her position by breaking relations with the Central Powers, the President did not accept it.[1] He kept at St. James's, as his most important agent in Europe, a representative who did not agree with him, whose sympathies were powerfully engaged by the British, and who supported American protests and demands with a reluctance that often destroyed their force.

It is possible, however, in spite of these unclarified divergences, that the President may not have been quite as impervious to Page's eloquence as he appeared to be. At heart he was, no doubt, sympathetic with England and, while impatient with her conduct, he may have nursed his irritation to keep from leaning too far in her favour while the chance of acting as peacemaker remained open; and when war later became inevitable, Page's arguments probably had their influence in his rationalization of his course of action.[2]

However indignant Wilson may have become as a result of the arbitrary and irritating course of the British, it was plain enough, from this period onward, that not only he but the entire American people[3] were beginning to draw distinctions, less subtle, more definite, in their attitude toward the British and the Germans. Wilson plainly diminished the force of his criticism of the British when, in his speech of acceptance, September 2nd, he emphasized the difference between offenses against property rights (as committed by the British) and offenses against the

---

[1] He sent word through Lansing, February 5, 1917, that he hoped Page would not "at the present time . . . press to be relieved from service."

[2] As Mr. Hendrick remarks. *The Life and Letters of Walter H. Page*, Vol. II, p. 196.

[3] See this volume, pp. 332 *et seq.*

"fundamental rights of humanity" (as committed by the Germans):

". . . property rights can be vindicated by claims for damages when the war is over,[1] and no modern nation can decline to arbitrate such claims; but the fundamental rights of humanity cannot be. The loss of life is irreparable. Neither can direct violations of a nation's sovereignty await vindication in suits for damages. The nation that violates these essential rights must expect to be checked . . . by direct challenge and resistance. . . . These are plain principles and we have never lost sight of them . . . whatever the stress or the perplexity of circumstance or the provocation to hasty resentment. The record is clear and consistent throughout . . ."[2]

Moreover, he vetoed Lansing's suggestion that a message be sent to the chargé at London "very frankly and very bluntly telling the truth about the present situation" —this to be unofficially shown to Grey:

"I had a talk with Walter Page of the most explicit kind . . . I covered the whole subject matter . . . in a way which I am sure left nothing to be desired in the way of explicitness or firmness of tone; and I think that our method had better stop with that for the time being. Let us forget the campaign so far as matters of this sort are concerned."

It was plain, indeed, that the President desired in every way possible to minimize diplomatic controversy during the heat of the presidential campaign, for in another letter he made it equally clear that he wished no dispute with Germany:

"At present I hope that the Department will confine itself as much as possible to routine matters. We should ourselves no doubt be unconsciously influenced by politi-

---

[1]This was the argument persistently advanced by Page.
[2]*The Public Papers of Woodrow Wilson*, Vol. IV, p. 282.

cal considerations and that would be most unfair to the country."[1]

Relations between Great Britain and the United States continued to be ruffled. The Washington *Post* declared that it was "a sorry day for the United States when it failed to put a stop to the first attempt to encroach upon its rights as a neutral. Every month since that time has witnessed further encroachment, with the result that the United States cannot now burst the ties that bind it without suffering great losses."[2] Apparent confirmation of the suspicion that the censorship of our mails was used for British trade advantage was given during August, and this too increased American disgust. On August 8th, Lloyd George replied as a Cabinet minister to questions in the House of Commons, first, that the British government held themselves free to make any use they chose of intercepted letters, and second, that pertinent information was passed on to various governmental departments.[3] But both Lloyd George and Grey made attempts to erase the impression that improper use of trade information was permitted.[4] News in September that American consular mail was being examined added to the irritation.[5] So tense did the nerves of American officials become that when in late September a member of the British embassy in Washington expounded the philosophy of the black list to a group of American business men, Lansing dispatched to the embassy a note marked by extraordinary asperity and challenge.[6]

---

[1]Lansing to Wilson, September 22, 1916; two letters, Wilson to Lansing, September 29, 1916; Savage, *Policy of the United States Toward Maritime Commerce in War*, Vol. II, pp. 520–521, 525–526.

[2]*Literary Digest*, Vol. 53, pp. 821–822 (September 30, 1916).

[3]*Foreign Relations*, 1916, Supp., p. 620; *House of Commons, Debates*, 5th series, Vol. 85, p. 851.

[4]*Foreign Relations*, 1916, Supp., pp. 621–622.

[5]*Ibid.*, pp. 622–623.

[6]September 28, 1916. *Ibid.*, p. 450.

Finally, on October 13th, the long-delayed British reply to the note of May 24th regarding seizure of mails arrived at the State Department.[1] Like our protest, the answer was legalistic and argumentative. No hint of surrender on any point could be found in it, although the Allied governments were able to promise by this late date, owing to their experience, that the process of censorship would be expedited. There the dispute sank into the limbo of accommodation, joining the contraband, blockade, and other interminable controversies. The issue was also blunted by the fact that German submarines were sinking many mail ships, in which case the mail was not merely delayed but lost irretrievably.[2] The bad versus the worst!

About ten days later officials in the State Department were busily poring over another long document just arrived from London; it was at last—after three months!—the British reply to the black-list note which we had addressed to them on July 26th.[3]

The President studied the British statement with great care. He double-marked the sentence declaring that Great Britain maintained the right, which in the present crisis they regarded as a "duty" to themselves and their Allies, "to withhold British facilities from those who conduct their trade for the benefit of our enemies." Necessarily the British disclaimed any intent to dictate to American citizens, a point in which Wilson saw a certain amount of validity. He placed large, emphatic question marks opposite two other statements, one, the claim of legal right to exclude goods belonging to "firms on the statutory list" from ships using British coal, and the other, the declaration that the British were "not unmindful of the obligations of those who possess sea-power, nor of that

[1]*Foreign Relations*, 1916, Supp., pp. 624–629.
[2]*Literary Digest*, Vol. 53, pp. 1096–1098 (October 28, 1916).
[3]Received October 24th. See *Foreign Relations*, 1916. Supp., pp. 461–465.

traditional policy pursued by the British Empire by which such power has been regarded as a trust and has been exercised in the interests of freedom."[1] It is plain that he was skeptical; but no reply was attempted. We were, as neutrals, growing daily more helpless in meeting impositions by either group of belligerents.

The last breath of life in the retaliation legislation was crushed out by an analysis submitted by the Secretary of Commerce, October 23rd. It was here shown that retaliation would probably be neither workable nor effective in obtaining a withdrawal of the objectionable regulations. Injurious counter-reprisals against our commerce would be "almost inevitable"; why, at this time, go beyond protest? "The restrictions are no more hurtful now than a year and a half ago." An embargo on "war munitions and supplies" that might earlier have been effective would now probably be ineffective. But the most telling argument was that for "success in commerce after the war we need the friendship of the belligerents," if this could be secured without "undue sacrifice."[2]

Whittled down by argument, dimmed by confusing newer problems, the crisis thus ebbed away, leaving the black list, except for negotiations on separate cases, in full force. Wilson had again found his hands tied—by international law, by uncompromising economic necessity, and by the need to keep the good will of the Allies if he was to realize his great hope for an enduring world peace after the war.

As usual, however, when irritating relationships with one belligerent seemed finally benumbed, new difficulties arose with the other.

On October 7th the startled citizens of Newport, Rhode

[1]Printed copy of the note in Mr. Wilson's private files.

[2]*Foreign Relations*, 1916, Supp., pp. 466–477. The possibility was also suggested of an "international congress of neutral powers . . . to discuss means of terminating or ameliorating the commercial restrictions imposed during the present war."

Island, saw in the harbour one of the giant cruiser submarines, the new terror of Germany's U-boat warfare.
The *U-53* delivered a letter for Bernstorff, took on board
a package of newspapers containing sailing lists, and,
putting at once to sea, sank nine vessels within twenty-
four hours.[1] While absolutely no violation of international
law had marked this astonishing raid, and no American
interest had been affected, it made a tremendous impression upon the popular mind—an impression not
unmixed with fear. It demonstrated emphatically that
our isolation was legendary; the danger was at our very
doors.[2] Prices tumbled on Wall Street; marine insurance
rates jumped 500 per cent. Further and far-reaching
complications seemed unavoidable when it was learned
that near-by American destroyers had taken on board the
passengers and crews set adrift in small boats. One of
them, the U.S.S. *Balch*, had passed across the line of
shellfire from the submarine.[3]

On the afternoon of the 9th Wilson received Bernstorff
at Shadow Lawn. The President "spoke very seriously . . .
and urged me to see to it that this incident was not repeated. Otherwise he could not be responsible for public
feeling in the United States, which might again become
very bitter."[4]

The British thought they saw in the raid of the *U-53* a
tolerated violation of American neutral obligations, and
in the manœuvring of our destroyers a desire not to
interfere with the deadly work. British feeling rose to
storm pitch.[5] The British naval attaché at Washington,

[1]*Foreign Relations*, 1916, Supp., p. 772; *Literary Digest*, Vol. 53, p. 940 (October 14,
1916); Bernstorff, *My Three Years in America*, p. 267.

[2]New York *Times*, October 9, 1916; *Literary Digest*, Vol. 53, pp. 1015–1017 (October
21, 1916).

[3]*Foreign Relations*, 1916, Supp., pp. 782–783; *Literary Digest*, Vol. 53, pp. 1015–1017
(October 21, 1916).

[4]Bernstorff, *My Three Years in America*, p. 267.

[5]*Foreign Relations*, 1916, Supp., p. 779.

Captain Gaunt, greatly perturbed, went at once to see Colonel House; and House "counselled calmness until we could see where we stood."[1] The roars of the British lion constrained Grey on October 17th to make an effort in the House of Lords "to hold back the almost fierce public feeling." The British people and government alike seemed especially to resent the silence of the American government.[2] Polk, temporarily Acting Secretary of State, thought that it was "up to the British to discuss this thing with us, if they wish any information." We had nothing to explain or to apologize for. "My own feeling is that they are sore and upset and do not know exactly what to take hold of. . . ."[3]

The President was surprised at what he considered the injustice of British opinion. When House informed him that Captain Gaunt believed that our good relations with Great Britain might be endangered, Wilson replied wearily:

"These are indeed deep waters . . . I can only say that if our friendly relations with England should be imperilled . . . it would be only another illustration of how difficult it is to be friends with Great Britain without doing whatever she wants us to do."[4]

British wrath was near the boiling point for several weeks. Even the King found occasion to make highly critical remarks.[5] Finally Polk smoothed official opinion somewhat by a confidential talk with Spring Rice, reminding him that British warships regularly patrolled off our North Atlantic coast, as it was their belligerent right—as

[1]October 9, 1916. *The Intimate Papers of Colonel House*, Vol. II, p. 323.

[2]Page to the Secretary of State, October 18, 1916; *Foreign Relations*, 1916, Supp., p. 779.

[3]Polk to House, October 19, 1916. *The Intimate Papers of Colonel House*, Vol. II, pp. 325–326.

[4]House to Wilson, October 9, 1916. Wilson to House, October 10, 1916.

[5]Page to the Secretary of State, October 20, 1916. *Foreign Relations*, 1916, Supp., p. 780.

it was also the German right—to do.[1] He also sent a personal letter to Page to be shown to the British, in which he embodied the substance of the American navy's report of the *U-53* incident.[2] This helped somewhat, but British public feeling was not mollified, and as late as middle November, Gaunt thought it still rising. House believed this to be serious; and, in his diary, blamed the President for his "tendency to offend the Allies." He thought it "likely to lead us into trouble with them. If we are to have war, let it be with Germany by all means."[3]

In this last phrase House was expressing an opinion that was becoming more and more common throughout America. Both sides were irritating us to the point of distraction: we wanted peace: but if war was inescapable, let it be with Germany.

III. WILSON AND THE EMOTIONS AND SYMPATHIES AROUSED BY THE WAR

Woodrow Wilson presents in the deepening summer of 1916 the tragedy that so often accompanies the power and responsibility of great place: not only the loneliness, but the essential helplessness, of supreme leadership.

He had come to the presidency at the age of fifty-seven with convictions soundly formed and deeply held. He had decided, in his own mind, after years of thoughtful study of history and of political science, what was right, what was just, what was honourable, in the conduct of a great state. His settled beliefs, based in large measure upon a deeply held religious faith, were of the stuff out of which the ancient principles of political democracy had been fashioned. All of his academic writings, his earlier ad-

---

[1] Polk to Page, October 22, 1916. *Ibid.*, pp. 780–781.
[2] *The Intimate Papers of Colonel House*, Vol. II, p. 326.
[3] *Ibid.*, p. 327.

dresses as governor and President, his state papers, are full
of his ideals, his vision. He believed, absolutely, a doctrine
that a considerable part of the world has now rejected,
that "force . . . never accomplished anything that was
permanent."

"I have not read history without observing that the
greatest forces in the world and the only permanent forces
are the moral forces."[1]

He believed in a government based upon the same
standards of reason, justice, duty, honour, demanded in
the highest type of individual conduct, and the great
storm in Europe was inexorably overpowering, defeating,
crushing, every such quality of civilized organization and
social relationship. He was criticized at the time, and in
the after-look it seems miraculous, that he should have
continued as long as he did to urge steadiness, reason,
duty, honour. For two years, in spite of every provocation,
he had persisted in seeking the solution of constantly
more difficult problems, not by going to war but through
the accommodations of diplomacy; and never for a moment during all of that time did he give over his determined efforts to bring about peace.

While he was continuing to talk of "the still small voice
of humanity" and "the moral judgment of mankind"[2]
there are plain evidences in the spring of 1916 that the
violent emotions generated by the war were also beginning
to affect him. It was easier to become irritated, if not
angry; he showed it in his attitude toward the British
black list and the German submarine sinkings. Whenever
he suggested what seemed to him wholly reasonable plans
for the beginning of peace negotiations, he was remorse-
lessly buffeted first by one belligerent and then by the

---

[1] Address before the Press Club, New York, June 30, 1916. *The Public Papers of Woodrow Wilson*, Vol. IV, p. 219.

[2] *Ibid.*, p. 158.

other; both accused him of partisanship if not of under-handed motives.

All his life long Woodrow Wilson had been fearful of emotion as a controlling influence in conduct. It was with complete sincerity that he had written, as a young man: "Hearts frequently give trouble . . . They must be schooled . . ."[1] It will be remembered that almost his first important advice to the American people after the out-break of the great war—for he dreaded the ungoverned emotions and sympathies which he knew would arise—was to be neutral *in thought* as in action. He knew that emotion if left uncontrolled would lead to every evil, of which military force was the final and most devastating expression.

And yet the forces of emotion and sympathy throughout the nation were steadily increasing: becoming more un-governable.

As early as January 1916 he was confessing that we were "finding it exceedingly difficult to be neutral" partly because "we have the deep passions of mankind in us."[2]

Two days later he was expressing the same idea in another form:

"So many men on this side of the water are seeing red that we seem to see in their thoughts the reflection of the blood that is being spent so copiously on the other side of the sea."[3]

Nevertheless he clung to his belief that Americans must maintain detachment of judgment; he of all men must keep his "passions disengaged."[4] America must, in the nature of things, become more or less a court of world opinion in which judgments must be as calm and well considered as in any court.

---

[1] *Mere Literature*, p. 45.
[2] *The Public Papers of Woodrow Wilson*, Vol. IV, p. 37.
[3] January 31, 1916. *Ibid.*, p. 57.
[4] *Ibid.*, p. 173.

"... I think it my duty to withhold all judgment concerning it [the violation of Belgium] until everything is made clear with regard to the war and its many distressing incidents."[1]

Another important reason why America should retain her self-possession was that the nations were looking to her for leadership in making peace and for the protection of the rights of humanity.

"... we cannot forget," the President said to the assembled Houses of Congress, April 19, 1916, "that we are in some sort and by the force of circumstances the responsible spokesmen of the rights of humanity, and that we cannot remain silent while those rights seem in process of being swept utterly away in the maelstrom of this terrible war."[2]

No neutral nation indeed was more deeply moved than we with sympathetic concern over the suffering of a blighted Europe so graphically presented every morning in the public press. American feeling responded as always in times of world disaster. The President himself had referred early in the war to his own "warmest sympathy" for those suffering "so grievously" in Belgium[3] and he welcomed the earliest opportunity to offer practical assistance. It was the one gate left open in the dike which neutrality had raised up against an expression of feelings in action. Always to be passive spectators was not enough.

"To feel and feel and feel and never to use that feeling is to grow distracted and worrisome, and to no end."[4]

---

[1]Wilson to Louis de Sadeleer, Minister of State, Belgium, October 7, 1914. Wilson's intercession in the matter of German aërial bombardments of cities, October 19, 1914, had been limited to an informal expression of opinion that such action was injuring the German cause among Americans. *Woodrow Wilson, Life and Letters*, Vol. V, *Neutrality*, p. 165.

[2]*The Public Papers of Woodrow Wilson*, Vol. IV, p. 158.

[3]To Hall Caine, October 26, 1914.

[4]Walter Lippmann, "Uneasy America," *New Republic*, Vol. V (December 25, 1915), p. 195.

Wilson had thus eagerly sponsored the proposal made as early as November 1914 for active help for the suffering people of Belgium. He asked Secretary Lane to give him information about the extraordinary American engineer who had stepped forward with such initiative and ability. The report regarding Herbert Hoover was "most interesting and satisfactory."[1] Some months later, when Hoover wrote to inform the President of the activities of the Commission for the Relief of Belgium, Wilson replied:

"It has commanded the admiration and confidence of every one who has had a chance to know of it . . ."[2]

When the difficulties increased during 1915, the President coöperated directly with Hoover in gaining the assistance of American business men and philanthropists, bidding him "Godspeed in the splendid work."[3]

As the war deepened, America saw the wave of suffering spreading out, engulfing not only individuals, but vast populations. The military spirit was absolutely ruthless, without pity, without remorse, consuming as with fire everything it touched. By 1915 the Young Turks had begun their attacks upon helpless Armenians and Jews, and the fate of millions of Poles was involved in the movements of the enormous Russian, German, and Austrian armies.

The President did everything possible to help mitigate these catastrophes. In February, Bryan warned the Turkish government that we would hold them responsible for massacres and looting.[4] Time and again, in the face of the resentment of the Grand Vizier, Bryan or Lansing author-

---

[1] Lane to Wilson, November 18, 1914; Wilson to Lane, November 20, 1914.

[2] Hoover to Wilson, February 26, 1915; Wilson to Hoover, March 19, 1915.

[3] Wilson to Hoover, November 3, 1915. Only a small part of the funds for Belgian relief, which cost $2,000,000 a week, came from the United States. Page to the State Department, January 11, 1916. *Foreign Relations*, 1916, Supp., p. 886.

[4] *Foreign Relations*, 1915, Supp., p. 979.

Belgian Relief Commission was permitted to ameliorate the hardships to some extent. The press in Allied countries and in America was filled with stories of personal crimes, many of which we now know were wildly exaggerated, but which at the time served to inflame American opinion. Late in April, Ambassador Gerard discussed the deportations with the Chancellor, and reported in June that they had been stopped.[1] To a suggestion that he offer sharp protests, Wilson answered:

". . . if I were to begin making protests along lines such as this, where would I stop? Where can you turn in the whole field of the war without coming upon instances of things so serious in their character and results as to raise in our own heart the impulse of protest?"[2]

Americans were beginning also in the spring of 1916 to be concerned at the serious plight of the Poles. Devastated by the Russian and German armies the year before, starvation and pestilence now possessed the land. Diplomatic negotiations were of no avail.[3]

"I know the terrible conditions, the tragical conditions, that exist there," Wilson told a delegation of Polish-American citizens, July 12, 1916, "and nobody could know them without feeling his heart torn with the knowledge."[4]

The next day, unable to endure the thought that nothing should be done to avert the starvation of millions of people, he wrote to Polk:

". . . I would like your very candid advice as to whether it would be wise or in any way efficacious . . . for me to address personal letters to the King of England, the Emperor of Germany, the Emperor of Austria, the Czar of Russia, and the President of France, appealing to them

[1]June 23rd. *Foreign Relations*, 1916, Supp., p. 859.
[2]Wilson to Robert Underwood Johnson, August 19, 1916.
[3]*Foreign Relations*, 1916, Supp., pp. 886 *et seq.*
[4]*The Public Papers of Woodrow Wilson*, Vol. IV, p. 247.

to cooperate with us in making arrangements which will enable the Polish citizens of the United States to send food to their suffering friends and kinsmen in Poland. That is the only thing I can think of that we have not yet done."

Polk replied by sending a proposed draft of such a letter. Wilson made verbal changes, and it was dispatched on the 20th:

". . . I confidently pledge the cooperation of the people of the United States, if only the way can be found to make their cooperation effective."[1]

The replies—polite personal letters from the futile heads of the governments of Europe—showed that the deadlock over military advantage made help impossible. Each belligerent accused the other.

"England entirely responsible for difficulties with regard to Polish relief," wired Bethmann-Hollweg to Bernstorff.[2] The Kaiser blamed the illegal actions of his enemies.[3] On the other hand, the King of England thought that the Allied demands were "moderate and reasonable."[4]

With extreme disappointment Wilson was forced to admit that the differences of opinion were still irreconcilable.[5] Increasingly, it seemed, the war was crushing every humanitarian instinct, even threatening the existence of civilization.

A similar fate met American efforts to feed the suffering Serbians. Despite the plea of the Serbian government that there was a "desperate state of starvation," Austria declared that they were supplying sufficient food. The

---

[1]From the original in Mr. Wilson's files.

[2]October 4, 1916. Bernstorff, *My Three Years in America*, p. 269.

[3]Emperor William II to President Wilson, August 22, 1916. *Foreign Relations*, 1916, Supp., pp. 909–910.

[4]King George V to President Wilson, August 12, 1916. *Ibid.*, pp. 907–908.

[5]Statement to the press. October 17, 1916. New York *Times*, October 18, 1916.

British government therefore dropped the matter, declaring that they would hold the Austrian government responsible for any distress.[1] This in turn led to ejection of the American Red Cross,[2] which had already begun to help the people.

All this pent-up feeling, this sickness of heart, was inevitably forcing the President and the American people into a new and dangerous attitude of mind. Wilson was all but overwhelmed at times with a painful sense of the "awful burden" of it all: the constant shock of its "appalling sacrifices." He shrank also from the possibility that these "hideous calamities" might be instrumental in forcing us also into the horror of the war:

"From these hideous calamities," he wrote, "we in this favored and beloved land of ours have thus far been shielded. I shall be profoundly thankful if, consistently with the honor and integrity of the nation, we may maintain to the end our peaceful relations with the world."[3]

More days were set aside in October for giving aid to Syrian and Armenian peoples,[4] and Wilson spoke publicly as well of the needs of Poles and other peoples who "are unorganized."[5] Americans knew that these oppressed minorities were fated to suffer most as deprivation increased. Their cause had already, as we have seen, found some championship in the Democratic platform.[6]

Emotional strain, which was steadily increasing, was capped in the last months of 1916 with the reports of what seemed, to Americans, a final outrage. German military

---

[1] W. H. Page to the Secretary of State, July 22, 1916. *Foreign Relations*, 1916, Supp., pp. 922–923.

[2] In November. Penfield to the Secretary of State, November 25, 1916. *Ibid.*, pp. 923–924.

[3] To the Jane Jefferson Club of Colorado, August 7, 1916.

[4] Proclamation dated August 31, 1916.

[5] October 26, 1916, at Cincinnati. New York *Times*, October 27, 1916.

[6] See this volume, p. 260.

authorities began in October to compel able-bodied Belgian workmen, in many cases employed men, to go to Germany to work. The German government asserted that the measure was designed to relieve unemployment in Belgium, but it was fully understood at the State Department that its purpose was to release German workmen for military service.[1] In effect, the Belgians were being compelled to fight against their relatives and friends on the Western Front.

A stronger tone in American protests at once reflected the rising feeling. Lansing, in view of the "seriousness of the consequences . . . aside from humanitarian considerations," instructed Grew to make informal representations to Germany.[2] The Chancellor promised no revocation of policy but did promise certain "points of amelioration."[3]

"He said that this question of Belgian enforced labor would never have arisen if his suggestions that Germany desired peace . . . had been taken up abroad. . . . He said 'What do these difficulties in Belgium matter compared to the hecatomb of lives lost on the Somme since last July?'"[4]

Bernstorff was well aware how bitterly American public opinion condemned Germany:

"The indignation of the press at this 'slavery' which is being imposed on Belgium is general, deep-rooted and genuine. Even newspapers which express themselves in pretty harsh terms on the subject of the English illegalities condemn these deportations in no measured terms. . . . The Philadelphia *Public Ledger* says: ". . . 'There has not been such a tragedy since the fierce barbarian tribes swept

[1]Lansing to Wilson, November 21, 1916; Grew, reports to the Secretary of State. *Foreign Relations*, 1916, Supp., pp. 859 *et seq.*; Whitlock, reports to the Secretary of State. *Ibid.*, pp. 863–865, 867–868.

[2]To Grew, November 2, 1916. *Ibid.*, p. 863.

[3]Grew to the Secretary of State, November 22, 1916. *Ibid.*, p. 866.

[4]Grew to the Secretary of State, a further report, November 22, 1916. *Ibid.*, p. 68.

over Europe' . . . such expressions as 'Huns,' 'Attila,' 'Hohenzollern slave trade,' and others of a similar nature are the order of the day . . ."[1]

Late in November, Wilson, realizing that this "very considerable opinion"[2] was gathering, and impelled by his own feelings, began to think favourably of making a strong declaration against the practice. Lansing was greatly stirred by the whole affair. Germany, he wrote, had reverted "to the barbarous methods of the military empires of antiquity."

"It arouses in me . . . an intense feeling of abhorrence . . ."

He suggested that "we ought to consider very carefully whether some way cannot be found to bring moral pressure upon Germany to cause her to abandon a policy which invites the protest of the civilized world, and which will greatly increase her difficulties when the time comes to negotiate a treaty of peace . . ."[3]

Wilson typed out the following reply:

November 26, 1916

MY DEAR MR. SECRETARY:

I think there is undoubtedly sufficient ground here for a very solemn protest, and I suggest that it be made orally, to the following effect:

That this Government has heard of this action with the greatest regret and wishes to enter its most friendly but most solemn protest as in contravention of all precedent and the long accepted principles of international practice;

That its effect upon Belgian relief, so humanely planned and so successfully carried out, will probably be fatal, to the great

---

[1]December 11, 1916. *My Three Years in America*, pp. 339–340. Of course the result was that Americans accepted the wildest atrocity stories more freely than ever. Any skepticism was hard to maintain in the face of such accumulating evidence of heartlessness.

[2]Wilson to Charles W. Eliot, November 22, 1916.

[3]Lansing to Wilson, November 21, 1916.

embarrassment, we should assume, of the German Government; and

That I feel that it has placed a new and very serious obstacle in the way of efforts looking towards peace which I had hoped made [sic] soon be made and which I was anxiously seeking an opportunity to make.

I hope that the suggestion of the last paragraph can be successfully withheld from any, even the least, publicity, by the most painstaking precautions. I believe, from Mr. Grew's recent despatches, that it will be the most persuasive part of the protest.

Faithfully yours,
W.W.

The formal communication was sent November 29th; the reference to jeopardizing peace was deleted in the protest itself, but Grew was directed to discuss it "confidentially and very earnestly" with the German Chancellor.[1]

It was "very earnestly worded," Wilson informed Senator John Sharp Williams in a confidential letter December 5th, and he would have liked to make it public:

"It is one of the most distressing and, I think, one of the most unjustifiable incidents of the present war, and I wish I were not obliged to express judgments of this sort in private only."

He intimated, however, to Former President Eliot, that he hardly expected Germany to abandon her policy:

". . . I am taking steps which I hope will be influential, if not effective."[2]

The doubt was well founded. The reply from Germany, December 11th, complained about the sending of a protest to them when none had been sent to the Allies when allegedly similar deportations had been made from East Prussia to Siberia. It claimed that the American govern-

[1]*Foreign Relations*, 1916, Supp., pp. 70–71.
[2]November 27, 1916.

ment must have been misinformed as to the facts. But Zimmermann, in handing the reply to Grew, said that conditions and means of carrying out the deportation measures were being ameliorated.[1]

There American efforts had perforce to stop:

". . . I think," wrote Wilson, "that what the Government has done is all that could possibly be done unless we are to go to the length of declaring war on Germany."[2]

The effect upon American opinion of these atrocities and of our helplessness in the whole situation is, of course, difficult to assess; it was unquestionably an important factor in preparing Americans to accept the idea that, if war came, it would not be an unmixed evil. The idea of participating in the conflict was gradually to become tolerable—in the guise of a war to end all war; to end Prussian militarism and barbarism; to save civilization and the rights of peoples—a war for liberty. The thought did not become fully conscious until Wilson gave it voice a few months later, but the eager response that met his declaration was being shaped by the experiences and agitations of the neutrality years.

"The one thing that is certain," declared the New York *Tribune* in November 1916, "is that there cannot be peace between Germany and civilization while Germany remains the exponent of all the things that mean the destruction of civilization and the denial of common humanity."[3]

Arthur Bullard understood the general state of mind:

"It is perhaps illogical for us to be more angry at German lawlessness than at that of the English, but there is no doubt that we are."[4]

---

[1] *Foreign Relations*, 1916, Supp., pp. 868–870. This meant little, however, for the power of Hindenburg and Ludendorff was rapidly rising to a point which subordinated control by the political authorities.

[2] To Dr. Hiram Woods, December 28, 1916.

[3] *Literary Digest*, Vol. 53 (November 25, 1916), p. 1397.

[4] Arthur Bullard, *The Diplomacy of the Great War* (1916), p. 297.

Americans found the inhumanities of the Central Powers far more reprehensible than the injustices of the Allies. Added to the horrors of submarine warfare and the belief that Germany bore at least the gravest share of responsibility for bringing on the war,[1] the case against Germany, as adjudged by Americans, was increasingly darkened.

The ties of friendship which in the past had bound Germany and the United States were far outweighed by those which linked Great Britain and France with the United States. There were cultural bonds with Great Britain: the common heritage, blood, political and social institutions, religion, and literature. With France there were warm memories of sympathy and assistance in the Revolutionary period. We had, moreover, during the war been able, despite severe strain, to keep our trade disputes with the Allies on a footing of accommodation, and our commercial and financial relations, close in peace times, had been enormously strengthened. Wilson and Page had worked more understandingly with the British on matters such as the Panama Canal tolls, relationships with Mexico, and peace plans, than it had been possible to do with Germany. Although in the previous two years we had only vague ideas of the Allies' material aims in the war, since we were not informed as to their secret treaties, we were essentially sympathetic, at least with the English liberals, as to moral views and goals. The easy interchange of ideas, made possible by language and better means of communication with the British, brought the American public increasingly to see the war through British eyes. Individual Americans who had gone to aid the Allies during the neutrality years[2] deepened our interest in the

---

[1] For official German report of the strength of this belief, see *Official German Documents*, Vol. II, pp. 869–871.

[2] *Cf. Foreign Relations*, 1916, Supp., pp. 287–288.

fortunes of the Allies. These fundamental factors were frequently alluded to by skillful speakers, both American and British:[1] and the ties were not only thus tightened, but Americans were made conscious of them.

By the winter of 1916 American antagonism toward Germany had greatly heightened; American irritation at the Allies had ebbed. Meanwhile, under great handicaps, Wilson was preparing the last great peace move of our neutrality period.

---

[1] *Cf.* Sir Gilbert Parker, head of the British propaganda in America, "The United States and the War," *Harper's Magazine*, Vol. 136 (1918), pp. 521–531.

CHAPTER IX

RENEWED STRUGGLES FOR PEACE

"I wish . . . that foreign affairs were as simple as agriculture."
Address at Washington, November 14, 1916.

"There must be a just and settled peace, and we here in America must contribute the full force of our enthusiasm and of our authority as a nation to the organization of that peace upon world-wide foundations that cannot easily be shaken."
Address at Shadow Lawn, New Jersey, September 2, 1916.

"Victory would mean peace forced upon the loser, a victor's terms imposed upon the vanquished. It would be accepted in humiliation, under duress, at an intolerable sacrifice, and would leave a sting, a resentment, a bitter memory upon which terms of peace would rest, not permanently, but only as upon quicksand. Only a peace between equals can last."
Address to the Senate, January 22, 1917.

I. THE BELLIGERENTS RESIST WILSON'S PEACE EFFORTS

THE conduct of the responsible statesman in the face of the inscrutable and inevitable is at once the touchstone of his character and the measure of his greatness. The future lifts only from hour to hour; he has no time for new thought: he cannot prepare: he is fated to act according to his essential nature, out of what the past has made him.

No period in the life of Woodrow Wilson, it seems to this biographer, made more exacting demands upon all the seasoned resources of his intellect, all the established qualities of his character, even upon his physical capacities, than the summer and fall of the year 1916.

At no time since the great war had broken in August

1914 had the situation in Europe looked blacker, and at no time had the emotional repercussions in America been more violent.[1] On the Western Front the bloody battle of the Somme was ending in a stalemate. Instead of bringing a speedy decision, as the Allies had ardently hoped and confidently expected, the war was everywhere spreading. During the last days of August, Roumania declared war against Austria-Hungary: Italy's declaration against Germany became effective on the 28th. And Greece, caught between the two coalitions, her people drawn toward the Allies, and her Hohenzollern monarch toward his kin, was slowly veering to the side of the Allies.[2]

An element not only of weariness but of desperation was entering into the appeals, the charges, even the prophecies of the time. There seemed no end to the tragedy.

In this crisis Wilson was finding himself driven more and more into an intolerable position: faced by problems he could not solve, asked for decisions he could not make. More and more the exhausted nations of Europe were looking to America and the American leader for help—if not for help to win the war, for help to stop it. The Germans in particular, standing firmly upon thousands of square miles of devastated France and Belgium, were not only demanding peace, but demanding that the American President institute negotiations—and threatening a renewal of indiscriminate submarine warfare, which Wilson thought curbed by the *Sussex* note, if they did not get it.[3]

---

[1] As the previous section of this volume has shown.

[2] For American disapproval of the aggressions by which the Allies forced this result, see the *Literary Digest*, Vol. 53 (October 28, 1916), pp. 1092–1094.

[3] A dispatch from the American embassy in Berlin, August 28th, warned that sentiment in favour of ruthless submarine warfare was swiftly gaining ground. Gerard telegraphed on the 25th that Germany was "anxious to make peace" and desired the President to act—at once. *Foreign Relations*, 1916, Supp., p. 55. The German General Staff, toward the end of September, was bringing pressure upon the government by a confidential memorandum which discussed recovering the freedom of action reserved in the *Sussex* note, May 4th, unless Wilson acted "soon," before the election in November. Hindenburg, *Out of My Life*, pp. 253–254.

With the most ruthless military leaders—Hindenburg and Ludendorff—coming into more dominating power, as against the milder civil authorities, the threats here implied might easily be carried out. If they were, what would happen to the American President who had already taken his stand upon an ultimatum? War?

On the other hand the British, just at this time, were, as we have seen, irritating if not infuriating American opinion by their demands and exactions in connection with their black lists, their blockade, their seizures of American mails. There was even talk, in Congress, of war with Great Britain![1] At the same time the Allies were resisting every effort of the President that remotely suggested peace. Only lately, August 23rd, he had had to inform the anxious Spanish government through Lansing that the Allies would reject any overtures until there was "a change" in their military situation:

"From the advices which have now been received from the capitals of the Allies the President does not feel that the Governments of the Entente have up to the present time changed their attitude in regard to proposals by neutrals looking towards peace, and that to make proposals, with knowledge that they would certainly be rejected and would in all probability cause irritation towards the . . . governments making them, would jeopardize the future usefulness of the proposers as agents in peace negotiations when an opportune time comes to offer friendly offices. . . ."[2]

It is difficult to overemphasize the pressure and anxiety under which the President was forced to live and to lead, during these tempestuous months. It must not be forgotten that his own personal and political fortunes during all this time were also at stake. He was in the midst of his

---

[1] See this volume, p. 315.
[2] *Foreign Relations*, 1916, Supp., pp. 46–47.

campaign for reëlection to the presidency, of which he was not only the potent director but in himself the principal issue.

Other problems were insistent and critical, not only the war in Europe but the Mexican imbroglio: in August and September, Pershing's army was still in an anxious position in the interior of Mexico; Villa was still at large. The plight of refugee Americans driven from Mexico was serious.[1] The treaty for the purchase of the Danish West Indies was sent from the President's desk to the Senate in August to face an uncertain voyage to ratification. He must decide promptly upon a new financial policy for Nicaragua.[2] And to cap the climax, a vast threatened railroad strike challenged to the utmost his executive leadership.

It is scarcely surprising that an expression of the strain and the weariness of the time should creep into his letters. Appended to a memorandum (August 14th) for Tumulty, regarding a certain delegation which desired to see the President, we find this note, in Wilson's handwriting:

"This seems literally impossible unless they come at 2 to-day and I ought to keep some free time for R. R. developments. I am desperately tired. W. W."

He wrote to one of his daughters in October:

"We are constantly on the move . . . and even when we are not away people are crowding here to have speeches made to them or to confer with me about all sorts of things. I have no doubt that when the campaign is over we shall feel the reaction and the fatigue very strongly."[3]

He frequently cut down upon his regular exercise, invaded his hours of sleep—though he knew that the payment of the toll to nature would have to be met later with

---

[1]Wilson to Newton D. Baker, August 25, 1916.
[2]Wilson to Lansing, August 22, 1916.
[3]To Mrs. Francis B. Sayre, October 16, 1916.

interest. Nevertheless, and this also was characteristic of the man, he sometimes found an unused moment to express his deep affection for his family:

"It was delightful to hear that Jessie and the babies are all right," he wrote to Frank Sayre. "I cannot tell you how often and with what deep love we all think of you. We are well, but in the midst of affairs so absorbing that I for one hardly have time to think whether I am well or not.

"All join in the warmest and tenderest love to you all. It would indeed be delightful if Edith and I could come up in November to see you."[1]

"How sweet and adorable of you," Mrs. Sayre wrote in August, "in the midst of all this dreadful business, to think of your little daughter's birthday! I could almost have cried when your telegram came, with its loving message . . . And then your wonderfully generous gift! . . . I will be giving myself and the children things with it for a long time to come."[2]

His letters of the time also tell of his "deep distress" occasioned by the death of his much-loved sister, Annie.[3]

"Your letter pleased and touched me very deeply," he wrote to his aunt, Mrs. Thomas Woodrow. "I knew you would be thinking of me when you heard of the loss of dear Sister Annie. I know, too, how deeply and sincerely she loved you . . .

"These are very trying times . . ."[4]

So far as he himself was concerned—his future plans and policies, his power of leadership—everything depended upon the political campaign. Even though the war in Europe might proceed to new extremities of ferocity,

---

[1] July 31, 1916.
[2] August 30, 1916.
[3] On September 16, 1916.
[4] September 30, 1916.

America must pause, according to the deliberate democratic method, to settle its own affairs, choose or reaffirm its leadership, and express its opinion as to policies for another four years. He expressed himself clearly upon this point in his speech of acceptance in September:

"From this time until the 7th of November it is going to be practically impossible for the present Administration to handle any critical matter concerning our foreign relations, because all foreign statesmen are waiting to see which way the election goes, and in the meantime they know that settlements will be inconclusive."[1]

In consonance with this conviction he avoided every possible controversy upon foreign affairs. When Lansing suggested on September 21st that the *Lusitania* negotiation be forced to a conclusion,[2] he replied:

". . . it may be well to take up a settlement of the *Lusitania* outrage with Bernstorff if he thinks it can be settled now without soon widening into the ancient difficulty. Let me warn you that negotiation at the present time is very dangerous because it affords the German Government an opportunity to play into the hands of the German mischief makers on this side of the water and supply them with campaign material by all sorts of false impressions. Please go very slowly in this critical matter. The atmosphere of the moment is a most unfavourable one for the handling of things of this kind and you are dealing with an astute and unscrupulous man."

The more Wilson thought about it the more he opposed action. He appended a definite instruction:

"Please keep me informed of any conversations you may have with him, and take no step without my advice."

---

[1] *The Public Papers of Woodrow Wilson*, Vol. IV, p. 330.

[2] Since, Lansing wrote, the delay which had occurred in the negotiations was being used by the Republicans as a point of attack.

Both the Allies and the Germans recognized the importance of this domestic crisis in American affairs. There was a brief easing of the debate within Germany on submarine policy,[1] done deliberately, as the American embassy learned, "to avoid embarrassing the President should he desire to act" for peace.[2] Bernstorff had notified Berlin on September 8th that if "Wilson is reelected I consider mediatory action by him as very likely to occur before the end of the year."[3]

What the President wanted, in short, was a clear new mandate from the people. As he said in a speech of September 30th: ". . . a great fundamental, final choice with regard to our foreign relationships is to be made on the 7th of November."[4]

His own general policy continued to be what it had been all along: to keep out of war, if it was a possible thing; to seek peace with the utmost diligence at every opening; and to proceed, guardedly, with military preparation to meet any eventuality.

During the campaign he set forth all these policies with vigour and continuity. In the matter of peace, however, which was uppermost in his mind, he confined himself largely, knowing the delicate situation abroad, to the advocacy of his plan for a league of nations:

". . . it is our duty to lend the full force of this nation, moral and physical, to a league of nations which shall see to it that nobody disturbs the peace of the world without submitting his case first to the opinion of mankind."[5]

". . . America is going . . . if other nations will join her,

---

[1]Grew to the Secretary of State, October 6, 1916. *Foreign Relations*, 1916, Supp., p. 293.

[2]Grew to the Secretary of State, October 7, 1916. *Ibid.*, p. 293; also same to same, October 20, 1916. *Ibid.*, p. 297.

[3]*Official German Documents*, Vol. II, p. 984.

[4]*The Public Papers of Woodrow Wilson*, Vol. IV, p. 331.

[5]October 5, 1916. *Ibid.*, p. 348.

to see to it that . . . the only thing ever fought for is the common rights of humanity."[1]

While he was thus expressing his glorified vision of a new peace, a new world, after the war, the belligerents in Europe were steadily making any immediate peace at all more remote and doubtful—and at the same time demanding that he act, one way or another, at once. The French in an official declaration on September 14th expressed their resolution to seek a "peace through victory," not, as Wilson hoped, a peace through negotiation:

"We ought to redouble our efforts . . .

"The union of all the living forces of the country is the essential condition of success; that is what will carry us to the end—peace through victory . . ."[2]

Briand on September 19th branded the idea of a peace by negotiation as "an outrage against the memory of so many heroes who had fallen for France":[3]

". . . if you wish the idea of liberty and justice to prevail, ask for victory, and not the peace obtainable to-day, for that peace would be humiliating and dishonouring."[4]

Such pronouncements incited equally truculent public responses from Germany:

"Does any one dare ask that to-day we make proposals to our enemies, inasmuch as M. Briand . . . said that consideration of peace now would be a humiliation and a disgrace to the memory of the dead?"[5]

And yet while the Chancellor was speaking these words, on September 28th, Ambassador Gerard was hurriedly embarking at Copenhagen on a secret mission. He had been asked by the German Secretary of State, Von Jagow,

---

[1]October 26, 1916. *Ibid.*, p. 380.

[2]Premier Briand, at the opening of the French Chamber of Deputies, September 14, 1916. *Current History*, Vol. V (November 1916), p. 285.

[3]*Ibid.*, p. 194.

[4]Quoted in *War Memoirs of David Lloyd George*, Vol. II, pp. 277–278.

[5]September 28, 1916. *Current History*, Vol. V (November 1916), p. 291.

to go to the United States to persuade the President to do something for peace! If Wilson did not hasten his long-awaited move, Von Jagow warned, "German public sentiment would compel the government to give in to the demands" for ruthless U-boat warfare.[1] Gerard immediately telegraphed a brief report[2] and departed for Washington.

Wilson was thus being torn—at a time when he could not act with authority—between the absolutely irreconcilable demands of the belligerents; the Germans ostensibly eager for peace by his initiation, but not desiring him to act as mediator, and the Allies bitterly rejecting any peace whatever. And the price of continued inaction, as he well knew, was the probable involvement of America in the war.

As it happened, the hardest possible blow to his peace hopes was delivered by the British Minister of War on the same day that Gerard embarked—September 28th. Lloyd George had for some time been listening to the remarks of his colleagues in the Cabinet and others who were with considerable justification becoming panicky regarding the Allies' deficiencies in shipping, finance, and food supplies. He decided that it was "vitally important to throw out a sharp challenge to the defeatist spirit which was working from foreign quarters [he meant America] to bring about an inconclusive peace, and which appeared to find an echo even in some responsible quarters" in England.[3] Accordingly, on his own initiative, he made a pronouncement directed to whomsoever it might concern. Page described his remarks as a "restrained expression" of English opinion.[4] One may wonder, as he reads the

---

[1]Memorandum prepared by Gerard for the author.

[2]Sent by Lansing to Wilson. Letter undated, but probably September 29th or 30th.

[3]*War Memoirs of David Lloyd George*, Vol. II, pp. 279–280.

[4]Page to the Secretary of State, October 11, 1916. *Foreign Relations*, 1916, Supp., p. 57. Lloyd George made his remarks through an interview with Roy Howard, president of the United Press.

Welshman's words, what a full expression would have been!

"Germany elected to make it a finish fight with England. . . . Now we intend to see that Germany has her way. The fight must be to the finish—to a knockout.

"The whole world, including neutrals of the highest purposes and humanitarians with the best motives, must know that there can be no outside interference at this stage. Britain asked no intervention when she was not prepared to fight. She will tolerate none now . . ."[1]

There was only one hesitation in the general approval which Grey gave to this interference in foreign affairs by the War Minister. He wrote to Lloyd George on the 29th that he was "apprehensive of the possible effect of the warning" upon Wilson. Briand's statements had "made any further warning to Wilson unnecessary for the present." One sentence of his letter illuminated Wilson's difficulties:

"It has always been my view that until the Allies were sure of victory the door should be kept open for Wilson's mediation. It is now closed forever as far as we are concerned."[2]

Wilson continually made the mistake of assuming that the chief end the belligerents sought was a just and durable peace. He himself took the better world order, which he was now passionately advocating, to be the highest goal. The Allies did not. The Central Powers did not. They not only sought military victory: they had far-reaching material purposes, some of them outspoken, others still concealed by undeclared secret treaties. Prestige, world power, commercial dominance, new territorial possessions!

Wilson's course was also made more difficult by another mistaken assumption—that victory was an impossibility

---

[1] *Current History*, Vol. V (November 1916), pp. 286–287.
[2] *War Memoirs of David Lloyd George*, Vol. II, pp. 282–283.

for either side, and that his mediation must therefore soon be accepted and negotiations started. Such pronouncements as those of Lloyd George, Grey, Bethmann-Hollweg, revealed how far any of the belligerents were from accepting, as yet, any such assumption. Wilson was thinking of the ultimate good of civilization: but civilization has always been secondary in military struggles. Progress and hope against fear and greed and ambition. Timeless conflicts!—they were crushing the possibility of an early peace. And they would later set grim limits to Wilson's league.

And yet the President continued stubbornly to affirm his intention to make peace—to which he was giving, he wrote on October 9th, "constant and most anxious thought."[1] Spring Rice might report to his government, as he did, that Lloyd George's announcement had an "immense and instantaneous effect in this country" and "put a stop" to peace rumours.[2] In fact the President proceeded as if the opposition were only a kind of distemper. Talking with Bernstorff on October 19th, he set forth his inmost convictions. He had, he said, "but the one wish, to remain neutral and to help bring the war to an end, since in his opinion a decision could not be reached by force of arms. . . . For this reason . . . it was better to make peace today than tomorrow . . ." He even warned Bernstorff that, should the United States be drawn in, "every opportunity of ending the war would vanish."[3]

When the interview concluded, the President must have been left with the unhappy realization that Bernstorff had given no hint whatever that there existed in Ger-

---

[1] Wilson to S. J. Blum.

[2] Spring Rice to Grey, October 6, 1916. *War Memoirs of David Lloyd George*, Vol. II, p. 285.

[3] Bernstorff's report to the German Foreign Office. *Official German Documents*, Vol. II, pp. 987–988.

many a willingness to make a sacrifice to obtain peace. No belligerent had any such enlightenment. The point had been reached where there seemed to be no effective instrument but the threat of force, or of war, which Wilson had already been compelled to use, with the Germans, in the submarine dispute. Pressure upon the Allies equally required force; but for what appeared to be compelling reasons, Wilson had already, as we have seen, rejected the policy of economic pressure—which was the only weapon he had left, so far as they were concerned.

The British continued to denounce a negotiated peace. On October 11th Prime Minister Asquith declared that the war "cannot be allowed to end in some . . . dishonouring compromise, masquerading under the name of Peace." It must go on to where a peace could be made that would give "adequate reparation for the past and adequate security for the future." Grey made a statement of a similar tenor two weeks later.[1]

The issue was finally being stripped clear for Wilson; if peace could not be won, the inevitable course of events would force America, also, to go to war. He was tortured by the narrowing choice and the stupendous responsibilities that confronted him.

"There is," he said in a moment of penetrating self-revelation, "a very holy and very terrible isolation for the conscience of every man who seeks to read the destiny in affairs for others as well as for himself, for a nation as well as for individuals. . . . That lonely search of the spirit for the right perhaps no man can assist."[2]

It is plain also from his speeches that he had, in facing at last the possibility, if not the probability, that America would be forced into the war, begun to consider the terms which we might exact—little knowing how slight, in the

---

[1] Quoted, *War Memoirs of David Lloyd George*, Vol. II, pp. 311–312.
[2] September 4, 1916. *The Public Papers of Woodrow Wilson*, Vol. IV, p. 295.

face of such savagery, was his chance of making any terms whatever:

"We are holding off . . . because when we exert the force of this Nation we want to know what we are exerting it for."[1]

We would not permit ourselves to be entangled in "the ambitions and the national purposes" of the nations now fighting. We could only fight—we would always be willing to fight—for "the rights of humanity." These rights were the "essence of free institutions"—our own institutions.[2]

With all this, in spite of the unanswerable logic of the situation, he was still clinging to his hope that he could make some turn, find some last desperate expedient to keep America out of war. He said, on October 21st:

"I am not expecting this country to get into war."[3]

Meanwhile, on the 10th, Gerard had arrived in New York harbour to the accompaniment of a fanfare of articles in the New York *World*. What he had to say—especially concerning Germany's intention of resuming ruthless submarine warfare—had been trumpeted abroad in the land. Little was left for the ambassador to report to Wilson!

The President, indeed, thought it best to delay seeing Gerard, possibly until after the election, "in order to dispel the idea that he was the bearer of a special message from Germany or was called home because of a possible crisis in the submarine matter." Lansing, however, argued that a longer delay might cause adverse comment;[4] and Wilson invited Gerard to visit him at Shadow Lawn.

In the two weeks that followed, developments grew steadily more ominous. Page telegraphed that the British

---

[1]October 5, 1916. *Op. cit.*, p. 346.
[2]*Ibid.*, p. 347.
[3]*Ibid.*, p. 371.
[4]Lansing to Wilson, October 16, 1916.

considered the Germans insincere in their desire for an early peace, hoping merely to gain evidence "to use at home and in propaganda in neutral countries to throw onus of continuing war on the Allies."[1] Moreover, there was really increasing reason to be fearful that a submarine crisis was not far distant. Already, in September, three ships with Americans on board had been sunk.[2] Grew reported from Berlin on October 12th that German naval officers had petitioned the Emperor for immediate resumption of unrestricted warfare.[3]

". . . God knows," wrote Wilson of our relations with Germany, "they are difficult . . ."[4]

Before the projected interview with Gerard, the German government had used their most aggressive argument to force Wilson to move. House received from Bernstorff on the 19th a secret memorandum, written by the Kaiser himself, and addressed to Gerard for use in his conversation with the President. House showed the document to Gerard[5] and sent it to the President the same day.

The memorandum read as follows:

"Your Excellency hinted to His Majesty in your last conversation at Charleville in April that President Wilson possibly would try towards the end of the summer to offer his good services to the belligerents for the promotion of peace. The German Government has no information as to whether the President adheres to this idea and as to the eventual date at which his step would take place. Meanwhile the constellation of war has taken such a form that the German Government foresees the time at which it will be forced to regain the freedom of action that it has

---

[1]October 11th. *Foreign Relations*, 1916, Supp., p. 57.
[2]*Ibid.*, p. 299.
[3]*Ibid.*, p. 296.
[4]To L. W. Nieman, of the Milwaukee *Journal*, October 16th.
[5]*The Intimate Papers of Colonel House*, Vol. II, p. 389.

reserved to itself in the note of May 4 last and thus the President's steps may be jeopardized. The German Government thinks it its duty to communicate this fact to your Excellency in case you should find that the date of the intended action of the President should be so far advanced towards the end of the season."[1]

While this was merely a restatement of facts already known, it was, for all that, an official notice from the highest authority that an action for peace must be taken quickly if the gravest submarine crisis of all was to be averted. It presaged disaster. Wilson's pent-up feeling against the inexorable pressure upon him, from both sides, found expression in a speech a few days later.

". . . this is the last war . . . that involves the world that the United States can keep out of.

"I say that because I believe that the business of neutrality is over . . . I mean this, that war now has such a scale that the position of neutrals sooner or later becomes intolerable."[2]

Ambassador Gerard's own report describes his interview with the President on October 24th—and incidentally gives an intimate glimpse of the President's poise in the midst of desperate uncertainty over peace and over his own reëlection:

"I arrived about eleven in the morning and . . . left about half past three or four. During all that time President Wilson was questioning in the greatest detail about affairs in Germany and did not let me go until he had extracted every bit of information I possessed . . .

"Mrs. Wilson was present during the interview and at times asked pertinent questions showing her deep knowledge of foreign affairs. . . .

---

[1] *Official German Documents*, Vol. II, p. 987.

[2] October 26, 1916. *The Public Papers of Woodrow Wilson*, Vol. IV, p. 381. Wilson was here expressing a conclusion that is now forcing itself, with intolerable insistence, upon all thoughtful students of the possibilities of future world wars.

"When the President finally dismissed me we were taken together on the porch of the house by several 'movie' men, the President saying to me, 'I'll show you how to act for the movies. I'm quite used to it now.'"[1]

The Kaiser's memorandum failed, however, to convince the President of the genuineness of Germany's willingness to make a peace that did not mean a mere harvest of the conquests her armies had already made. It was sheer threat[2] without any information whatsoever as to peace terms—without so much as a general acceptance of the principles Wilson had laid down, May 27th, as the basis on which he would be glad to mediate.[3] The Kaiser spoke, in fact, only of the earlier suggestion in April—before Wilson's world peace plan had been announced. It was also clear that the Germans suspected and opposed Wilson as a mediator: Bethmann-Hollweg informed Bernstorff on October 14th that mediation by Wilson was not desirable, but "a spontaneous appeal for peace . . . would be gladly accepted by us."[4]

On the eve of the election, Wilson received a letter from Colonel House, which, if he placed credence in its views, must have increased his doubt as to any further effort to secure peace—which was, of course, what House desired.

"He [Roy Howard] tells me that Germany almost to a man is wishing for your defeat and that France and England are almost to a man wishing for your success. Lloyd George, Northcliffe and others are particularly keen to have you win."[5]

---

[1]Memorandum written by Gerard for the author.

[2]In spite of the fact that Bethmann-Hollweg, in transmitting it, said that it was not "to be understood as constituting a threat of U-boat war." *Official German Documents*, Vol. II, p. 987.

[3]*Cf. The Public Papers of Woodrow Wilson*, Vol. IV, p. 188.

[4]*Official German Documents*, Vol. II, p. 989.

[5]November 6, 1916. Within two weeks House had to revise his statement. He reported to Wilson on the 20th that he had "indisputable evidence that Bernstorff used

He went on to indict Germany on other grounds. "They sneer at such proposals as a league to enforce peace, and believe, as they have believed heretofore, that large military armaments are necessary to enforce peace."

Only three days after House was writing, however, Bethmann-Hollweg told the Reichstag that Germany would "honorably co-operate in investigating every attempt to find a practical solution and collaborate toward its possible realization. . . ."[1] And finally, in cold truth, the Germans' reliance at this time upon "large military armaments" was fully matched by the Allies.

Wilson appears to have been impervious to every influence which countered either of his two fixed purposes: to make a peace which would bring a durable improvement in world relationships, and to keep America out of the war.

As the campaign came to a close, Wilson's anxieties were increased by still more threatening submarine attacks. Would he get across the line on November 7th without a genuine new crisis? On October 30th Lansing began an investigation of the sinking of the freighter *Rowanmore*. The next day he requested the German government to explain the torpedoing of the *Marina* without warning. Nine Americans had been killed or wounded. On the day before the election Page telegraphed that the liner *Arabia* had been sunk without warning.[2] Whether these had been clear-cut violations of the German pledge of May 4th was a question: the *Marina* and the *Arabia* aroused grave apprehension. One thing, however,

---

in a quiet way what influence he could bring to bear in favor of your re-election." And in a letter of the 21st he enclosed a message from Sir Horace Plunkett, dated November 2nd, saying: ". . . I hope you will not be annoyed, if the President's re-election is badly received by British public opinion."

[1] *Current History*, Vol. V (February 1917), p. 870. According to some reports, he interpolated the objectionable words, "even to place herself at the head" of a league of nations. New York *Times*, November 10, 1916.

[2] *Foreign Relations*, 1916, Supp., pp. 298–299, 308–309.

was plain: the naval authorities in Germany were preparing to force matters. Wilson was pessimistic over the outlook:

". . . I have done all that it was possible to do," he wrote, October 30th, "to bring Germany to a better way of action."[1]

However, neither these threats nor any other influence served to turn him from his purpose. He intended to make at least one more desperate effort to secure peace.

"The minute the campaign is over," he wrote November 4th, "I shall be obliged to prepare some of the most important papers I have yet had to prepare . . ."[2]

It was to be one of the noblest expressions during his entire administration of his vision and of his wisdom—however doomed to failure.

II. THE CRISIS DEEPENS

Wilson had confidently hoped that when the election was over, and he had obtained a new mandate from the people, his problems relating to the European war would be appreciably simplified. Doubt both at home and abroad as to the continuance of his leadership and his policies would be stilled. His voice in world affairs, sustained by the renewed approval of the most powerful of neutral nations, would take on new authority. He could not only suggest peace: he could even demand it. A cessation of the war, as he now clearly perceived, was the only sure escape from American participation in it.

His hope of simplification, however, was wholly unwarranted. Instead of simplification, there was increasing complication: a steadily narrowing range of possible action. Events, like the jaws of some monstrous, inexorable vise, were closing in upon him.

[1] To Professor G. M. Harper.
[2] To William Edlin, managing editor of *The Day*.

He knew, he had known for some time, that he must launch a new and powerful peace move. His proposals for a league of nations were too vague. They looked to the security of the nations after the war. A league might satisfy idealistic America, for we were not at war; it did not meet the urgent crisis in Europe. Something sharper, more definite, was called for. He told House on November 13th that unless he acted immediately the United States would "inevitably drift into war with Germany upon the submarine issue."[1]

But the old problem as to the best time, the most favourable occasion, still persisted. Immediately following the election all the old irritations, all the explosive issues, which had been somewhat restrained by both belligerents during the campaign, broke with new ferocity upon the President—the more insistent because they had been delayed. War is no respecter of the deliberate processes of peace. The Germans, impatient under the limitations imposed by the *Sussex* pledge, were preparing to renew their submarine warfare. The forced resignation of Von Jagow, German Minister of Foreign Affairs, who had been the chief opponent in Berlin of unrestricted submarine warfare, struck an ominous note.[2]

On the other hand British relationships, which had somewhat improved since the explosions of American irritation over the black list, were approaching a new and far more fundamental crisis. The Allies were running out of money! They could not go on with the war without a continuous flow of supplies from America, for which they could no longer pay in cash, or in repatriated securities,

---

[1] *The Intimate Papers of Colonel House*, Vol. II, p. 390.

[2] News of the resignation came on the 23rd. New York *Times*, November 24, 1916. The official American representatives in Germany gave no evidence of recognizing the significance of this event. Grew, to the Secretary of State, November 23, 1916. *Foreign Relations*, 1916, Supp., pp. 67–68; Gerard's reaction, as described by Bernstorff, *My Three Years in America*, pp. 310–311.

or in temporary bank loans. A radical new policy for credits—involving vast new financial machinery—appeared absolutely necessary if one or both of two catastrophes were to be avoided: either the speedy defeat of the Allies, or an industrial and financial crisis of the first magnitude in America—since our economic system was now overwhelmingly dependent upon trade with Great Britain and France.

In Great Britain, also, as in Germany, the forces of moderate action were rapidly losing ground. On December 5th the Asquith government was overthrown and succeeded the next day by the pugnacious Lloyd George, who had committed himself to the policy of the "knockout blow." It was indeed a most unpromising, if not desperate, outlook that the President was facing in the weeks that followed the election.

With these great problems of war and peace to solve— as serious as any in his administration—he was overwhelmed with the maddening, superficial, trivial interruptions which assail a newly elected President. He could not get away from "the things that have been gripping me so tight and so constantly."[1] Thousands of warm-hearted, if thoughtless, supporters, who had shared the "heat and dust of the battle," were rushing to Washington partly to offer their congratulations and partly to make sure they were remembered. Other thousands who were writing or telegraphing were prepared to be offended if they did not instantly receive personal replies. Innumerable decisions, delayed by the campaign, must now be met; cabinet members must be appointed or reappointed, important diplomats must be received, necessary secretarial places must be promptly filled. He must begin immediately the preparation of a most important annual message to Congress, which would assemble early in December.

---

[1] To Mrs. Sayre, October 16, 1916.

Worn out by the campaign, the President had been feeling for weeks the absolute need of a respite from his overwhelming burdens. He had begun to say as long ago as August that he was "greatly in need of rest,"[1] and his physician, Dr. Grayson, was now demanding it. Accordingly he seized upon the occasion of the christening of a grandchild recently arrived at the home of the Sayres at Williamstown, Massachusetts, for a brief vacation. It was a forlorn hope. Crowds greeted him everywhere: he had to make two speeches, and he returned to Washington utterly worn out. A few days later he was confessing that he had had a "bad night,"[2] and on November 23rd he was ill.

However merciless the strain upon the President, events would not wait. No one could tell at what moment some incident might fire the train of violence that would force us into war. Six days after the election Wilson made a desperate effort to get the time to consider the new peace move he had been contemplating. He pencilled a memorandum for Tumulty (November 13th):

"Please say to *all* that the President is so engrossed just now with business of the most pressing sort that it is not possible for him to make appointments unless the matter *cannot* be postponed."

He began at once to think and work upon a note to the belligerents, demanding that the war cease.[3] House, who had been summoned to Washington, urged delay—as usual —fearing that the Allies would consider a peace movement at that time an unfriendly act, but without shaking the President's determination to go forward as soon as possible. A few days later[4] we find Ambassador Bernstorff

---

[1] To Royal Meeker, August 21, 1916.

[2] *The Intimate Papers of Colonel House*, Vol. II, p. 392.

[3] *Ibid.*, pp. 390 *et seq.*, in which Colonel House gives an account of his conferences with the President.

[4] November 21, 1916.

reporting to Berlin that Wilson would move for peace "probably between now and the New Year."

"Wilson," added Bernstorff, on the basis of his conversations with House, "still hesitates to intervene . . . while House urges it strongly . . ."[1]—exactly the reverse of the real fact! As Berlin must have understood Wilson's attitude, based on such reports, there was extreme doubt as to whether he would act at all—hence the more reason to resume their unrestricted submarine policy— hence the more immediate likelihood of American involvement.

In the meantime the President was avidly seeking information from other sources. A report, November 21st,[2] indicated that war weariness was far advanced in France, both among civilians and the men in the trenches, but that owing to governmental espionage such views were well suppressed. The President replied:

". . . I am sure that it is probably very near to being an assessment of the actual facts. Human nature, after all, is the same everywhere and there are some things we can take for granted."[3]

Wilson was encouraged. In spite of House's most unfavourable reports of interviews with a member of the British Parliament[4] and a French publicist, he wrote on November 21st:

"Your letter about your interviews with Whitehouse, Carver, Bernstorff et al, has given me a great deal to think about . . . corroborating in some degree the impression I

---

[1]Bernstorff to his government, November 21, 1916. Bernstorff, *My Three Years in America*, p. 305. House also discussed with Bernstorff the rising crisis over submarine sinkings. "I told him," House reported to Wilson in a letter of November 20th, "that we were on the ragged edge, and brought to his mind the fact that no more notes could be exchanged, that the next move was to break off diplomatic relations."

[2]From John Palmer Gavit, of the New York *Evening Post*.

[3]November 22, 1916.

[4]J. H. Whitehouse, a Liberal and pacifist, said that a peace move then would be disastrous. "A military dictatorship would probably ensue . . ."

expressed to you, that this is very nearly the time, if not the time itself, for our move for peace. . . .

"I . . . am just about to sketch the paper . . . I will make the best haste I can consistent with my desire to make it the strongest and most convincing thing I ever penned."

The actual situation, however, was not encouraging. Northcliffe, powerful supporter of Lloyd George, wired the New York *Times:*

"The suggestion that Great Britain should consider peace can only be regarded as hostile. . . .

"There are no peace discussions in this country at all and there will be none while Germany occupies any portion of the Allied territory."[1]

Nor was the situation in Germany much better. Wilson himself considered the relations so "very unsatisfactory" that he replied to a query as to a possible American loan to certain German cities:

". . . convey to Kuhn, Loeb & Co. through Mr. Schiff, who would be sure of my personal friendship, the intimation that our relations with Germany are now in a very unsatisfactory and doubtful state, and that it would be most unwise at this time to risk a loan."[2]

The attitude of both belligerents, indeed, was most exasperating to the President. He directed House to "write to Lord Grey in the strongest terms" that the people of the United States were "growing more and more impatient with the intolerable conditions of neutrality, their feeling as hot against Great Britain as it was at first against Germany and likely to grow hotter still against an indefinite continuation of the war if no greater progress could be shown than now appears, either for the Allies or the Central Powers."

He felt so strongly upon this subject that he wanted

---

[1] November 23rd. New York *Times*, November 24, 1916.
[2] To House, November 24, 1916.

no softening of pressure by the intervention of Page, and suggested that it be intimated to Grey that "Page no longer represents the feeling or the point of view of the United States . . ."

Certainly a most astonishing statement from the head of a great state regarding his ambassador at the court of another!

"It might even be well," he added, "to intimate that we, in common with the other neutral nations, look upon the continuation of the war through another winter with the utmost distaste and misgiving."[1]

At this time, indeed, Wilson seemed to be far more irritated by the Allies than by the Germans. It was the Allies who were opposing any opening toward peace, while the Germans, however dubiously, seemed willing at least to begin talking. Bernstorff had received a confidential notice from Berlin, sent the 22nd, that the German government would, if the military situation justified it, "announce forthwith our willingness to enter upon peace negotiations."[2] A hint to Wilson that the German government itself was now preparing to move for peace on its own initiative would probably have hastened his own action, and thus have given it a more favourable hearing than it had later; but Bernstorff held to the letter of his instruction to keep silent.[3]

By the 25th, working against innumerable obstacles, and still not fully recovered from his illness, the President had completed a first draft of his proposed demand for peace:

"I think things are thickening and we should choose our course at once, if we have data enough to form a judgment on.

---

[1]House did not, so far as the author can discover, write such a letter.
[2]*Official German Documents*, Vol. II, p. 992.
[3]Bernstorff, *My Three Years in America*, p. 314.

"I am better. I hope that I had a clear head enough for the draft."[1]

Things were indeed thickening! The situation as it related to both belligerents was rapidly getting out of hand. He put it eloquently in the tentative draft of the note he was working upon, expressing not only his anxiety for America as a neutral nation, but that deeper anxiety, which had from the beginning inspired his programme of domestic reform—for the "poor" to whom his heart went out, who form "the bulk of mankind."

> The war is disturbing the whole life of the world, making it hard everywhere for governments to serve and safeguard the life of the nations they serve, and all but impossible for the poor to live at all (governments are for the poor if they are for the bulk of mankind)
> The war is making the task of neutrals impracticable, the position of neutrals intolerable.

It is important here, since the President was so unalterably determined, even against the urgings of some of his closest advisers, to make one last great effort for peace, to see exactly what conditions he was then having to face. It is important to see why he took no sides: assessed no blame: appealed alike to all the warring nations. To no other note or address of his entire career, perhaps, did he give more concentrated thought, a greater passion of earnestness: and in few was he able to rise more completely out of the turmoil of the time, to the serenity of a wholly objective view, and base his plea for peace upon fundamental principles. His nearest adviser might urge him to add something "which would make the Allies believe he sympathized with their viewpoint"[2]; he was determined to see and to set forth the situation with utter impartiality and candour.

---

[1] Wilson to House, November 25, 1916.

[2] House's diary entry. *The Intimate Papers of Colonel House*, Vol. II, p. 394.

While it is true that he was alarmed by the German attitude—the unrestrained violence of which cried from the housetops—he was not less worried by the British and French situation, little known either then (or since) to the public, but clearly understood by him in most of its complicated ramifications.

He expressed himself strongly again and again—at the very time that he was working on his note—regarding the German offenses. Both the Belgian deportations and the submarine sinkings had shocked the entire world:

". . . I feel that it has placed a new and very serious obstacle in the way of efforts looking towards peace which I had hoped . . . [would] soon be made and which I was anxiously seeking an opportunity to make."[1]

Grew in Berlin was directed to inform the German government of this fact and to point out also that ". . . the President . . . has been repeatedly distressed to have his hopes frustrated and his occasion destroyed by such unhappy incidents as the sinking of the *Marina* and the *Arabia* . . ."[2]

His entire conversation with Gerard at the White House, November 29th, was concerned with the gravity of the German situation.

"The President said that he did not think our people wanted war and that he would do everything possible as long as our national honor was preserved to keep us out of war. He said also, and quite truly, that the Germans did not seem to appreciate the power of the United States and the warlike character of the people once aroused."[3]

But it is clear from a study of the documents that the President was giving even more concentrated attention to the economic and financial pressure which the Allies were,

---

[1]Wilson to Lansing, November 26, 1916.
[2]Lansing to Chargé Grew, November 29th. *Foreign Relations*, 1916, Supp., p. 71.
[3]Memorandum written by Gerard for the author.

during the feverish weeks that followed the election, bringing to bear upon the United States. These are customarily dull subjects, not as spectacular as submarine outrages, not easily understood by the public, but of enormous potency in affecting the destiny of the world.

Only three weeks before the election the British Chancellor of the Exchequer displayed the bare bones of the situation when he declared (October 19th) that the British would need to spend nearly $10,000,000 daily, for every working day, for their purchases in America.[1]

Wilson had already been concerned with this developing situation and had referred to it repeatedly in his campaign speeches. Two billion dollars' worth of foreign-owned American securities, he told the people of Cincinnati,[2] had been brought back to America; in two years we had accumulated one third of the entire supply of gold in the world—and the trend was still sharply upward.

He felt acutely the tremendous new power of the American people—and his own responsibility as their leader:

"We can determine to a large extent who is to be financed and who is not to be financed."[3]

Lloyd George conceded the accuracy of this statement in a memorandum prepared early in November 1916:

"Our dependence upon America is growing for food, raw material and munitions. We are rapidly exhausting the securities negotiable in America. . . . The problem of finance is the problem of victory . . ."[4]

This extraordinary situation, coming to a head just after the election, also had disquieting repercussions at home. Allied demand for our goods was increasing costs of

[1]New York *Times*, October 20, 1916.
[2]October 26, 1916. *The Public Papers of Woodrow Wilson*, Vol. IV, p. 379.
[3]Speech at Shadow Lawn, November 4, 1916. *Ibid.*, p. 391.
[4]*War Memoirs of David Lloyd George*, Vol. II, p. 340.

living so rapidly that on November 14th the President was considering an investigation, which he later ordered.[1] At the same time, the heavy return flow of gold and securities into the United States was creating risks of instability and inflation. More and more the money of American banks began to be tied up in secured but long-term loans to the Allies.[2]

In November, however, the British were reaching the end of their ready resources. What they now demanded was an unsecured loan—that is, a loan not backed by gold or pledged securities, but based upon government credit only, such as the Anglo-French loan of October 1915.[3] New York bankers were loath to make such loans, but they feared that unless the British could be thus financed their expenditures in America would rapidly drop off— as the Chancellor of the Exchequer plainly declared on November 23rd.[4] This would necessarily work havoc with American industry and finance, by now far more closely dependent upon the Allies' purchasing than a year before when imperious economic requirements had been strong enough to alter Wilson's loan policy.[5]

In these circumstances, J. P. Morgan & Company devised a new plan for financing the Allies: renewable short-term treasury notes of the British and French governments. Renewable! That practically eliminated the short-term aspect. And treasury notes! Notes of a government

[1]For Wilson's address on the responsibility of the middlemen for the condition, November 14, 1916, see *The Public Papers of Woodrow Wilson*, Vol. IV, pp. 396–399. See also Wilson to W. J. Harris, chairman of the Federal Trade Commission, February 7, 1917.

[2]From August through November $550,000,000 to the British; $100,000,000 to Canada; $50,000,000 to the city of Paris; $36,000,000 to Bordeaux, Marseilles, and Lyons. *Hearings, Senate Munitions Investigation*, 74–2, Pt. 28, p. 8708.

[3]See *Woodrow Wilson, Life and Letters*, Vol. V, *Neutrality*, pp. 380–383.

[4]Morgan Grenfell & Company to H. P. Davison, November 23, 1916. *Hearings, Senate Munitions Investigation*, 74–2, Pt. 28, p. 8725.

[5]*Ibid.*, pp. 8732–8733; and *cf. Woodrow Wilson, Life and Letters*, Vol. V, *Neutrality*, pp. 380–383.

and therefore not secured.[1] In effect it was a plan involving unsecured long-term loans, with no set limit to the amount: a half-billion, a billion!

The President, who had become much concerned, conferred on the 18th with H. P. Davison, of the Morgan firm. He was altogether cordial, so much so that Davison thought him even a little encouraging; nevertheless the banker left Washington without gaining real hope "for easy future financing."[2] The President asked him during their conference for information on the external debts of Great Britain and France. He learned from Davison's letter a week later that Great Britain's had risen to about 7 per cent of her total indebtedness, and France's to 7.8 per cent of the entire obligations of the French Republic, including those of the Bank of France! These percentages were "higher than I had supposed," the banker admitted.[3]

Meantime, on November 25th, just as he was completing the first draft of his peace note, Wilson had informed himself of the attitude of the Federal Reserve Board in an interview with W. P. G. Harding.[4] He found the members anxious to give out some warning against financing by treasury notes, fearing the danger of becoming so deeply involved with Great Britain that we could no longer command our own affairs.[5] In a statement prepared for the press, the board advised that members of the Federal

---

[1]A treasury note of the British government had behind it, of course, the usually solid credit of that government; but in 1916 that government was risking the gamble of a desperate war.

[2]Davison conferred the same day with the Federal Reserve Board. (Davison to J. P. Morgan, in London, November 20, 1916. *Hearings, Senate Munitions Investigation*, 74-2, Pt. 28, p. 8730.) Davison defended their plan as checking the dangerous flow of gold into the United States and as maintaining our advance to a position of financial dominance.

[3]H. P. Davison to Wilson, November 25, 1916.

[4]Governor of the board. Diary of C. S. Hamlin, of the board, November 25, 1916. *Senate Reports*, 74-2, No. 944, Pt. 5, p. 206.

[5]Warburg to Benjamin Strong, November 23, 1916. *Hearings, Senate Munitions Investigation*, 74-2, Pt. 28, pp. 8732-8733.

Reserve System "should pursue a policy of keeping themselves liquid; of not loaning down to the legal limit, but of maintaining an excess of reserves . . . banks should proceed with much caution in locking up their funds in long-term obligations or in investments which are short term in form . . . but which, either by contract or through force of circumstances, may . . . have to be renewed until normal conditions return."[1]

Wilson was not only in full agreement with this policy, but after thinking the matter over, and reading Davison's report, he wrote to Harding that the proposed warning was "not strong enough." It would be "very embarrassing to have banks invest in this kind of security, if there should be any change in our foreign policy."[2] He offered two suggestions for sharpening the warning; advising that it was not "in the interest of the country at this time" for banks to invest in foreign treasury bills of this character, and that the private investor "should receive full and authoritative data—particularly in the case of unsecured loans—in order that he may judge the future intelligently in the light of present conditions and in conjunction with the economic developments of the past."[3] A hard-hitting blow!

Both the President and the board understood thoroughly that this "slowing down" of credit extensions might curtail "our abnormally stimulated export trade to certain countries." But if the Allies wanted loans, let them put up for collateral the "hundreds of millions of our own and foreign securities" which they still held. If they did not wish to do this—as the Chancellor of the Ex-

---

[1] Copy given to the President by Harding on November 25th.

[2] Hamlin diary entry, November 27, 1916. *Senate Reports*, 74–2, No. 944, Pt. 5, p. 207. The President told Harding on the 25th that "our relations with England were more strained than with Germany." Hamlin diary, November 30, 1916. *Ibid.*

[3] Statement made public November 27, 1916, by the Federal Reserve Board. The President's suggestions are underlined in the copy which remains in his files.

chequer had made plain—"trade can be stimulated in other directions." In any case our present financial strength must be kept unimpaired: the world would have to be rehabilitated after the war, and our banks must be constantly ready to meet our home requirements, the "scope of which none can foresee."[1]

New York bankers saw in this statement "the most serious financial development in this country since the outbreak of the war and one likely to be of far-reaching consequence."[2] Foreign bonds sagged on the market, British exchange dropped so far on the 28th that the Morgan company had to buy nearly $20,000,000 of sterling to keep the price from slumping to a danger point.[3] On November 29th the Chancellor of the British Exchequer declared he did not wish to disregard the warning, and asked that no treasury bills be issued.[4] Henceforth the British must ship gold to pay for their purchases, or borrow on secured loans.[5] Wilson was pleased with this result:

"The developments which have come from the statement of the Board have certainly been most interesting and I shall watch their progress with the keenest interest."[6]

---

[1]Statement made public November 27, 1916, by the Federal Reserve Board.

[2]J. P. Morgan & Co. to Morgan Grenfell & Co., London, November 28, 1916. *Hearings, Senate Munitions Investigation*, 74–2, Pt. 28, p. 8738.

[3]*Ibid.*, p. 8739.

[4]Morgan Grenfell & Co. to J. P. Morgan & Co., November 29, 1916. *Ibid.*, p. 8742.

[5]The next secured loan was for $250,000,000, made late in January 1917 to the United Kingdom. The second and last was a secured loan of $100,000,000 to the French government. (From information supplied by Thomas W. Lamont.)

[6]Wilson to W. P. G. Harding, December 5, 1916. Although the statement had not reflected upon the credit of the Allies, M. Jusserand, the French ambassador, hurried in excitement, on December 3rd, to complain to Colonel House, who suggested that Jusserand cable his government, among other things, "that we were trying to undo the harm which the Federal Reserve Board has done regarding their credits." House diary entry, December 3, 1916. *Hearings, Senate Munitions Investigation*, 74–2, Pt. 28, p. 8750. The "we" could have had no reference to the President, who had not corresponded with Colonel House on the financial situation. House's letter to Wilson, December 4th, telling of the interview with Jusserand, said on this point merely this: "He was excited over the action of the Federal Reserve Board. I tried to smooth it over." (Original letter. This excerpt is omitted, with indication, in *The Intimate Papers of Colonel House*, Vol. II, p. 396.)

But the actual crisis, if delayed, still persisted; it was indeed sharpened, so far as the British were concerned, by poor harvests and heavy losses of ships by German submarine attacks.[1] It was only a question of months, probably only of weeks, before the problem would again present itself with renewed coercive force. The British could not keep on indefinitely spending $10,000,000 a day for American goods; when their gold was gone and all the American securities sent home, what next? The British would probably have to sell or pledge their very industrial empire to American bankers in the form of stocks and bonds of British factories: and beyond that, since the complicated economic structure of the United States would then rest still more heavily upon Allied purchases, might there not be widespread bankruptcy in America? All these were threatening possibilities unless peace came promptly, or the United States entered the war.

But Wilson did not want war with any nation; and was indignant at the inexorable forces which were beginning to make war seem inevitable—on the one side, the rising emotions of the American people (his own included), and on the other, the unrelenting pressure of economic compulsion. It is small wonder that Wilson exclaimed in the introduction to the peace note he was now drafting that the "position of neutrals" was becoming "intolerable."

He had toiled mightily on the preliminary memorandum for his note to the Powers. The writer has before him the bulky folder containing the documentary material upon which he worked—expressive evidence of his care and thoroughness. Here are magazine and newspaper articles, clippings of editorials, flimsies of dispatches, selections from the speeches of the leading foreign statesmen, and

---

[1]*War Memoirs of David Lloyd George*, Vol. III, pp. 44–48. The President of the British Board of Trade concluded on November 10th that a complete breakdown in British shipping would come before June 1917. *Ibid.*, Vol. II, p. 374.

his own memoranda and notes.[1] These papers were mostly concerned with the attitude of public opinion at home and abroad; beneath them, of course, the solid foundation for his new project, lay his own comprehensive knowledge— supported by innumerable documents—of the problems of the war itself. In short he knew well the dominant economic and emotional forces (already referred to), and he had before him a more complete picture of the diplomatic situation, possibly, than any other living statesman, because he himself at every step had played such an important part in it.

He read his proposed draft aloud to House on November 27th. He had written it out first in shorthand, on sheets of paper $5\frac{1}{2}$ x 8 in size, and then typed it out on his own typewriter on the other side of the sheets. He had added comments in shorthand here and there on the margins. The document itself, having never before been published, is so important, reveals so clearly the actual original thought of the President in this time of crisis, that it is here presented in full:[2]

Reasons why I have the right to speak:
The war is disturbing the whole life of the world, making it hard everywhere for governments to serve and safeguard the life of the nations they serve, and all but impossible for the poor to live at all (governments are for the poor if they are for the bulk of mankind)
The war is making the task of neutrals impracticable, the position of neutrals intolerable.

---

[1]An editorial from the *New Republic*, November 25, 1916, was studied with especial care, and those sentences underlined which declared that public opinion in neutral and in belligerent countries alike needed to know "the precise nature of the political objects" for which each of the belligerents would insist upon continuing the war, and whether or not the readiness of the United States "to participate on certain express terms in the waging of war or in the structure of peace will serve to appease the apparent irreconcilability of the attitude of the belligerents."

[2]Bracketed words and sentences in these notes were crossed out by the President himself.

The character to which the war has settled down: a war of exhaustion and attrition, and the result to be expected.

The professions of each side: that they do not desire conquest or the destruction of their antagonists: that they wish to safeguard the rights of small nations and of peoples: that they desire to end war (which cannot be done by conquest or destruction of nationalities)

The danger that the whole future will be prejudiced.

> A common object has been professed by the leaders of the governments at war, viz. such a league to enforce peace as will make the future secure.

> The United States is willing to lend its whole force of every kind to that end, with equal resolution and enthusiasm.

> A little while and it may be too late to realize this object, because of exhaustion and *reaction*.

> Triumph and hate cannot accomplish it.

In such circumstances and in the interest not only of all concerned directly in the war itself, of the whole world, rather, I feel that I have the right, with the utmost respect for the rights of all, to call for a parley, [without even a suggestion of terms of peace, which, probably only the belligerents have the right to name.]

My objects:

To stop the war before it is too late to remedy what it has done;

> To reconsider peace on the basis of the rights of the weak along with the rights of the strong, the rights of peoples as well as the rights of governments;

> To effect a league of nations based upon a peace which shall be guaranteed against breach by the common force and an intelligent organization of the common interest.

I take the liberty of addressing to you very frankly certain questions which seem to speak out almost of themselves from the circumstances and present progress of the war and of which I feel justified in making myself the spokesman not only because I am privileged to speak as the head of a great nation whose vital interests are being more and more seriously and profoundly affected with each week of the war's continuance but also because both my heart and my reason tell me that the time has come to take counsel lest a violence be done civilization itself which cannot be atoned for or repaired.

In every quarter of the world the life of mankind has been altered and disturbed. Everywhere it is hindered and perplexed, rendered harder, more hazardous, more difficult to plan or to live upon any terms. The task of every government, the task of caring for and promoting the interests of its own people, has been hampered and impeded, and the burden falls, as always, upon those least prepared, least able to bear it.

The position of neutral nations, in particular, has been rendered all but intolerable. Their commerce is [hampered] interrupted, their industries are checked and diverted, the lives of their people are put in constant jeopardy, they are virtually forbidden the accustomed highways of the sea, their energies are drawn off into temporary and novel channels, they suffer at every turn though disengaged and disposed to none but friendly and impartial offices.

And yet [the reasons for this upheaval of the world remain obscure, and] the objects which would, if attained, satisfy the one group of belligerents or the other have never been definitely avowed. [As it is not known what motives led to the war's sudden outbreak so it is not known, the] The world can still only conjecture what definitive results, what actual exchange of guarantees, what political readjustments or changes, what stage or degree of military success even, would bring it to an end. If any other nation now neutral should be drawn in, it would know only that it was [forced] drawn in by some force it could not resist, because it had been hurt and saw no remedy but to risk still greater, it might be even irreparable, injury, in order to make the weight in the one scale or the other decisive; and even as a participant it would not know how far the scales must tip before the end would come or what was being weighed in the balance!

Authoritative spokesmen of the nations engaged have, indeed, spoken [very definitely] in general terms of the issues involved; [They are fighting, they have declared, to be quit of aggression and of peril to the free and independent course of their peoples' lives.] but they have nowhere, so far as I know, made any definite statement of the measures which would in their judgment bring those issues to a practical settlement.

Reasons why I have the right to speak:

The war is disturbing the whole life of the
world, making it hard everywhere for
governments to serve and safeguard the
life of the nations they serve, and all
but impossible for the poor to live at
all (governments are for the poor if they
are for the bulk of mankind)

The war is making the task of neutrals impracticable, the position of neutrals intolerable.

The character to which the war has settled
down: a war of exhaustion and attrition,
and the reslt to be expected.

The professions of each side: that they do not
desire conquest or the destruction of their
antagonists: that they wish to safeguard
the rights of small nations and of peoples:
that they desire to end war (which cannot
be done by conquest or destruction of nationalities)

The danger that the whole future will be prejudiced.

A common object has been professed by the
leaders of the governments at war, viz.
such a league to enforce peace as will

First page of one of President Wilson's preliminary drafts of his
message to the belligerent nations, asking for their peace terms,
finally sent on December 18, 1916. It was written first on his own
typewriter and then corrected in his own shorthand notes.

Whatever may have brought the war on, they believe the very life and political integrity of the nations they represent to be involved. They are fighting, they have declared, to be quit of aggression and of peril to the free and independent [course] development of their peoples' lives and fortunes. They feel that they must push the conflict to a conclusion in order to make themselves secure in the future against its renewal and against the rivalries and ambitions which brought it about. But to what conclusion? These are very general terms. What sort of ending, what sort of settlement, what kind of guarantees will in their conception constitute a satisfactory outcome, promising some prospect of permanency and safety?

Leaders on both sides have declared very earnestly and in terms whose sincerity no one can justly doubt that it was no part of their wish or purpose to crush their antagonists, make conquest of their territories or possessions, deprive them of their equal place and opportunity among the great peoples of the world. They have declared also that they are fighting no less for the rights of small and weak nations and peoples than for those of the great and powerful states immediately involved. They have declared their desire for peace, but for a peace that will last, a peace based, not upon the uncertain balance of powerful alliances offset against one another, but upon guarantees in which the whole civilized world would join, that the rights and privileges of every nation and people should be the common and definite obligation of all governments.

With these objects the people and government of the United States whole-heartedly sympathize. //[1] and they are struck by the circumstance that, stated in the general terms in which they have been stated, they are the same,—are the same even in specific detail, as, for example, the security of all nations alike, whether they be weak or strong, against aggression and competitive force. We ⟍ [They] are ready to join [any] a league of nations that will pledge itself to their accomplishment and definitely unite in an organization not only of purpose but of force as well that will be adequate to assure their realization. They are ready to lend their every resource, whether of men or money or substance to such a combination, so purposed and organized. If that be the object of the present war, they are

---

[1]Passages marked by // ⟍ added by Wilson to the original draft.

ready when the right moment comes to cooperate to bring it about. But how are they to know when that moment comes unless they be apprised by what test the nations now at war will judge the time of settlement and definition to have come? What must constitute victory by the one side or the other, and what must that victory mean?

The conflict moves very sluggishly. Only upon one or two separated fields here and there do armies move with definite success. Along the main lines of battle, so far as we can judge, there can be no rapid change, until ——? Must the contest be decided by slow attrition and ultimate exhaustion, the slow expenditure to millions of human lives until there are no more to offer up on the one side or the other? Triumph so gained might defeat the very ends for which it had been desired. Upon a triumph which overwhelms and humiliates cannot be laid the foundations of peace and equality and good will. A little while and it may be too late to realize the hopes which all men who love peace and justice entertain and which all statesmen must see to be the only hopes worthy to serve as the motive of great and permanent plans for mankind. Exhaustion, reaction, political upheaval, a resentment that can never cool would make such hopes vain and idle. An irreparable damage to civilization cannot promote peace and the secure happiness of the world.

In such circumstances and moved by such considerations, I deem myself to be clearly within my right as the representative of a great neutral nation whose interests are being daily affected and as the friend of all the nations engaged in the present struggle, and speaking with the utmost respect for the rights of all concerned, in urging, as I do most earnestly urge, that some means be immediately taken, whether by conference or by a separate formulation of demands and conditions, to define the terms upon which a settlement of the issues of the war may be expected. It has become necessary that the nations that are now neutral should have some certain and definite guide for their future policy. It is necessary that they should have some certain means of determining what part they shall henceforth play should the terms defined be impossible of realization and the end of the war be indefinitely postponed.

The simplest means of arriving at this end would be a con-

ference of representatives of the belligerent governments and
of the governments not now engaged in the war whose interests
may be thought to be most directly involved, and it is such a
conference that I take the liberty of urging, whatever its outcome
may be. If that be not feasible, it is possible that other means
may be found which will in effect accomplish the same result.

My object, my sole object, in pressing this essential issue
now is to assist, if I may, in bringing the war to an end before
it is too late to remedy what it has done; to bring about an
early reconsideration of peace on the basis of the rights alike of
the weak and of the strong, the rights of peoples as well as of
governments; and to afford an opportunity to form such a
league of nations as all now desire, a league united and powerful
enough in force and purpose to guarantee the peace of the
world against further breach by injustice or aggression,—
guarantee it by the sheer [force] might of an intelligent and
irresistible organization of the major force of mankind in the
common interest of civilization.

Let me say, in order that there may be no danger of any
misunderstanding, that I am not renewing or seeking to press
my offer of mediation made at the outset of the war. I then
expressed my desire to be of service to the belligerents by any
offices of accommodation looking towards an end of the contest
that they might any of them suggest or encourage; and that
offer of course stands. But I am not now returning to that.
Neither am I proposing peace. I am doing a very simple, a
very practical, and a very different thing. I am asking, and
assuming that I have the right to ask, for a concrete definition
of the guarantees which the belligerents on the one side and
the other deem it their duty to demand as a practical satisfaction of the objects they are aiming at in this contest of force,
in addition to the very great and substantial guarantee which
will, I feel perfectly confident, be supplied by a league of nations
formed to unite their force in active cooperation for the preservation of the world's peace when this war is over. To answer
these questions need not commit any belligerent to peace at
this time; but until they are answered no influential nation
of the world not yet involved in the struggle can intelligently
determine its future course of action. The United States feels
that it can no longer delay to determine its own.

No one with any knowledge of the crisis that then existed can read this note in its original form, before it had been whittled down by the fears and sympathies of his advisers, without regarding it as one of the strongest papers Wilson ever wrote. It expressed in terms of consummate statesmanship a feasible way out of the misery the world was suffering—but it was unfortunately addressed to reasonable human beings, when reasonable human beings had momentarily disappeared from off the earth. What could have been more sensible than to ask the fighters to stop for a moment, discuss what the war was all about, and define what each wanted as the price of peace?

The President's friend House expressed admiration—then doubt. He objected to the clause that "the reasons for this upheaval of the world remain obscure."[1] The Allies were certain, he said, that they had made those reasons crystal clear; they would be angered. Very true, they would be. The President struck out that clause and another similar to it. House next urged him to add something "which would make the Allies believe he sympathized with their viewpoint." The document itself shows that Wilson refused. Then, again, in order not to offend the Allies, House suggested adding a statement saying that the President was not offering mediation, and not demanding peace. Wilson at last agreed to make this great alteration; although we have no record of the arguments leading him to do so.[2]

It is plain that the President's original purpose was to demand a definition of terms, preferably in a conference. As a result of his talks with House and Lansing, and his own reconsideration of the difficult situation in Europe at

[1] This clause was rendered somewhat differently in House's diary notation. *The Intimate Papers of Colonel House*, Vol. II, p. 394.

[2] This first draft may be compared with the final note, published in *Foreign Relations*, 1916, Supp., pp. 97–99.

that moment, the emphasis of the note was toned down to a mere request for terms. Some of his advisers thought he was even then going too far—and he himself, reconsidering the passionate unreasonableness on both sides, knew that if he asked too much he would get nothing, except the abuse that is often the only reward of the peacemaker.

Moreover, his closest advisers were constantly urging delay. House wrote to him on November 30th:

"I have been thinking a lot of your proposed note to the belligerents and I cannot bring myself to believe that it should be done immediately or without further preparation. . . .

". . . if you do not act too hastily you can bring about the desired result. If you do it now there does not seem to me one chance in ten of success and you will probably lose your potential position for doing it later."[1]

And Lansing, to whom Wilson submitted a draft of the note on December 1st, damned it with faint praise: it was "far less objectionable than the one originally proposed."[2]

The delay may or may not have been unfortunate— probably any peace move at that time had become hopeless—but this we know, that the situation, instead of improving, grew steadily worse.

On December 2nd the President went to New York to deliver an address on the occasion of the illumination of the Statue of Liberty in New York harbour. The popular ovation accorded him gave renewed evidence, if any was necessary, of the eager acceptance of his leadership. Booming guns, the cheering thousands that lined the walls of the Battery as the *Mayflower* steamed down the harbour, might well have satisfied a more ambitious leader

---

[1]Original in Mr. Wilson's files. Only a few days later Bernstorff, who had just been to see House, reported to his government: ". . . House is continually urging Mr. Wilson to take action." December 4, 1916. *War Memoirs of Robert Lansing*, p. 179; *cf.* also paraphrased report. Bernstorff, *My Three Years in America*, pp. 308–309.

[2]*War Memoirs of Robert Lansing*, p. 178. This draft is not in Mr. Wilson's files.

than Wilson if he had not been weighed down with a heavy sense of the gathering woes of the world and his own special responsibility in meeting them. His address that evening gave a sobering sense of the penetration of his thought, probing those fundamental truths which lie deeper even than statesmanship—words of eternal purport:

"The peace of the world is not going to be assured by the compact of nations, but by the sympathies of men."

". . . peace is going to come to the world only with Liberty."

". . . peace cannot come so long as the destinies of men are determined by small groups who make selfish choices of their own."[1]

It is forever the problem of the idealist, however clearly he may see the ultimate truth, to act so that his action counts in a bitterly practical and selfish world. How puny must his utmost efforts for peace have seemed to Wilson, when he knew, deep down, that where there is no sympathy there can be no peace, where there is no liberty there can be no peace, where civilization is dominated by selfish groups there can be no peace.

It was in meeting and dealing with problems such as these, that go down to the roots of human life, that Wilson differed from Bryan. Wilson was as great an idealist as Bryan: he was a far greater statesman.

It is perhaps unfortunate that after Bryan's resignation Wilson had no adviser near him who was *primarily* an idealist—there was more than a sufficiency of those who were not. Again and again, however, even after Bryan had left him, we find Wilson watching him narrowly, listening to what he was saying, for he knew well how profound were the Commoner's instincts for those deeper truths that are often so potent in dominating human

[1] New York *Times*, December 4, 1916.

action. He himself agreed fundamentally with Bryan: his most effective appeals to the people were based upon ideals common to both of them.

It is a singular thing, then, that at this very juncture, when Wilson was deeply in doubt, not as to what he thought, but as to what he should do, that Bryan should step suddenly into the picture. Not indeed in person, but in the low-voiced confidences of Ambassador Gerard, who stood beside him on the bridge of the *Mayflower* as they steamed down the harbour. Gerard, plainly disturbed, even alarmed, told the President that Bryan was about to launch a peace movement on his own account. While it was fantastic in its details, scarcely worthy of serious consideration, Wilson knew what lay behind it, knew also what a powerful hold Bryan had upon the American people. He thought aloud in a memorandum for Colonel House, written the next day:[1]

"One of the reasons why early action is necessary is W.J.B. Gerard told me yesterday: 1. that W.J.B. was intent (as you already know) on going abroad to fix the whole matter up himself and wanted him (Gerard) to prepare the way for him by getting the consent of the Kaiser and the men at the Foreign Office to see him. I instructed Gerard to do nothing of the kind; but simply to show him every courtesy if he came but let it be distinctly understood that he represented nobody but himself.

"2) That W.J.B. had told him in a previous interview that he was going actively to oppose me in this country if I showed any signs of breaking off diplomatic relations with Germany.[2]

"3) that he had (I think most indiscreetly) told W.J.B. (in a later interview) that he could not consistently oppose

---

[1]December 3, 1916.

[2]As a matter of fact, when this country went to war with Germany four months later, Bryan was one of the earliest to telegraph assurances of his support to the President.

me if I merely insisted on knowing what they were fighting for, showing W.J.B. a declaration of that very policy in the COMMONER; and that it was evident that W.J.B. took to a renewal of that line of action very quickly and would probably make it the basis of his own mediation. I did not gather that he actually told W.J.B. what I had in mind; but that he must have made it easy to guess that I had talked to him along those lines. . . .

"Mr. B. told him that he would 'expect' to be the peace commissioner if any were at any time appointed by me; but that, whether a commissioner or not, he would go and act as he thought best,—substantially what he said to you."

In the same letter the President responded to House's letter of November 30th in which House had advised him to delay his peace move:

"The situation is developing very fast and if we are going to do the proposed thing effectively we must do it very soon. . . .

"Gerard hopes that I will do what we discussed, and do it at once, and thinks, with us, that it is not what Germany wishes and not what either side could object to or decently decline if done in the terms I suggested,—as a neutral demand."

In short, the President was still as strongly determined as ever to send his proposed note, but still doubtful as to the right occasion. A week later a most unexpected event occurred, which was to affect, profoundly, Wilson's plans. This was a peace proposal on the part of the German government itself, news of which reached Washington on December 12th. The Germans were prepared, now that they occupied an advantageous military position, to talk peace.[1]

In making his offer Bethmann-Hollweg argued that if

[1]Berlin had, however, decided upon it on the 9th. Bucharest had fallen three days earlier and the military situation was, in appearance at least, favourable to the vic-

Wilson should make an immediate peace move, Germany would "have two irons in the fire."[1] While he refused to admit that the President's proposals would be impaired by the German offer, they were in reality robbed of that initiative and unembarrassed neutrality which Wilson needed to secure a fair hearing from the Allies.[2]

Americans in general were in doubt how to appraise the German offer. Some were skeptical of its sincerity. Some thought Germany was admitting that she could not win. Others were hopeful that the ice had been broken.[3]

The comment of spokesmen of the Allied powers regarding the German offer, even before they had been formally notified, was one of furious rejection. Page wired that British public opinion held the language and tone of the offer to be "insulting because of its boastfulness and its threat"; the proposal an indication of weakness and economic strain; the whole unworthy of consideration until

---

torious armies of the Central Powers. So far as the German government knew at that time, from Bernstorff's misleading reports after his conversations with House, Wilson could not be persuaded to make his proposed move because of such obstacles as Belgian deportations and submarine incidents. Lansing also mentioned these obstacles, as has been seen. *Official German Documents*, Vol. II, pp. 1053-1073.

[1]Bernstorff, *My Three Years in America*, p. 311.

[2]The German offer simply suggested negotiations. No terms were declared. The four Central Powers felt "sure that the propositions which they would bring forward and which would aim to assure the existence, honor, and free development of their peoples, would be such as to serve as a basis for the restoration of a lasting peace." But this assurance was embedded in a mass of arrogant affirmations of the purely defensive character of their aims, the invincibility of their armed forces, and their determination, in case their offer was refused, to fight on "to a victorious end." *Foreign Relations*, 1916, Supp., p. 94. Bethmann-Hollweg himself later admitted that this wording was harmful to the success of the note. It was "due to our anxiety on the point of giving an appearance of weakness . . ." *Official German Documents*, Vol. I, p. 335. The Kaiser aggravated the damage done by a speech to his troops in Alsace, December 13th: "In the conviction that we are the absolute conquerors," he had proposed negotiations. If the enemy "still think that they have not had enough, this much I know, that you" —and here the Emperor stopped, according to the German account, "with a soldierly turn which brought out a grim smile on the faces of the soldiers." The Kaiser also twitted the British in a reference to wheat bought by the British and captured recently: "The English have paid for it, we are eating it, and that is what they call a war of starvation." *Official German Documents*, Vol. I, pp. 420-421; Vol. II, p. 1077; New York *Times*, December 16, 1916.

[3]*Cf.* press comment, New York *Times*, December 13, 1916.

definite terms were put forward. It might be an attempt to "prepare an excuse for further deliberate frightfulness."[1]

"The Russian Government repudiates with indignation the mere idea of suspending the struggle . . ."[2]

Briand, of France, speaking in the Chamber of Deputies, placed his country "on guard against possible poisoning." "Take care!"[3]

Baron Sonnino, of Italy, left the door to negotiation slightly ajar.[4] Lloyd George brusquely closed it, but without finality.

"We must keep a steadfast eye on the purpose for which we entered the war. . . .

"We will . . . wait until we hear what terms and guarantees the German Government offers . . . Meanwhile we ought to put our trust in an unbroken army rather than in a broken faith."[5]

The sum of the Allies' spontaneous answers to Germany was, "No!"

As for Germany, Grew reported that the "reception of Germany's peace offer in the [German] press is in general favorable," though Pan-Germanist papers expressed "misgivings" because no precise statement of peace terms had been made.[6]

Wilson was himself at first much disturbed by the German move. His second reactions were on the whole favourable. He said, in a draft of a communication to Grew at Berlin, that the government of the United States would "very cheerfully" transmit the note, and that it "wel-

---

[1]Page to the Secretary of State, December 15, 1916. *Foreign Relations*, 1916, Supp., pp. 92–93.

[2]December 15, 1916. *Current History*, Vol. V (January 1917), pp. 590–591.

[3]December 12, 1916. *Ibid.*, p. 590.

[4]December 19, 1916. *Ibid.*, pp. 591–592.

[5]December 19, 1916. *Ibid.*, p. 594.

[6]Grew to the Secretary of State, December 13, 1916. *Foreign Relations*, 1916, Supp., p. 91; Stovall to the Secretary of State, December 14, 1916, copy in Mr. Wilson's files.

comes this expression of the willingness of the Imperial German Government to discuss terms of peace . . ."[1] His early draft of a letter to the American ambassadors who were to communicate the German note to the Allied nations spoke of the offer as "a very welcome surprise because it seems to . . . promise at least a beginning of interchanges of view . . ."[2]

But his final feeling was that the offer really embarrassed him in making his proposals for peace,[3] for it served to bring out and solidify the uncompromising position of the Allies who now had their backs to the wall: their resources dwindling, war costs rising, and the Russian Premier, according to common report, negotiating for a separate peace. Disruption of the Entente even seemed possible. In such a crisis France and Great Britain stiffened in the face of threatened disaster; what might superficially have seemed favourable to a peace discussion actually bred a grim determination to go on with the war.

On the other hand, there was undoubtedly great war weariness in both England and France. As Charles Trevelyan wrote to the President, there was a "yearning for a great solution" to the war, for a moderate peace based on international coöperation—and a weariness with fighting as a way to get it. Wilson was the hope of those who desired this.[4] And J. H. Whitehouse reasoned that fear of radical reform would unite the divided opponents of Lloyd George—moderates in Parliament and the country—and thus create a favourable opportunity for action by the President.[5] Wilson was encouraged at this prospect:

---

[1]Draft on Wilson's own typewriter, undated, presumably December 14th.

[2]Tentative draft on Wilson's own typewriter, undated, presumably December 14th.

[3]See the President's note to the Allies, December 18, 1916. *Foreign Relations*, 1916, Supp., p. 98.

[4]November 23, 1916.

[5]Memorandum written by Whitehouse, and transmitted to the President by House, December 7, 1916.

"That was a most impressive letter from Mr. Trevelyan, —and a most interesting memorandum from Mr. White-house. The time is near at hand for *something!*"[1]

The assembly of Congress on December 4th and the necessity of completing and delivering his annual address caused still further delay.

"Members of Congress have been sucking the life out of me, about appointments and other matters affecting the destiny of the world, and I have been prevented from per-fecting the document. I shall go out of town (on the MAYFLOWER no doubt) for the purpose, if it can be done in no other way."[2]

Lansing was again demanding that relationships with Germany be broken. Merchant vessels were being sunk without warning: we must "live up to" the first *Sussex* note:

"Delay, in my opinion, will accomplish no ultimate good, as there seems to be a very definite determination on the part of the German Government to make submarine warfare more effective by pursuing more reckless methods, which I am convinced will increase as more submarines are launched."[3]

However, no advice on House's part to delay his peace offer or, on Lansing's, not to delay breaking relations, seems to have made any impression on Wilson. The next day he sent Lansing a revised draft of his proposed note:

"Here is the demand for definitions. I would be very much obliged if you would give me your detailed criticism of it . . .

"I think that the time is at hand for something of this kind . . . Affairs may disclose it at any moment."[4]

---

[1] Wilson to House, December 8, 1916.
[2] *Ibid.*
[3] To Wilson, December 8, 1916.
[4] Letter written on the President's own typewriter.

The emphasis had now been altered fundamentally. The note no longer proposed a conference between the belligerents themselves; each belligerent was simply asked "to define" its terms. Consequently the note was gravely weakened; either belligerent could make a reply differing but little from the statements of terms which Wilson had already said were unsatisfactory. Yet, there was a possibility that it would find an opening in the belligerents' armour, perhaps through a discussion of Wilson's league of nations as the basis for future security.

Lansing wrote to the President after reading it:

"We cannot continue much longer to attempt by peaceable means to secure our rights. We are certainly drifting nearer and nearer . . .

". . . it is probably the only step which can be taken offering a possible way to prevent an open rupture in the near future with one side or the other."

Lansing was afraid the Allies might send a less satisfactory reply than Germany and Austria:

". . . suppose that the unacceptable answer comes from the belligerents whom we could least afford to see defeated on account of our own national interest and on account of the future domination of the principles of liberty and democracy in the world—then what? . . . I think that we must consider the possibility of such a situation resulting . . ."[1]

Lansing here subtly presented the two reasons why we should go to war on the side of the Allies: our economic interests, our love of democratic institutions.

This latter consideration especially—the future of democracy in the world—had begun to have great weight with the President.

---

[1]Lansing to Wilson, December 10, 1916. Lansing argued again against Wilson's suggestion that the league be supported by force, and suggested some verbal alterations in the note.

"I am convinced," he had said a month earlier, "that only governments initiate such wars as the present, and that they are never brought on by peoples, and that, therefore, democracy is the best preventive of such jealousies and suspicions and secret intrigues as produce wars among nations where small groups control rather than the great body of public opinion."[1]

Wilson was here moving toward a personal acceptance—where Lansing had already arrived—of the thesis Walter H. Page had so often written into his letters, that the war was a contest between democracy and autocracy.

The President seems not to have replied to the Secretary's letter; but Lansing's comments may well have induced him to hesitate until he had thought them through.

In the meantime the economic aspects of the war were again in ugly evidence—at least behind the scenes. The Comptroller of the Currency, John Skelton Williams, informed Wilson on December 6th that he was about to issue a statement showing the enormous resources of our national banks and the amount of their investments in foreign securities.[2] The President at once asked that such an announcement be withheld for the time being.[3]

"I am not sure what indirect effect the publication might have on some of our foreign relations."[4]

The most important fact about these foreign investments was that they were almost entirely bonds of the Allied governments. Wilson was obviously anxious lest this condition be interpreted wrongly as an influence making for unneutral action on the one hand against Germany, and, on the other hand, in favour of the Allies. We know that Wilson himself saw in the rising financial strength of

---

[1] Unsigned interview with the President, probably early in November. Washington *Post*, November 5, 1916.

[2] $239,566,000 as of September 12, 1916, and rapidly increasing.

[3] December 8, 1916.

[4] Wilson to John Skelton Williams, December 11, 1916.

the United States, and its increasing control of foreign finance, only an opportunity to improve world conditions. He wrote, a few weeks later, when a modified statement was put out by the Comptroller showing that the full resources of our national banks on November 17, 1916, had reached the astonishing figure of $15,520,000,000:[1]

"It is indeed extraordinary and I believe ought to make the whole country think all the more soberly about the very critical question what we are going to do with the money for the real benefit of the country and the world."[2]

In the face of these gathering difficulties, the situation by the middle of December was growing positively ominous. Chargé Grew reported on December 13th that the prevailing opinion in Berlin was that "if the peace offer should fail, as is generally expected, the Chancellor would be subjected to greater pressure than ever before to reopen the ruthless submarine campaign."[3]

Wilson decided to act at once "before it be too late to inject new elements into the debate now going on among the nations at war."[4]

The note was dispatched on December 18th.

III. WILSON DEMANDS DEFINITION OF TERMS

While Wilson's note of December 18th to the Powers had been often reworked, and some of its strength diminished by changes, it was still a powerful document.

[1]Press copy, December 27, 1916, in Wilson's files. The increase of resources in the past two years and seventeen days was $4,028,000,000, as of date November 17, 1916.

[2]Wilson to John Skelton Williams, December 28, 1916.

[3]Received the 14th. *Foreign Relations*, 1916, Supp., p. 89. The effectiveness of the present restricted submarine warfare gave some indication of what ruthless warfare would do. In four months during 1916, submarines sank about 632,000 tons of British shipping—three times more than the British could build. *War Memoirs of David Lloyd George*, Vol. III, pp. 75, 77.

[4]Letter to Lansing, written on the President's own typewriter, December 17, 1916. The President intimated his doubts whether Walter H. Page would give proper support to the note, but Lansing thought that in this instance there need not be alarm. *Cf. War Memoirs of Robert Lansing*, p. 184.

He made one assertion that was shocking to the warring nations at that moment, since each belligerent considered its objectives high and pure, and those of its opponents vile and low. He called attention "to the fact that the objects which the statesmen of the belligerents on both sides have in mind in this war are virtually the same, as stated in general terms to their own people and to the world."

While this sentence was torn out of its context and made the target of fierce attacks, the context itself, full of un-conscious irony, did not much mitigate the devastating truth which it contained. For how could it have been less than ironical to say at that time of violent passion that each side "desires to make the rights and privileges of weak peoples and small states as secure against aggression or denial in the future as the rights and privileges of the great and powerful states now at war. Each wishes itself to be made secure in the future, along with all other nations and peoples, against the recurrence of wars like this and against aggression or selfish interference of any kind. Each . . . is ready to consider the formation of a league of nations to insure[1] peace and justice throughout the world."[2]

He also asked a question that neither side would for a moment have considered answering with candour—that is, "such an avowal of their respective views as to the terms" upon which the war might be ended and the peace guaranteed "as would make it possible frankly to compare them."

He declared that he was not offering mediation or pro-posing peace, but he made it clear that he hoped his re-quest would lead to an interchange of views, and this in turn to a conference. He declared that he would "be

---

[1]The President's draft used the word "enforce." Lansing suggested "insure," a less explicit commitment.

[2]Quoted from the note as finally sent. *Foreign Relations*, 1916, Supp., pp. 97-99.

happy himself to serve or even to take the initiative in its accomplishment. . . ."

In his original draft of the note there had been a warning, even a threat, that the United States must have this information so as to determine its future course. Now he simply pointed out that the United States had an "intimate interest" in the ending of the war, lest the struggle go on until resentment and despair would be so great that a durable peace would become impossible, the situation of neutrals "be rendered altogether intolerable," and "more than all, an injury be done civilization itself which can never be atoned for or repaired."

The publication of the note was followed throughout the world by the harshest criticism and the most unstinted praise: a test in itself of the virility of the truth presented. It had cut down through folly and fustian to reality.

The President had anticipated the criticism:

"Neither side in the war is pleased with anything I write unless it can be construed as favourable in feeling to them . . ."[1]

The first reaction in Europe was one of bewilderment. Journalists, statesmen, and the general public seemed unable to conceive what the President really intended.[2]

Did he not yet know what the war was being fought for?

The British read his words with dismay and consternation. Their feeling of outraged virtue at once sought an outlet in personal attacks. The London *Morning Post* declared the President's detachment "reminiscent of the attitude of the antique gods." The *Daily Chronicle* detected an insult. The editor of the London *Times*, peering

---

[1] To Roy W. Howard, January 2, 1917.

[2] George D. Herron, "The Note of President Wilson," an article published in the *Journal de Genève*, December 31, 1916, and reprinted in Herron's *Woodrow Wilson and the World's Peace*, pp. 81–83.

across the Atlantic, pronounced the President sincere but sadly deluded.[1]

". . . the King wept . . ."[2]

Sir William Wiseman informed Colonel House that "an insistent demand" had arisen in England "that some sort of propaganda be started in America to properly put" the British case before the American people[3]—when, as a matter of fact, British propaganda in America since the beginning of the war had been consummate in its skill and success.[4]

The basic fact was, of course, that in their patriotic fervour the British read into Wilson's reasonable words a lack of appreciation of their efforts in a cause which they believed was also America's cause.[5] He seemed to throw unbearable doubt upon their motives, and to cheapen their sacrifices and sufferings. From the start, however, liberal and moderate forces in England began to rally in support of the wisdom of stating specific aims; and shortly there began to emerge a fairer understanding of the President's purpose and the disinterestedness of his appeal for the rights of humanity and civilization.[6]

The French were much less excited than the English, however sharply Wilson was criticized for his remarks about the "objects" being the "same."[7] But from the French point of view Wilson's efforts toward peace nego-

---

[1]Press comments, New York *Times*, December 22, 1916.

[2]Walter H. Page to Lansing, December 22, 1916. *Foreign Relations*, 1916, Supp., pp. 108–109.

[3]House to Wilson, January 13, 1917.

[4]Sir Gilbert Parker was "responsible for American publicity" for Great Britain from the beginning, practically, of the European war. For his own account of his activities in the period of American neutrality, see *Harper's Magazine*, Vol. 136 (1918), pp. 521–531.

[5]Sir Horace Plunkett to Colonel House, December 27, 1916, in Mr. Wilson's files.

[6]J. H. Whitehouse, "Moderate Opinion in England," January 12, 1917, sent to Wilson by House, January 13, 1917.

[7]New York *Times*, December 23, 1916; December 24, 1916.

tiation seemed Utopian; battles were being fought on their soil: the invader had to be driven out and punished. Peace negotiations would mean defeat: on with the war!

Editors of German newspapers were divided between suspicion that the President was scheming to protect England from defeat, and approval that he had taken a step which might "bring peace appreciably nearer."[1]

Meanwhile, America was speaking out both its approval and its indignation. Bryan telegraphed to the President:

"You have rendered an invaluable service . . . Accept . . . my earnest wish for the success of the movement which you have had the honor to inaugurate."[2]

The *New Republic* declared that if "there was one thing more than any other which the note is meant to initiate it is an era of plain speaking." The President "has sounded a call which will restore the morale of liberalism." "Those who have cried for a leadership expressive of American idealism and interest have it now."[3]

On the other hand the note was held by some to be inopportune, and it was felt that it "might do more harm than good, by irritating the Allies with the belief that it was part of the German program."[4] Pro-Ally Americans were indignant that the President was not satisfied to accept the Allies' general statements of their war aims.[5] Secretary Baker sent the President a letter showing such a feeling. Wilson replied:

"I have read this letter of Professor Johnson's with a great deal of interest.

"I wish every day that there were more *mere* Americans in this country. Almost all of our fellow citizens this side

---

[1]Gerard's report, December 23, 1916. *Foreign Relations*, 1916, Supp., p. 113.
[2]December 21, 1916.
[3]*New Republic*, Vol. IX (December 30, 1916), pp. 227, 232.
[4]*Current History*, Vol. V (January 1917), p. 602.
[5]*Cf. New Republic*, Vol. IX (December 30, 1916), p. 228.

the Mississippi seem to think in terms set by the thinking or the prepossessions of one side or the other across the water. If Professor Johnson had lived with the English statesmen for the past two years and seen the real inside of their minds I think he would feel differently."[1]

The most vitriolic criticism was offered by Major General Leonard Wood, stormy advocate of war with Germany. Stalking into a cheering dinner meeting in the interest of preparedness, his face set like flint, he said:

"Gentlemen, I have just received word that the President has today dispatched another note to the German government. In this note he states that, so far as he can see, the aims of Germany and of the Allies are the same." Exclamations of disgust! "Gentlemen," he continued, "we have no leadership in Washington."[2]

Congressmen in general praised the President's bold action: "good," "fine," "timely."[3] Champ Clark, Speaker of the House, wrote to the President on the 25th that it was "the best of all your good performances, saying precisely what should have been said . . ." In order to place Senate support squarely behind the peace move, Senator G. M. Hitchcock, of Nebraska, on the 21st introduced a resolution of endorsement. Borah, objecting ostensibly to the passage of such a resolution without the fullest deliberation, blocked an immediate vote.[4] The next day Hitchcock submitted another, similar, resolution—the one on which the great fight was to be made in January:[5]

"That the Senate approves and strongly indorses the action taken by the President in sending the diplomatic notes of December 18 to the nations now engaged in war

---

[1]December 26, 1916.

[2]Hagedorn, *Leonard Wood*, Vol. II, p. 200.

[3]New York *Times*, December 21, 1916.

[4]*Cong. Rec.*, 64-2, p. 635. The resolution was referred to the Committee on Foreign Relations.

[5]See this volume, following section.

suggesting and recommending that those nations state the
terms upon which peace might be discussed."[1]

Again the resolution failed of immediate consideration,
going over this time until January 2nd when the Senate
met again after the Christmas holidays.

Wilson was somewhat nettled by the reports of the
"discordant voices" that denounced his message at home
and abroad. He thought he had made "its true meaning
and purpose" clear to "all those who know how to judge
generously."[2] But in such a time of unreason and fiery
passion, how many men were there in the world who were
still able—like the President—to "judge generously"?

Lansing had been immediately aware of the doubts expressed as to the real meaning of the note, and in a spirit
of mistaken helpfulness, undertook to explain in an interview published on the morning of the 21st. He said in
part:

". . . more and more our own rights are becoming involved by the belligerents on both sides . . .

"The sending of this note will indicate the possibility
of our being forced into the war. That possibility ought to
serve as a restraining and sobering force safeguarding
American rights. It may also serve to force an earlier
conclusion of the war."[3]

When these remarks were flashed to the large cities, they
caused tense excitement.

". . . the government was contemplating abandoning its
neutrality and was about to enter the war!"[4]

Lansing was taken by surprise at this interpretation,
reasonable though it was. Presumably he had been so intent upon trying to make plain that we did not fear to go

---

[1]*Cong. Rec.*, 64–2, p. 668.
[2]Wilson to H. A. Garfield, December 27, 1916; *War Memoirs of Robert Lansing*, p. 91.
[3]*Ibid.*, pp. 186–187.
[4]Lansing's statement of what was thought to be the meaning of his remarks. *Ibid.*,
p. 187.

to war that he had overemphasized and oversimplified the likelihood of our early entrance.

The President, though he agreed with certain of the statements,[1] at once wrote Lansing a letter which, while courtesy itself, conveyed a reproof and a command:

"Would it not be possible for you to issue another statement . . . saying that you found that your utterance of this morning had been radically misinterpreted, and explaining that your intention was merely to suggest the very direct interest the neutral nations have in the question of possible terms of peace and that it was not at all in your mind to intimate any change in the policy of neutrality which the country has so far so consistently pursued in the face of accumulating difficulties. You will know how to phrase it and how to give your unqualified endorsement to the whole tone and purpose of our note."[2]

During a later talk Wilson declared that Lansing had given "the impression that this government had actually decided to enter the war in case the terms proposed by one group of belligerents appeared to be more just and lenient than those of the other group."[3] Lansing argued that his remarks told the truth—as, essentially, they had, if properly qualified—but he made a corrective statement which followed in general the phrasing of the President's own letter to him.[4]

The excitement thereupon quieted, but the significance of the first statement was not lost: America was near to war with Germany! Officials in Berlin decided that mediation by Wilson was more than ever a thing to beware of.[5] On the other hand Lansing's statement, however modified

[1] *Ibid.*

[2] Wilson to Lansing, December 21, 1916.

[3] *War Memoirs of Robert Lansing*, pp. 187, 190.

[4] *Ibid.*, pp. 187–188; New York *Times*, December 22, 1916, for both statements.

[5] See testimony of Dr. Karl Helfferich, November 14, 1919. *Official German Documents*, Vol. II, p. 701.

by his later explanation, had greatly cheered the Allies. They could be more certain than ever of American support! Why bother with Wilson's demands as to peace terms? Spring Rice told Lansing three weeks later that it was "the only thing that saved the situation"; without it, the President would have received the unbounded resentment of Great Britain "for his untimely attempt to inject himself into the peace movement of the Central Empires."[1]

If relations between Great Britain and the United States continued to be disagreeable, relations between Germany and the United States were becoming actually alarming. Submarine warfare was constantly overstepping the restrictions guaranteed in the *Sussex* settlement; and the Germans were rushing the construction of new U-boats.[2]

Late in December, Lansing returned to his attack upon Wilson's neutrality policy, writing a letter to the President that was positively harsh, asserting that it was time to make good our threat at the time of the *Sussex* incident: we should "determine at once upon a definite course of action."

But Wilson would not be rushed, either in this case or in the matter of the British detention and censorship of mails, which was also troubling Lansing:

"I will be glad to discuss this and other kindred matters with you when we have seen just what the several belligerents are willing to do about discussing terms of peace."[3]

His patience was unending: on December 24th he instructed Lansing to send a confidential suggestion to the belligerent powers, designed to make their responses more favourable, that they give their replies to him in "strict

[1] See *War Memoirs of Robert Lansing*, p. 190.

[2] Secretary Lane to Wilson, December 21, 1916, reporting comment of the consul general for the Netherlands at San Francisco, who had recently been in Germany.

[3] December 27, 1916. Savage, *Policy of the United States Toward Maritime Commerce in War*, Vol. II, p. 539.

confidence; it being understood that the Government of the United States may in its turn convey it in like confidence to the governments of the other group of the belligerents, in order that it may in that way be ascertained without publicity whether there is any present ground or basis to hope for negotiations or conferences of any kind."[1]

This was a thoroughly practical move, but in the end the replies were all made publicly.[2] This was especially regrettable in the case of Germany. If she had thus disclosed her aims secretly and the Allied governments had refused to follow her lead, it would have made clear to the President as well as to their own peoples that they were opposed to any negotiated peace. Furthermore, Germany stood to see her own peace offer fail utterly unless she accepted Wilson's suggestion: she knew that the Allies would not consent to a conference without having a statement of her terms.[3] Her refusal to divulge her terms even in confidence was thus costly, if not fatal. In deciding to gamble for victory on the debatable effectiveness of unrestricted U-boat warfare, she lost a possible chance for peace. Probably her decision was at that time inevitable. She had her own public opinion to consider; by the end of 1916 the German mind had become accustomed to the picture, seen through the rose-tinted spectacles of the German Admiralty, of absolutely certain future victory—and beyond that, the material rewards for the blood spilled and the treasure expended.

---

[1] *Foreign Relations*, 1916, Supp., p. 112. Draft sent by Wilson to Lansing, December 23rd.

[2] This instruction of December 24th may not have arrived in Germany in time to affect their hasty reply on the 26th. But the same suggestion, made to Bernstorff by Lansing and reported to the German government as early as the 21st, had arrived in time to be considered. *Official German Documents*, Vol. II, pp. 1004–1005.

[3] Lloyd George had expressed that opinion pointedly: To enter on Germany's invitation, "without any knowledge of the proposals she proposes to make, into a conference is to put our heads into a noose with the rope in the hands of Germany . . ." House of Commons, December 19, 1916. *Foreign Relations*, 1916, Supp., p.

These tremendous issues of a war-torn world were momentarily and blessedly laid aside by the President at the approach of Christmas Eve.

Late on that pleasant Sunday afternoon President and Mrs. Wilson, accompanied by friends and relatives, walked over to a community gathering on the south steps of the Treasury Building, where they joined in singing Christmas carols. Christmas in the White House was much like Christmas in the homes of millions of less anxious Americans: relatives gathered together, gifts unwrapped, good talk, games—the old, satisfying joys of "home folks."

"It was sweet of you to think of us and send us such charming Christmas presents," wrote Wilson in a letter to his old friends, the Misses Lucy and Mary Smith.[1] "I hope that you will enjoy the Littell. I have not seen it recently but it ought just now to have rather poignant interest as reflecting the thoughts of the nations at war.

"We had a very happy Christmas. Jessie and Frank[2] came down (leaving the precious little ones in good hands, you may be sure) and at our Christmas dinner we had all three of the girls, all Edith's family who are here,—in all twenty-two very jolly people. After dinner we had a fine time playing charades, and, as usual, the three Wilsons showing alarmingly finished histrionic gifts! Stock.[3] was here, too, and did some 'tough' parts in the scenes with great ability! It was fine to see him so well.

"Little Josephine[4] is the only little one in the house, so that the Christmas tree was not so exciting a function as usual. Some of the toys she received have been played with more by Stock. and Frank than by her. 'Boys like that kind of thing,' was her comment as *she* played happily

---

ecember 28, 1916.

and Mrs. Francis B. Sayre.

[4]A or Stockton Axson.

ece.

putting her new doll to bed in a charming four-poster toy
bed.

"All join me in the most affectionate messages. May the
best conceivable things of the new year come to you both,
along with what you are already sure of, the continued love
of your friends!"

The President's birthday followed on the 28th: his
"sixth ten year milestone."

"I remember ten years ago when we celebrated your
fiftieth birthday," wrote Cleveland Dodge. "How big the
lively scraps of those days seemed at the time, and how
small they seem now. . . .

"You have tackled a good many large jobs in your life,
but you now have on your hands the hardest proposition,
even you ever undertook. . . .

"We thank God for all you mean to the World . . ."[1]

On the day following this charming and quiet and
homely celebration, the President returned to the grim
problems of war and peace.

On the 27th the discouraging German reply to his request for peace terms[2] was placed in his hands. It indicated plainly that the group in Germany who demanded
unrestricted U-boat warfare had won the dominant voice.[3]

Moreover, there was little doubt that the crisp reply
was deliberately calculated "to prevent any meddling on
the part of President Wilson in peace negotiations."[4] It
was only after the present conflict was ended by negotiations between victorious Germany and her enemies that

---

[1]December 27, 1916.

[2]Dated December 26th; received in Washington on the evening of December 27th.
Foreign Relations, 1916, Supp., pp. 117–118. The remaining Central Powers replied
in terms similar to those of Germany. *Ibid.*, pp. 118–120.

[3]*Official German Documents*, Vol. I, p. 136.

[4]*Ibid.*, Vol. II, p. 1087. *Cf.* also *Ibid.*, Vol. I, pp. 398, 434–437; Vol. II, pp. 1085–1088.
Bernstorff, however, interpreted this reply as not doing away wholly with the possibility of peace mediation by Wilson. He continued to work to bring about such
"mediation." (Testimony of Bernstorff. *Ibid.*, Vol. I, p. 265.)

"the Imperial Government" would be "ready" to coöperate with the United States in the "sublime task" of preventing future wars.[1] The reply was not only a rebuff to the President but a body blow to any hope of peace negotiations. It deepened American suspicions of Germany's war aims and of the genuineness of her desire for a better world order.

" . . . the German government can not or does not care to understand the democratic view of the war."[2]

Bernstorff was disappointed, agreeing with the President that the terms of his country should have been communicated confidentially. He even cabled to Berlin[3] that he believed the confidential mediation of Wilson ought to be accepted, for with "the exception of the Belgian question the American Government ought to bring us more advantage than disadvantage as Americans have only just come to realize what England's mastery of the seas means." If Germany would give guarantees regarding "disarmament by land and by sea (freedom of the seas), provisions for arbitration and a peace league," Wilson might be able to bring about a conference. He repeated that the United States would participate—as had been tacitly accepted for the past year and a half—only in the general conference dealing with those guarantees.[4]

This additional, explicit offer of mediation was therefore thrown into the final debates of the political and military authorities in Germany as to unrestricted submarine warfare. But unfortunately its influence was overborne by the withering formal reply of the Allies to the peace offer of the Central Powers. It was a joint answer,

---

[1]*Foreign Relations*, 1916, Supp., p. 118.

[2]Editorial, *New Republic*, Vol. IX (December 30, 1916), p. 226.

[3]Following a conference with House, in which House was acting on Wilson's instructions.

[4]Bernstorff to the German Foreign Office, December 29, 1916. Bernstorff, *My Three Years in America*, pp. 323–325. The telegram arrived in Berlin on January 3, 1917.

and Wilson received an advance copy of it December 30th. The Allies declared that the German object was base: to deceive neutral opinion, to "trouble" opinion in the Allied countries, to strengthen public opinion in Germany, and to justify new crimes in advance. They refused curtly "to entertain a proposal without sincerity and without import." A statement of the general war aims of the Allies was given in conclusion: "the reparation of violated rights and liberties, the acknowledgement of the principle of nationalities and of the free existence of small states," and "guarantees for the security of the world."[1]

It was thus that, after weeks of anxious and laborious effort, only the slenderest threads of hope were left to the President. Two possibilities, however, still remained. Would Germany accept the urgent advice just sent by Bernstorff—to give their terms to Wilson confidentially? Would the Allies' reply to his own request for terms be such as to lead to negotiations? Wilson anxiously awaited the responses to these crucial questions, but the Allies did not reply until January 10th, and the Germans delayed still longer. Every day the prospect of realizing his hope of peace was lessened. He studied the situation constantly. He was baffled by tremendous forces wholly beyond his control. It was with a spirit overborne by apprehension that he wrote on the third day of January:

"My heart aches that no way can be found out of the present wilderness of war . . . May the New Year bring to you and to us all unexpected blessings!"[2]

[1] *Foreign Relations*, 1916, Supp., pp. 124–125, 139.
[2] To Lady Mary Paget.

CHAPTER X

APPEAL TO THE PEOPLE OF THE WARRING NATIONS

"The real people I was speaking to was neither the Senate nor foreign governments . . . but the *people* of the countries now at war."
Letter, January 29, 1917.

"I hope with all my heart that something can be worked out that will assure the world of peace and justice."
Letter to William Jennings Bryan, February 2, 1917.

"The right state of mind, the right feeling between nations, is as necessary for a lasting peace as is the just settlement of vexed questions of territory or of racial and national allegiance."
Address to the Senate, January 22, 1917.

"Undoubtedly, at present there is a universal excitement of opinion which is unfavourable to calm international understandings, but I think that is merely temporary . . ."
Letter, January 25, 1917.

1. "PEACE WITHOUT VICTORY"

REBUFFED by both belligerents in his efforts to make peace, discouraged by his most intimate advisers, bitterly reviled by those who demanded immediate war, Woodrow Wilson might, as early as January 1, 1917, have given up further peace efforts, accepted the inevitable. If he had, the world would have lost a sublime declaration of the fundamental ideals of just dealings among the nations—and of the democratic principles upon which they rest; a state paper which will ultimately be numbered among the noblest utterances of American statesmanship. This was the "peace without victory" address of January

22nd. Like so many lasting human achievements, it came after the lesser men had given up hope: for it rested upon a deeper faith than theirs.

It was a deeper faith because it had its foundations in an authority more fundamental than that of diplomats or of soldiers: it rested upon a profound belief in the people: that the people, if they could be informed, would judge more righteously than most of the leaders who represented or governed them. Specifically, he believed that the people of all nations wanted peace. This may or may not have been true. His whole system of political philosophy, fundamentally democratic, is now under attack from various sources; but the fact remains that Woodrow Wilson believed in it to the depth of his being. His conviction never weakened to the end of his life; and it is in this light that his record must in all fairness be studied.

Again and again in his life, then, we find Woodrow Wilson appealing from the decision of the authorities to the people themselves: it was the last resort when everything else had failed: and these appeals, since they expressed the truths in which he believed most fundamentally, remain his greatest utterances, the most likely to survive as instruments of future progress. He seemed to rise above the turmoil of the moment to the serene atmosphere of ultimate truth. It happened at Princeton, it happened repeatedly during his political career, it was the final resort at the Paris Peace Conference when the decisions were going against him: and it was the last desperate appeal to the American people, the ghastly campaign from coast to coast in September 1919, in behalf of the League of Nations, that caused his untimely death.

So now, in January 1917, every other resource having been tried, he decided on a great appeal to the people of the world. It had been long in his mind. He said in the address of January 22nd:

"I would fain believe that I am speaking for the silent mass of mankind everywhere who have as yet had no place or opportunity to speak their real hearts out concerning the death and ruin they see to have come already upon the persons and the homes they hold most dear."[1]

As a result of his position as the free leader of the most powerful of the neutral nations, he felt a peculiar and deep obligation to the people of the world:

"Perhaps I am the only person in high authority amongst all the peoples of the world who is at liberty to speak and hold nothing back."[2]

He was even more explicit in the definition of his purpose in a letter written after his great address:

"The real people I was speaking to was neither the Senate nor foreign governments, as you will realize, but the *people* of the countries now at war."[3]

The President had begun working on his proposed address immediately after the disappointments, already narrated, that followed the Christmas season. The writer has before him the bits of White House paper upon which he wrote in shorthand characters a series of memoranda of what he wished to say. However fragmentary, one of them, headed "General Notes" illuminates his process of clarifying his thought:[4]

1) Why did the war occur? Because ultimate alignment was unknown, the processes established insecurely, the objects conjectural.

2) Our interest only in law and such justice as it was supposed international law had secured. Our whole moral, and if necessary physical, force ready to be used to sustain these.

3) "Entangling Alliances" which we cannot escape. We

---

[1]*The Public Papers of Woodrow Wilson*, Vol. IV, p. 413.

[2]*Ibid.*

[3]To John P. Gavit, January 29, 1917.

[4]The transcription of these hasty shorthand notes may be defective in some of the minor words, but it is as accurate as it can be made.

INFORMAL PICTURE OF PRESIDENT WILSON, TAKEN IN
OCTOBER 1916.

have become entangled, whether we would or not, in affairs
of the world. Its general interests are ours. Our interests touch
those of other nations at every point. We are deeply concerned
in what can be secured only by the co-operation of nations,
namely in a peace which comes from justice and places the
rights of humanity above motive of gain and national advantage.[1]

At this very time Colonel House was making various
critical confessions in his diary, to the effect that Wilson
had lost all "punch," that "things were drifting in an
aimless sort of way," that the President was "for peace at
almost any price."[2] When House, intent upon war,
brought up the question of preparedness, Wilson responded:

"There will be no war. This country does not intend to
become involved in this war. We are the only one of

[1] It is an interesting fact that while the President was working on these notes, he
had before him a remarkable original memorandum (which remains still in his files)
written by President Monroe in his own hand when he also was facing the painful
dilemma of a war in Europe. This highly important document, which, so far as the
author knows, has never before been published, was sent to him on January 1st by a
young man who was then Assistant Secretary of the Navy. His name was Franklin D.
Roosevelt, and his letter was as follows: "I came across the enclosed memorandum
while going over some papers I acquired many years ago. It is in the handwriting of
James Monroe, and was evidently written in 1814 when the Congress of Vienna was
about to meet. I have been unable to discover that it was actually used in any official
message or document; but it is in many ways so interestingly parallel to events of
the day that I thought you would like to add it to your collection of historical material."

Monroe's memorandum, which must have greatly interested Wilson the President
as well as Wilson the historian, and would have interested him still more if he had
known that this document of the President of 1814 had been sent to him, the President
of 1917, by the future President of 1937, was in part as follows: "A war in Europe,
to which Great Britain with her floating thunder, and other maritime powers, are
always parties, has long been found to spread its calamities into the remotest regions.
Even the U.S. just and pacific as their policy is, have not been able to avoid the
alternative of either submitting to the most destructive and ignominious wrongs from
European Belligerents, or of resisting them by an appeal to the sword: or to speak
more properly, no other choice has been left to them but the time of making the
appeal; it being evident that a submission too long protracted, would have no other
effect than to encourage and accumulate aggressions, untill they should become altogether intolerable; and untill the loss of honor being added to other losses, redress
by the sword itself would be rendered more slow and difficult." The memorandum
is dated 1814 and initialed "J.M."

[2] Diary entries, January 2 and 4, 1917. The Intimate Papers of Colonel House, Vol. II,
p. 413.

the great white nations that is free from war to-day, and it would be a crime against civilization for us to go in."[1]

He was not here arguing against preparedness; but he was pinning his hope upon the appeal to the people upon which he was then at work with such persistence of faith and of patience.

Meanwhile the inexorable forces of unreasonable and intractable human nature were gathering in power: making it less likely, every day, that the President, for all his power and all his eloquence, could counteract them. And, unhappily, it was not only the intractables of Europe that were balking him. There were developing doubts and opposition at home—represented in the Senate by the two most vocal of the Republicans, Borah and Lodge, and by the most virulent of Wilson's critics outside of Congress, Theodore Roosevelt.

The controversy had begun with the Hitchcock resolution of December 22nd already referred to[2] which had asked for senatorial endorsement of Wilson's note of December 18th. The issue did not concern the President's request for peace terms; upon that the Senate was in substantial agreement; it was Wilson's suggestion that a league of nations should be formed "to insure peace and justice throughout the world" that fired his critics. This was new, it was disturbing, it would make an excellent campaign issue!

Since May 1916 the proposal for an international organization had been the central pillar of Wilson's peace programme.[3] The Democratic platform had pledged the good faith of the party to join with other nations in "any

---

[1] *The Intimate Papers of Colonel House*, Vol. II, p. 412.

[2] See this volume, pp. 403–404.

[3] The league idea had, of course, been in his mind since August 1914, at least. See *Woodrow Wilson, Life and Letters*, Vol. V, *Neutrality*, pp. 73 *et seq.*

feasible association" that would secure "settled peace and justice," the freedom of the seas, and such principles as self-determination and respect for the rights of small nations. He himself had preached it vigorously in many of his campaign addresses; he believed that the election had sanctioned his proposals.

He had been the more confident of the ultimate success of the league idea since it had earlier been espoused and strongly commended by many of the most powerful Republican leaders, among them Roosevelt, Taft and Lodge.[1]

Roosevelt was the first to attack: writing in the *Metropolitan Magazine* for January 1917, he attempted to explain away his former allegiance to the principles of a league, combining with his explanation a vindictive personal attack on Wilson and on Taft.[2]

Senator Lodge promptly supported Roosevelt. With a vehemence no doubt born of embarrassment, he repudiated his earlier endorsement of the idea. He was now, January 3, 1917, manifesting profound concern about the "abandonment of the policy we have hitherto pursued of confining ourselves to our own hemisphere . . ."[3]

---

[1]See this volume, pp. 205-206.

[2]"The Election." Roosevelt followed this with a criticism of that part of Wilson's note which said that the objects of the belligerents were the same, as stated to their peoples; the note, he said, was "profoundly immoral." New York *Times*, January 4, 1917. For Roosevelt's early belief in a league with force, *cf.* Roosevelt, *America and the World War* (1915), p. 62.

[3]*Cong. Rec.*, 64-2, p. 794; *cf.* also *ibid.*, pp. 2368, 2370. The President recognized all too well the personal and political animosity of Lodge. In the course of a courteous refusal of a certain invitation, late in December, there occurred this terse paragraph:
"I find upon examining the programme . . . that Senator Henry Cabot Lodge of Massachusetts is announced as one of the speakers. Senator Lodge's conduct during the recent campaign makes it impossible for me with self-respect to join in any exercise in which he takes part or to associate myself with him in any way." (Wilson to Dr. Roland Cotton Smith, December 29, 1916.) As early as January 31, 1915, during the Shipping bill debate, Wilson had spoken of Lodge and Root as men who would stoop to "twist the truth," who had no consciences, and who used "insincere and contemptible methods of fighting." See *Woodrow Wilson, Life and Letters*, Vol. V, *Neutrality*, pp. 126-127.

In short, it was just at this moment of supreme international crisis, in January 1917, that the most fundamental issue in American foreign policy since the time of Washington and Jefferson was called forcibly to the attention of the American people. There followed the most bitterly protracted political debate in our history since the Civil War. Should America enter a world alliance to keep peace *collectively*—because every other method had failed?

Every argument of the forthcoming struggle, indeed, was developed in January 1917. Senator Gallinger feared that the Monroe Doctrine might be endangered, Lodge announced that Hitchcock's resolution "projects Congress into the field of European politics, and involves us in the affairs of Europe," Borah argued that it would place American naval and military forces behind the national integrity of every little nation in Europe or Asia, placing us in "the storm center of European politics"; the advice of Washington and Jefferson would be abandoned and the Monroe Doctrine destroyed.[1]

Senator Hitchcock, who was supporting the President, was forced, after four attempts to pass his resolution of endorsement, to accept a substitute resolution approving only that part of Wilson's note which requested the terms upon which peace might be discussed. Even so, seventeen senators voted "nay" and thirty-one abstained from voting. It was a formidable, portentous opposition to the peace policy of the President.

Wilson might well write on January 17th:

". . . it is hard to see how to guide Congress successfully."[2]

But in spite of these furious attacks, the President never

---

[1] *Cong. Rec.*, 64–2, pp. 736, 792, 893–895. Even Senator Hitchcock, upon whom fell the brunt of the battle for the League in the Senate in 1919, admitted now in his reply to Borah: "I might not differ so much with the Senator from Idaho upon the construction which he places upon the note." *Ibid.*, p. 895.

[2] Wilson to House, January 17, 1917.

wavered for a moment in his determination to carry through his programme: his faith in the essential truth of his principles, his confidence in the reasonableness of his practical proposals, were never for a moment dimmed. If he could get his ideas to the people of the world, would they not prevail? He turned with new enthusiasm and new hope to the preparation of his appeal.

Before he could finally complete it, however, on January 10th, Briand finally delivered to the American ambassador in Paris the Allied reply to his note of December 18th with the explanation that it would be published in Europe on the 12th rather than communicated confidentially, as Wilson had hoped.[1] The reply was obviously expected to put an end to any further talk of negotiation.

". . . war," said Lloyd George in London while Wilson was reading the Allies' note in Washington, "is better than peace at the Prussian price of domination over Europe. We made it clear in our reply to Germany; we made it still clearer in our reply to the United States."[2]

The defeat of Germany, said the note, was necessary in order to assure the Allies reparation, restitution, and guarantees of a durable peace. That was to say, the conflict between Wilson's hope of a negotiated peace and the Allied—and the German—determination to force a peace through victory was as sharp as ever, if not sharper. The Allies declared that Germany and Austria-Hungary were stained with moral guilt for beginning the ruinous war; the peace settlement must protect Europe from another outbreak of such "brutal covetousness." Belgium, Serbia, and Montenegro must be restored and indemnified; French, Russian, and Roumanian territories evacuated and reparation given; past conquests from the Allied

---

[1]Sharp to the Secretary of State, January 10, 1917. *Foreign Relations*, 1917, Supp., 1, pp. 5–6.

[2]Spoken at Guildhall, January 11, 1917. New York *Times*, January 12, 1917.

nations returned; Italian, Slav, Roumanian, and Czecho-Slovakian minorities liberated; peoples subject to the Turks freed and Turkey expelled from Europe; Poland given autonomy under the Czar; Europe reorganized under a league of nations and territorial guarantees given to small and large nations alike, and liberty and free economic development given to all."[1] In a letter to Spring Rice which reached the Department of State January 16th, Balfour made the establishment of international sanctions to support international law and treaties one of the chief aims, though the primary goal he spoke of was complete victory over the enemy.[2]

This was the crushing reply of the Allies. While it was, indeed, more explicit in its statement of terms than the German reply had been, it was not less peremptory. It was followed a few days later by certain explanations and mitigations by the German government, made in response to Bernstorff's vigorous appeals. While open to question upon several points these seemed, at first, somewhat hopeful. House reported Bernstorff's responses to the President on January 15th:

"(1) His Government are willing to submit to arbitration as a means of peace. [Wilson put a question mark opposite "arbitration."]

"(2) They are willing to enter a league of nations for the enforcement of peace and for the limitation of armaments both on land and sea.

"(3) They propose that you submit a program for a peace conference and they agree to give it their approval.

"(4) To show their good will they are willing to sign the

---

[1]Sharp to the Secretary of State, January 10, 1917. *Foreign Relations*, 1917, Supp., I, pp. 6–8. Belgium made a separate answer which asked special consideration as to reparation and security in the peace settlement. *Ibid.*, pp. 8–9.

[2]January 13, 1917. *Ibid.*, pp. 17–21.

arbitration treaty immediately (that is the so called Bryan Treaty.)"[1]

House also reported the statement that the German terms were "very moderate" and did not include an annexation of Belgium; and added that Bernstorff thought Germany was ready "to agree to the formation of an independent Poland and Lithuania," but would insist upon the Bulgarian and Austrian frontiers touching:

"This . . . is in line with what I thought they would demand—that is an uninterrupted route from Berlin to Constantinople.

"Bernstorff said he believed if Lloyd George had stated that there should be *mutual* restoration, reparation and indemnity, his Government would have agreed to enter negotiation on those terms."[2]

Wilson's first reply was made at once, on the spur of the moment, and in some confusion as to the meaning of House's letter. Naturally, he could not believe his eyes as he read Bernstorff's first point.

"Do I understand you to mean," he wrote to House, "that they are willing to submit the terms upon which the war is to be concluded to arbitration or only that they are willing to conclude a 'Bryan treaty' with us?"[3]

---

[1] A Bryan treaty was not an arbitration treaty: it went beyond arbitration, which it was intended to complement.

[2] About this time, also, the President received from the State Department a copy of a dispatch from Ambassador Elkus in Turkey, reporting a conversation with the German ambassador there who had just returned from Berlin. The pertinent paragraph follows:

". . . Germany is perfectly willing to confidentially state her peace terms; that Germany [is] willing to give up Belgium retaining certain rights of travel on the Meuse; that Holland, Denmark and Belgium should remain as neutral or buffer states for England; that French coast land be retained by France in its entirety so that she remain an important and absolutely independent power; that Russian territory be restored; that Servia and Roumania be treated properly; and that Belgium be indemnified although her conduct as neutral was not correct." (Cablegram dated January 12, 1917, attached to House's letter in Mr. Wilson's files.)

[3] January 16, 1917.

Arbitration to end the war was of course what the German government was set on avoiding, as the past negotiations had proved.

Wilson, still suspicious, wrote the next day:

"Did Bernstorff . . . touch at all upon the question what his government would be willing to do *during* the year of investigation . . . suppose the subject of controversy which has exhausted the resources of ordinary diplomacy to be her use of submarines in the way we have objected to, would she, or would she not, feel herself obliged to discontinue such practices while the inquiry of the international commission into the merits of the case was in progress? That with me is the vital question. I do not want to walk into a trap and give them immunity for the next year."[1]

House replied with a brief account of the complete unwillingness he had found in Germany, on his earlier visits, to consider signing a "Bryan treaty," but he added:

"Since then the Government is completely in the hands of the liberals and the war has cut so deeply into the very heart of the nation that their entire attitude seems changed, and today, if we are to believe Bernstorff, they are willing to reverse their former position and take a stand as advanced as any of the democracies. . . .

"In my opinion, the best interests of the Allies and ourselves would be met by taking Germany at her word and concluding peace as speedily as possible. . . .

"Would it not be well for me to send Balfour and Lloyd George a cable covering the points enumerated in this letter? To this might be added that the German Government had proposed an immediate signing of an arbitration treaty with us, and that they had proposed submitting the question of peace to arbitration, or, as an alternative, that you submit proposals yourself for a conference.

---

[1]Wilson to House, January 17, 1917.

"I wrote Bernstorff in detail and expect his confirmation or denial by tomorrow."[1]

Wilson was much interested.

"Your letter . . . certainly does set forth a very striking and significant change of attitude on the part of the German authorities since the old confident days before the war . . .

"Yes, I hope that you *will* prepare and code for prompt use a message to Balfour and Lloyd George, making a similar review in summary form and setting forth, as you get them in writing from Bernstorff, the terms and methods the Germans now indicate their willingness to accede to. But hold it until I can consult Lansing, and until the address I am about to make to the Congress[2] has had time to sink in a little."[3]

Bernstorff's letter, however, which House sent to the President on the 19th, proved a great disappointment.

". . . the idea of my Government was, that the President submit a program *for the general conference* concerning the guarantees for the future.

"As you know, my Government thinks, that a conference of *the belligerents* about the terms of peace should precede the general conference about the guarantees."[4]

"Of course," remarked House as he forwarded this letter to the President, "it is a long way for them to go . . . but it does not give you the opportunity to force peace now as my first interpretation of it would have done."

In a second letter, which House also sent on immediately, Bernstorff expressed his fear that the situation in Berlin was "getting out of our hands." And in answer to a question as to the "Bryan treaty," he pointed out that if

---

[1]House to Wilson, January 18, 1917.
[2]January 22, 1917, to the Senate.
[3]January 19, 1917.
[4]Letter dated January 18, 1917.

the German government were "obliged to meet the British *illegal* starvation policy with the same kind of warfare by employing submarines, they would certainly not be ready to discontinue the practice during the investigation. At the present time, however, our submarines are not used in the way to which the American Government has objected, so that the question of principle is not involved . . ."[1]

With this, the plan for cabling Balfour and Lloyd George was dropped. The Germans, House wrote to the President, were "slippery customers"![2]

The President did not in the least know, at the time, what was actually going on in Germany, or how far the Germans were from considering any peace proposals whatsoever—as will presently be shown.

In short, both belligerents scorned real negotiation: both were determined upon victory and a dictated peace. Nevertheless, the President did not waver in his determination to appeal to the people of the world. If the governments would not yield to reason, perhaps the people would! On January 11th he read the first draft of his proposed address to Colonel House.

"As usual," commented House afterward, "he struck the wrong note in one instance, which he seems unable to avoid. He said, 'This war was brought on by distrust of one another.'"

That, as Wilson's shorthand notes showed, was one of his firmest convictions. He believed it to be true; but it did not affect the essence of his proposals, and it might irritate rather than convince the people to whom he was appealing. He struck it out.

House also criticized the assertion: "Both sides say they have no desire to humiliate or destroy the other." Wilson struck out "humiliate."

[1] January 20, 1917.
[2] January 20, 1917.

House records no discussion of the keynote phrase of the address, "peace without victory," which was soon to fly from one end of the world to the other.[1] The idea was, of course, the core of the President's peace proposals, and, regardless of any argument of expediency or diplomacy, he refused to compromise it. It said in the fewest possible words that he believed in peace by negotiation as against the determination of both belligerents to secure a "knock-out blow." Looking into the future, Wilson dreaded what such a victory might mean.

When Lansing objected to the phrase as easily subject to "hostile criticism" and misinterpretation in the Allied countries, Wilson replied that that was not "at all likely . . . in view of the context."[2] Lansing dropped the matter, turning away with the feeling that the whole speech was questionable, since it was an appeal to the peoples of Europe over the heads of their governments.[3]

Page, in London, was by no means so compliant. Sharing wholly the British view, he was seized with consternation when the address reached him. Putting the two belligerents on the same moral plane! This must not be! He let his indignation cool for some days, and then dispatched a cablegram—"strictly confidential and of immediate importance to the President"—protesting that the phrase "peace without victory" was ruinous. He feared a "storm of criticism that may greatly lessen your influence hereafter"; it might even appear "as an interference on behalf of Germany." Better say "peace without con-

[1]Probably it was an editorial in the *New Republic*, December 23, 1916, pp. 201–202, in which this phrase was used, which had caught the attention of the President, and to which he referred in a letter to Herbert Croly, January 25th: "I was interested and encouraged when preparing my recent address to the Senate to find an editorial in the New Republic which was not only written along the same lines but which served to clarify and strengthen my thought not a little." A comparison will show, however, that the argument of the editorial was distinctly not the argument developed in Wilson's address.

[2]*War Memoirs of Robert Lansing*, p. 193.

[3]*Ibid.*, p. 194. The address was sent to our ambassadors in Europe on January 15th.

quest," he advised[1]—though how this could be reconciled with certain of the Allied terms he did not explain. Lansing threw his support to Page's plea. But again Wilson cut off discussion abruptly.

"I'll consider it."[2]

He wrote to his old friend Cleveland Dodge:

". . . I have an invincible confidence in the prevalence of the right if it is fearlessly set forth."[3]

And he refused to make any modification.

On Monday, the 22nd, at 12:45 P.M., the President left the White House for the Capitol.[4] He walked down the Senate aisle to the rostrum accompanied by a man soon to part company with him on his policy, Stone of Missouri. In that historic room, Wilson faced an audience made up of men widely differing in their beliefs—among them convinced supporters, others yet undecided, and many bitter foes of his policy. His world audience was cut by the same lines. It was no easy task, measuring his own strength of faith and power of eloquence against the inexorable fate then challenging the world, and against the inertia of entrenched tradition in his own government.

"I spoke," he said of his request for peace terms, December 18th, "on behalf of humanity and of the rights of all neutral nations . . . The Central Powers united in a reply which stated merely that they were ready to meet their antagonists in conference to discuss terms of peace. The Entente Powers have replied much more definitely . . . We are that much nearer a definite discussion of the peace which shall end the present war. We are that much nearer the discussion of the international concert which must thereafter hold the world at peace."

---

[1] *The Life and Letters of Walter H. Page*, Vol. III, pp. 317-318.
[2] *War Memoirs of Robert Lansing*, p. 195.
[3] January 25, 1917.
[4] Mrs. Wilson heard the address from the executive gallery.

12 January, 1917.

THE WHITE HOUSE,
WASHINGTON.

My dear Mr. Secretary,

I saw Senator Stone this evening and
he is generously ready to cooperate in our
plan.

I am, therefore, sending you with this
the address, which I beg that you will set
Mr. Sweet to put into code at once for transmission as we planned at theearliest possible
hour.

I am sending the original because I do
not want to take the time to make a copy and
do not wish to have anyone else make one. I
would be very much obliged if you would send
it back to me when Mr. Sweet has finished putting it in code.

I will then myself make a copy to be
sent later to the printer for distribution
to our press immediately after I shall have
delivered it to the Senate.

Meanwhile I feel that <u>time is of the</u>
<u>essence.</u>

Faithfully Yours,

W. W.

The Secretary of State.

President Wilson made somewhat elaborate plans for the widespread circulation of his appeal to the people of the warring nations
on January 22, 1917. This letter of January 12th to Secretary Lansing
shows how important he considered it to get the exact text into the
hands of American representatives in Europe.

There must follow a peace which would make it impossible for such a war as this to come again:

"Every lover of mankind, every sane and thoughtful man must take that for granted."

With that he turned powerfully to a discussion of the responsibility of America:

"It is inconceivable that the people of the United States should play no part in that great enterprise. . . . They cannot in honor withhold the service to which they are now about to be challenged. . . .

"That service is nothing less than this, to add their authority and their power to the authority and force of other nations to guarantee peace and justice throughout the world. . . .

"If the peace . . . is to endure, it must be a peace made secure by the organized major force of mankind."

Here were bold and original proposals! Since we would assist in guaranteeing the future peace, "our judgment upon what is fundamental and essential as a condition precedent to permanency should be spoken now, not afterwards when it may be too late."

The terms must "create a peace that is worth guaranteeing . . . not merely a peace that will serve the . . . immediate aims" of the warring nations.

"Only a tranquil Europe can be a stable Europe."

To bring about a "tranquil Europe," the peace would have to provide, "not a balance of power, but a community of power." On the basis of the assurances made lately, Wilson believed that neither belligerent wished to crush the other. That fact gave hope for a sound peace built on such a community of power. This, above all, meant one thing: ". . . it must be a peace without victory."

Here he set forth the immutable truth as he saw it, that a "victor's terms" would "leave a sting, a resentment, a bitter memory upon which terms of peace would rest, not permanently, but only as upon quicksand. Only a peace between equals can last."

Speaking "for liberals and friends of humanity in every nation," Wilson laid down the fundamental principles of a great and permanent peace:

"I am proposing, as it were, that the nations . . . adopt the doctrine of President Monroe as the doctrine of the world: that no nation should seek to extend its polity over any other nation or people, but that every people should be left free to determine its own polity, its own way of development, unhindered, unthreatened, unafraid, the little along with the great and powerful.

"I am proposing that all nations henceforth avoid entangling alliances which would draw them into competitions of power . . . There is no entangling alliance in a concert of power. . . .

"I am proposing government by the consent of the governed[1] . . . freedom of the seas . . . and that moderation of armaments which makes of armies and navies a power for order merely, not an instrument of aggression or of selfish violence."

His conclusion rang with the emotion of his deepest convictions:

"These are American principles, American policies. . . . They are the principles of mankind and must prevail."[2]

The address gave President Wilson the moral leadership of liberals the world over. It represented a crystallization of his ideas and ideals for the peace settlement that was not modified until after the close of the conflict. In some measure it transformed the war into a great crusade for an ideal peace.

---

[1]Poland was mentioned as an example of the working of this principle: ". . . there should be a united, independent, and autonomous Poland . . ."

[2]*The Public Papers of Woodrow Wilson*, Vol. IV, pp. 407–414.

Posterity—whether friendly or unfriendly to Wilson—has acclaimed it:

". . . perhaps the most important international document of all history."[1]

"No greater state paper than this exists in the records of modern states." He spoke as "the one dispassionate voice of mankind."[2]

Almost the whole press at the time also approved it:

"In the stateliness of its expression, as well as in the elevation of its thought and the grandeur of its theme, the President's address is one of the most notable in the history of modern statesmanship."[3] "A bold utterance."[4] "Possibilities of vast service."[5]

The phrase "peace without victory" has been well compared with Lincoln's "with malice toward none." Both Presidents had much the same thought in mind—a desire that no bitterness and revenge should follow the close of the war. Lincoln's second inaugural, in which the phrase occurs, and Wilson's speeches in 1918 make clear that each intended to prosecute war with full vigour; each wished that the peace terms should be such that post-war bitterness and a desire to "get even" would be minimized or obliterated. The tragedy of reconstruction was the result of overthrowing Lincoln's magnanimous plans; the chaos of post-war Europe was the result of the defeat of Wilson's aspiration.

But neither "peace without victory" nor Lincoln's "malice toward none" satisfied extremists. Pro-Ally Americans were critical—German ideals and the German spirit must be profoundly changed before peace was

---

[1]G. Lowes Dickinson, *The Choice Before Us*, p. 264.

[2]E. A. Alderman, address before Congress, December 15, 1924.

[3]Springfield *Republican*, January 23, 1917.

[4]Baltimore *Sun*, quoted in the New York *Times*, January 23, 1917.

[5]Cleveland *Plain Dealer*, quoted in the New York *Times*, January 23, 1917.

made.[1] Theodore Roosevelt was vociferous in his criticism[2] and even Bryan, as an idealistic pacifist, was fearful of a league with force—though pleased with the remainder of Wilson's effort.[3] But it satisfied those Americans who wanted most of all to see the war end in an enduring peace. The address, as the writer noted in his diary at the time, seemed "curiously common and familiar, expressing exactly the inner beliefs of thousands of Americans."

While Wilson was pleased with the nation's acceptance—"The country has responded very nobly to what I said . . ."[4]—he could not forget what he considered the "ignoble" response of certain senators. He unburdened his heart in a letter to Cleveland Dodge:

". . . I have been a little low in my mind the last forty-eight hours because of the absolute lack of any power to see what I am driving at which has been exhibited by the men who are looked upon as the leading Republican members of the Senate. After all, it is upon the Senate that I have to depend for the kind of support which will make acts possible, and there are sometimes hours of discouragement connected with trying to lift things into a better air."[5]

While Wilson's caustic comments on the reaction of the Republicans in the Senate were no doubt coloured by his disappointment at their attitude, there was more than a grain of truth in what he said. They at once centred their criticism on the league proposal, and especially upon the idea of force behind it; and bitter things were said. Senator Cummins on the 23rd intimated that the President had chosen the Senate "simply as a conduit through which to

[1] See editorial, New York *Times*, January 25, 1917.
[2] Interview given to news correspondents. *Ibid.*, January 23, 1917.
[3] *Ibid.*, January 24, 1917.
[4] Wilson to Samuel Seabury, January 25, 1917.
[5] January 25, 1917.

pass this new doctrine to the ministers of foreign affairs
and the newspapers of the world," though he added that
he did not hold this belief himself![1] Two days later Borah
threw out a challenge to the President in the form of a
resolution, designed to be laid on the table, to reaffirm the
faith of the Senate in the permanent wisdom of the isolation policies of Washington, Jefferson, and Monroe:[2] the
world, it seemed to the Senator from Idaho, was still the
kind of world in which the United States could be isolated.

An editorial in the *New Republic* a few days later put
the matter succinctly:

". . . to-day it is a Democratic President who grasps
the truth that isolation is over and strives to guide our entrance into world politics towards stability and safety. It
is the Republican party which proposes to crouch at its
own fireside, build a high tariff wall, arm against the whole
world, cultivate no friendships, take no steps to forestall
another great war, and then let things rip."[3]

The address was received in Europe with a mixture of
emotions. "Peace without victory" rang harshly through
the ranks of the Allies. "Government by consent of the
governed" rang as harshly through Germany, Austria-
Hungary, and Turkey. Wilson's ideas had cut both ways—
and both sides seemed to think the gains not worth the
price. Let Wilson "undeceive himself," said a London
paper. This war could not be ended "without bitterness."[4]

"What a pity," groaned Gustav Hervé, that the speech
had been "almost disfigured" by that phrase "peace
without victory."[5]

Although many liberals in England were sympathetic,[6]

[1]*Cong. Rec.*, 64-2, p. 1880.
[2]January 25, 1917. *Ibid.*, p. 1950.
[3]February 3, 1917.
[4]*Daily Chronicle*. Quoted in the New York *Times*, January 23, 1917.
[5]In *Victoire*. Quoted in the New York *Times*, January 24, 1917.
[6]Press comment. *Ibid.*

the French Socialists approved,[1] and the Russian Foreign Office gave its endorsement to the address,[2] underneath there was deep resentment.

"They [the British] consider it," wrote House on the 25th after talking with Wiseman, "inconsistent for us to want to let Germany go free from punishment for breaking the very rules we wish to lay down for the future."[3]

Official Germany, whose attitude Wilson did not know at the time, merely found the speech no "step in the direction of a peace acceptable to us."[4] The Kaiser had decided six days before the address that he placed "absolutely no" reliance on Wilson's peace move.[5]

But Wilson's appeal had been made above all to "the *people* of the countries now at war."[6] He centred his hopes in them.

"I think it ought to have been said, no matter what comes of it."[7]

Since his appeal was primarily to the people, he now sought help outside the political field, writing to several trustees of the Carnegie Foundation for Peace "to ask whether it would or would not in your opinion be possible and wise to get the consent of the Foundation to back my recent address to the Senate up with a systematic propagation of the ideas and the implicit programme which it embodies.

"I feel that the task of the moment is the rousing of a great body of opinion to very definite thought and pur-

---

[1]Ambassador Sharp to the Secretary of State, January 27, 1917. *Foreign Relations*, 1917, Supp. I, pp. 33–34.

[2]New York *Times*, January 27, 1917.

[3]From original. See also *The Intimate Papers of Colonel House*, Vol. II, pp. 420–421.

[4]Testimony of Bethmann-Hollweg after the war. *Official German Documents*, Vol. I, p. 455.

[5]Von Lersner to the German Foreign Office, January 16, 1917, from Pless. *Ibid.*, Vol. II, p. 1106.

[6]Wilson to John Palmer Gavit, January 29, 1917.

[7]Wilson to Charles W. McAlpin, January 26, 1917.

pose, not only in this country but in the countries most immediately involved in the present terrible struggle . . ."[1]

But he did not wish to have "any particular *plan*" presented, as he wrote to a friend:

"I have purposely put forth only the idea, the principle, with the feeling that it could be best advanced by leaving the whole question of organization and detail to the international conference which I hope will some day meet to determine the ways and means of concerted action in the support of peace. If we leave this field clear, we can hope for such an ultimate acceptance of the idea as will create the most favorable possible atmosphere."[2]

Meanwhile, the German government had already made a decision which rendered every peace effort futile.

II. GERMANY'S FATAL DECISION

Ironic tragedy marked Woodrow Wilson's supreme effort of January 22nd to seek peace by an appeal to the people of the world. It was too late. Power had long since passed out of the hands of the people. Everywhere in Europe it was exercised, in secret, by groups of iron-jawed soldiers who knew nothing, demanded nothing, but unremitting force, or by political leaders who, if more diplomatic, were scarcely less determined. Wilson had appealed to reason and to moderation: that also was too late. It might convince Americans, since we were not yet at war: it was utterly lost upon Europe.

It was as ironic as it was tragic that even while Wilson was desperately pleading for peace at Washington, the issue, all unknown to him or to any of his advisers, had been irrevocably decided against him. Two weeks before his impassioned appeal to the people, this order, signed

---

[1]January 29, 1917.
[2]To Edward A. Filene, January 30, 1917.

by the Emperor of Germany, had been secretly promulgated:

General Headquarters, January 9, 1917

I order that the unrestricted submarine war be launched with the greatest vigor on the 1st of February. You will immediately take all the necessary steps, taking care, however, that this intention shall not prematurely come to the knowledge of the enemy and the neutral Powers. . . .

WILHELM I.R.[1]

The drift toward such action, indeed, had been going on for months. The diplomats might continue to talk peace: but as early as August (1916) Hindenburg and Ludendorff had taken over the Supreme High Command of the German army, and they considered that "the unrestricted U-boat war was essential."[2]

Bethmann-Hollweg might, and did, argue moderation and due consideration for the sanctity of treaties—as on October 1st:

"It is well known that we have promised the United States to carry on the U-boat war under the rules of prize. We can recede from this promise only after an impressive statement of our reasons therefor, and after providing for the lapse of a period of time in which the United States would be enabled, in theory at least, to prevent the sailings of American ships and passengers to England."[3]

He might and did continue to fight for delay. He might and did encourage the discussion of peace proposals, even though handicapped by Wilson's postponements—which were mainly due to the opposition of the Allies, and somewhat to the obstruction of Lansing and House.

But the military authorities, now wholly in control, were insisting upon meeting the problems as they saw

---

[1] *Official German Documents*, Vol. II, p. 1210.
[2] Von Hindenburg's testimony, November 18, 1919. *Ibid.*, p. 855.
[3] *Ibid.*, Vol. I, p. 363.

them: and meeting them by the only instruments they knew: powder and shot.

Admiral von Holtzendorff argued on December 22nd that Germany must, for her own survival, bring an end to the war before August 1917; the loss of life, loss of morale, loss of commercial connections, and the rise of political unrest compelled action. In advocating unrestricted naval warfare he was not only moved by wrath against the starvation blockade of England,[1] but he demanded that England be brought "to her knees" and compelled to "accept a useful peace."

What about world opinion?

"Hatred and bitterness," wrote the admiral, ". . . are least of all to be overcome by making concessions or manifesting consideration for others. . . . The success of the strong man has really always been the element before which the world has bowed its head."

What about the United States in particular?

"We can meet the hypocritical arguments which speak of suffering humanity with the remark that it is indeed far more inhuman to sacrifice additional hundreds of thousands of German nationals for the purpose of sparing an infinitesimal number of seamen who, in spite of all warnings, hasten on to their doom."[2]

In any case, as Holtzendorff had written on December 10th:

"There is reason to hope that . . . the United States will confine itself to the use of big words . . ."[3]

He counted on a sudden resumption of unrestricted war-

---

[1]And yet the German food "dictator," Dr. Batocki, announced on January 27, 1917, that Germany had "food enough. . . . In fact, we have a considerable reserve . . .

"I tell you there is absolutely no question of starvation for the German people. In point of fact, there is less starvation in Germany today than there is in the United States . . ." New York *Times*, January 28, 1917.

[2]*Official German Documents*, Vol. II, pp. 1259 *et seq.*

[3]*Ibid.*, p. 1183.

fare to inject "panic and fear" into the enemy and "into neutrals as well."[1] Finally he argued that ". . . the abnormally poor results all over the world of this year's harvest of breadstuffs and provender has placed in our hands a very unique opportunity . . ." He predicted that by February 1917 North America would be practically unable to ship more wheat to England, and Argentina but little. The destruction of "cargo space" would cut down supplies of "metals and woods" with the result, first, that mining and manufacturing would be curtailed, and second, importation of ammunition from neutrals would be effectively stopped. Fear would complete the havoc.[2]

To show how utterly he misunderstood the American people, he concluded by arguing that when Germany had won the war, "an understanding" could be brought about with the United States, "by virtue of which alone she will be able to recover her commercial prosperity, and which will not necessarily result in political sacrifices upon her part."[3]

No doubt the German decision, influenced by conditions that were becoming desperate, was a hard one. Von Hindenburg, looking back later, thought it the most difficult of the whole war except for the decision late in 1918 to ask for an armistice.[4] The German peace move of December 1916 had brought no results satisfactory to Germany; and Wilson's peace note had intimated a kind of concern over peace terms which was unpalatable to the German government.[5]

The German decision, in fact, all unknown to Wilson, was made early in January. On January 6th the Kaiser

[1] *Ibid.*, p. 1218.
[2] *Ibid.*, pp. 1215–1219.
[3] *Ibid.*, p. 1270.
[4] *Ibid.*, p. 877.
[5] *Cf.* testimony of Bethmann-Hollweg. *Ibid.*, Vol. I, p. 351.

exhorted his soldiers to be "from now on . . . men of steel."

"The enemy have rejected my proposal. Their thirst for power dictates Germany's ruin. Let the war take its course."[1]

This was four days before the Allied reply to Wilson's peace note—which the German government itself had urgently encouraged the President to make. They were not waiting even for the possibility of negotiation!

On January 9th the formal announcement that unrestricted submarine warfare was to be resumed[2] was issued, significantly not by the German political leaders, not even in Berlin, but at the military headquarters of the Crown Council at Pless. Secrecy to insure the surprise of the enemy was regarded as of such importance that even Bernstorff at Washington did not receive notice of it until January 19th—when Wilson's appeal for peace had already been decided upon.

Bernstorff had no misconceptions regarding the effect of such a declaration in the United States. He knew how serious the crisis was, and, like Lichnowsky at London in 1914, he fought valiantly and sincerely to avert what he feared to be the impending doom. His reply to his government, sent immediately, went straight to the point:

"War unavoidable if we proceed as contemplated. . . .

"If military reasons . . . are absolutely imperative, a postponement would be urgently desirable . . . Wilson believes he will be able to obtain peace on the basis of the principle announced by us of equal rights to all nations. House told me even yesterday that Wilson was preparing to go ahead in the immediate future . . ."[3]

When Wilson delivered his address to the Senate, January 22nd, Bernstorff thought it not unfriendly to the Cen-

---

[1]*Op. cit.*, Vol. II, p. 1094. Published in the New York *Times*, January 7, 1917.
[2]Printed at the beginning of this section.
[3]January 19, 1917. *Official German Documents*, Vol. II, p. 1021.

tral Powers; but Berlin read it with distorted vision and a mind set upon a crushing victory within six months.

It was perfectly plain, indeed, that the German leaders were contemptuous of American military prowess. The Kaiser said on January 16th that if a break with America was unavoidable, "matters can not be changed; we shall go ahead."[1] They believed that their submarines could win the war before America could become an effective factor.

"Looked at from the military standpoint," said Admiral von Capelle, "I consider that the assistance which will result from the entrance of the United States into the war on the side of our enemies will amount to nothing."[2]

Wilson knew well enough, even while he was delivering his appeal for peace, how desperate the chances really were. He had seen Bernstorff's warning of January 20th that the situation in Berlin was "getting out of our hands"; he had read Gerard's report of January 21st that demands for resumption of "reckless submarine warfare" were becoming so overpowering that it was doubtful whether the government could withstand them;[3] and he knew that submarines were sinking an increasing number of vessels.[4] He wrote to House on the 24th that if the Germans would not assist in making peace possible at once, danger loomed ahead:

". . . with the preparations they are apparently making with regard to unrestrained attacks on merchantmen . . . there is a terrible likelihood that relations between the United States and Germany may come to a breaking point and everything assume a different aspect."

---

[1]*Ibid.*, p. 1106.

[2]February 1, 1917. *Ibid.*, Vol. I, p. 525.

[3]Savage, *Policy of the United States Toward Maritime Commerce in War*, Vol. II, p. 542. Wilson wrote to Lansing on the 24th: "It is only too probable that Gerard's conjectures in this matter are well founded." *Ibid.*, p. 548.

[4]Lansing sent to him on the 15th a list of the cases up to and including the 12th of January.

Few of the President's letters of the time, indeed, so revealed the depth of his feeling of thwarted good will, the measure of his discouragement.

"Feelings, exasperations are neither here nor there. Do they want me to help? I am entitled to know because I genuinely want to help and have now put myself in a position to help without favour to either side."

He was "convinced" that peace was yet possible:

". . . if Germany really wants peace she can get it, and get it soon, *if she will but confide in me and let me have a chance*. What Bernstorff said to you the other day as trimmed and qualified by what he wrote afterwards amounts to nothing so far as negotiations between the belligerents are concerned. It occurs to me that it would be well for you to see Bernstorff again at once (not where your meeting can be noted, as the last one was, but at some place which is not under observation) and tell him that this is the time to accomplish something, if they really and truly want peace; that the indications that come to us are of a sort to lead us to believe that with something reasonable to suggest, as from them, I can bring things about . . .

"I feel very lonely sometimes and sometimes very low in my mind, in spite of myself."

This letter, written to House on January 24th, was only a week away from the deadline set by the Germans—of which the President had not as yet even been informed.

Bernstorff cabled his government on the 25th, again pleading for delay;[1] then he hurried to New York to see House for what was to be his last conference—but he did not tell him of the German ultimatum! He let him think that there was still a chance for peace: he even agreed to telegraph again to his government.

"I told him," wrote House to Wilson on the 26th, "you

---

[1] *Official German Documents*, Vol. II, p. 1027.

wished something to use with the people of the Allied countries, so that public sentiment might force the governments to discuss peace. . . .

"He is to suggest to them that the terms include complete evacuation of Belgium and France.[1] In addition to this he is suggesting that they make an offer to go into a peace conference on the basis of your address to the Senate."

We know now how completely both Wilson and House were being hoodwinked. We know what irony, deepening into tragedy, marked those fatal last days of January. Bernstorff had been informed of the ultimatum and did not warn either Wilson or House! But, as the documents clearly reveal, the British also knew and did not inform either Wilson or House![2]

As to the attitude of the British, House reported hopefully to Wilson on the 26th[3] that Sir William Wiseman, who was attached to the British Embassy in Washington, had called.

"His whole tone had changed. He said the atmosphere had cleared wonderfully since yesterday."

House naïvely told Wiseman of "Bernstorff's visit and what you [Wilson] had asked him to do. This pleased him and we got down to a discussion of actual peace terms . . .

"He told me in the *gravest confidence* . . . that he is in direct communication with the Foreign Office, and that the Ambassador and other members of the Embassy are not aware of it. . . .

"He went so far as to discuss with me where the confer-

---

[1]Bernstorff, wrote House in his long letter, "rather shied" at House's reference to "*mutual* 'restoration, reparation and indemnity,'" though Bernstorff had himself suggested it "in a former conversation."

[2]The famous Zimmermann note of January 16th, to be discussed later, which the British intercepted, contained this sentence: "It is our purpose on the 1st of February to commence the unrestricted U-boat war." *Official German Documents*, Vol. II, p. 1337.

[3]In a letter not published in *The Intimate Papers of Colonel House.*

ence should be held, and whether or not there should first be a preliminary conference and afterwards a general one. I take it he has heard directly from his government . . . for he seemed to speak with authority."

Wilson was encouraged by these communications: it seemed that both sides were willing still to talk peace!

But Wiseman, although "in direct communication with the Foreign Office" and on "confidential" relations with House, said nothing, so far as House reveals, about the absolutely vital matter of the German decision. It is a subject painful to contemplate! Did the British *want* the German announcement to be sprung without warning upon America? Did they think that the resulting shock would help to drive us into the war?

It was now the 28th—with the deadline three days off. Bernstorff had been as good as his word and sent a last desperate appeal to Berlin:

"If the U-boat war is commenced forthwith the President will look upon this as a slap in the face, and war with the United States will be unavoidable . . . if we meet Wilson's proposition and if, in spite of that fact, these plans are brought to naught by the obstinacy of our opponents, it will be a very difficult thing for the President to undertake a war with us, even if we were then to start the unrestricted U-boat warfare. Thus . . . all we need is a brief delay . . . we can get a better peace by means of conferences than if the United States should join our enemies."[1]

Whatever Bernstorff may have done in the past—and he had a hard post to fill—one must admire his courage and his ability in these last days of January.

Bethmann-Hollweg read the dispatch in a "state of contained excitement" over this prospect of peace,[2] and

---

[1] *Official German Documents*, Vol. I, pp. 302–303.
[2] *Ibid.*, Vol. II, p. 695.

hurried to headquarters to discuss it. But the decision was irrevocable. Twenty-one U-boats were already at sea—there was no possible way, it was said, of making sure that a message would reach all of them. They could not be recalled.[1] The glory of a swift, decisive stroke was more promising, more intoxicating than the prospect of a doubtful victory by mediation.

Bethmann-Hollweg still saw a bare possibility, however, that Wilson might, if he were given the German terms, keep on seeking peace. He therefore dispatched a relatively specific telegram to Bernstorff on the 29th.

On the 30th House reported to the President:

"Bernstorff has just called me up to say that he is sending over by messenger tomorrow, a *very important* letter. I asked him if it was an answer. He replied: 'a partial one.'"

Bernstorff's letter was indeed important—or would have been, earlier. It was dated January 31st, and House took it to Washington forthwith, leaving on the night train. It was to be considered, as will be shown presently, after it was too late.[2]

The deadline was now scarcely two days off—and Wilson still knew nothing of the German ultimatum!

"It is hard," as he wrote to an old friend, "to see in the present murky air any landmarks by which to steer."[3]

On the morning of the 31st the President and his physician, Dr. Grayson, played a round of golf. There were a number of appointments at the Executive Office in the afternoon—and the day's correspondence to be taken care of. He studied a recent letter from Lansing on Far Eastern matters and again approved the policy of refusing international coöperation in China except on matters ab-

---

[1]*Ibid.*, Vol. I, pp. 560–564.
[2]See this volume, pp. 450–451.
[3]To E. P. Davis, January 30, 1917.

solutely free from political motives. Still unaware how little such minor irritations any longer counted, he wrote a letter to Lansing regarding the British practice of arming merchant ships—a letter that also revealed his determined intention of holding even the scales between the belligerents in Europe.

"This is, to my mind, quite the most puzzling and difficult question we have had to deal with. It is becoming pretty clear to me that the British are going beyond the spirit, at any rate, of the principles hitherto settled . . . and that the method in which their ship captains are instructed to use their guns has in many instances gone beyond what could legitimately be called defense. It appears that they have more than once attacked. . . . I would be glad to know the progress of your own thought in this matter.[1]

In a response that afternoon Lansing revealed his deep anxiety:

"You may see, Mr. President, from what I have written that I am greatly agitated . . . I am indeed more anxious than I have been since the *Sussex* affair."

Before the President left his office that afternoon, his Secretary, Mr. Tumulty, brought an Associated Press bulletin which had just come by telephone. It was a bald statement of fact: on the following day unrestricted submarine warfare would begin.

"As I entered," Tumulty writes, "he looked up from his writing, casual inquiry in his eyes. Without comment I laid the fateful slip of paper on his desk, and silently watched him as he read and re-read it. I seemed to read his mind in the expressions that raced across his strong features; first, blank amazement; then incredulity . . . then gravity and sternness, a sudden grayness of colour, a

---

[1]Savage, *Policy of the United States Toward Maritime Commerce in War*, Vol. II, p. 549.

compression of the lips and the familiar locking of the
jaw which always characterized him in moments of supreme resolution. Handing the paper back to me, he said
in quiet tones: 'This means war. The break that we have
tried so hard to prevent now seems inevitable.'"[1]

These words—if Tumulty records them correctly—were
the expression of Wilson's first strong reaction. While the
possibility of such a course was not unexpected, the utter
ruthlessness of a warning without preliminary notice, after
the promises made in the *Sussex* case, was a shocking
surprise.

At ten minutes past four the German ambassador arrived at the State Department. Lansing noticed that
"though he moved with his usual springy step, he did not
smile with his customary assurance." He sat down; drew
a number of papers from a large envelope and passed them
over to the Secretary. Lansing read them with deliberation. Bernstorff, watching his two and a half years of
effort to preserve friendly relations breaking down, said,
as Lansing turned again toward him:

"I am sorry to have to bring about this situation but
my government could do nothing else."

". . . you must know," responded Lansing, "that it
cannot be accepted."

"Of course; of course, I understand that. I know it is
very serious, very, and I deeply regret that it is necessary."

Bernstorff arose, offered his hand, bowed a little tiredly,
and left the room.[2]

Lansing immediately sent the papers to the White
House, but it was not until after eight o'clock that they
came to Wilson's hand and he read the formal notification

---

[1] Tumulty, *Woodrow Wilson As I Know Him*, pp. 254–255.

[2] Lansing's memorandum, made on February 4, 1917. *War Memoirs of Robert Lansing*,
pp. 210–212.

from the Imperial German government which was to become effective at midnight.[1]

". . . Germany will meet the illegal measures of her enemies by forcibly preventing after February 1, 1917, in a zone around Great Britain, France, Italy and in the Eastern Mediterranean all navigation, that of neutrals included . . . All ships met within that zone will be sunk."

Only neutral ships already on the seas would be "spared during a sufficiently long period" to provide for their return.

". . . one steamer a week," not carrying contraband as defined by Germany, might sail to and from Falmouth, provided three markings were made alternately red and white in "vertical stripes 1 meter wide" on the hull and superstructure, and provided the American flag was flown on the stern and red and white flags on the masts, and the ships were "well lighted" at night[2]—provisions for the control of ships and shipping of the United States that most Americans, when they heard the terms, considered outrageous and insulting.

The President turned to his telephone and asked Lansing to come at once to the White House.

---

[1]Because of the difference in time it was, of course, already midnight in the zone marked out by Germany, and the new ruling was therefore already in effect when the papers reached the President.

[2]Bernstorff to the Secretary of State, with enclosures, January 31, 1917. *Foreign Relations*, 1917, Supp., I, pp. 97–102.

CHAPTER XI

THE BREAK WITH GERMANY

"We are the sincere friends of the German people and earnestly desire to remain at peace with the Government which speaks for them. We shall not believe that they are hostile to us unless and until we are obliged to believe it; and we purpose nothing more than the reasonable defense of the undoubted rights of our people."

Address to Congress, February 3, 1917.

"I hope that I need give no further proofs and assurances than I have already given throughout nearly three years of anxious patience that I am the friend of peace and mean to preserve it for America so long as I am able. . . . War can come only by the wilful acts and aggressions of others."

Address to Congress, February 26, 1917.

I. SEVERING DIPLOMATIC RELATIONS

IT WAS a solemn and momentous meeting there in the quiet study of the White House on the night of the 31st of January 1917. The Secretary of State, summoned by the President, arrived at a quarter of nine. In the zone marked out, German submarines were already beginning a ruthless campaign of unrestricted warfare. Of this the German government, though still formally bound by their *Sussex* pledge, had given no preliminary warning. Scores of American ships were on the high seas subject to possible attack: hundreds of American lives were newly endangered. The finality of the German challenge had been deliberately emphasized that forenoon by the swift disabling of the interned German ships in American ports.[1] The ominous news of the new crisis, half fact, half wild

[1]Bernstorff had given the order at ten o'clock that morning.

447

rumour, was already being cried on the streets of New York.

Wilson's first reaction to the German declaration had been one of "astounding surprise."[1] He could not at first believe it. Only a little more than a week before, in his address to the Senate, he had made a passionate appeal to the people of the world. He had firmly believed, had been led to believe by both belligerents, that there was still a chance for peace. All his hopes were fallen now in utter confusion; the bitter disappointment occasioned by his repeated rebuffs sharpened by the knowledge that he had also, at the last, been hoodwinked.

Upon few occasions in our history have profounder responsibilities rested upon the shoulders of an American President. What was he to do? What alternatives were there? He had already, more than nine months before, sternly warned the German government:

"Unless the Imperial Government should now immediately declare and effect an abandonment of its present methods of submarine warfare against passenger and freight-carrying vessels, the Government of the United States can have no choice but to sever diplomatic relations with the German Empire altogether."[2]

The Germans had grudgingly given their pledge—which they had now broken.

If he severed relations, as he had threatened, it was all but inevitable that war must follow. The Germans themselves, by scuttling their ships, plainly indicated their belief that the end had come. In this crisis the President could not divide responsibility: it rested initially with him, and him alone, to decide whether the youth of America should be ordered to the bloody fields of France.

He discussed the situation anxiously with Lansing

---

[1] *The Letters of Franklin K. Lane*, p. 233.

[2] April 18, 1916. *Foreign Relations*, 1916, Supp., p. 234.

that evening at the White House. Lansing had no doubt as to what the decision should be: he had had no doubt for months. He was for an immediate break with Germany: "any lesser action would be impossible." But the President, quite as "deeply incensed at Germany's insolent notice" as the Secretary, was still thinking of American responsibilities and duties as well as of American rights. His brooding, prophetic mind, looking before and after, was considering what was right, what was just, what, in the long run, would be best for the world. It would be easy to fight: one could fight at any time. It would settle nothing. Lansing records that he talked of the future of "white civilization," of how the world, after the war, was to be reconstructed. Who was to help restore the nations "ravaged by the war"? Was it not probable that America could do a greater service if she kept out than if she went in?

"He said," reports Lansing, "that as this idea had grown upon him he had come to the feeling that he was willing to go to any lengths rather than to have the nation actually involved in the conflict."

Lansing argued that "if we failed to act" we would be disgraced, and would in the future be "treated with contempt by both the Allies and Germany."

But the President was still not convinced. He said that if he "believed it was for the good of the world for the United States to keep out of the war in the present circumstances, he would be willing to bear all the criticism and abuse which would surely follow our failure to break with Germany; that contempt was nothing unless it impaired future usefulness; and that nothing could induce him to break off relations unless he was convinced that, viewed from every angle, it was the wisest thing to do."

Moreover, bitter as was the offense of the Germans, he was still obstinately convinced that right was not all on one side. He showed, even during this discussion of German "insolence," "much irritation over the British disregard for neutral rights."

Finally, he must, he told Lansing, have more time to think; meanwhile he directed the Secretary to draw up, for further consideration, a tentative note breaking relations.[1]

On the next morning, February 1st, House arrived bringing Bernstorff's letter about which he had telegraphed Wilson on the day before. Bernstorff had called it "a *very important* letter"; it represented, indeed, the last desperate appeal of all that was left of the moderate party in Germany.

". . . my Government," wrote Bernstorff, "begs the President to continue his efforts to bring about peace . . ."[2]

Wilson read aloud this belated appeal: ironic now, in the light of the newly disclosed intentions of the Germans.

---

[1] *The War Memoirs of Robert Lansing,* pp. 212–213.

[2] The essential parts of the letter are here published, from the copy in Mr. Wilson's files: "I have received a telegram from Berlin, according to which I am to express to the President the thanks of the Imperial Government for his communication made through you. The Imperial Government has complete confidence in the President and hopes that he will reciprocate such confidence. As proof I am to inform you in confidence that the Imperial Government will be very glad to accept the services kindly offered by the President for the purpose of bringing about a peace conference between the belligerents. My Government, however, is not prepared to publish any peace terms at present, because our enemies have published such terms which aim at the dishonor and destruction of Germany and her allies. My Government considers that as long as our enemies openly proclaim such terms, it would show weakness, which does not exist, on our part if we publish our terms and we would in so doing only prolong the war. However, to show President Wilson our confidence, my Government through me desires to inform him *personally* of the terms under which we would have been prepared to enter into negotiations, if our enemies had accepted our offer of December 12th.

"'Restitution of the part of Upper Alsace occupied by the French.

"'Gaining of a frontier which would protect Germany and Poland economically and strategically against Russia.

"'Restitution of Colonies in form of an agreement which would give Germany Colonies adequate to her population and economic interest.

"'Restitution of those parts of France occupied by Germany under reservation of strategical and economic changes of the frontier and financial compensations.

"'Restoration of Belgium under special guarantee for the safety of Germany which would have to be decided on by negotiations with Belgium.

"'Economic and financial mutual compensation on the basis of the exchange of territories conquered and to be restituted at the conclusion of peace.

"'Compensation for the German business concerns and private persons who suffered by the war. Abandonment of all economic agreements and measures which would form

"He saw at once," wrote House in his diary, "how perfectly shallow it was. Bernstorff's protestations were almost a mockery when the substance of the cable from his Government was considered."[1]

But the letter throws no little light upon the difficulties which Wilson all along had to face in dealing with the European belligerents. What was he to believe? Whom was he to trust? Here was Bernstorff struggling up to the last moment to prevent a final break, and encouraging, even begging, Wilson to go forward with his peace efforts; and over against him, in Berlin, the diabolical forces of unrestrained militarism. It is scarcely surprising that Wilson should all along have doubted, because he could not know, Bernstorff's motives. He had written to House in 1915:

"He is a most extraordinary person. In his letters to you he is one person, in his interviews (particularly in his confidential interviews) with the newspaper men he is quite another. I wish I knew which, if either, is the genuine Bernstorff."[2]

On another occasion he had said:

"I do not feel that Bernstorff is dealing frankly with us . . ."[3]

---

an obstacle to normal commerce and intercourse after the conclusion of peace, and instead of such agreements reasonable treaties of commerce.

"'The freedom of the seas.'

"The peace terms of our allies run on the same lines. My Government further agrees, after the war has been terminated, to enter into the proposed second International Conference on the basis of the President's message to the Senate.

"My Government would have been glad to postpone the submarine blockade, if they had been able to do so. This, however, was quite impossible on account of the preparations which could not be canceled. My Government believes that the submarine blockade will terminate the war very quickly. In the meantime my Government will do every thing possible to safeguard American interests and begs the President to continue his efforts to bring about peace, and my Government will terminate the submarine blockade as soon as it is evident that the efforts of the President will lead to a peace acceptable to Germany. . . ."

[1]*The Intimate Papers of Colonel House*, Vol. II, p. 438.

[2]September 20, 1915.

[3]Wilson to House, July 29, 1915.

But what hope was there for those individual virtues, those nobilities of understanding, which Wilson craved, when war, having smothered every civilized tradition, dealt only in suspicion and deceit?

House reports of his conference on February 1st that the President was deeply irritated and spoke of Germany as "a madman that should be curbed." House asked "if he thought it fair to the Allies to ask them to do the curbing without doing our share." But Wilson again argued, as he had argued the night before with Lansing, that "it would be a crime" to become involved in the war if it were humanly possible to avoid it. Who would be left to "save Europe"?

It was indeed a bitter day for the President. He felt "as if the world had suddenly reversed itself . . . and that he could not get his balance."

". . . I did not succeed at any time . . . in lifting him into a better frame of mind."

He walked the floor: "nervously arranged his books." He waited anxiously for Lansing to bring the draft of the proposed note to Germany. Mrs. Wilson, understanding the agony of spirit the President was undergoing, suggested that he get out of doors—play a game of golf. House, however, said "the American people would feel that he should not do anything so trivial at such a time."[1]

Newspapers all over America resounded with the crisis. Outside, on the streets of Washington, curiously quiet men and women looked inward to the White House—who knows with what tumultuous, expectant, fatalistic thoughts? Many knew of the decision that was in the making; it might affect them for the remainder of their lives. At the other end of Pennsylvania Avenue, the Senate was stolidly discussing appropriations, and, bitterly, a league of nations; the House was preparing to pass the

[1] *The Intimate Papers of Colonel House*, Vol. II, pp. 439-441.

Immigration bill over the President's veto.[1] In Wall Street, stocks were falling precipitously; American ships, awaiting the fateful decision at Washington, remained at their docks, not daring to risk the chance that a submarine might be on guard to destroy them.[2]

It was not until noon that Lansing arrived with his draft of the note:

"I went further in this conference," he reports, "than I did in the previous one by asserting that in my opinion peace and civilization depended on the establishment of democratic institutions throughout the world, and that this would be impossible if Prussian militarism after the war controlled Germany. The President said that he was not sure of this as it might mean the disintegration of German power and the destruction of the German nation. . . .

"When I left the conference I felt convinced that the President had almost reached a decision to send Bernstorff home."[3]

House's report of the conference shows that he was even more convinced than Lansing that the President had made his decision;[4] but Wilson was as yet by no means committed; he still hoped for a peace without victory. That very afternoon, desperate as was the crisis he was facing, we find him recurring to one of the possibilities which he had in the past rejected: that is, a joint declaration by neutral nations. He conferred with Minister Ritter, of Switzerland, asking if his country still adhered to the sug-

---

[1] *Cong. Rec.*, 64-2, pp. 2361 *et seq.*, 2442 *et seq.*

[2] New York *Times*, February 2, 1917.

[3] *War Memoirs of Robert Lansing*, p. 214. House, wrote Lansing, "as is customary with him, said very little, but what he did say was in support of my views." *Ibid.*

[4] *The Intimate Papers of Colonel House*, Vol. II, p. 441. It was probably at this time, also, that it was decided not in any case to break relations with Austria-Hungary if it could be avoided. *Ibid.*, p. 449. The Austro-Hungarian note declaring unrestricted submarine warfare was not received until the morning of February 3rd. *Foreign Relations*, 1917, Supp., I, pp. 104-105.

gestion made on January 9th that all neutrals unite to assert their rights and lay down the bases of peace they proposed to support. Was it possible that such a plan might after all open a way to peace? Ritter immediately communicated with his government, but the reply did not arrive in time to affect the immediate crisis. The incident shows, however, that the President was still hoping against hope that something, somewhere, would give him a way of escape. His letters on the following morning (February 2nd) reveal his continued indecision and his agony of spirit:

"Just now it looks as if the cause of peace were all but desperate, but words of encouragement such as you are generous enough to send help immensely in these dark hours."[1]

To an old friend:

"Alas, even you don't realize how I am overwhelmed . . . My thought is under seas."[2]

Three times he talked with Lansing by telephone, discussing the sailing of American ships, the issuance of passports, and the possibility of securing identic action by other neutrals in case of a break. Lansing pressed him hard, orally and by letter, arraigning Germany mercilessly, and suggesting that the President ought not to stop with a mere break, but should deliver a message to Congress asking for a declaration of war.[3]

It was indeed beginning to appear that public opinion favoured a break. In the East the feeling could be summarized by the phrase "we cannot temporize." The Middle West was becoming almost as belligerent: "Facts must be dealt with"; it "is inconceivable" that the United States should give tacit approval to Germany. The far

---

[1]To the Rev. Dr. Charles S. Macfarland.
[2]To Lawrence C. Woods.
[3]*War Memoirs of Robert Lansing*, pp. 219–220.

West thought it better to delay action until we were "specifically injured," though the Denver *Post* declared there was "no other choice" but to break.[1]

Up to this time the President had not consulted with his cabinet; he usually delayed such action until he was nearing a decision himself. Upon that Friday afternoon at two-thirty when he walked into the conference room every member of the cabinet, aware of the momentous problem confronting the country, rose to his feet.

The President began by reading aloud "in measured tones, giving weight to every significant syllable,"[2] the text of the German declaration of unrestricted submarine warfare.

"I can see now the faces of some of my Cabinet colleagues . . . feelings of mingled amusement and wrath . . . Everybody seemed to feel, if not to say, 'That settles it' . . ."[3]

Each in turn was ready to discuss the issues, but hesitated, in the presence of a crisis of such magnitude, to offer specific advice. The President finally broke out almost impatiently:

"What is the concrete suggestion? What shall I propose? I must go to Congress. What shall I say?"[4]

Someone asked which side he wished to see win. He did not, he replied, "wish to see either side win . . ." He still believed profoundly in a peace without victory! He added that he "would like to see the neutrals unite."

After some further discussion, Lane suggested the likelihood of a German-Russian-Japanese alliance after the war—which would be dangerous to the United States. The President responded with a prophetic suggestion, astonish-

[1]News comments, quoted in the New York *Times*, February 1, 1917.

[2]Daniels, *Our Navy at War*, pp. 21–22.

[3]Redfield, "Woodrow Wilson, An Appreciation," in the *Review of Reviews*, April 1925.

[4]Houston, *Eight Years With Wilson's Cabinet*, Vol. I, p. 230.

ing at that moment, that "the Russian peasant might save the world this misfortune."[1]

He also declared with emphasis, as he had previously told Lansing, that if "in order to keep the white race or part of it strong to meet the yellow race . . . it was wise to do nothing, he would do nothing, and would submit to . . . any imputation of weakness or cowardice . . ."[2]

The President adjourned the cabinet meeting, after a long session, without disclosing his final decision. It was clear, however, that the members generally agreed upon the necessity of a break.[3]

Having the unanimous opinion of his official family, the President was now prepared for the next step he commonly took in facing the gravest of his decisions. He went at once to the Senate building for a long conference with Stone of Missouri,[4] chairman of the Foreign Relations Committee, and with other senators. Some urged waiting for an overt act, but most of those with whom he consulted were in favour of breaking relations.

"They thought," read a news report, "this was the dignified thing to do and were sure that their constituents would applaud that course."[5]

The President returned that evening to the White House to make the irrevocable decision, alone, in the quiet of his own room. Apparently the cabinet and the Senate both favoured the drastic course. But he was still stubbornly plagued by the deeper, more fundamental questions: What was right? What was wise? Even though the

---

[1]*Letters of Franklin K. Lane*, p. 234.

[2]Houston, *Eight Years With Wilson's Cabinet*, Vol. I, p. 229.

[3]Daniels, *Our Navy At War*, pp. 21–22; W. B. Wilson in a letter to the author, September 17, 1932. But Lane left the meeting believing that Wilson would await an "overt" act before doing anything. *The Letters of Franklin K. Lane*, p. 234.

[4]Who had been summoned back from St. Louis by a telegram from the President. *The Intimate Papers of Colonel House*, Vol. II, p. 441.

[5]New York *Times*, February 3, 1917; *Current History*, Vol. V (March 1917), p. 970.

people generally assented, as he now believed that they would, could he regard it as a final mandate? Mere popular approval had never satisfied him; he had confessed the depth of his feeling in this regard in a letter written nearly two years before:

"I know . . . there is nothing to tie to or live on in popular approval: and I know that I must hold myself ready to do the right thing at the immediate sacrifice of it all, if the occasion should arise."[1]

What, after all, was the final authority? We know what it was in the case of Woodrow Wilson. We know not only the thoroughness of his preparation as a scholar, especially his knowledge of history, but how deep and sincere were his religious foundations.

"*My* life would not be worth living if it were not for the driving power of religion, for *faith* . . ."[2]

His convictions had been bred in the bone: inherited through generations of Scotch Presbyterian ancestors, many of whom had been ministers of the gospel. They had been the teachings of his earliest youth; and however the reality of such a faith may have been dimmed in the popular mind, its verities remained, with all their antique power, as a sovereign resort with Woodrow Wilson.

The next morning (February 3rd) he had made his decision. He planned to address Congress at two o'clock that afternoon; we know, from the letters he wrote during the forenoon, how profoundly he was affected. He thanked his brother "from the bottom of a very troubled heart" for his "God be with you."

"It is a hard decision to come to," he wrote to a friend, "but one which has been forced upon me."[3]

He explained in the same letter that he had been "deal-

---

[1] To Lucy M. Smith, May 23, 1915.
[2] *Woodrow Wilson, Life and Letters*, Vol. V, *Neutrality*, p. 144.
[3] To Mrs. Anita McCormick Blaine.

ing so intimately and so long with the German authorities that I feel that any course except the one I am pursuing today would be practically useless."

Reports that the President would address Congress had drawn thousands of people, who, unable to get into the chamber of the House, crowded the corridors and overflowed to the streets. Justices of the Supreme Court occupied the front row to the left of the Speaker's desk; cabinet members were scattered wherever they could find places.[1] Chairs had to be placed in the aisles for some of the senators. At two promptly the President entered, his face "drawn," set in "grave lines."[2] There was sporadic handclapping as he went to the rostrum, then silence. He reviewed the *Sussex* notes—the threat to break relations, the refusal to accept a conditional pledge. He read briefly from the new German announcement of unrestricted submarine warfare. That declaration, he continued in tones of absolute conviction, left us "no alternative consistent with the dignity and honor of the United States" but to break relations.

"I have, therefore, directed the Secretary of State to announce to His Excellency the German Ambassador that all diplomatic relations between the United States and the German Empire are severed . . ."

His listeners broke into applause, but the President waited only a moment. It was no agreeable task for him to do this thing.

". . . I refuse to believe that it is the intention of the German authorities to do in fact what they have warned us they will feel at liberty to do. . . . Only actual overt acts on their part can make me believe it even now."

If such acts were committed, in violation of law and

---

[1]Lansing was not there; he was attending to the necessary diplomatic correspondence —passports, invitations to the neutral governments to take identic action. *War Memoirs of Robert Lansing*, p. 216; *Foreign Relations*, 1917, Supp. I, p. 108.

[2]Robert J. Bender, *Woodrow Wilson*, pp. 29–30.

humanity, ". . . I shall take the liberty of coming again before the Congress, to ask that authority be given me to use any means that may be necessary for the protection of our seamen and our people . . ."

Again there was cheering.

"I take it for granted that all neutral governments will take the same course."

Then he concluded:

". . . we purpose nothing more than the reasonable defense of the undoubted rights of our people. . . . We seek merely . . . to vindicate our right to liberty and justice and an unmolested life. These are the bases of peace, not war. God grant we may not be challenged to defend them by acts of wilful injustice on the part of the Government of Germany!"[1]

The public response to his address left no doubt in the President's mind that he had expressed the overwhelming sentiment of the nation. There was hardly a murmur of criticism either of his stand or of the manner in which he had handled the crisis. "Admirably done" was the sum of opinion in Congress and among the people at large.[2] Four days later the Senate gave convincing evidence of the widespread approval by passing a resolution endorsing his action by a vote of 78 to 5.[3]

While Wilson had been speaking, Bernstorff was handed passports for himself and his staff. He met the situation stoically:

"I am not surprised. . . . There was nothing else left for the United States to do."[4]

Immediately after the President's return to the White House, the grounds were closed to the public; a few min-

---

[1] *The Public Papers of Woodrow Wilson*, Vol. IV, pp. 422–426.

[2] Press comment, New York *Times*, February 4, 1917.

[3] The five who voted against the resolution were Gronna (N. Dak.), Kirby (Ark.), La Follette (Wis.), Vardaman (Miss.), Works (Calif.). *Cong. Rec.*, 64–2, pp. 2749–2750.

[4] *War Memoirs of Robert Lansing*, p. 217; New York *Times*, February 4, 1917.

utes later the State, War and Navy Departments were likewise closed. At three o'clock the Secretaries of War and Navy arrived at the White House for a hurried conference with the President. That night all American naval vessels were ordered to report their readiness for war.[1] No one knew what might now happen.

II. LAST DESPERATE EFFORTS TO MAKE PEACE

Wilson's message breaking relations released the pent-up feelings of millions of Americans. He had feared all along that even precautionary and preparatory measures would fan the war spirit; his address proved far more decisive in this respect than he had anticipated. It seemed that he had phrased for the first time what many Americans had "only half worked out in their minds." Evidence accumulated that people were accepting the severance of relations with Germany as presaging immediate war.[2] By February 8th long lines of young men were waiting to enlist—in Iowa![3]

It was indeed a vicious circle in which the President found himself enmeshed. One defiant step, since it implied possible danger, inevitably led to another. In a time of intense emotion, with the wildest rumours eagerly circulated, it was impossible to neglect protective measures. Protective measures meant soldiers to guard public buildings, munitions factories, unfortified boundaries. Soldiers meant headlines. However forcibly the President might direct that "no troops under Federal control be stationed or used in a manner which will excite apprehension or suggest anticipated trouble, and especially that no basis should be given for opinion abroad that we are mobil-

[1]Daniels, *Our Navy at War*, pp. 22–23.

[2]This biographer wrote in his diary on February 4th: "While of course war is not begun, no one now believes that we can escape it."

[3]Letter from Ida M. Tarbell, February 8, 1917, from Des Moines, Iowa, in Mr. Wilson's files.

izing,"[1] the fact that Pershing rode out of Mexico on February 5th with ten thousand men and that the mustering out of the National Guard was being delayed[2] was exciting to the public mind.

There was still other and even more solidly convincing evidence. A huge naval appropriation bill was being pressed in Congress; railroad companies began to coördinate their services to meet military exigencies;[3] the Council of National Defense organized committees on industrial mobilization.[4] Even the pulpits of the nation resounded with sermons which would have delighted the pagan gods of war. The astonished President exclaimed:

". . . I think our ministers are going crazy . . ."[5]

The President was not only astonished by these overwhelming evidences of popular feeling, but he was also alarmed. This was especially evident when messages of support from the powerful financial and industrial interests of the nation began to flood the White House. The United States Steel Corporation, the Bethlehem Steel Company, the Remington Arms Company, Henry Ford, J. P. Morgan & Company were among those who sent immediate word of their readiness to place all their resources at the disposal of the government.

Wilson's cool reply to J. P. Morgan typified his reaction to these messages:

"It is not yet clear what is ahead of us but I am sure that all America will have but a single spirit in meeting any crisis that may develop."[6]

What Wilson desired most, of course, was the unified

---

[1]Secretary Baker to General Wood, February 3, 1917, stating the President's instructions.

[2]*Ibid.*

[3]New York *Times*, February 17, 1917.

[4]Grosvenor Clarkson, *Industrial America in the World War*, pp. 28-29.

[5]Wilson to Tumulty, February 1917.

[6]February 5, 1917.

support of the people of America: but the avalanche of approval and the offers of assistance from interests that had fought him bitterly in the past were disturbing.[1] Overtures were even being made by Republicans for a coalition cabinet!

In short, he saw the whole structure of economic and political liberalism he had been striving to build up in danger of being undermined by reactionary forces creeping in with the wave of primitive emotion occasioned by the fear of war. He expressed his indignation about this coöperation "from certain once hostile quarters," in a letter to House:

"You notice the suggestion is being actively renewed that I call their crowd into consultation and have a coalition cabinet at my elbow. It is the *Junkerthum* trying to creep in under cover of the patriotic feeling of the moment. They will not get in. They have now no examples of happy or successful coalitions to point to. The nominal coalition in England is nothing but a Tory cabinet such as they are eager to get a foothold for here. I know them too well, and will hit them straight between the eyes, if necessary, with plain words."[2]

Wilson knew well, as an historian, the powerful recessive forces inevitably unleashed by war: the destruction of deliberative democratic action, the rise of more primitive forms of dictatorship. He feared these tendencies; it was the principal reason for his stubborn resistance to the invasion

---

[1] There was nothing personal in this feeling. It represented his anxiety lest a point of view in the matter of domestic reform which he had been opposing since the beginning of his administration should reassert itself. He felt, as he had written to the chairman of the Minnesota Democratic State Central Committee, that "reaction now might set the cause back a generation." (September 22, 1916.)

[2] February 12, 1917. Once the war began, and the new problem of fighting it had to be faced, the President of course welcomed the help of everyone, Republican or Democrat, bankers, industrialists, labour leaders, farmers. Many of the "dollar-a-year men" belonged to the class who had been his critical opponents. But he always opposed a "coalition cabinet."

8 February, 1917.

My dear Daniels,

So many people who want to run our foreign affairs for us are trying to communicate
with the German Government that it has occurred to me that they might try to employ the
wireless stations, which are under the control
of your Department. I hope that you will very
carefully guard against that and issue very
strict and definite orders about it.   There
is extreme danger in everything of that kind.
Impressions are apt to be made which will be
so misleading as to make war more rather than
less likely, by leading the German authorities
to a wholly wrong impression,- especially as
they know that no messages go through that we
do not officially let through.

I hasten this over to you, because it
is a matter which I had omitted to cover in our
conferences.

Faithfully Yours,

Woodrow Wilson

The Secretary of the Navy.

Original letter written on his own typewriter by President Wilson
to Secretary Daniels, February 8, 1917.

of the war spirit: and for his passionate, even desperate, effort until the very last to avoid becoming involved.

Nevertheless the sequence of events he was facing was inexorable and irresistible. However he might resist extensive military preparation,[1] he was forced constantly to plan for any eventuality; we find him directing Daniels and Baker to "get and keep" the ablest men they could find for responsible positions in their Departments.[2] In the weeks following the severance of relations it was clear —painfully clear to those in his cabinet and in Congress who were ready to go to war—that the spearhead of resistance was the White House.

". . . I am doing everything that I honorably can to keep the country out of war . . ."[3]

In answer to an offer of personal service if war came he wrote:

"I pray God there may be no need to call for you . . ."[4]

Wilson did not, however, wait supinely for the "overt act." He never for a moment during all of these anxious weeks ceased his efforts to find some plan, some formula, that would prevent a final decision for war.

Even before he delivered his address of February 3rd, as we have seen, he had turned his attention to the long-rejected plan for action on the part of the neutral nations of the world. A favourable report from the Swiss minister, after consultation with his government (February 4th) momentarily encouraged the President. He wrote out a remarkable draft of the "Bases of Peace" as a foundation for discussion among neutrals. It is so significant not only of the President's strong purpose at the time, but of the sweeping comprehensiveness of his thought, that it is here

---

[1]February 15, 1917. *The Letters of Franklin K. Lane*, p. 236.
[2]February 5, 1917. Daniels, *Our Navy at War*, pp. 23-24.
[3]Wilson to C. S. Hamlin, February 15, 1917.
[4]To his nephew, George Howe, February 13, 1917.

presented in full as finally completed on February 9th.[1] It was essentially his first outline of a constitution for the League of Nations.

I.

Mutual guarantee of political independence,—absolute in all domestic matters, limited in external affairs only by the equal rights of other nations.

II.

Mutual guarantee of territorial integrity.

Note.

The application of this guarantee to the territorial arrangements made by the terms of the peace by which the present war is to be ended would, of course, necessarily depend upon the character of those arrangements, that is, upon their reasonableness and natural prospect of permanency; and, so far as the participation of the United States in the guarantee is concerned, would depend upon whether they were in conformity with the general principles of right and comity which the President set forth in his address to the Senate on the twenty-second of January.

Such a guarantee would not affect natural expansion peaceably accomplished.

III.

Mutual agreement not to take part in any joint economic action by two or more nations which would in effect constitute an effort to throttle the industrial life of any nation or shut it off from fair and equal opportunities of trade with the nations thus in concert or with the rest of the world.

Note.

This would of course not apply, as its terms indicate, to the laws of an individual state intended for the regulation and development of its own industries or for the safeguarding of its own resources from misuse or exhaustion, but only to cooperative action between states intended [to operate outside territorial limits?] or which would operate to injure particular rivals or groups of rivals.

---

[1]An earlier draft (February 7th) has been published, with Lansing's comments, in the *War Memoirs of Robert Lansing*, pp. 199–201.

IV.

Mutual agreement to limit armaments, whether on land or sea, to the necessities of internal order (including, of course, the internal order of an empire) and the probable demands of cooperation in making good the foregoing guarantees and agreements.

Note.

> PROVIDED the nations which take part in these covenants may reasonably be regarded as representing the major force of mankind.

GENERAL NOTE. It is suggested that it would not be necessary to set up at the outset any permanent tribunal or administrative agency, but only an office of correspondence through which all matters of information could be cleared up, correspondence translated by competent scholars, and mutual explanations and suggestions exchanged. It would in all likelihood be best, in this matter of executive organization, to await the developments and lessons of experience before attempting to set up any common instrumentality of international action.

Attached to this final statement of the "Bases" was a sheet headed: "Points to be made in reply to the suggestion of the Swiss Federal Council":

The probable physical impossibility of holding an actual conference.

The embarrassments which it is now evident many neutral governments would feel in seeming to come together to influence the present course of events.

The desirability, nevertheless, of a frank interchange of views. SUGGESTION, therefore, that the Swiss Federal Council communicate to the Government of the United States its views as to any present feasible course of cooperative action and any common bases upon which neutrals might at this time draw together in a League of Peace. The United States would be very glad in its turn, or at the invitation of the Council, to submit its own views on these vital and important subjects.

Wilson had undertaken the project with great hope: he was doomed to speedy disappointment. The neutral nations, who were quite as eager as the President himself for some solution of their difficulties, were afraid. They were small and weak! Wilson had expressed the hope in his address of February 3rd that they would join the United States in breaking relations. They had utterly failed to respond. However uncomfortable their status as battered neutrals, they dreaded the still more dangerous position of unfriendly or belligerent powers. Moreover, they were piqued by Wilson's refusal to coöperate with them during the past two years.[1]

The final blow to the project was the discovery that Ritter, the Swiss minister, was hand in glove with Bernstorff.[2] The whole effort exploded!

Wilson had also seized eagerly upon another desperate possibility—that a separate peace might be made with Austria-Hungary. At first there seemed to be good reason to hope for success. Austria-Hungary was nearly exhausted. Czernin, Minister for Foreign Affairs, had begged Wilson to continue to work for peace.[3] The new Austrian ambassador-designate, Count Adam Tarnowski, had recently arrived full of hope for friendly relations and

---

[1]The opinion of the Dutch minister, reported by House in his letter to Wilson, February 10, 1917. China was the only great neutral to respond favourably, and she desired guarantees of American support if she broke relations with Germany. *Foreign Relations*, 1917, Supp. 1, pp. 407–408. Wilson decided it would be best for China, owing to her grave difficulties at home and with Japan, not to follow our lead. He wrote to Lansing, February 10th: "I think that it would be well to let Reinsch tell the Government of China how sincerely we desire to help China and that we are constantly trying to shield her against the selfishness of her neighbor. I do not want them to get the idea that we are unappreciative of their present willingness to stand with us, which is singularly generous and enlightened." For Lansing's telegram to Reinsch, on the same day, see *ibid.*, p. 408.

[2]On February 10th Ritter presented a proposal which he said he had obtained from the German government, to negotiate on any point in the present imbroglio except the submarine war. *Foreign Relations*, 1917, Supp. 1, p. 125. On February 21st, Ritter confessed that his suggestion for negotiating came from Bernstorff, an admission which henceforth barred him from being considered a reliable agent in peace negotiations. *Ibid.*, pp. 139–141. Wilson had written to House as early as February 12th: "Give yourself no uneasiness about the Swiss-German move; it will not work."

[3]Ambassador Penfield to the Secretary of State, February 5, 1917. *Foreign Relations*, 1917, Supp. 1, pp. 38–39.

thoroughly well aware of the effect that American entrance into the war might have upon his country's future.[1] Like the American people in general, Wilson was not hostile to Austria, regarding her as an unfortunate pawn of Germany.

On the 8th, Lansing, at the President's direction, instructed Page at London to discuss with "the leading members of the British Government"[2] his hope of bringing Austria to accept peace.

"The chief if not the only obstacle is the threat apparently contained in the peace terms recently stated by the Entente Allies that in case they succeeded they would insist upon a virtual dismemberment of the Austro-Hungarian Empire. . . .

"The President still believes and has reason to believe that, were it possible for him to give the necessary assurances to the Government of Austria . . . he could in a very short time force the acceptance of peace upon terms which would follow the general lines of his recent address to the Senate . . ."[3]

Lloyd George was at first evasive. Because of "military expediency regarding the war as a whole" the British government could not, he said, at that time receive a proposal of peace from Austria; nor could the British government "authorize any representations on its behalf," though he stated that it "sees no reason to dismember Austria by removing Hungary and Bohemia . . ."[4]

By the 20th of February, however, the agile Prime Minister had had one of his quick changes of mind; he ap-

[1]Lansing to Wilson, February 10, 1917.

[2]The President, Lansing explained, "speaks of the leading members of the Government rather than of the Foreign Office because he does not intend this as in any sense an official but only as a personal message . . ."

[3]*Foreign Relations*, 1917, Supp. I, pp. 40–41, for entire message, including the President's specific suggestions.

[4]Page to the Secretary of State, February 11, 1917. *Ibid.*, pp. 41–44.

proved of Wilson's mediation with Austria, at the same time confirming his earlier assurances.[1]

Wilson relied upon these assurances and at once began the negotiations.[2] He felt that he was dealing honourably with Austria in submitting the proposal, and honourably with Great Britain in frankly asking her views. Whether the intentions of the Allies were equally sincere was another matter: Wilson was not told of their secret negotiations for breaking up the Central Powers.[3] Wilson indeed, then and earlier, was too trustful. He was not subtle minded: he had little of the politician's defensive readiness for suspicion, and no gift at all for intrigue.

The hopelessness of the negotiation was apparent within a few days. Czernin refused to discuss peace apart from Austria's allies.[4] Desperately unwilling to see this hope of peace lost, Wilson renewed his proposal on March 3rd; Czernin repeated his refusal ten days later.[5]

Meantime it became necessary to raise the issue of breaking with Austria over her submarine policy. In order not to jeopardize the peace negotiation, Lansing had inquired casuistically whether Austria's note of January 31st— which was almost identical with the German declaration— meant that she would disregard her *Ancona* pledge to give warning to unresisting ships and provide safety for life.[6] Quite as casuistically, Czernin replied that he thought his answer would be satisfactory but asked for time to make a

---

[1] Page to the Secretary of State, February 20, 1917. *Foreign Relations*, 1917, Supp. 1, pp. 55–56.

[2] Lansing to Penfield, February 22, 1917. *Ibid.*, pp. 57–58.

[3] For a study of these so-called "Prince Sixtus negotiations," see *War Memoirs of David Lloyd George*, Vol. IV, Chapter VII. The purpose of the Allies, of course, was to weaken the enemy by the old stratagem of dividing them: Wilson's purpose was to open a way to peace.

[4] Penfield to the Secretary of State, February 27, 1917. *Foreign Relations*, 1917, Supp. 1, pp. 62–63.

[5] *Ibid.*, pp. 63–66.

[6] Lansing to Penfield, February 14 and 23, 1917. *Ibid.*, pp. 131–133, 143.

formal reply. He waited until March 2nd and then submitted a discursive *aide-mémoire*, putting so many glosses
on the Austrian position that, despite the declaration of
unrestricted warfare, he was able to reach the surprising
conclusion that the *Ancona* pledge still held![1] This remarkable answer left the American government free to
think just what it wished. The upshot was that Tarnowski
continued to cool his heels outside the State Department;
and relations were not broken.

It is probable that Wilson never placed much hope in
separate peace negotiation with Austria, but the failure
of his project for joint neutral action was a great disappointment. It brought him, indeed, to the end of his resources as a peacemaker—with events driving him
irresistibly toward an outright declaration of war which he
dreaded. His nearest advisers were clamouring for it—
and if the feeling expressed in newspapers and in Congress
could be believed, there was now a widespread public
readiness for immediate and decisive action.

But the President still resisted; he was considering one
more intermediate step—no longer for peace, but to delay
war.

III. WILSON AND THE ZIMMERMANN NOTE

Only one step between American neutrality and outright war—and that one short and shaky—still remained.
A last ditch of defense! Woodrow Wilson determined to
hold it: it would at least delay capitulation. This was to
demand, not war, but armed neutrality. It would give the
American people a little more time. A miracle might still
happen!

Since the beginning of February there had been tremendous pressure brought to bear upon Wilson to arm

---

[1] Penfield to the Secretary of State, February 26 and March 2, 1917. *Op. cit.*, pp. 151,
161–168.

American ships. This was not because of submarine attacks, for only the *Housatonic* and the *Lyman M. Law* had been sunk, and those with ample warning and no loss of life. But fear of Germany had in effect blockaded the whole eastern American seaboard. Ports were crowded with ships riding at anchor. Business was slowing down. Ship-owners naturally declared it was the government's duty to protect them. Wilson continued to refuse for three weeks, with pressure for action, however, becoming more and more insistent.

The cabinet was nearer open revolt upon this issue than it had been at any other time during Wilson's administration. In the meetings in early February the President took the position that the ships might arm but that he must have authority from Congress to place navy guns and gunners on them.[1] By the middle of the month several members[2] had become insistent on action.[3] Customary mild discussion began to give way to emphatic argument and patriotic oratory. The meeting on the 23rd came as near being a cabinet crisis as the American system is able to produce. Houston declared that Germany would attack us if she won the war unless we enforced our rights. Lane asked whether it was true that German authorities had stripped the wives of American consuls to search for "writing on their flesh."

"This," he commented bitterly in a personal letter, "the President took as a suggestion that we should work up a propaganda of hatred against Germany."

Lane, McAdoo, Houston, and Redfield argued that Americans were entitled to know the facts. Wilson "re-

---

[1]*Letters of Franklin K. Lane*, pp. 234-235; Houston, *Eight Years With Wilson's Cabinet*, Vol. I, p. 233.

[2]Especially Houston, Lane, and McAdoo.

[3]*Letters of Franklin K. Lane*, p. 236; Houston, *Eight Years With Wilson's Cabinet*, Vol. I, pp. 234-235.

proached all of us with appealing to the spirit of the *Code Duello*."

Lane wrote later: "We couldn't get the idea out of his head that we were bent on pushing the country into war."

But in fact, what else was it? After the meeting Houston talked of resigning. Lane believed that McAdoo also would resign.[1] It was as plain as day that Wilson's resistance had been carried as far as it could be. Moreover, the arguments had begun to convince even him that American ships really should be armed.[2]

Another potent reason for action also developed just at this time. The Republicans in the Senate held a caucus February 23rd to consider plans for delaying legislation and thereby compelling an extra session—that is, a filibuster. Republicans who yearned for war were determined

---

[1]Houston, *Eight Years With Wilson's Cabinet*, Vol. I, pp. 235–237; *Letters of Franklin K. Lane*, pp. 239–240.

[2]Houston, *Eight Years With Wilson's Cabinet*, Vol. I, p. 237. Two documents seem also to have influenced Wilson to alter his position. Lansing sent him a long, closely reasoned memorandum declaring that, since Germany ignored international law, our rights fell back upon "the same primitive law of self-defense that justifies an individual in arming and defending himself from a highwayman in a region which is known to be without police protection." The United States government had a duty not only to give "full sanction" and advice to its merchant vessels "to arm and resist" illegal attacks, but to give arms and gunners to such vessels to defend the lives of those on board. Whether it would be expedient was another problem—"It would certainly entail a certain measure of danger of creating a state of war . . ."—but not to do so was actual submission to Germany. (Memorandum written February 20, 1917, sent by Lansing to Wilson February 21st. Savage, *Policy of the United States Toward Maritime Commerce in War*, Vol. II, pp. 565–568.)

The other document was a plan drawn up by Professor Carlton J. H. Hayes, of Columbia University, presenting a plausible argument for a league of armed neutrals to defend their rights. (Enclosed in a letter from House to Wilson, February 8, 1917.) There might be pitched battles, but there would not need to be war: the armed neutrals would be so powerful that they could ignore any declaration of war aimed at them. There were precedents for this in European history, but the most telling precedent was from American history. In 1798 the United States had broken relations with France, and Congress had authorized American frigates to capture any French vessel guilty of depredations on American commerce. Within a year France had given in to the American demands. The advantages of such a course now would be that war could be avoided at the same time that we maintained our rights, and it would pave the way for an improvement in international law. The main proposal, an armed league, was ruled out by Wilson: neutrals had not shown any real desire to join us. But the argument of American precedent for armed neutrality seemed to be a sound basis for action. It supported the very demand that the cabinet was making.

not to leave a "pacifist" President in control for nine months. On the other hand, it soon appeared that those who wanted peace were equally determined on forcing an extra session to prevent any war move on the part of the President.[1]

Political opposition alone, however, even the filibuster that began to develop in the Senate on February 24th, would probably not have moved the President. He had met many such emergencies; he was a resourceful and determined fighter. But just at that time an utterly astounding document was sent to him by Page from London. The war had been fertile in startling disclosures of the length to which infuriated nations would go: but he had never before seen anything so barefaced as this. He was shocked and indignant. He could scarcely believe the disclosures made!

It was the note, signed by Zimmermann, German Foreign Minister, offering in case of war with the United States to make an alliance with Mexico with "an understanding on our part that Mexico is to reconquer the lost territory in Texas, New Mexico, and Arizona." Japan was to be invited by Mexico to join.[2]

The authenticity of the note was established almost immediately: although, as we shall see, the President did not know until several days later the full enormity of the offense committed by the Germans. It had, in fact, been in the possession of the British for some three weeks, having been intercepted by their consummately efficient Naval Intelligence Service on January 16th;[3] the British had now with equal skill chosen exactly the right moment

---

[1]See New York *Times*, February 24, 1917. Lodge led the war group. La Follette led the peace group; he had already introduced a resolution to prevent the arming of ships. *Cong. Rec.*, 64–2, p. 3064.

[2]Germany was also to give financial support to Mexico. *Foreign Relations*, 1917, Supp. 1, pp. 147–148.

[3]Hendrick, *Life and Letters of Walter H. Page*, Vol. III, pp. 336–337.

to hand the document to Page for transmission to the President.[1]

Wilson knew well what publicity for such an intrigue, planning an actual attack upon American territory, with a foreign alliance of Germany, Japan, and Mexico to support it (however chimerical the plan itself might be), would have upon the American people—as it did have when it finally appeared on March 1st.

It was probably the stupidest diplomatic blunder of the entire war period. No statesman in the world at that moment was more anxious to be genuinely helpful to the Germans, if they really wanted peace as they had said they did, than Woodrow Wilson. This document, following so closely upon their declaration, issued without warning, of the resumption of unrestricted submarine warfare, immediately and completely disillusioned him. He felt that they had insulted us in their note of January 31st: and now, while still urging us to work for peace, they were planning an underhanded invasion of our territory! It convinced the President, then and there, that the German leaders could not in any circumstances be trusted. It seemed that they had not been in earnest about peace at all. They did mean, then, to dominate the world by a crushing victory! They would use any means that served their purpose! No single, more devastating blow was delivered against Wilson's resistance to entering the war.

The President's first instinct was to make the Zimmermann declaration immediately public. Lansing being absent from Washington, Polk urged delay: and Wilson, upon second thought, feared that the explosion of public feeling following such a disclosure might force his hand—might even arouse a demand for measures far more drastic than armed neutrality.

However, it fixed his determination to act immediately.

[1] It reached him February 25th.

THE WILSON CABINET OF 1916

Lower row, left to right: WILLIAM C. REDFIELD, SECRETARY OF COMMERCE; ROBERT LANSING, SECRETARY OF STATE; DAVID F. HOUSTON, SECRETARY OF AGRICULTURE; PRESIDENT WILSON; WILLIAM G. McADOO, SECRETARY OF THE TREASURY; ALBERT S. BURLESON, POSTMASTER GENERAL. *Upper row, left to right:* JOSEPHUS DANIELS, SECRETARY OF THE NAVY; WILLIAM B. WILSON, SECRETARY OF LABOR; NEWTON D. BAKER, SECRETARY OF WAR; THOMAS W. GREGORY, ATTORNEY GENERAL; FRANKLIN K. LANE, SECRETARY OF THE INTERIOR.

On the following day, the 26th of February, he went before Congress and asked for the power to arm American ships.[1]

The chamber of the House of Representatives was crowded. War or peace might depend upon what the President said. Everyone knew that he must take some decisive step; any retreat was now out of the question. When he entered he was warmly welcomed by the members of his own party. The Republicans, violently divided between those who wanted war and those who did not, were, for the most part, tensely silent.

The President read his message "in a clear, steady, calm voice . . . without gesticulation of any kind, without emphasis at any point . . ." The audience was expectant, motionless, like a crowd caught by an instantaneous photograph.[2] He recounted how shipping had sought refuge in port; declared that the Germans in effect were successfully invading our rights.

"No thoughtful man can fail to see that the necessity for definite action may come at any time, if we are in fact, and not in word merely, to defend our elementary rights as a neutral nation."

Congress would soon adjourn. Before it did so, he needed to have assurance of the authority he might at any moment need to exercise:

"No doubt I already possess that authority . . . by the plain implication of my constitutional duties and powers; but I prefer, in the present circumstances . . . to feel that the authority and the power of the Congress are behind me in whatever it may become necessary for me to do.

---

[1] Further evidence of the ruthless purpose of the Germans came to the State Department while the President was actually speaking. The Cunard liner *Laconia*, carrying many Americans, had been sunk without warning. Two American passengers were lost. It was clearly an "overt" act. The first report arrived at the State Department at 1:10 P.M. *Foreign Relations*, 1917, Supp. 1, p. 149; *cf.* also p. 151.

[2] From notes made at the time by the author, who was present.

We are jointly the servants of the people and must act together . . ."

The government's duty was unmistakable:

"Since it has unhappily proved impossible to safeguard our neutral rights by diplomatic means against the unwarranted infringements they are suffering at the hands of Germany, there may be no recourse but to *armed neutrality* . . ."

This was not, however, to seek war:

"War can come only by the wilful acts and aggressions of others."

The form in which action might become necessary could not be foreseen. For this reason, he hoped, his hearers would understand why he could "make no definite proposals or forecasts of action now and must ask for your supporting authority in the most general terms."

La Follette was sitting with his hands folded across his breast; Lodge, "quite characteristically with his hands clasped in front of him just under his chin."[1] Both were bitterly opposed, for directly contrary reasons, to the recommendations of the speaker, the first because the President was going too far, the second because he was not going far enough.

"I believe that the people will be willing to trust me to act with restraint, with prudence . . . it is in that belief that I request that you will authorize me to supply our merchant ships with defensive arms, should that become necessary, and with the means of using them, and to employ any other instrumentalities or methods that may be necessary . . . to protect our ships and our people . . . on the seas."

La Follette threw up both hands instinctively as though hope were gone. Lodge "unclasped his fingers and gently

[1] Author's memorandum.

tapped the points of them together, not, apparently, in applause, but as one would say, a little cynically, 'Well, well!'"[1]

In conclusion Wilson rose, as he rarely failed to do, above the confusion of the moment to the clear atmosphere of eternal principles:

"I am thinking of those rights of humanity without which there is no civilization. . . . rights which our hearts support and whose foundation is that righteous passion for justice upon which all law, all structures alike of family, of state, and of mankind must rest . . . I cannot imagine any man with American principles at his heart hesitating to defend these things."[2]

The President walked quickly out of the chamber after the conclusion of the address. The applause died away; the floor began to clear; a babel of comment arose. Jealousy of congressional prerogative, problems of peace and of war, political complications—all cropped up in that comment. The Congress was in turmoil. Opposition from both extremes had become momentarily futile. Pacifist opponents of the President were helpless because they could offer no practical alternative programme; extremists like Lodge, doubtful of emphatic popular support for actual war, hesitated to go further. In the wild confusion of opinion, Wilson alone had an immediate and practical plan of action. This fact gave him tremendous power.

The public, which seemed generally to support the President, did not realize that he himself still had misgivings about the wisdom of his course; that it had been forced upon him by inexorable events.

"These are days," he wrote on the day following his address, "when none of us can feel absolutely certain of a

[1]Author's memorandum.
[2]*The Public Papers of Woodrow Wilson*, Vol. IV, pp. 428–432.

correct judgment because there are so many things to stir passion and so many things to distress the mind and throw it off its right balance."[1]

Wilson had himself painstakingly drafted the bill he wanted passed; and it was introduced in the House by Representative Flood.[2] When it became clear that amendments would be insisted upon, Wilson declared that he would fight to the limit for his measure as he framed it.

". . . I shall use every legitimate influence I can exercise to bring about a 'show down'. . ."[3]

"I hope very much," he wrote to Burleson, "that none of these amendments will be adopted. The original language was most carefully studied."[4]

But there was no possibility of a full victory even in the generally tractable House of Representatives, split as it was by dissension, and with a calendar crowded by a host of last-minute legislation. Members of the House objected to the insurance of munition cargoes or ships carrying munitions. Nearly half the Western representatives were not even in favour of authorizing the President to arm munition ships at all.[5]

At this moment of hesitation and opposition Wilson made certain further discoveries regarding the Zimmermann note which immensely increased the sternness of his purpose. On the day after his address to Congress, Lansing returned to Washington and the President asked him for particulars regarding the transmission and interception of the inflammatory German document, and what connection Bernstorff had with it. He listened with utter amazement and growing indignation to Lansing's reply.

[1]To George Foster Peabody.
[2]Chairman of the Committee on Foreign Affairs of the House.
[3]Wilson to Representative Jouett Shouse, February 27, 1917.
[4]Handwritten note by Wilson, undated.
[5]Cf. the analysis made in the New Republic, Vol. X (March 24, 1917), p. 218.

It seems that in early January, when the President had been so ardently seeking some method of instituting peace negotiations—with German encouragement—Bernstorff had complained that his efforts were hopelessly frustrated because he had no means of prompt secret communication with his government. The British, having complete control of cables and radio, blocked everything. Bernstorff had thereupon, "in view of this reasonable statement," been granted the extraordinary privilege of sending cipher messages through the American State Department.[1] So great was the President's hope that he could find even a small opening toward negotiations!

This privilege, however, had been abused both by the German Foreign Office and by Bernstorff in transmitting the Zimmermann note which proposed an attack upon the United States.

"Good Lord!" exclaimed the President several times while this extraordinary story was being unfolded.[2]

A little later Zimmermann himself destroyed the last doubt as to the authenticity of the note by brazenly admitting that he had sent it.[3]

Both Wilson and Lansing agreed, however, that it would be better to continue to hold back the publication of this highly sensational news for fear it would be charged that publication was designed "to influence opinion on the bill for arming merchant vessels."[4] But with the increasing obstruction in Congress, and the date of necessary adjournment (March 4th) rapidly approaching, the facts

---

[1] This was in itself a technical violation of neutrality, but in the interest of the emergency peace negotiations Wilson had decided it was the right thing to do. Peace efforts might fail unless negotiations could be speeded up. The Allies, it will be recalled, had taken over the German cables early in the war, leaving Germany without swift means of communication.

[2] *War Memoirs of Robert Lansing*, pp. 227–228.

[3] New York *Times*, March 4, 1917; *War Memoirs of Robert Lansing*, p. 232.

[4] *Ibid.*, p. 228.

were given to the public on March 1st. Indeed, the public had a right to know them! And it caused quite as much of a furor as the President had feared.

When the House bill finally came to a vote it passed by an overwhelming majority, 403 to 14.[1] In the Senate, however, the obstruction begun earlier by the Republicans to force an extra session was a grave obstacle to any action at all. By March 2nd a non-partisan filibuster was under way, led by the Progressive Republicans, Norris and La Follette, and joined by several Democrats. Fear of war dominated this group. The Senate's vote to adjourn late on the night of the 2nd until the next day at ten was the beginning of defeat for Wilson.

"We've got them beaten," said Norris to La Follette. "We can hold out now. We've enough speakers to filibuster from tomorrow on."[2]

He was right—they had more than enough!

After "one of the bitterest parliamentary wrangles in the history of the country,"[3] a manifesto was signed by seventy-five senators—stating that they favoured the armed ship bill but were prevented by a small minority—twelve votes—from expressing their support of the measure.[4]

Wilson was thoroughly angry. The end of the 64th Congress had come: the filibuster had succeeded: an extra session which he had been most anxious to avoid would be necessary. He commented on the "vanity" of La Follette and the "slipperiness" of Stone.[5] It did not help matters to reflect that he himself had opened the way for the attack, since he had asked for an endorsement of authority

---

[1] *Cong. Rec.*, 64–2, p. 4692.
[2] Memorandum of conversation, Senator Norris with Harley A. Notter, May 1936.
[3] New York *Times*, March 5, 1917.
[4] *Cong. Rec.*, 64–2, pp. 4988–4989.
[5] Houston, *Eight Years With Wilson's Cabinet*, Vol. I, p. 240.

which he considered that he as President already possessed under the terms of the Constitution.

In the midst of the excitement and confusion of this tremendous political battle, the fact that it was March 4th and the beginning of a new four-year term of office for the President seemed half forgotten. The actual ceremony of inauguration had been set for Monday, the 5th, but Wilson took the formal oath, administered by Chief Justice White, at noon on Sunday the 4th. Afterwards he returned to the White House, deeply wrought up by the action in the Senate. When he denounced the filibusterers to House, the Colonel suggested that he say "to the public what he was saying to me, and . . . say it immediately."[1]

Late that evening the President issued the angriest, least premeditated, statement of his career—which he was afterwards to regret:[2]

". . . the Congress has been unable to act either to safeguard the country or to vindicate the elementary rights of its citizens. . . .

"A little group of willful men, representing no opinion but their own, have rendered the great Government of the United States helpless and contemptible."[3]

He declared that a special session of the 65th Congress would be useless unless the rules were changed so that vital measures might be passed.

"There is but one remedy . . . the rules of the Senate shall be so altered that it can act. The country can be relied upon to draw the moral. I believe that the Senate

---

[1]*The Intimate Papers of Colonel House*, Vol. II, p. 457.

[2]Just before issuing the statement Wilson called Burleson, McAdoo, Tumulty, House, and McCormick into consultation. They approved. *Ibid.*; New York *Times*, March 5, 1917.

[3]*The Public Papers of Woodrow Wilson*, Vol. IV, pp. 433–435. The twelve Senators were: Norris (Nebr.), La Follette (Wis.), Clapp (Minn.), Stone (Mo.), Cummins (Ia.), Kenyon (Ia.), Gronna (N.D.), Works (Calif.), Kirby (Ark.), Lane (Ore.), O'Gorman (N.Y.), Vardaman (Miss.). Kenyon took no active part in the obstruction and the reference to "eleven senators" in Wilson's statement of March 4th was presumably based upon this fact.

can be relied upon to supply the means of action and save the country from disaster."[1]

The country was in an uproar. The "willful men" were showered with criticism—some of it nothing short of violent—from nearly every newspaper and by nearly every gathering in the United States. So bitter was the feeling on all sides that when President Wilson rode to the Capitol the next day to give his inaugural address he was guarded more heavily than any President since the days of the Civil War. Roofs were manned by soldiers; troopers and police formed a hollow square about the carriage as he and Mrs. Wilson were driven along Pennsylvania Avenue.

His address bore no signs of the hot indignation that now burned within him.

"This is not the time for retrospect," he said. "It is time, rather, to speak our thoughts and purposes concerning the present and the immediate future."

The war had affected every aspect of our lives. We had already turned to "armed neutrality"[2] to protect our rights:

"We may even be drawn on, by circumstances . . . to a more . . . immediate association with the great struggle itself."

The great thing he wished to declare, however, was his faith that, no matter what lay ahead, "nothing will alter our thought or our purpose" on the principles of America. Whether "in war or in peace," America would stand for her beliefs. He reiterated those beliefs, some of which were:

"That all nations are equally interested in the peace of the world and in the political stability of free peoples, and equally responsible for their maintenance;

---

[1] *The Public Papers of Woodrow Wilson*, Vol. IV, p. 435. By March 8th, compelled by the irresistible pressure of a country almost unanimously behind the President, the Senate had passed a bill providing for a limitation of debate.

[2] However, the notice that merchant vessels would be armed was not sent out until March 12th.

"That the essential principle of peace is the actual equality of nations in all matters of right or privilege;

"That peace cannot securely or justly rest upon an armed balance of power;

"That governments derive all their just powers from the consent of the governed and that no other powers should be supported by . . . the family of nations;

"That the seas should be equally free and safe for the use of all peoples . . . and that, so far as practicable, they should be accessible to all upon equal terms . . ."

This was his last word on a peace programme while America was still a neutral. He closed with an appeal for American unity in support of that programme, and asked for "tolerance" in judgment as to the tasks ahead. He was sure that if America was but true to herself, the "shadows that now lie dark upon our path will soon be dispelled and we shall walk with the light all about us . . ."[1]

The poignancy of this appeal, the difficulties and struggles for which the President asked understanding and tolerance, seemed to have passed all but unnoticed in that moment of tense excitement. This was nothing but another inaugural address: it was his denunciation of the "willful men" that rang in all ears: it was the fateful crisis confronting the nation that stirred all hearts.

Although Wilson was still angry over the defeat of his plans, he regretted having lost his self-possession.

"Do you know what is the hardest job in being President?" he asked a friend who called.

"No," was the reply, "never having been President!"

"I'll tell you," said Mr. Wilson. "It is the difficulty of keeping your temper."[2]

The little tempest of the filibuster soon passed into his-

---

[1] *The Public Papers of Woodrow Wilson*, Vol. V, pp. 1-5.

[2] Memorandum of conversation between Robert Weeks and the author, October 2, 1925.

tory; the problem of arming the ships remained. The pressure upon the President for further action steadily increased. Deadly efficiency marked the raids of the German submarines upon Allied shipping, and while no more American vessels had been sunk, a new crisis might at any moment develop. Something had to be done.

The difficulties involved in the armed ship policy were all too numerous: Wilson had seen many of them for weeks; the "willful men" had seen them; Daniels and the naval experts saw them.[1] How far could we go without an actual declaration of war?

Lansing presented most forcibly the arguments for immediate action at whatever cost. So far as armed neutrality was concerned, he held that if an "armed guard" were placed on American vessels proceeding to the German "danger zone" with permission to resist unlawful attack outside that zone, the policy would be legally sound.[2] But, he maintained, the existing state of affairs was "hopeless."

". . . we ought to proceed on the theory that we will in a short time be openly at war with Germany. . . .

"As I read the public mind there is an impatient desire to go forward. . . . I am firmly convinced that expediency as well as duty lies in action."[3]

Telling arguments to a President harassed by pressure and unable to find any peaceful way of escape! He had the power,[4] and the need, and the legal justification to enforce American rights. Most of the people and most of Congress were increasingly unwilling to drift.

He acted finally and definitely on March 12th. The

---

[1]*Cf.* Daniels to Wilson, March 9, 1917. Savage, *Policy of the United States Toward Maritime Commerce in War*, Vol. II, pp. 577–580.

[2]Lansing to Wilson, March 9, 1917. *Ibid.*, pp. 580–581.

[3]Lansing to Wilson, March 8, 1917. *Ibid.*, pp. 575–577.

[4]Wilson had issued a call on March 9th—the day after the Senate limited debate—for Congress to meet April 16th to pass necessary financial and other legislation. He could not, however, delay action on armed ships until April 16th; and he felt that authorization was not legally necessary.

American government gave notice that an armed guard would be placed on "all American merchant vessels sailing through the barred areas."[1]

It was the beginning of the end. From this time onward the President, however reluctant he might be to take the final step, knew that war was all but inevitable.

---

[1] *Foreign Relations*, 1917, Supp. 1, p. 171. The *Algonquin* was sunk on the very day the new policy was announced; and within the next two weeks other ships were sent down, most of them without warning. Fifteen lives were lost in the sinking of the American ship *Vigilancia* on March 16th. *Ibid.*, pp. 174 *et seq.*

CHAPTER XII

ACCEPTING THE INEVITABLE

"There are, it may be, many months of fiery trial and sacrifice ahead of us. It is a fearful thing to lead this great peaceful people into war, into the most terrible and disastrous of all wars, civilization itself seeming to be in the balance. But the right is more precious than peace . . ."

Address to Congress, April 2, 1917.

". . . a state of war exists between the United States and the Imperial German Government . . ."

War proclamation, April 6, 1917.

I. WILSON'S CONVERSION TO WAR

WOODROW WILSON'S valley of decision, the most critical, the most heart-breaking, of the entire period of his leadership of the American people, was in the three weeks from March 12th, when he ordered the arming of ships to meet attacks of German submarines, to April 2nd, when he asked Congress for a declaration of war. Historians of the future may well look back upon these weeks as among the most decisive of the century. The destinies of two of the most powerful nations of the world were in process of being shaped into new courses of profound import and significance. While the American leader, the representative of the newest idealisms in statecraft, was deciding to bring his country into the European conflict, breaking its historic tradition of isolation, the Russian Czar, symbol of all that was old, was abdicating, and a new regime, of still unfathomed potentialities, was beginning.[1]

It was an agonizing ordeal for the President, personally.

---

[1]The Czar abdicated on March 15th.

486

The latter days of February and early March had been peculiarly trying both mentally and physically. Explosive foreign problems had been made more difficult by dissension at home: the filibuster in the Senate, the attack of the "little group of willful men," and finally the strain of the second inaugural on March 5th. On March 7th the President fell ill with a cold, and his physician, Dr. Grayson, ordered him to remain in bed. It was not, however, the slight physical ailment that so much distressed him, but the irrevocable decision that he was facing. Was war inevitable? If it was inevitable, when was the declaration to be made? Above all, how were the issues to be presented to the American people?

For about ten days he remained almost constantly in his room: he saw few visitors: he wrote scarcely a dozen indispensable letters. His schedule for a week (based for the most part upon the diary of the head usher of the White House) gives some idea of the daily routine:

Friday, March 9th. The President remained in his bedroom during the entire day and evening. The regular Friday cabinet meeting was not held; but the Postmaster General called early in the afternoon, and in the evening the President received Secretary Daniels.

Saturday, March 10th. The President again remained in his room during the day and evening, receiving only Secretary McAdoo and the Attorney General.

Sunday, March 11th. The President remained in his room during the forenoon, but lunched downstairs with members of the family.

Monday, March 12th. The President remained in his room during the forenoon, receiving at 9 o'clock Senator Martin, and at 9:45 Secretary Lansing. The only afternoon caller was Senator Swanson.

It was on this day that the Department of State, by order of the President, announced the arming of American merchant ships.

Tuesday, March 13th. The President remained in his private

apartments during the morning and afternoon. The regular cabinet meeting was again postponed, and there were no callers at any time.

News arrived of the sinking, without warning, of the American ship *Algonquin* by a German submarine.

Wednesday, March 14th. The President "remained in private room all forenoon, coming down to lunch. Afternoon same." There were no callers.

Thursday, March 15th. The President spent the morning in his room. At six o'clock in the evening Ambassador Gerard called. Of this meeting Gerard writes (in a memorandum for the author):

"He was in a most serious mood:—he said that he had done everything to preserve peace and even yet he hoped that the Germans would abandon the ruthless submarine war . . ."

This was the day on which the first news of the Russian revolution reached the Department of State—in a cablegram from Ambassador Francis.

At this time, also, the railroad crisis was becoming acute: a nation-wide strike threatened.

During these bitter days in which the President remained secluded we know with what painful thought he was considering the decision he must soon make. A relentless flood of letters, memoranda and reports regarding the crisis in Europe, as well as the repercussions at home, continued to flow in upon him. We know that he watched every turn of events: considered anxiously each proposal for action to meet the swiftly growing emergency. For example, on March 12th, when Lansing was about to transmit the announcement of the order for arming American ships, the President wrote (on his own typewriter), urging that the regulations as to American armed merchant vessels, which Secretary Daniels had prepared, be kept secret:

"I would be very much obliged if you would give the most emphatic orders that no part of any of this is to be given even the least publicity. I should feel justified in ordering a court martial for disobedience to such an order."[1]

He received and considered further dispatches regarding the possibility of peace with Austria and reports of the Russian revolution, and on the 16th, aware of the disaster that might follow a national railroad strike, he appealed in a telegram to Elisha Lee, chairman of the Conference Committee of Managers; and to the Railway Brotherhood heads:

"I deem it my duty and my right to appeal to you in this time of national peril to open again the questions at issue between the railroads and their operatives with a view to accommodation or settlement. . . . The safety of the country against manifest perils affecting its own peace and the peace of the whole world makes accommodation absolutely imperative and seems to me to render any other choice or action inconceivable."

On the 19th he was conferring with Mr. Lansing on the latest and most ruthless of the German submarine attacks upon American ships.[2] Lansing, as usual, argued that war was inevitable, and that "the sooner we openly admitted the fact" the better; but he found the President still doubtful, still anxious, still seeking some way to avoid the final catastrophe.

"I felt that he was resisting the irresistible logic of events . . ."[3]

We know also, from direct evidence, something of what those days must have meant in terms of mental agony from the report of Frank I. Cobb, editor of the New York *World*, who had a long night conference with the President only a few hours before the final step was taken.

[1]Wilson to Daniels; for the regulation, see Savage, *Policy of the United States Toward Maritime Commerce in War*, Vol. II, pp. 582–584.

[2]Word had come on March 18th of the sinking of three American ships: the *City of Memphis*, the *Illinois*, and the *Vigilancia*. New York *Times*, March 19, 1917.

[3]*War Memoirs of Robert Lansing*, p. 233.

"For nights, he said, he'd been lying awake going over the whole situation; over the provocation given by Germany, over the probable feeling in the United States, over the consequences to the settlement and to the world at large if we entered the mêlée. . . .

"He said he couldn't see any alternative, that he had tried every way he knew to avoid war. 'I think I know what war means,' he said, and he added that if there were any possibility of avoiding war he wanted to try it. 'What else can I do?' he asked. 'Is there anything else I can do?'

"I told him his hand had been forced by Germany, that so far as I could see we couldn't keep out.

"'Yes,' he said, 'but do you know what that means?' He said war would overturn the world we had known; that so long as we remained out there was a preponderance of neutrality, but that if we joined with the Allies the world would be off the peace basis and onto a war basis. . . .

"The President said a declaration of war would mean that Germany would be beaten and so badly beaten that there would be a dictated peace, a victorious peace.

"'It means,' he said, 'an attempt to reconstruct a peace-time civilization with war standards, and at the end of the war there will be no bystanders with sufficient power to influence the terms. There won't be any peace standards left to work with. . . .'"[1]

Many Americans had not found it so difficult to reach a decision: they were prepared to go to war because they were angry, or because they felt that the United States had been insulted or vitally injured—for pride, for fear, even for greed—but Woodrow Wilson was still considering the profounder questions:

What is it right to do? In the long look, what is best for civilization? How can America most helpfully serve the world?

[1] *"Cobb of* The World", pp. 268–269.

It was with him no new attitude of mind or of spirit. We recall that he was moved by the same ideals many years before when he delivered his inaugural address as president of Princeton University. It was not the pride or the glory of that great educational institution which he was considering, but "Princeton for the Nation's Service." And in one form or another he had been demanding of the greater institutions of the state and the nation the same high purpose. "The idea of America is to serve humanity . . ."[1]

There were not wanting critics who attacked Wilson as a "pacifist."[2] He was as far as possible from being a pacifist! He seemed, indeed, in those weeks of struggle to have given no consideration whatever to war as war—as being either good or evil in itself. Roosevelt might sing the virtues of war as heroic discipline: Bryan might denounce it as being wholly evil: Wilson agreed with neither. It was in his view a "crude instrument" which it might be necessary for civilized nations from time to time to employ. He had said in 1911:

"... there are times in the history of nations when they must take up the crude instruments of bloodshed in order to vindicate spiritual conceptions . . . liberty is a spiritual conception, and when men take up arms to set other men free, there is something sacred and holy in the warfare."[3]

For months he had been giving profound consideration to the various reasons that might necessitate the entrance

---

[1] Address to the graduating class of the United States Naval Academy, Annapolis, June 5, 1914. *The Public Papers of Woodrow Wilson*, Vol. III, p. 127.

[2] In this very week, when Wilson was struggling with these problems involving "the moral standards of mankind" which he considered of primary importance, Theodore Roosevelt was writing to his friend, Senator Lodge:

"I regard Wilson as far more blameworthy than the 'wilful' Senators. I am as yet holding in; but if he does not go to war with Germany I shall skin him alive. To think of the folly of having cursed this country with the really hideous misfortune of four years more of Wilson in this great and terrible world crisis!" (March 13th. *Selections from the Correspondence of Theodore Roosevelt and Henry Cabot Lodge*, Vol. II, p. 503.)

[3] *The Public Papers of Woodrow Wilson*, Vol. II, p. 294.

of the United States into the European war. It is astonishing in studying the Wilson documents to see the care and
thoroughness with which he was able, in the midst of so
many world-rocking events, to work out, in his own mind,
every contingency. Many of these considerations he presented in his public addresses: we might have to go to war
to maintain American self-respect and the principles of
liberty and justice for which she had always contended;[1]
to keep her moral influence intact in order to carry out
her mission in the world;[2] to protect her sovereignty and
the rights of her people against direct attacks;[3] to protect
the liberty of government and the independence of the
Western Hemisphere;[4] and to uphold the rights of mankind and the principles of humanity.[5]

All these possibilities he could consider, but the all-
important time factor remained still undecided. *When*
should the break be made? He had said in an address in
February:

"Valor strikes only when it is right to strike. Valor with-
holds itself from all small implications and entanglements
and waits for the great opportunity when the sword will
flash as if it carried the light of heaven upon its blade."[6]

These, then, were the questions—when the "crude instrument" should be used, when the "great opportunity"
had arrived, when valour should strike—which plagued
him during those tormenting weeks of March. For it was
proving utterly impossible to simplify the factors involved;
they could not even be separately examined, let alone
quantitatively measured. The rights and the wrongs could
not be clearly sifted out.

---

[1] *The Public Papers of Woodrow Wilson*, Vol. IV, pp. 4, 8, 72, 213–214.
[2] *Ibid.*, pp. 171, 202.
[3] *Ibid.*, pp. 282, 426.
[4] *Ibid.*, pp. 67–68, 205–206.
[5] *Ibid.*, pp. 127, 158, 194, 282.
[6] *Ibid.*, p. 128.

At least three groups of problems presented themselves:

1. Critical economic considerations, chiefly our financial and commercial entanglements with the Allies, upon which our own prosperity now depended.

2. Overt acts of war, rapidly growing intolerable, upon the part of the Germans.

3. Swiftly developing emotion and sympathy in America.

At the last moment, also, there was the influence, of great importance in the thinking of the President, of the sudden overturn in Russia and the abdication of the Czar.

In considering Wilson's conversion to war each of these influences must be examined.

As to the first, we find among Wilson's letters and papers no reference to the commercial or financial interests of the United States as a reason for war. He denied repeatedly, indeed, any such interest:

"The Government of the United States is contending for something much greater than mere rights of property or privileges of commerce. It is contending for nothing less high and sacred than the rights of humanity . . ."[1]

He had held from the beginning of his presidency that it was "a very perilous thing to determine the foreign policy of a nation in the terms of material interest. It not only is unfair to those with whom you are dealing, but it is degrading as regards your own actions."[2]

It was not that he underestimated the power and the importance of the economic elements—he himself had said, "There is no man who is more interested than I am in carrying the enterprise of American business men to every quarter of the globe"[3]—but these property interests were not to dominate our decisions:

"Property we have found to be the indispensable foun-

[1]June 9, 1915. *The Public Papers of Woodrow Wilson*, Vol. III, p. 344.

[2]October 27, 1913. *Ibid.*, p. 67.

[3]*Ibid.*, p. 143.

dation of stable institutions, but the rights of humanity are the essence of free institutions, and nothing can take precedence of them."[1]

And yet, however the President may have striven to subordinate or moralize the economic factors of the conflict, they were there, as always, enormously potent influences behind the scenes. At the beginning of the European war he had tried to curb their influence by a "moral" loan policy but had found it, by September 1915, impossible to maintain.[2] The effect of our rapidly expanding wartime trade—trade that was then perfectly legal—was to entangle us vitally with the welfare of the Allies. The President saw clearly and feared this tendency; he considered that there was "a moral obligation laid upon us to keep free the courses of our commerce and of our finance"[3] from entanglements with either group of belligerents that we might use our increasing economic power for the benefit of the world.[4] It may seem, in the after-look, the unwarranted vision of an altruist, but no one studying the life and thought of Woodrow Wilson can doubt that he considered it a profoundly reasonable and practical course of action. It was the way truly civilized human beings should act—as, indeed, they might have acted if this had been a truly civilized world!

Whether these vast economic forces were to be used selfishly or altruistically, there they were—realities, facts —and the President himself saw that "we have interests which we see being drawn slowly into the maelstrom of this

---

[1]*The Public Papers of Woodrow Wilson*, Vol. IV, p. 347.

[2]See *Woodrow Wilson, Life and Letters*, Vol. V, *Neutrality*, pp. 382–383.

[3]*The Public Papers of Woodrow Wilson*, Vol. IV, p. 91.

[4]He said in July 1916: "We have more of the surplus gold of the world than we ever had before, and our business hereafter is to be to lend and to help and to promote the great peaceful enterprises of the world. We have got to finance the world in some important degree. . . . We cannot cabin and confine ourselves any longer, and so I . . . congratulate you upon the great rôle that lies ahead of you . . ." *Ibid.*, p. 229. For similar views, see also pp. 302, 314, 353, 391.

tremendous upheaval."[1] The war, indeed, had reached the point where everything that happened in Europe immediately affected America.

The President was being constantly impressed with the gravity of this developing economic crisis. Page sent him a long telegram, March 5th, stating that the international condition was "most alarming to the American financial and industrial outlook." Franco-American and Anglo-American exchange was in "almost immediate danger" of being disturbed, "and there will be almost a cessation of transatlantic trade. This will, of course, cause a panic in the United States. . . . France and England must have a large enough credit in the United States to prevent the collapse of world trade and of the whole of European finance.

"If we should go to war with Germany the greatest help we could give the Allies would be such a credit. . . .

"Unless we go to war with Germany our Government of course cannot make such a direct grant of credit, but is there no way in which our Government might indirectly, immediately, help the establishment in the United States of a large Franco-British credit without a violation of armed neutrality?

"Perhaps our going to war is the only way in which our present preeminent trade position can be maintained and a panic averted. The submarine has added the last item to the danger of a financial world crash."[2]

Wilson sent no reply to this alarming appeal. Three days later the Federal Reserve Board, no doubt sensitive to the ruinous effect which the collapse of the Allies[3] might have upon the entire economic structure of American life,

[1]*The Public Papers of Woodrow Wilson*, Vol. IV, p. 37.

[2]*Foreign Relations*, 1917, Supp. 2, Vol. I, pp. 516–518.

[3]McAdoo had seen Page's cablegram of March 5th and reported it to the Federal Reserve Board on the 8th. *Senate Report*, 74–2, No. 944, Pt. 5, p. 210, extract from the diary of C. S. Hamlin.

had encouraged "foreign loans," though they frowned, as in the previous November, on unsafe methods.[1]

He soon learned from other sources further details regarding the condition of the Allies. On March 10th he had before him a letter from Arthur H. Frazier, of our embassy in Paris, and another from W. H. Buckler in London. Not only was England threatened by financial collapse, but French morale was cracking.

"What Frazier says is disturbing," wrote House, "and I fear is true. If France should cave in before Germany it would be a calamity beyond reckoning."[2]

Ten days later, he added:

"Everybody I have talked to connected with the English and French Governments tell me that if we intend to help defeat Germany that it will be necessary for us to begin immediately to furnish the things the Allies are lacking."[3]

These desperate appeals for economic and financial assistance, coming at the very time that the President was trying to decide the course for America, had a strong influence upon his thought. If America adopted the cause of the Allies it was plainly her duty, irrespective of her interest, or in furtherance of it, to extend all the assistance possible: and we find him declaring in his war message of April 2nd that it would be necessary to extend to those governments "the most liberal financial credits" and to supply them with "the materials which they can obtain only from us or by our assistance."[4]

Complications, as they affected American relationships with the Germans, were less intangible and perhaps of less fundamental importance than the economic entanglements

[1]Savage, *Policy of the United States Toward Maritime Commerce In War*, Vol. II, pp. 574–575.

[2]House to Wilson, March 9, 1917, enclosing letters from Frazier and Buckler.

[3]House to Wilson, March 19, 1917.

[4]*The Public Papers of Woodrow Wilson*, Vol. V, pp. 9, 10.

with the Allies, but they were far more clamorously insistent, noisy, dangerous. They were dramatic: they were terrifying: they appealed instantly to the public mind. And these also had come to a head during the dismal weeks of March. "Overt" acts by German submarines had begun to accumulate, sinkings without warning, losses of American life. Even Belgian relief ships were sent down! Also, word filtered over that Gerard was being detained and ill treated in Berlin, that consuls and their wives had been humiliatingly searched as they left Germany—stories which, in that moment of emotional excitement, were given wide credence.

The record was indeed terrifying. Germany had sunk 781,500 tons of vessels in February,[1] including two American vessels, with due warning, and the British liner *Laconia*, carrying Americans, without warning. Here were actual evidences of attack upon us at sea. Evidence of a secretly planned attack upon land had also been discovered, as already set forth, in the Zimmermann note.[2] Added to the news of subversive German activities in the United States, this "astounding" intrigue, boldly authenticated by Germany, fixed in Wilson's mind the conclusion that further peaceful dealings with Germany were impossible.[3] It did even more. Because it seemed to reveal a basic German policy, Wilson saw in it a final confirmation that German aggression and intrigue had started the war,[4] and that if the Germans won, a reasonable peace, at the close of it, would be impossible of attainment.

The influence of all these facts upon Wilson's thinking at this time can scarcely be exaggerated. He had declared,

---

[1] *Official German Documents*, Vol. I, p. 544.

[2] See this volume, p. 473.

[3] See Wilson's address to Congress, April 2, 1917. *The Public Papers of Woodrow Wilson*, Vol. V, p. 13.

[4] *Ibid.*, p. 12.

as early as May 1, 1916, that the "danger of our time is nothing less than the unsettlement of the foundations of civilization."[1] Was not America's immediate entrance into the war necessary then to save civilization? If Germany won and dictated a peace based upon the conceptions that dominated her present course, would it not mean a temporary and utterly hopeless settlement? Would not this war lead swiftly to another? Would it not be better to go in now and insist upon a just peace?

The thought that America could and should participate in, and in some measure dominate, the peace conference was indeed highly persuasive with Wilson.[2] He was encouraged by Lloyd George's statement—reported at once by Page—"If you are drawn into the war I shall be glad for many reasons but especially because your Government will then participate in the conference that concludes peace. I especially desire this because of your President's cool and patient and humane counsel which will be wholesome for us all."[3] This was the kind of challenge that appealed strongly to the President, to serve the world by helping to bring about a permanent, sound peace![4] The point naturally gained strength during March as the likelihood—and the threat—of German victory continued to rise.

While both of these conditions—the acute economic crisis and the evidence of German aggression—had vast

---

[1]Address at the opening of the National Service School Military Encampment for Young Women. New York *Times*, May 2, 1916.

[2]House hammered home this idea in letter after letter in February and March 1917. (February 4 and 10, and March 17 and 29, 1917.)

[3]Page to Lansing, February 6, 1917. *Foreign Relations*, 1917, Supp. 1, pp. 119-120.

[4]Wilson unquestionably planned to take a prominent part in the making of peace after America entered the war, backed by the moral authority and financial and military power of the United States. He hoped that, with the coöperation of Great Britain, a good peace could be made. House wrote to him that Lloyd George had said recently: "Great Britain will be fighting for moderate terms at the conference. Some of her allies will be grabbing. We want America in to back up England." (House to Wilson, March 29, 1917.)

influence upon the President's thinking, there were other considerations of great importance.

Public opinion in America was becoming highly inflamed. The people were speaking out in March as never before. The submarine sinkings, the Zimmermann note, the excitement incident to the arming of American ships, emblazoned in every newspaper, stimulated both anger and fear. The widespread popular irritation aroused by the opposition of the "willful men" indicated that a readiness to fight existed in practically all parts of the nation.

"Germany is already waging war against us," wrote Henry Watterson.[1]

The Boston *Globe* maintained that our attitude from now on "must be that if Germany wants war with us she shall have it."[2]

". . . the issue shifts from Germany against Great Britain to Germany against the United States. . . ."[3]

Defense committees began to organize all over the country, spontaneous growths that showed the changing temper.[4] Sermons prodded laggards. Pacifists were denounced.[5] A conference of official representatives of American labour met on March 12th and, after one day's deliberation, pledged support in case of war, with America's "ideals of liberty and justice . . . as the indispensable basis for national policies."[6] Leading Socialists joined the ranks of those "willing to fight for democracy."[7]

[1] In the Louisville *Courier-Journal*. Quoted in the *Literary Digest*, Vol. 54 (March 10, 1917), p. 605.

[2] *Ibid.* (March 17, 1917), p. 690.

[3] Omaha *World-Herald*. Quoted in the *Literary Digest*, Vol. 54 (March 17, 1917), p. 689.

[4] Author's memorandum, March 6, 1917.

[5] See the New York *Times* of this period.

[6] Samuel Gompers, *Seventy Years of Life and Labor*, Vol. II, pp. 359–360.

[7] "Democratic Defense: A Practical Program for Socialism," statement by W. J. Ghent, Mrs. Jack London, Charles Edward Russell, Mary C. Sinclair, Upton Sinclair, George Sterling, J. G. Phelps Stokes, William E. Walling. *New Republic*, Vol. X (March 31, 1917), pp. 262–263.

The idea of fighting to defend democracy, indeed, received sudden and powerful support when the news of the miraculous Russian revolution burst upon the world. Democracy had overthrown the only autocratic government among the Allies! From the beginning of the war it had been impossible to believe that the Allies with the Russians supporting them were really fighting, as the British and French had declared, for democracy. Now, abruptly, all the Allies seemed to be democratic. Americans exulted: "William of Germany is now the only living exponent of absolutism that the democracies of the world need fear."[1] An imperialistic peace would now be impossible, unless Germany won!

By the middle of March the dominant conviction among the American people was undoubtedly that war was inevitable, imminent, and at last, desirable. The actual existence of a state of war had begun to be accepted; "War is already upon us . . . we have decided to fight . . ."[2]

There were, of course, vigorous and persistent voices of dissent. Bryan, David Starr Jordan, Jane Addams, and various peace organizations made a tremendous but hopeless fight to avoid war—by a public appeal to Germany for her terms, by a conference of neutrals, by mediation, by a referendum. A vast majority in Congress—where if anywhere ears are attuned to the opinions of the mass of silent voters—certainly favoured war. Senator Norris, himself opposed to war, admitted that the country was "war-mad."[3] And the overwhelming majority of the appeals and opinions reaching Wilson prior to his decision agreed that the people were ready for war—ready *before* he was!

---

[1] Springfield *Republican*, quoted in the *Literary Digest*, Vol. 54 (March 31, 1917), p. 885.

[2] Arthur Bullard, *Mobilizing America*, preface, written March 26, 1917.

[3] *Cong. Rec.*, 65–1, p. 215. *Cf.*, *ibid.*, this period.

A reading of comments of the time indicates that the preponderant war sentiment was not based, among the people at large, upon enthusiasm for war, but upon the deliberate decision that war was now unavoidable. And there was the widest divergence of opinion on just why we were being forced to go in! Some thought it was to protect our rights of travel on the high seas; some, to save the Allies; some, to punish the Germans; some, to safeguard democracy; some, to preserve our economic interests; some, because we had not "minded our own business." The confusion continued for months afterwards.[1]

Nothing, perhaps, better fitted in with Wilson's conviction that war, if it were accepted, must be based upon constructive ideals, than the amazing news that came out of Russia on March 15th[2]—while he was still seeking a decision as to his own course. The Russian autocracy fallen! A new democratic regime in control!

Wilson plainly regarded the event as profoundly encouraging, for he approved immediate instructions to extend recognition of the new government (March 22nd) making the United States the first nation to welcome the new democracy.[3]

It is probable indeed that important elements of Wilson's war address on which he was then at work would have been different had there not been a democratic revolution in Russia. And yet, even on March 20th, so hard was he struggling against the final defeat of his hope to keep out of the war that he took issue sharply with Lansing's remarks that "the revolution in Russia removed the last obstacle to viewing the war as one for democracy and against absolutism," and that the "only hope for

---

[1] See the author's "Are We in the War?" New York *Tribune*, June 17, 1917.

[2] See *Foreign Relations*, 1918, *Russia*, Vol. I, p. 1.

[3] *Ibid.*, pp. 12–13. President Wilson had also been the first to recognize the new government in China. *Foreign Relations*, 1913, pp. 109–110.

permanent peace . . . was in the establishment of world-wide democracy, and by entering the war now, the United States would be battling for the democratic ideal."[1]

All of these complicated influences played a part in the decision which the President finally made. Comment since the war has tended unfortunately to over-simplification: American participation, it has been said, was due solely to economic and financial pressure; to the brutal violence of the German submarines; to the Russian revolution; to political pressure at home! All of these influences were present, all were deep-seated. As a matter of fact most of them had been so long at work that the decision of March 1917 was not at all a decision as to our entry into the war—our hands had already been forced!—but as to the time, the immediate occasion, and the reasons which the President was to give to the people.

The days of decision were March 20 and 21, 1917.

The President had been secluded for ten days, debating destiny, fighting fate: a solitary man of vast power and awful responsibility. He had resisted the pressure for war to the point of panic among his advisers.[2]

The cabinet met in regular session at two-thirty on Tuesday the 20th: the President sat at the head of the great oval table. It was as solemn a gathering as the Wilson cabinet had ever known.

There were almost no preliminaries. The President went directly to the problem that was agitating every mind. Although, as Daniels reports, he was still "disinclined to the

---

[1]Remarks at cabinet meeting. *American Secretaries of State and Their Diplomacy*, Vol. X, "Robert Lansing," p. 97. House had forwarded to the President, January 30, 1917, a letter from James Bryce, January 14, 1917, in which Bryce set forth one of the important implications of the issue: Prussian militarism must be discredited at home, and Germany brought nearer to a democratic government, before she "can enter and ought to enter" a league of nations to keep peace. "Till this happens, she could not do so with any likelihood of her becoming a trustworthy member of it, prepared to abide by her engagements."

[2]House diary, March 22, 1917. *The Intimate Papers of Colonel House*, Vol. II, p. 461.

final break," the two questions he asked indicated that he
had practically given up hope of keeping out of the war:

Should Congress be called into extra session earlier than
April 16th? If so, what should he say?

He reviewed the situation, the events which had led up
to it, and the steps he had already taken to protect American lives and rights. He said that overt acts had been
committed by Germany. What was the next move? He
asked each member in turn to give his views.

Some spoke at length, some but little. All realized the
tremendous responsibility of the moment. All agreed that
war was inevitable, all that Congress should be called to
meet before April 16th.

"No two of the Cabinet on that day," wrote Daniels
afterward, "gave expression to precisely the same reasons . . . But all were convinced that the character of the
warfare being waged by the Central Powers could no
longer be tolerated . . ."

Burleson read several telegrams conveying the impression that public opinion favoured war.

"We are not governed by public opinion in our conclusion," responded the President. "I want to do right
whether it is popular or not.[1]

When the meeting ended, after two and one half hours
of discussion, the members solemnly left the room. The
cabinet had shown its undivided conviction: but the President still indicated no positive decision. He asked Burleson
and Lansing to wait after the others had gone: inquiring
how long it would take, if war should be declared, to prepare the necessary legislation for submission to Congress.
After some discussion it was agreed that it would require
more than a week.[2]

---

[1]Daniels, *Our Navy at War*, pp. 30–32; Houston, *Eight Years With Wilson's Cabinet*,
Vol. I, pp. 241 *et seq.*; *War Memoirs of Robert Lansing*, pp. 236–237; *The American
Secretaries of State and Their Diplomacy*, Vol. X, "Robert Lansing," p. 97.

[2]*War Memoirs of Robert Lansing*, pp. 236–237.

The President acted decisively on the next morning, March 21st, by convening Congress April 2nd "to receive a communication by the Executive on grave questions of national policy which should be taken immediately under consideration."[1]

From that time onward all doubt as to American action —save in the President's own anxious mind—had disappeared. To all intents and purposes the United States government acted as though war had already been declared.

For example, on the evening of the 24th the President signed an order increasing the enlisted strength of the navy, and it was announced that the American minister to Belgium and all diplomatic and consular officials had been withdrawn the day before. Upon the 24th, also, voluntary censorship regulations were announced—sure sign of the imminence of the catastrophe.[2]

The President had undoubtedly, during the days of his seclusion, given much thought to the immediate action that would be necessary in case hostilities began. One of the most important of these was a plan for practical coöperation with the Allies, especially Great Britain. Page had sent an urgent message on the 23rd, suggesting that a naval officer of high rank be sent to England at once. Balfour had strongly approved the idea.[3] The President at once wrote Daniels—showing that he had already carefully considered the details of such coöperation:

"The main thing is no doubt to get into immediate communication with the Admiralty on the other side (through confidential channels until the Congress has acted) and work out the scheme of cooperation. As yet sufficient attention has not been given, it seems to me, by the authori-

[1] New York *Times*, March 22, 1917.
[2] *Ibid.*, March 25, 1917.
[3] March 23, 1917. *Foreign Relations*, 1917, Supp. 2, Vol. I, pp. 5–6.

ties on the other side of the water to the routes to be followed or to plans by which the safest possible approach may be made to the British ports. As few ports as possible should be used, for one thing, and every possible precaution thought out. Can we not set this afoot at once and save all the time possible?"[1]

The immediate result was that Rear-Admiral William S. Sims was ordered to sail for England. He left March 31st, incognito.[2]

Even with all these preparations Wilson did not for several days inform his Secretary of State as to what he planned to say to Congress. Lansing finally appealed to House for help.[3]

But the great decision had already been made, and the President had been working on his proposed address to Congress for several days. Nevertheless the necessity of leading his people into war continued to occasion the President the acutest anguish. Even after he had completed his message on April 1st, the doubts that besieged him were all but overwhelming. Feeling, apparently, that he must talk them out with someone, as he could not talk even with the members of his cabinet, he sent for Frank I. Cobb, of the New York *World*, a trusted friend, a man of honest mind and shrewd judgment.

Cobb reported this extraordinary interview:

"I was late getting the message somehow and didn't reach the White House till 1 o'clock in the morning. 'The old man' was waiting for me, sitting in his study with the typewriter on his table, where he used to type his own messages.

"I'd never seen him so worn down. He looked as if he

---

[1]March 24, 1917.

[2]Sims, *The Victory at Sea*, pp. 3–4.

[3]*The Intimate Papers of Colonel House*, Vol. II, p. 462. House told the President that he was not well fitted to conduct a war, "too civilized, too intellectual," not coarse enough. *Ibid.*, p. 464.

hadn't slept, and he said he hadn't. He said he was probably going before Congress the next day to ask a declaration of war, and he'd never been so uncertain about anything in his life as about that decision."

The President outlined the essence of his problem, as
already referred to in these pages,[1] and Cobb comments:

"W.W. was uncanny that night. He had the whole
panorama in his mind. He went on to say that so far as he
knew he had considered every loophole of escape and as
fast as they were discovered Germany deliberately blocked
them with some new outrage.

"Then he began to talk about the consequences to the
United States.[2] He had no illusions about the fashion in
which we were likely to fight the war.

"He said when a war got going it was just war and there
weren't two kinds of it. It required illiberalism at home
to reinforce the men at the front. We couldn't fight Germany and maintain the ideals of Government that all
thinking men shared. He said we would try it but it would
be too much for us.[3]

"'Once lead this people into war,' he said, 'and they'll
forget there ever was such a thing as tolerance. To fight
you must be brutal and ruthless, and the spirit of ruthless

---

[1]Pp. 489–490.

[2]Secretary Daniels quotes Wilson as saying, during the latter part of the neutrality
period:

"Every reform we have won will be lost if we go into this war. We have been making
a fight on special privilege. We have got new tariff and currency and trust legislation.
We don't know yet how they will work. They are not thoroughly set. War means
autocracy. The people we have unhorsed will inevitably come into the control of the
country for we shall be dependent upon the steel, oil and financial magnates. They
will run the nation." (Josephus Daniels to the author.)

[3]Wilson told Judge Adamson, prophetically, that "in addition to disorganization of
business and expenditure of treasure and the possible loss of life in the field, he dreaded
the general disorganization consequent upon war . . . He said that a state of war
suspended the law, and legal and moral restraints being relaxed . . . industry would
be so demoralized, profiteering run rampant, robbery would become the order of the
hour and prices would soar so high that even after peace should be restored, it would
require a generation to restore normal conditions." (W. C. Adamson, in a memorandum
for the author.)

brutality will enter into the very fibre of our national life, infecting Congress, the courts, the policeman on the beat, the man in the street.' . . .

"He thought the Constitution would not survive it; that free speech and the right of assembly would go. He said a nation couldn't put its strength into a war and keep its head level; it had never been done.

"'If there is any alternative, for God's sake, let's take it,' he exclaimed. Well I couldn't see any, and I told him so."[1]

There was no alternative! The decisive morning of April 2nd was already dawning.

II. THE DECISION: WAR

The broad streets of Washington filled early on the morning of April 2nd. Citizens had come by thousands to hear the President speak or to see him go by on his way to the Capitol. Congress was to convene at noon. Crowds moved slowly along the streets; swarmed about the White House; gathered in the hotels. Hundreds carried little American flags. The very atmosphere was explosive with excitement. Pacifists, come for a last-ditch stand against war, jostled ardent militarists in the corridors of the Capitol. One of them, in a violent argument, called Senator Lodge a coward.

"You are a liar!" retorted Lodge.

The pacifist—a Princeton athlete—forsook his principles and struck the aging Senator. Without a moment of hesitation the Senator retorted in kind.[2]

There had been unusually provocative news in the news-

---

[1] "*Cobb of* The World", pp. 268–270, transcription by Maxwell Anderson of Cobb's report of his interview.

[2] New York *Times*, April 3, 1917; *Selections from the Correspondence of Theodore Roosevelt and Henry Cabot Lodge*, Vol. II, p. 506.

papers that morning. Germany was calling to the colours every available man, even those above forty-five; the great Allied drive on St. Quentin was in progress; and the people of America that day were about to marshal their millions of men, their wealth, their power, for immediate war.

The President had slept little or none that night.[1] He sought to relieve an overwrought mind by an hour or so of golf with Mrs. Wilson on a quiet Virginia course. When they returned, shortly after eleven, Colonel Brown and the President's cousin, J. A. Wilson, came in for luncheon, joined a little later by Colonel House.

The afternoon dragged, everyone impatiently expectant, until the new Congress, in process of hasty organization, should summon the President. Wilson read aloud his proposed address to Colonel House, admitting that he doubted the wisdom of one phrase, "until the German people have a government we can trust."[2] After discussion, the words were eliminated.

When four-thirty arrived and still no summons, Wilson walked across the street to the State, War, and Navy Building. He was outwardly calm: but some activity had become imperative. After talking with Daniels for a few minutes, he went down the corridor to Lansing's office, where he discussed the form of the war proclamation presently to be issued. Lansing urged him to have an ample military escort provided on his way to the Capitol. Attorney General Gregory, who was with Lansing, agreed. Wilson scoffed at their fears, but after he was gone, Lansing arranged with Secretary Baker to add a cavalry squadron to the usual police protection.[3]

Dinner was served at six-thirty—early, for word had

---

[1] Cobb did not leave him until toward morning.

[2] House's diary entry, *The Intimate Papers of Colonel House*, Vol. II, p. 467.

[3] *War Memoirs of Robert Lansing*, pp. 238–239; New York *Times*, April 3, 1917.

come from Congress that the President would be received at eight-thirty. No one spoke of the matter in hand.

At ten minutes past eight Mrs. Wilson and the various house guests started for the Capitol; ten minutes later the President left the White House, accompanied by Dr. Grayson, Colonel Harts, and Mr. Tumulty.

It was a rainy evening, the Capitol illuminated from below—white against a black sky.

The House of Representatives was prepared for the momentous, if not unprecedented, event. Directly in front of the Speaker's desk the justices of the Supreme Court were solemnly seated. At one side were the cabinet officials; behind them the diplomatic corps, a brilliant group gathered for the first time on the floor of the House. Mrs. Wilson and the ladies of the cabinet were among the throng in the galleries. The representatives of the people having taken their places, the senators, as representatives of the states, filed in, all except La Follette and two or three others carrying or wearing little flags. Five minutes later the Speaker announced:

"The President of the United States."

The Supreme Court justices arose, followed by the entire gathering. The applause that followed was the greatest that Wilson had ever received in that historic room.

The President walked directly to the rostrum and faced the audience. Men remarked his distinguished bearing, his gravity, the deep lines of purpose in his face.

He shifted the small sheets of his address, waiting somewhat impatiently until the applause died away. An intense stillness fell upon the room.[1]

The President rested his arm on the high green-covered

---

[1] *Cf.* Redfield, "Woodrow Wilson, An Appreciation," *Review of Reviews*, April 1927; Daniels, *The Life of Woodrow Wilson*, pp. 277–280; Houston, *Eight Years With Wilson's Cabinet*, Vol. I, pp. 253–256; David Lawrence, *The True Story of Woodrow Wilson*, pp. 207–208; *War Memoirs of Robert Lansing*, pp. 239–243; New York *Times*, April 3, 1917.

desk and began to read, at first in a voice that was husky with feeling. Occasionally he looked up: it was the only gesture he made. In recounting the stark elements of the crisis that confronted the nation, he avoided every oratorical emphasis, lest he arouse unwarranted emotion. The record itself was enough—the unarmed ships that had been ruthlessly sent to the bottom without warning and without thought of help or mercy for those on board— even "hospital ships and ships carrying relief to the sorely bereaved and stricken people of Belgium."

"International law had its origin in the attempt to set up some law which would be respected and observed upon the seas, where no nation had right of dominion and where lay the free highways of the world. By painful stage after stage has that law been built up, with meager enough results . . . but always with a clear view, at least, of what the heart and conscience of mankind demanded. This minimum of right the German Government has swept aside under the plea of retaliation and necessity and because it had no weapons which it could use at sea except these which it is impossible to employ as it is employing them without throwing to the winds all scruples of humanity or of respect for the understandings that were supposed to underlie the intercourse of the world."

German submarine warfare was warfare against mankind. It cut to the roots of human life. Each nation must decide how to meet the challenge of it. We ourselves must act without "excited feeling," with no desire for revenge.

The crowded room was intensely silent.

"There is one choice we cannot make, we are incapable of making: we will not choose the path of submission and suffer the most sacred rights of our Nation and our people to be ignored or violated."

At the word "submission" Chief Justice White "dropped the big soft hat he had been holding, raised his hands high in the air, and brought them together with a heartfelt bang; and House, Senate, and galleries followed him with a roar like a storm."[1] With this, Wilson's voice began to clear, he became vibrant and firm.

"With a profound sense of the solemn and even tragical character of the step I am taking and of the grave responsibilities which it involves, but in unhesitating obedience to what I deem my constitutional duty, I advise that the Congress declare the recent course of the Imperial German Government to be in fact nothing less than war against the government and people of the United States; that it formally accept the status of belligerent which has thus been thrust upon it; and that it take immediate steps not only to put the country in a more thorough state of defense but also to exert all its power and employ all its resources to bring the Government of the German Empire to terms and end the war."

This would involve "the immediate full equipment of the navy in all respects." It would involve the immediate raising of an army of a half-million men, chosen "upon the principle of universal liability to service." It would involve "the utmost practicable cooperation in counsel and action with the governments now at war with Germany" —not an alliance—supplying them with credits and materials they needed. "They are in the field and we should help them in every way to be effective there."

Holding faithfully to his vision of America's mission in the world, and believing that our unselfish, enlightened purposes would usher in a new world order of peace, freedom, and international morality, Wilson called America to war for the noblest purposes for which any war was ever undertaken.

"Our object . . . is to vindicate the principles of peace and justice in the life of the world as against selfish and

[1]New York *Times*, April 3, 1917.

autocratic power and to set up amongst the really free and self-governed peoples of the world such a concert of purpose and of action as will henceforth insure the observance of those principles. . . . We are at the beginning of an age in which it will be insisted that the same standards of conduct and of responsibility for wrong done shall be observed among nations and their governments that are observed among the individual citizens of civilized states."

We would fight the system which menaced these things; we would not fight the German people:

"We have no feeling towards them but one of sympathy and friendship. It was not upon their impulse that their government acted in entering this war. It was not with their previous knowledge or approval."

The world must be governed, for the sake of peace and morality, by the rule of the people:

"A steadfast concert for peace can never be maintained except by a partnership of democratic nations. No autocratic government could be trusted to keep faith within it or observe its covenants. It must be a league of honor, a partnership of opinion. Intrigue would eat its vitals away; the plottings of inner circles who could plan what they would and render account to no one would be a corruption seated at its very heart. Only free peoples can hold their purpose and their honor steady to a common end and prefer the interests of mankind to any narrow interest of their own."

Russia had made herself fit for the new freedom:

"Does not every American feel that assurance has been added to our hope for the future peace of the world by the wonderful and heartening things that have been happening within the last few weeks in Russia? . . . the great, generous Russian people have been added in all their naive majesty and might to the forces that are fighting for freedom in the world, for justice, and for peace. Here is a fit partner for a League of Honor."

The German autocracy had proved itself a "natural foe to liberty" by its conduct in the war, its subversive activities in the United States, its intrigues and its plots, as evidenced in the Zimmermann note. We must, "if necessary, spend the whole force of the Nation to check and nullify its pretensions and its power."

"We are glad, now that we see the facts with no veil of false pretense about them, to fight thus for the ultimate peace of the world and for the liberation of its peoples, the German peoples included: for the rights of nations great and small and the privilege of men everywhere to choose their way of life and of obedience. The world must be made safe for democracy. Its peace must be planted upon the tested foundations of political liberty."

We would fight for no material objects:

"We have no selfish ends to serve. We desire no conquest, no dominion. We seek no indemnities for ourselves, no material compensation for the sacrifices we shall freely make. We are but one of the champions of the rights of mankind. We shall be satisfied when those rights have been made as secure as the faith and the freedom of nations can make them. . . .

"It is a distressing and oppressive duty, Gentlemen of the Congress, which I have performed in thus addressing you. There are, it may be, many months of fiery trial and sacrifice ahead of us. It is a fearful thing to lead this great peaceful people into war, into the most terrible and disastrous of all wars, civilization itself seeming to be in the balance."

In these sentences, delivered with the deepest emotion, the President not only confessed his own anguish over the necessity of going to war, but foreshadowed the after-cost in terms of trial and sacrifice to the nation and to civilization as he saw it with prophetic vision. It was not, however, these considerations that stirred his hearers to wild applause, but the hard-hitting charges of outrage and insult by Germany in the earlier part of his address. War demands brutal simplification!

The objectives which the President himself had chiefly in mind, though they won no such immediate and tumultuous approval, were expressed in the last powerful and solemn paragraph of his address:

"But the right is more precious than peace, and we shall fight for the things which we have always carried nearest our hearts,—for democracy, for the right of those who submit to authority to have a voice in their own Governments, for the rights and liberties of small nations, for a universal dominion of right by such a concert of free peoples as shall bring peace and safety to all nations and make the world itself at last free. To such a task we can dedicate our lives and our fortunes, everything that we are and everything that we have, with the pride of those who know that the day has come when America is privileged to spend her blood and her might for the principles that gave her birth and happiness and the peace which she has treasured. God helping her, she can do no other."

"God helping her, she can do no other!" It was a cry from his heart. He was doing his uttermost to transmute a hated war into a crusade for noble ends.

The message was ended. The act he had dreaded to do was done. For seconds the stillness remained unbroken. Then, as with a single impulse, the audience broke into tumultuous, roaring, deafening applause. Hard-hearing John Sharp Williams, who had been sitting "huddled up, listening attentively and approvingly, with one hand to his ear, removing it frequently for an instant, just long enough to give a single clap,"[1] now applauded enthusias-

---

[1] Houston, *Eight Years With Wilson's Cabinet*, Vol. I, p. 255.

tically. The approval was indeed all but unanimous. But La Follette, opposition etched in every grim look, was silent, arms folded high on his chest, contemptuous of the defeat that the moment held for him.

The President quickly left the room, stopping only an instant here or there when someone spoke to him. Even Senator Lodge shook his hand warmly:

"Mr. President, you have expressed in the loftiest manner possible the sentiments of the American people."[1]

Secretary Houston congratulated him heartily, reporting that he had been watching the Supreme Court and that it had decided on the spot to give him a favourable verdict on any proposal necessary to beat the Germans! "He smiled, thanked me, and passed on."[2]

When Colonel House told him that he "had taken a position as to policies which no other statesman had yet assumed," the President replied that Webster, Lincoln, and Gladstone had believed the same things.[3]

Two days later Wilson wrote a revealing letter to his old friend, Cleveland Dodge:

". . . it was necessary for me by very slow stages indeed and with the most genuine purpose to avoid war to lead the country on to a single way of thinking. I thank God for the evidences that the task has been accomplished. I think I never felt the responsibilities of office more profoundly than I feel them now, and yet there is a certain relief in having the task made concrete and definite."

As comments began to filter in, it could be seen that Wilson's address had worked "a miracle of crystallization and unification in American sentiment."[4] He seemed to

---

[1]New York *Times*, April 3, 1917.
[2]Houston, *Eight Years With Wilson's Cabinet*, Vol. I, p. 256.
[3]*The Intimate Papers of Colonel House*, Vol. II, p. 470.
[4]*Literary Digest*, Vol. XIV (April 14, 1917), p. 1043; *cf.* press comment in the New York *Times*, beginning April 3, 1916.

have expressed what the people had been thinking but could not put into words.

"Until yesterday," wrote a Kansas editor, "America was divided into many different groups on the solemn question . . . Today we stand behind the nation's chosen leader in his weighty responsibility and in his reluctant decision to meet war by war."[1]

It was recognized from the beginning that the war resolution would carry overwhelmingly in Congress.

Debate began in the Senate on the morning of April 4th, continuing until after eleven at night. The vote, when it was finally taken, was 82–6. Promptly on the morning of the 5th the House took up the discussion, keeping doggedly at it until the early hours of the following day. Shortly after three o'clock on the morning of April 6th, the resolution passed, 373 to 50.[2]

The vote probably reflected closely the opinion of the people: that is, not more than ten or twelve in a hundred, the country over, were definitely opposed to the war. The size of this huge majority was the measure of the country's support of Wilson and its confidence in him as a leader. His long and patient struggle against war had convinced the country, as nothing else could have done, that war, now that he had asked for it, was necessary. He had charted the course; he had led his people; and the nation supported him now with a nearer approach to unanimity than had ever before been achieved in any American crisis. At eighteen minutes past one, on the afternoon of Friday, April 6th, President Wilson had before him the joint resolution, signed by Champ Clark, Speaker of the House, and Thomas R. Marshall, president of the Senate, by which "the state of war between the United States and

---

[1]Topeka *Capital*, April 3, 1917. Quoted in the *Literary Digest*, Vol. XIV (April 14, 1917), p. 1043.

[2]*Cong. Rec.*, 65–1, pp. 200 *et seq.*, 305 *et seq.*

the Imperial German Government which has thus been thrust upon the United States is hereby formally declared . . ."

He wrote at the bottom of the page:

"Approved 6 April, 1917
WOODROW WILSON"

The neutrality of the United States had ended. Wilson's long struggle to avoid war was over. He was now to begin his effort to achieve by war what he had been unable to achieve during neutrality: a new world order, in which the rights of mankind and the rule of the people would be safeguarded. The nobility of that vision was the source of the tremendous personal power he exerted during the history-making years that followed. In him, in his thought, in his faith, and in his courage, the hopes of the peoples of the Western world were soon to centre, hopes that raised him for a time to the challenging, perilous, awful height of World Liberator.

INDEX

INDEX

[COMPILED BY JOHN CRAIG]

Wilson, Woodrow—*Continued*

for peace, 453–454; Lansing presses him hard and suggests that he ask Congress for a declaration of war, 454; consults his cabinet on the German crisis, 455–456; confers with Senator Stone and other senators, 456; his deep and sincere religious foundations, 457; addresses Congress on Feb. 3 and says he has directed the Secretary of State to sever diplomatic relations with Germany, 457–459; by a vote of 78 to 5 the Senate endorses his action, 459; confers with the Secretaries of War and Navy, 460

LAST DESPERATE EFFORTS TO MAKE PEACE

Evidence that people are accepting the severance of relations with Germany as presaging immediate war astonishes and alarms him, 460–462; opposes the suggestion of a coalition cabinet, 462; asks Daniels to guard against unauthorized use of wireless stations, 463; resists extensive military preparation, but directs Baker and Daniels to "get and keep" the ablest men they can find for responsible positions in their departments, 464; receiving a favourable report from the Swiss minister, he writes a draft of "Bases of Peace" as a foundation for discussion among neutrals, 464–466; but the effort explodes when he finds that the Swiss minister is hand in glove with Bernstorff, 467; decides it is best for China not to break relations with Germany, 467 *footnote*; seizes upon the possibility of a separate Austro-Hungarian peace, 467–469

THE ZIMMERMANN NOTE

His cabinet is near to open revolt on the issue of arming American merchant ships, 471–472; receives from Page the Zimmermann note, intercepted by the British, offering to make an alliance with Mexico in case of war with the U. S., 473; the intercepted Zimmermann note immediately and completely disillusions him, 474; on the following day he goes before Congress and asks for power to arm American ships, 475–477; painstakingly drafts the bill (for arming ships) that he wants Congress to pass and declares he will fight to the limit for it as he has framed it, 478; he learns of Bernstorff's connection with the Zimmermann note—which Zimmermann now admits sending—and the sensational news is made public, 479–480; the House overwhelmingly passes his armed-neutrality bill, but the filibuster of "a little group of wilful men" defeats it in the Senate, 480–481; takes oath of office for second term as President on Sunday, Mar. 4, 481; issues an angry statement regarding the "little group of wilful men" which he was afterwards to regret, 481–482; guarded heavily, gives his second inaugural address Mar. 5, 482–483; on Mar. 12, believing that he possesses the executive power, he orders American merchant vessels armed, 484–485

CONVERSION TO WAR

His three-weeks valley of decision one of the most decisive periods of the century, 486 *et seq.*; ill with a cold on Mar. 7, remains in his room for about ten days, 487; urges that regulations as to American armed merchant vessels be kept secret, 488–489; his mental agony over the German crisis, 489–490; attacked as a "pacifist," is as far as possible from being one, 491; his reasons, presented in public addresses, why America might have to go to war, 492; the influences in his conversion to war, 493 *et seq.*; Page cables him regarding the necessity of establishing a large Franco-British credit in the U. S., 495; learns from other sources that England is threatened by financial collapse and that French morale is cracking, 496; the intercepted Zimmermann note fixes in his mind the conclusion that further peaceful dealings with Germany are impossible, 497; encouraged by Lloyd George's statement regarding the place of the American government at the peace conference that will conclude the war, 498; the overwhelming majority of appeals and opinions reaching him agree that the people are ready for war before he is, 500; approves immediate instructions to extend recognition to the new government in Russia after the revolution, 501; was the first to recognize the new government in China in 1913, 501 *footnote*; on March 20 reviews the German situation in a cabinet meeting, and the cabinet members are agreed that war is inevitable and that Congress should be called to meet before April 16, 502–503; on March 21 convenes Congress for April 2, 504; signs an order increasing the enlisted strength of the army, 504; studies a plan for practical coöperation with the Allies, 504; besieged with overwhelming doubts about his decision to ask Congress for a declaration of war, 505–507

THE DECISION: WAR

Reads his proposed address to Congress aloud to House, 508; on the evening of April 2 addresses Congress and asks for declaration of war, 509 *et seq.*; his address to Congress crystallizes and unifies Amer-